LION SONGS

LION SONGS

Thomas
Mapfumo
and the Music
That Made
Zimbabwe

BANNING EYRE

DUKE UNIVERSITY PRESS • DURHAM AND LONDON • 2015

Library of Congress Cataloging-in-Publication Data
Eyre, Banning.
Lion songs : Thomas Mapfumo and the music that made Zimbabwe /
Banning Eyre.
pages cm
Includes bibliographical references and index.
ISBN 978-0-8223-5908-1 (hardcover : alk. paper)
ISBN 978-0-8223-7542-5 (e-book)
1. Mapfumo, Thomas. 2. Popular music—Political aspects—Zimbabwe.
3. Popular music—Zimbabwe—History and criticism. 4. Blacks
Unlimited (Musical group) 5. Revolutionary ballads and songs—
Zimbabwe. I. Title.
ML3503.Z55E97 2015
781.63092—dc23   2014042426

Frontispiece: Thomas Mapfumo performing in the United Kingdom in 1985. Photo: Ian Anderson/fRoots.

Cover: Thomas Mapfumo, New York City, 2012. Photo by Banning Eyre. All photos by Banning Eyre unless otherwise noted.

TO SEAN,
who started me
on this path
and stuck with me
the whole way

A lot of historians write about this country completely forgetting a vital dimension of the African spirit. And that is music. That is song. When people are under stress—colonial stress, as laborers on the farms, in the mines, in the domestic industry, or as peasants suffering the brunt of oppression and forced resettlement—at every turn, Africans had recourse to one artistic medium. That is music. That is song. They sought to express their anxieties, their joys, their fears and hopes, their satire and mockery of the system. Even as they were going into war, they played music. And it is a glaring gap in the history of this country that no one has sought to establish the role of music in the lives of the common people.

MUSA ZIMUNYA

CONTENTS

Galleries appear after pages 122 and 228.

PREAMBLE Chimurenga Nights

When are you leaving?

A PATRON AT THE SEVEN MILES HOTEL

The Rixi cab driver wanted 130 Zimbabwe dollars, just over ten bucks US. That seemed high for a trip from downtown Harare to the Seven Miles Hotel, but if the meter was rigged, there was nothing to do about it. As I paid and got out, two women, laughing and arguing in tipsy Shona, edged in to take my place in the beetle-like Renault 4, which pulled out of the crowded parking lot and headed back to town. In the midnight warmth, patrons moved in and out of the hotel's worn, wooden entryway, and the air reverberated with the pulse of a live band. Metallic thrumming from electrified mbira rebounded off walls and washed over low rooftops as notes plinked in isolation and clustered like iron raindrops.[1] These handheld African instruments made of wooden slabs and iron tongues spoke power. Mbira could heal sickness. In ceremonies, they could rouse spirits of the dead to possess the living. Here, fed through guitar amplifiers, they clanged like hammers on anvils, infusing the air with a righteous din. Blasts of bass guitar drove a lashing rhythm, rooted in heartbeat kick drum and restlessly chattering hi-hat. An electric guitar crested through with a bright cry, then submerged again. A low-pitched voice boomed within the storm. Whispering thunder. Only one band in the world sounded like this: Thomas Mapfumo and the Blacks Unlimited.

It had been more than a quarter century since that baritone voice had first rocked the nation. Every black Zimbabwean knew it, and most adored it. Beyond the iconic sound, Thomas Mapfumo's words had succored a people wracked by a century of invasion, theft, cultural sabotage, brutality and despotism. During the bloody struggle for independence in the 1970s, Mapfumo's sinewy songs had told Zimbabweans who they were—farmers, fighters, and artists, rightful inheritors of a stolen African pastoral.

To me, the hundreds gathered at Seven Miles that night seemed more like congregants than fans. Yes, they were drinking and dancing in a secular beer hall, but the music, especially the mbira songs, evoked a sacred realm. People don't become possessed by spirits at Thomas Mapfumo shows, and that distinction is important in a world where Shona religion is still widely practiced in its traditional form. Still, with his explicit references to the sacred mbira repertoire and the philosophical cast of his lyrics, Mapfumo and his band provided a singular brand of psychic sustenance to people whose lives were increasingly filled with challenges and suffering. Some at the Seven Miles that night were poor, choosing to nourish their souls rather than their bellies. Some had left loved ones hungry at home. All faced danger amid the criminality of the townships, and few would sleep before sunrise. Those who could manage it would return again soon, for the Blacks Unlimited faithful gathered often—four or five nights a week—mostly in crowded suburbs and "growth points" outlying the metropolis of nearly three million that was Harare in November 1997.

No guest had stayed at the Seven Miles Hotel in years. This bungalow-style, English garden inn had become a nightclub with an inside bar and pool table and a walled garden in back. Seven Miles was the new headquarters for Thomas Mapfumo and his band, the place they rehearsed in four days a week and performed at twice monthly. Thomas's Sekuru Jira presided at the gate, his leathery, masklike face suitably menacing when needed.[2] With a flicker of recognition, Jira brushed a patron aside to let me pass without paying the Z$50 cover. I slid down the dim hallway lined with prostitutes and drunks. The music grew louder as I approached the garden, and I quickened my pace, avoiding strangers until I could find friends.

I had returned to Zimbabwe at a tense moment. Earlier that year, liberation war veterans had interrupted President Robert Mugabe's Heroes Day speech, taunting him for his failure to redistribute land from whites to blacks. Veterans, sometimes hand in hand with local chiefs and spirit mediums, had begun quietly seizing white-owned farms. They had extorted money from a government with a guilty conscience, and the resulting payout to their families was triggering a decline in the Zimbabwean dollar that would have consequences for all, and would continue ruinously for more than a decade. Dormant caches of bitterness and racism were resurfacing. You could feel it on Harare's streets. There were fewer whites than there had been five years earlier, and they seemed newly wary. A car had nearly run me down that afternoon; a black onlooker had hissed at the black driver, winning his attention, then giving him a grim thumbs-up.

But the tensions of the city faded as I entered the garden at Seven Miles. I had spent the years of Zimbabwe's independence (1980–97) immersed in African music, wedging my way into African crowds to get close to performers in Mali, Senegal, South Africa, the two Congos—anywhere the music had taken me. I had navigated a river of African songs, one in which the swiftest currents and deepest eddies belonged to Thomas. His songs had pulled me in completely. I wanted to sing and dance to them, to play them on guitar, to immerse myself thoroughly in their swirling waters. I also wanted to understand their history, and how they had made history in this gorgeous, troubled land. I had returned to Zimbabwe for a third time, and over the next six months, I would live the nocturnal life of Thomas Mapfumo, his entrancing musicians, and entranced fans.

Obscure on the unlit stage, the Blacks Unlimited were lost in their work. Brothers Bezil and Ngoni Makombe and Chaka Mhembere sat side by side gazing down as their calloused thumbs and forefingers caressed the slender keys of their mbira, hidden inside huge, halved calabashes and plugged into guitar amplifiers. Barely five feet tall, Allan Mwale, on bass, looked older and more ragged than his years, but he thumped out his lines with titanic force. Samson Mukanga, the lanky, rail-thin drummer, was the first to spot me and flash a smile. Then Thomas tossed his four-foot dreadlocks aside, caught my eye, and waved coyly. Leaning a bit precariously to the side and holding his microphone upright, he nudged the lead guitarist, Joshua Dube, who, without missing a note, came beaming to the edge of the stage and offered a quick bow.

Three dancing, singing "girls" were new, as was the keyboard player, a second guitarist, and two of the three horn players. In fact, of the seventeen musicians and dancers at Seven Miles that night, only two had stood on stage with Thomas when I had first met the band in 1988. Exhaustion, rebellion, and disease—AIDS in some cases—accounted for the turnover. Yet Mapfumo's mystic *chimurenga* sound held true. Therein lay a hard truth. However gifted they might be, the players of the Blacks Unlimited could sicken, die, run away, or simply vanish into Harare's township ghettos. As long as Thomas remained, Zimbabweans would gather for the catharsis of his all-night vigils, and the chimurenga movement—the title of Thomas's twentieth album, out that fall—would continue.

This book tells the stories of an artist and a nation, with music as the thread that binds them together. For in the end, there is no way to understand Thomas Mapfumo without understanding Zimbabwe, and no better way to know Zimbabwe than through an examination of the life and work of Thomas Mapfumo.

But this is no simple task. Even his name is a conundrum. His mother called him Michael, and as Michael, he adopted his maternal grandfather's surname, Munhumumwe. His father's kin were the Mupariwas of the Makore clan, and he has sometimes said that one of these should be his rightful surname, though he has never used either. His passport says Chikawa, a name that comes from his mother's maternal clan. Mapfumo is his stepfather's surname, and it means "spears" in Shona. Thomas was an uncle's name, which the boy adopted when he enrolled in school at age nine as Thomas Mapfumo. Over the years, Zimbabweans have bestowed their own names: Mukanya, after his totem, the monkey; also Tafirenyika, meaning "we die for our country," an honorific garnered during the liberation war. Zimbabwe's journalists may call him the Chimurenga Guru, or Hurricane Hugo after a storm he survived on tour in America, or, more recently, Gandanga, "the guerrilla," or Mudhara, "the old man." I simply call him Thomas, as I always have.

The broad framework of the man's story is a set of facts all can agree upon. Thomas was born in 1945 in Southern Rhodesia. He began writing and recording music in 1962 and has never stopped. He earned national prominence during the liberation war with piquant, subversive songs that turned dreamers into fighters who, in turn, brought down one of colonial Africa's fiercest white regimes. Had he died at independence in 1980, at the age of just thirty-five, Thomas would already have earned a place of pride in Zimbabwe's artistic pantheon. Instead, over the next twenty years, he created a second legacy as one of the boldest and most tireless critics of Robert Mugabe's ZANU-PF regime. Harassed by the very government he once helped to empower, Thomas moved his family into exile in Eugene, Oregon, in 2000. At first, Thomas returned to Zimbabwe for highly anticipated year-end concerts, but since 2004 he has not gone home, reaching his most loyal fans only through pointed public remarks, concerts attended by Zimbabweans in places like London and Johannesburg, and recordings made in exile.

Beyond these clear markers lie debates, for this is a tale of beginnings, not resolutions. In these pages, Thomas's version of events is paramount—what he hears, what he sees, what he feels and decides. But dissenters and critics also have their say, as they must in such a contentious and unsettled history.

Even the term Thomas has long applied to his oeuvre, "chimurenga music," stirs controversy and confusion. Thomas and many who have written about him translate *chimurenga* as "struggle." The precise meaning is deeper.

Murenga Sororenzou was a Shona warrior and a revered ancestor spirit—some would say the "Shona high spirit."[3] The word *chimurenga* literally means "Murenga's thing," sometimes rendered as "Murenga's war." It is a venerated term, applied first to the Shona uprising of the 1890s, and then to the liberation war of the 1970s, the Second Chimurenga. The "chimurenga songs" sung by freedom fighters of the 1970s were devised as the property of all Zimbabweans, so for a single man to apply this mantle to his own work strikes some as arrogant. But as often as that charge has been leveled, it has never dissuaded Thomas Mapfumo from wearing his chimurenga crown.

Thomas stood at center stage at Seven Miles, hunched forward, dreads framing his face, his microphone held aloft as if it were a sacred object. Serene and unglamorous, he delivered his lines straight, more like a mystic saint than a preacher or an entertainer. The crowd—thick, sweat-soaked, and pressed tight against the stage—sang along with ritualistic fervor. They were Jamaicans in the presence of Marley, Pakistani Sufis awash in the ecstatic incantations of Nusrat Fateh Ali Khan, Elvis fans reveling in Memphis in the summer of 1962—people for whom music had become the essence of being.

In preparation for the rains, the hotel had strapped dusty, blue-and-white canvas to the rafters over the stage and the concrete dance floor, where two hundred people, mostly men in their twenties and thirties, danced with heads tossed back, eyes closed, arms up. Brown bottles of beer—Castle and Lion Lager—dangled from tightly clenched fingertips. Foreheads glittered with sweat in the light cast by a hovering string of bare bulbs. Spilled beer, fresh sweat, cigarette smoke, and cheap perfume mingled in the air. In the past, Mapfumo shows had always attracted a handful of *murungus* (whites), usually tourists. Now I was the only one, and the object of attention. At the bar, busy hands scoured my trouser pockets. "Buy me a beer," demanded a man in a muscle shirt. I said I would and laid a Z$10 bill on the bar. In the instant I looked for the bartender, my bill was gone.

On the dance floor, a man with beery breath pressed his face close to mine and snarled, "Are you enjoying?" The approach was aggressive but friendly—the curiosity of a confident host to an uninvited visitor. Before the stranger could say more, a familiar sequence of jazzy chords in clipped rhythm rang from the stage—the signal for a break. Soon Thomas's musicians surrounded me. Allan bought me a beer, Sam shook my hand vigorously, and Ngoni launched into comical reminiscences about adventures in the United States. "Do you still remember how we paid less at Payless?" There was laughter, a staple of life with the Blacks Unlimited.

Bezil, Ngoni's young brother and the most gifted of the three mbira players, took my hand and pulled me aside. "I must speak with you," he purred. Bezil was a handsome man of twenty-two with soft features and moonlike eyes, now clouded with alcohol. After five years in the band, he had traded his farm-boy shyness for the slouch of a dandy. He wore a gray suit jacket purchased at a thrift shop in Seattle. His fluty voice broke with excitement as he commanded me, "You must meet my friend, Evans. He has a car. A BMW. It can be *yours*. And you must stay at his place." Bezil corralled me toward a stocky thirtysomething man with a drooping eye, a hard look, and a torn combat jacket. Despite his ragged appearance, Evans in fact programmed mainframe computers at Zimbank, one of Harare's largest banks. There were others like Evans in this crowd, urban professionals living out parallel lives as would-be warriors, hunters, perhaps even spirit mediums, in the magical space only Mapfumo could provide.

A gin and tonic in hand, guitarist Joshua Dube (doo-BAY) rescued me from a wordless stare-down with Evans.[4] In the past, Dube had been my guitar teacher, sharing his mastery at transposing mbira melodies onto the fretboard. Though his history with Thomas went back to Zimbabwe's liberation war, Dube had more than once left the Blacks Unlimited. Yet, here he was again, on stage with Thomas and playing with heart. "What can I do?" he deadpanned, half smiling. "That's how it is."

We were interrupted by a round-faced man with no left eye, just closed lashes skirting a sliver of red. He smiled benignly and said, "Thomas is calling for you." This was Anton, a battle-scarred onetime *tsotsi* (hooligan) and a key member of the Blacks Unlimited's formidable cadre of "doormen." These were a rough crew, Sekuru Jira's boys, charged with moving and assembling the sound system, collecting money at the door, breaking up fights, clearing the hall at the end of the show, and packing up for the next one. Once, at the Nyamutamba Hotel, there was pandemonium at the end of the night when the doormen announced that an entire roll of tickets had been stolen. Angry shouting echoed through the deserted hall. Jira got involved, then Thomas himself, both roaring with outrage. Dube just shook his head and smiled. If tickets disappeared, so could money. "All these doormen," said Dube. "They are tsotsis. They steal from Thomas. You can't avoid it. They're professionals."

Anton led me on a vaguely familiar route out of the garden, up the ramp into the hotel proper, through the pool table bar, and out along a concrete walkway to the bungalow where Thomas retreated between sets. We knocked, the door opened, and there was the Lion of Zimbabwe wearing a blue-and-white soccer jersey and sweatpants. He lay sprawled on an unmade bed minus his left shoe. His calloused left foot was plunked in the lap of a pretty young girl—not much over twenty—who was dutifully massaging his big toe. Thomas leapt up and threw his arms around me. "How are you, my brother?" he bellowed. "Did you travel well?"

Thomas was on. He introduced me to officials from his soccer team, the Sporting Lions. I greeted his brother William, dressed Cotton Club style in a gray suit and fedora, nursing a Bols and Coke. "We are good here," said Thomas, adding after a pause, "except that we lost Jonah." Though just forty-five, Jonah Sithole (sih-TOH-lay), the original Blacks Unlimited lead guitarist, had passed away in August 1997. A depressing number of Zimbabwean musicians had been dying of late, but Sithole's absence loomed large. No other instrumentalist had ever received such personal recognition on the Harare scene. Among all Zimbabwe's fine guitarists, Sithole's sweet and sure lines had cut closest to the spiritually charged core of mbira music, and this had made him an icon. During twenty years together, Sithole had sometimes clashed with Thomas, even bitterly, over the direction of the band, the way songs were credited, and, as in all bands, money. But when it came to music, Thomas would be the first to tell you: no one could touch Sithole on guitar. Almost four months later, this loss still felt fresh.

When ten minutes passed with no sign of smoking preparations, I began to wonder whether Thomas had abandoned his ceremonial habit. Then Sekuru Jira appeared at the door carrying a floppy duffle bag. He produced from it six cigar-sized "cobs" of Malawian marijuana—*mbanje, fodya, ganja*—each wrapped neatly in dried corn husk and bound with a strip of raffia. Jira unraveled three bundles and began separating seeds and stems from deep brown leaves and flowers. He constructed three enormous spliffs, each five inches long and as thick as a man's thumb on the fat end. Jira lit one, passing it to Thomas, who puffed once, twice, and then passed it to me before turning to Jira for the second. The rich, woody aroma brought back memories of my earliest meetings with Thomas. A few puffs of "Malawian Gold" soon immersed me in pleasant, uncomplicated euphoria. Now Jira lit the third, drawing deeply to burn through a good half inch of it, then releasing thick coils of smoke that curtained his face, closed-eyed, rapturous, and stoic as a Shona stone sculpture. I looked at the room's faded yellow walls, the gathering clouds of smoke, the girl pressing her thumbs into the arch of Thomas's foot while his ropy dreadlocks draped over a pillow against the wall, and I felt a singular peace.

Thomas launched into banter, mixing Shona with English. He reported that Bob Coen, one of his managers from back in the 1980s, had resurfaced after a long absence. "Bob is making films for CNN now, in Somalia and Liberia. These are war zones!" he exclaimed, impressed and amused. "I'm telling you—that Bob. He is very *adventurous*." We laughed at the understatement, and Thomas's guffaws resolved into rhythmic, hornlike wheezes. Rocking with choked hilarity, he extended his fingertips to touch mine, a Zimbabwean custom when friends share a joke.

"What are you drinking?" asked Thomas.

"Lion."

"Here," he said, handing me a Z$100 bill. "Buy your beers with that. Anton will take you out. It is time to go to the stage." Thomas reached for his bottle of Bloplus Cough Syrup and Anti-Fatigue Tonic. Two spoonfuls soothed his throat, and he was ready to go. A smoldering spliff remained in the ashtray. It would not go to waste.

Back in the garden, the scene was jumping as the Blacks Unlimited moved into the brass-section segment of their warm-up set. Dancers on the floor crouched and spun, raising elbows and striking poses as only Zimbabwean revelers do. Yet the mood remained heavy. Like the stage where the band played, this garden was full of ghosts—many of them AIDS ghosts. Thomas began with "Ngoma Yekwedu (Our Music)," not a traditional mbira song but one that tapped the mbira's uncanny blend of wistfulness and joy.[5] "I love this song," said a female friend of the band. "It says, '*When our music starts playing, everyone is going to come out. Everyone is dancing, even the dead.*' Thomas is singing about the ones who have gone, like Jonah Sithole."

Thomas closed his eyes and held the microphone in front of his face for a long time before singing. He was gathering himself for spiritual exertion, and it taxed him. As he began to sing, he moved to the front of the stage and pressed his right ear—his good one—close to the speaker. His voice sounded weary but strong, and tuned to perfection.

Strangers approached me, compelled to explain the songs. A man who had earlier pinched a notebook from my shirt pocket, then discarded it by the stage, returned without shame to say, "Thomas is singing, '*Money, money. Everybody wants money. Give us money. We need money.*'" A shirtless drunk came stomping over and made me hold his hand while we danced. Anton interrupted this absurd tango to say, "Joshua is calling you." I looked to the stage and saw Dube shaking his head vigorously as he played his guitar. "He says you are talking with tsotsis," Anton said serenely. A self-proclaimed "liberation war hero" came next. "I too am a citizen," he slurred, adding that he was "in intelligence." He took my hand and pressed it against the cold handcuffs in his trouser pocket, that I might savor his importance.

Though the hour grew late, the crowd never thinned. As always, the night ended in trance with the musicians suspended in mbira time for thirty minutes or more while dancers communed in a blissful union of beer and heritage. These celebrants drank "clear beer," but its effect was little different from that of the milky millet brew that has always been central to the *bira*, the Shona spirit possession ritual, wherein secrets of the past are revealed through contact with the spirits of the dead. The sacred ways of the Shona past echoed in this decidedly secular space. Here—amid crime, alcoholism, infidelity, and brazen escape from the darkening realities of life in "liberated" Zimbabwe—there was a kind of grace that is rare in popular music performances anywhere. At Blacks Unlimited shows, tsotsis, spiritualists, bureaucrats, intellectuals, dreamers, ideologues, prostitutes, and poets all communed. And, as routine as this communion seemed at the time, there was nothing quite like it in the world. "People never recognize what they have until they lose it," one fan told me. "When Mukanya is gone, they'll be crying for him."

With a languid tumble of drums, the final song trailed off around 3:30 AM— an early night. If the show were a *pungwe* (an all-nighter), a third set would have kept the faithful dancing past dawn.[6] Now the garden emptied fast. Thomas slipped away; the doormen set about ejecting drunks; and musicians scrambled for transport back to town. Bezil Makombe, the mbira player, ushered me into Evans's tangerine-colored BMW, and we headed off to Mbare, the ghetto, in search of beer.

So began my longest stay in Zimbabwe.[7] Soon I would be spending my days rehearsing with the band at Seven Miles, watching as Thomas developed new songs for a new era, sculpting his signature creations from the collective ideas of his singularly talented musicians. I would learn guitar with Dube and work the parts he taught me into the Makombe brothers' mbira songs at informal all-night parties at their mother's rural homestead in Seke, some twenty miles south of Harare. I would attend some seventy-five Blacks Unlimited shows all over Zimbabwe, joining the band on stage with my guitar for their warm-up sets, and even playing a few songs when Thomas sang.

I would become known to the band's Harare fans for my Shona guitar playing. A few even called me "Murehwa," after a town famous for its music and dance traditions. Many of those fans had arresting English-language names: Lonely, Last, Never, Loveless, Decent, Winsome, Whither, Gift, Kindness, Patience, Marvelous. Such names, common in Zimbabwe, reflect an old fascination with the West. In this uneasy time of rising anti-Westernism, I found their notes of moral clarity both charming and incongruous. For me, feeling my way anew through this changing land, the only real clarity lay in Thomas's music, and in the sacrifices so many had made to create and sustain it. Thomas is a siren, and his song has lured not only fans but also musicians, managers, journalists, and adventurers. Those enraptured by his call have surrendered much—jobs, health, marriage, fortune; for some musicians, arguably, their lives.

One moment stands out amid all my interactions with Thomas. He is sitting on the back porch of a motel in Salmon Arm, British Columbia, on a hot summer afternoon during a season of wildfires in 1998. The smoke from his spliff mingles with smoke peeling off burning mountains to the east. He launches into an impolitic speech about the inherent inequality of women and men—*a woman must keep house for her husband; she must serve him; she must not wear short skirts and provoke unwanted attention*. It's a familiar rant. I don't argue, but somehow convey skepticism. "It was not me who decided that," Thomas parries as if challenged. "God made men and women this way." This is neither the first nor the last time our worldviews sheer off one another. But this time Thomas seizes the nettle. "We have different cultures, Banning. We can work together, but we can never be the same. And we must protect that difference." This book is both enriched and hobbled by "that difference." It is the work of an outsider with access, a lifelong fan searching for truth in a world—it must be acknowledged—he can never fully understand.

Thomas Mapfumo is one of the most brilliant African creators of the past century. He is also the embodiment of a tumultuous history rooted in a head-on collision of Western ambition and African culture. More than a hitmaker or a pop icon, Thomas has created a tapestry of civil trauma, gnarled with imperfections and gilded with genius. He has achieved greatness his way, without guidance or training, taking what pleases him from the idioms and musicians around him, and weaving all of this, along with his own incisive poetry, into the fabric of his "chimurenga" oeuvre. Buoyed by insight, vision, passion, and humor, Thomas's art unfolds the saga of his wounded nation. The unfolding continues, for Zimbabwe is young, though its story is already an epic of innocence, beauty, and pain.

And it all begins with the land.

RHODESIA

1 / England Is the Chameleon, and I the Fly

> I may die, but my bones will rise again.
>
> MBUYA NEHANDA AT HER EXECUTION IN 1897
>
> We are the bones.
>
> THOMAS MAPFUMO IN 1988

The Zimbabwe plateau is a territory apart, a stone house aloof from its neighbors. Two big rivers surround it, the slow, silty Limpopo in the south, and the churning Zambezi up north, which plunges over the ledges of Victoria Falls and thunders into a series of bone-crushing rapids before flowing east into Mozambique. Along the plateau's eastern edge, the Chimanimani Mountains throw up a rugged wall one hundred miles short of the Indian Ocean. For centuries, this geography protected the Shona clans in their peaceful pastoral. While tsetse flies savaged herds in surrounding lowlands, the Shona thrived amid wind, sun, fertile grasslands, and robust livestock. Even in the mid-nineteenth century, when Ndebele interlopers surged up from the south, followed soon by the Rhodesians, and the plateau became a place of conflict and killing, Shona agrarians still herded and harvested, raising their children under the watchful gaze of their ancestors. The elders who saw Thomas Mapfumo through his boyhood in the Marandellas Tribal Trust Lands were among these—people of the past, both protected and constrained by their spirits.

Janet Chinhamo delivered her first child on July 2, 1945. The boy's father, Tapfumaneyi Mupariwa, was a Korekore Shona man from Guruve in the remote rugged valleys of Dande. An itinerant musician and "one-man band," Tapfumaneyi made a scant living driving tractors at farms in Mashonaland. He was too poor to pay Janet's *lobola* (bride-price), so no marriage could occur. "When I was pregnant," recalled Janet, "Thomas's father paid a little lobola, but not enough. And then he went for good." At age seventeen, Thomas would seek out and befriend his real father, and come to think of himself too as a "Korekore man." Thomas would always revere his mother's people who raised him in Marandellas (now Marondera), but the Shona pray to the spirits of the paternal clan, so Thomas's true "rural area" would always lie in Dande. The elasticity of African life rendered these facts all but invisible to most people Thomas encountered in his youth. But long after he achieved stardom, fans would still whisper about his "illegitimate" birth, revealing in hushed tones a strand of mystery concealed within the fabric of his celebrity.

In the beginning, though, things are simpler. The first light ignites towers of boulders, huge faun-colored Easter eggs as much part of the azure sky as the apple green earth. It brightens dewdrops on curved blades of grass, racing to vaporize the water before the rough tongues of groggy cattle arrive. The herd boy's switch keeps everything in motion, the rising breeze, the hoof-fall of cows, the fleeting surreality of dawn's panorama. The boy sings a song he learned from his *ambuya* (grandmother), something about the great ancestor spirit Chaminuka, something about glory. There are words he can't understand—ancient phrases whose meanings have been lost—but he sings them anyway. A smoke flag flies above a thatched mud-and-pole roundhouse. Ambuya is cooking *sadza* (stiff cornmeal porridge). He claps his cupped hands together to greet her. The spirits are not seen, but they notice, and now he can reach out to ambuya and know she will smile and feed him, and the real work of the day will begin.

Janet herself grew up on a farm. It was owned by a white man she remembered only as "Mr. Brown." She first met Tapfumaneyi through his sister, a domestic worker at a white household in the Avondale district of Salisbury. In the 1940s, rural people were drawn to the cities by work, and African townships bloomed at the edges of white Salisbury (now Harare) and Bulawayo. Janet and Tapfumaneyi came together in the shuffle between farm and city. When she discovered she was pregnant, she went to see him in Seke, and he told her he could never satisfy the financial demands of her family. Janet returned alone to her post at Imbwa Farm in Kandege and gave birth there. She brought the baby to her parents, Hamundidi and Kufera Munhumumwe, in Marondera. She named the baby Michael, for no reason anyone could recall. Michael Munhumumwe (Thomas's childhood name) would remain with his mother's people for almost ten years, while she prepared a home and family of her own fifty miles away.

Nights are cold and days hot around harvest time. Then comes *chisi*—a strictly enforced day of rest. No one works the soil during chisi. The *n'anga* arrives with his furs and snuff, ready to fulfill his shamanic role. The *sekurus*—uncles—drink their millet beer and start telling funny stories, these hard men all of a sudden jokesters.[1] And at night the mbira sound for the elders, but the music is so loud at times that the youngest children can catch the melody and sense the depth, even gravity, it conveys. Older boys play the *ngoma* drums, and all the children dance. Moonlight is best. No workday is too long, no rain too cold nor sun too hot, no elder too mean—as long as everything ends with dancing and songs, laughter and moonlight, and the all-encompassing embrace of a big family.

Janet's people were peasant farmers in the "communal lands" that the Rhodesians had set aside for rural Africans. Marondera lies in Mashonaland East, about a hundred kilometers southeast of Salisbury, along the road that leads to Manicaland and the city of Mutare before crossing the mountains into Mozambique. Janet's parents produced eleven children, she being the eldest, followed soon by Jira. The youngest, Marshall Munhumumwe, would one day be a famous musician, like Thomas.[2] Three of Janet's siblings died as children when a hut caught fire in a heavy wind. Their bodies were burned and swept away amid smoke and ashes, an aching reminder of what spirits can do when riled to anger.

When they received young Michael, Hamundidi and Kufera lived on the farm of a white man named Simons. Soon afterward, they were granted village land of their own, and they moved the family there. This is the first place Thomas Mapfumo can remember, and it is a place of enchantment, full of animals, spirits, open spaces, and natural delights. On just a few acres of land, his grandparents grew maize, rapoko, groundnuts, wheat, and sweet potatoes and kept cattle, pigs, goats, and donkeys. They lived tight with the children in a traditional round hut, subjects now of a village headman rather than a white farmer. Hamundidi and Kufera would drift into old age this way, at a distance from the churning tumult of the liberation struggle. They would die a few years short of Zimbabwe's independence.

Michael was put to work as soon as he could wield a stick and mind goats and cows. His constant companion was his uncle Peter, almost the same age as him. "We used to take our cattle a long distance to grazing places," Thomas recalled, starting well before sunrise, as "the cows would love to graze on that wet grass." The boys would spend the day whistling after animals, foraging for wild fruits—*hacha* (wild cork fruit), *matamba* (monkey orange), and *mapfura* (marula)—and fishing in streams and ponds. For Thomas, it was "an exciting life," if austere. Once he recalled asking his grandfather permission to bathe. The old man replied, "You want to wash? Is it Christmas?"

At Thomas's birth in 1945, Southern Rhodesia was as settled and peaceful as it would ever be. Whites had their farms and cities, Africans their reserves and townships. If anything seemed to threaten the Rhodesians' ordered world, it was the meddling British, not Africans. Rhodesians believed deeply in their own permanence, even though nothing had ever been permanent on the Zimbabwe plateau.

Historians lament the scarcity of knowledge about ancient doings in this part of Africa. The people collectively called the Shona—more precisely, the Manica, Korekore, Kalanga, Zezuru, and others—originated in the Cameroon highlands more than three thousand years ago.[3] They are part of the great Bantu river of humanity that flowed across most of Africa long before any white man set foot on the continent. Between 500 BC and AD 500, Bantu immigrants infiltrated Khoisan-speaking hunter-gatherer communities on the plateau, and their shared descendants became today's Shona clans. The plateau was a place of bounty. Herds of elephants, laden with ivory tusks, roamed freely, and there were gold reefs one could mine with simple hand tools. The Bantu built fixed settlements, farmed the land, and forged iron tools and weapons. By AD 700, they were trading with Muslims on the East African coast. Shona archaeological sites have yielded beads of Syrian glass, Persian faience and carpet, and Chinese celadon and porcelain. The thirteenth-century Arab explorer Ibn Battuta found gold dust for sale in the port city of Sofala and reported that it had come from "Yufi in the land of the Limiyin . . . a month's journey" inland.[4] The place-names are mysterious, but the gold likely came from the Shona. Through Arab middlemen, Shona exchanged gold, ivory, copper, and leopard skins for goods and knowledge. Weaving methods gleaned from coastal Muslims allowed them to make cloth heavy enough to protect them from the greatest killer they faced on the plateau—the cold winds of June and July.

"Zimbabwe" means "house of stone," a reference to the structures found in ruins throughout the country. The most extensive is Great Zimbabwe, with its circular, granite-walled enclosure and cone-shaped boulder tower. Great Zimbabwe was the only real city in this part of Africa in precolonial times, built by the Shona between 1250 and 1450, and probably home to some eighteen thousand people at its height.[5] Its massive walls and mysterious tower apparently served beauty or religion, not defense. Decorated walls and stone pillars topped with bird figures carved from soapstone suggest a scene of ritual, but no firsthand description of any rite survives, tantalizing the imaginations of poets and allowing prominent Rhodesian scholars to claim that Arabs or Phoenicians—anyone but Africans!—created Great Zimbabwe. Why the city was abruptly abandoned around 1500 remains a stubborn unknown.[6]

The face of human power begins to come into focus only with the reign of the Munhumutapas, a series of authoritarian kings who rose in the wake of Great Zimbabwe.[7] The Munhumutapas refused to deal in slaves, an admirable choice that likely contributed to their sparse representation in recorded history. Shona oral accounts go back only to about 1700 and have been corrupted by successive rewritings, as historian David Beach notes, "omitting rulers, condensing and altering events and generally making them fit the political needs of the day, whether in 1763, 1862 or 1958."[8]

The Portuguese dominated the plateau briefly, only to be forced out by the Changamire Rozvi state, the last great Shona polity and the strongest military force in southern Africa at the end of the seventeenth century. Over the next hundred years, Changamire too would fade as the gold fields of the southwest became depleted.[9] Trade with Shona goldmines stopped entirely after 1800, and the elephant population was all but gone. War and dwindling wealth had devastated the northern plateau, leaving behind isolated communities plagued by disease and disunity. Beach writes of "a bewildering variety of Shona territories" at the dawn of the nineteenth century.[10]

In this weakened state, the Shona confronted a foe more disruptive than any they had known. The *mfecane*, or "crushing," was a violent outpouring of people from the Nguni language group, who surged north as they fled the militant rampages of warrior king Shaka Zulu (1787–1828). The resulting effulgence of bloodletting reached as far north as the equator and left an indelible legacy on the Zimbabwe plateau in the form of two new states—Gaza in the southeast and Ndebele in the southwest.[11]

The Ndebele seized Shona land. They purveyed a culture of expansion and conquest quite alien to the Shona. This inspired fear but also a certain admiration. The Ndebele lifestyle—"distinctively clad and armed young men enjoying a life of raiding, increased access to young women and beef eating"—dazzled Shona men. The Shona had no hope of defeating such an enemy, especially after 1837, when the Ndebele king Mzilikazi arrived with his *impis* (armies).[12] Displaced from their land and menaced by raids, many Shona embraced Mzilikazi.

As internal divisions destabilized his regime, Mzilikazi famously beheaded disloyal chiefs, a ritual that gave the Ndebele capital its name: Kwa Bulawayo, "the killing place." Rhodesian propaganda would later sensationalize Ndebele brutality, portraying the Shona as hapless victims of an unstoppable Ndebele juggernaut. Schoolbooks would fraudulently suggest that only English benevolence had saved the Shona from complete destruction. In fact, the arrival of the English amplified mistrust between Shona and Ndebele, motivating each to betray the other's interests to gain advantage with a new enemy. Today's Shona and Ndebele inherit this thorny legacy of fact and myth, bitterness and awe, a legacy that complicated the liberation war and remains a dark undercurrent in the affairs of Zimbabwe.

The first English prospectors, missionaries, and adventurers began filtering onto the plateau around 1866. David Livingstone's magnificent description of Victoria Falls, and the potential riches of this untamed land, proved irresistible. It was late in the colonial game, but one more frontier remained. Shona towns and villages were now islands amid a sea of dangers. Great swaths of the plateau lay unused and unprotected.[13] Anthony Thomas writes that the nineteenth-century Shona had no concept of "owning" land: "Land was where cattle grazed and wild animals were hunted. Like sunshine and rain, it had been provided for everyone."[14] Land also held the bones of ancestors, and people had to return to certain places at certain times in order to appease family spirits. Restricted movement was thus a cruel fate for the Shona.

"I am the owner of this land," Thomas Mapfumo said once, speaking for his Shona forebears in their first encounters with Europeans. "They found me here, and I was generous enough to give them space to live also. 'Live with me like a brother.' But instead, they didn't see that. They had to enslave me, to make me work hard for my own life, for protection. For everything that I needed, I had to sweat." Thomas's generation of Zimbabweans grew up with this history, but for him, raised on a farm and working the land with his own hands, the truth of it cut deep.

The first Ndebele, a people born of war, built armies to fight the English. Mzilikazi, after all, had taken on Shaka Zulu himself. But when he died in 1868, Mzilikazi left his kingdom and impis to his less experienced son, Lobengula, whose fate it was to defend or lose all his father had established. Though the two men would never meet, Lobengula's true adversary in this struggle would be Cecil John Rhodes.

History offers up few men like Rhodes. The son of an English vicar, he was a sickly boy with a defective heart and big dreams. He went to South Africa in 1870 to convalesce with his older brother Herbert, who oversaw a diamond claim near Kimberly. Rhodes arrived a "shy, solemn, delicate-looking, fair-haired, gangling boy of eighteen." Eight years later, when Herbert died in an explosion, Cecil took over what would become the most profitable diamond empire in the world, De Beers. In those days, Rhodes divided his time between the Kimberly mines and Oxford. He showed little interest in study—ironic, considering the scholarship that bears his name—and historians wonder why he bothered with university at all when adventure and fortune awaited him in Africa. One satisfies himself with the conclusion that Rhodes "never grew up."[15] Others look deeper, speculating about his secret homosexuality, likely; and his mercurial will to power in many forms, undeniable.[16]

There are flashes of humanity in Rhodes's early story. He earned the respect of African workers on a cotton farm in Natal, insisting that they be paid in advance.[17] He wrote admiringly of their customs and the value they placed in a man's trust. He once intervened to prevent a chief from being forced off his farm by settlers. Later, wielding real power, Rhodes became hardened. He enacted racist regulations at the Kimberly mines and discriminatory laws in the Cape Colony, and he seized more than one million square miles of African land, riling critics with remarks like "I prefer land to niggers!"[18]

Rhodes had Machiavellian powers of persuasion—a combination of charm, character judgment, and a willingness to bribe or deceive anyone who stood in his way. At key moments, he was able to change the minds of businessmen, politicians, journalists, and African chiefs. Though his methods were devious, he largely escaped judgment, dying an English hero of mythic proportion in 1902.

Few could have foreseen this. Edward Fairfield of the Colonial Office asserted early on that Rhodes was "not to be regarded as a serious person." He was "grotesque, impulsive, schoolboyish, humorous and almost clownish."[19] Rhodes, with his disheveled attire, squeaky voice, fidgety manner, and explosive falsetto laugh certainly lacked the iron hand, but he made up for his deficits in other ways, rising in power and stature from the moment he stepped onto African soil. Thomas Parkenham writes that at his height Rhodes lived four lives at once: "Bismarck of the diamond mines" at Kimberly, dean of the gold miners around Johannesburg, popular prime minister of the Cape Colony, and strategist with a master plan to establish an African empire, "from Cape to Cairo," as the phrase went.[20]

Rhodes knew the key to northward expansion lay in subverting Lobengula, who commanded some fifteen thousand warriors in Bulawayo. Ndebele fighters favored the short, stabbing spear called *assegai*, and they had shown ferocity and discipline in battle. However, Lobengula had seen what modern weaponry could do, and though he was willing to fight, he preferred to talk. Rhodes staked his bet on a delegation led by Charles Dunell Rudd, a mining expert, in 1888. Also on board was the explorer Frank Thompson, who as a boy had watched Ndebele raiders kill his father by forcing a ramrod down his throat. Their mission was nothing less than to trick the king into giving up his kingdom.

Lobengula's principal advisers were his *indunas* (chiefs), but he also took council from a group of missionaries and European adventurers in his entourage. During the crucial palaver, one of these interlocutors elicited verbal assurances from the Rudd delegation that the land would remain Lobengula's, that only *ten* miners would come, and that they would obey the king's laws. Meanwhile, the actual words in the Rudd Concession granted "complete and exclusive charge over all metals and minerals situated in my kingdom ... together with full power to do all things that they [the concessioners] may deem necessary to win and procure the same."[21] The king knew he had been duped, saying afterward, "England is the chameleon and I [am] the fly."[22]

Rhodes and his followers read the mining concession as a license to occupy not only Lobengula's territory but also the Shona lands, which they classified as an Ndebele dependency and, therefore, fair game under the agreement. The queen of England granted Rhodes his charter, and the British public celebrated his achievement as a match to "the great civilizing mission of King Leopold in the Congo."[23] If "civilizing" means the ability to pass craven deception and mass slaughter off as charity, the comparison is apt.

In June 1890, Rhodes conducted the decisive movement in his symphony of guile. He assembled 196 "Pioneers"—farmers and prospectors lured by promises of land and gold, men chosen by Rhodes to be "the complete nucleus of a civil population."[24] The column was guided by renowned big-game hunter Frederick Selous. It advanced more than one thousand miles in less than three months, skirting Lobengula's impis to the west and cutting a road that would soon feed a colony. Swift and stealthy, the Pioneers also outflanked the Portuguese, who had secured the vast colony of Mozambique and were about to move on the plateau themselves. Had Rhodes delayed mere months, Zimbabweans today would speak Portuguese instead of English.

Selous had scouted the site for the column's destination, Fort Salisbury, a hill "at the center of a great grassy plain ... fertile and full of promise."[25] Many Pioneers believed this place to be the biblical land of Ophir, where King Solomon's mines had been abandoned, full of gold. On September 13, 1890, Lieutenant Tyndale-Biscoe hoisted the Union Jack up the tallest tree he could find, twenty-one shots sounded over empty fields, and the Pioneers, along with their African laborers, began building a settlement. On hearing this, Rhodes glowed with satisfaction, convinced that he had claimed "the richest gold-field in the world" without a fight.

Cowed by the Ndebele and estranged from their imperial past, the Shona greeted the white interloper with naive trust, "as a brother," in Thomas's words. The Pioneers would suffer a season of record rainfalls, generating disease, hunger, shortages, and death during that first winter. Many would survive only through the graces of their Shona benefactors. Shona leaders probably imagined they were having it both ways, earning the trust of the British, who in turn kept the Ndebele at bay. Meanwhile, Lobengula clung to the fantasy that his people were living in a state adjacent to the British one. But as Pioneers began pegging out land claims, forcing Africans into settlements and then hard labor, white intentions gradually became clear. Forced labor was anathema to the Shona, "the most humiliating experience of all," noted Zimbabwean writer Chenjerai Hove, who said that "only the downtrodden would *work* for somebody."[26]

Rhodes's colonial administrator, Leander Starr Jameson, swiftly rallied the country's first black militia and mounted a surprise attack on Lobengula's impis, laid low with smallpox at the time and ripe for the taking. The humiliated Ndebele king killed himself with poison soon afterward, leaving his people with these bitter words: "You have said it is me that is killing you. Now here are your masters coming. . . . You will have to pull and shove wagons; but under me you never did this."[27] Jameson's men seized some ten thousand square miles of rich, red-soiled high veldt in Matebeleland and inaugurated the city of Bulawayo in 1894.

The Ndebele now joined the Shona in a state of shredded dignity, and their shared fight to stop the Rhodesians began in earnest. The First Chimurenga was sparked by reckless audacity on Jameson's part. On December 29, 1895, he led the entire Rhodesian police force—510 troopers—into the Transvaal in a bold attack on the Boers that was to have culminated in the taking of Johannesburg. But word of the plan had leaked, and the column was surrounded, ambushed, and forced to surrender just outside the city. While Jameson and his party's survivors languished in a Johannesburg jail, Rhodesia was left with just forty-eight policemen. An aggrieved African population saw its chance. The uprising started with the Ndebele, who began killing whites indiscriminately, intent on their complete elimination. Caught off guard and without resources, the colony was slow to react, but when it did, the first independence war of the late nineteenth-century "scramble for Africa" was under way.

An African victory was within reach in March 1896. Then, in April, six hundred mounted riflemen deployed out of Bulawayo, changing the game. Rhodes then led a column from Salisbury in mid-June. When the Shona defied expectations and joined the Ndebele fight, the column turned tail to reconnoiter with British and Portuguese forces coming in from the coast. Beach argues that the Shona and Ndebele set their sights too low, seeking only to return to their former separate worlds rather than unite and form a state that might have held off the Europeans. Some Shona in the south actually helped the British quell the Ndebele. Divide and rule had worked once again.

The Shona leaned on their spirit mediums, valuing the leverage of watchful ancestors over military strategy.[28] It is easy to dismiss a war party's reliance on spirits contacted through ceremonies with mbira and beer, but the mediums brought a certain logic to the fight. Shona elders had been fooled by the Rudd Concession in part because it talked about mining and minerals, things that did not interest them. As Chenjerai Hove put it, "The Shona elders said, 'We want the soil. We want to farm. If [Rudd] wants to dig, let him dig.' However, when Cecil John Rhodes and his gang didn't find gold, they began to realize they must take the land. That's where trouble started, because the land is a shrine. You don't mess with it."

For the Shona, the First Chimurenga revolved around two supreme spirit mediums, Kaguvi and Nehanda. These were both religious and military leaders who focused the fighters' minds on the need to reclaim the land that held the bones of their ancestors. Mbira songs fortified Shona warriors, reinforcing their tangible link with aggrieved ancestral spirits. The mass killing that ensued on all sides—Shona, Ndebele, and Rhodesian, including civilians—was on a scale the region had not known in two hundred years. This uprising ended only when Kaguvi and Nehanda were captured and hanged in 1897.[29] Before she died, Nehanda uttered the phrase known to all Zimbabweans: "I may die, but my bones will rise again." Streets in Harare bear the names of Kaguvi and Nehanda today.

Rhodes continued to recruit settlers for his colony until his death in 1902. He promised them adventure, glory, and wealth. Frustrated by Shona and Ndebele intransigence, colonial administrators imported trainloads of more willing workers from Malawi to the north. "You could see Malawians sleeping in the street," said Chenjerai Hove. "My father would *die* to think of that—sleeping in the street!" But by the 1920s, a new generation of Shona and Ndebele were coming up, more amenable to the colony's labor practices. Two decades after their founder's passing, Rhodesians had concluded that their territory contained little gold and perhaps no diamonds at all. Settlers arriving from South Africa now expected to farm rather than mine. This meant displacing more and more Africans, year after year after year.

The Rhodesian state had long sought to create a malleable black elite, a central goal of its Department of Native Education, established in 1928.[30] The right upbringing would give "natives" a worldview tailored to make them love British culture more than their own. It would provide a loyal, technically skilled workforce to drive the nation's economy. This nation-building instinct distinguished Southern Rhodesia from other British holdings in Africa, especially West Africa. In Ghana, Gambia, and Nigeria, for example, simmering ethnic conflicts and the prevalence of diseases like malaria made settlement dangerous and unattractive. Rhodesians were fashioning a homeland, and its longevity relied on molding African minds and spirits. Missionaries had made a start. State education and strict discipline would do the rest. This is the world into which Michael Munhumumwe—aka Thomas Mapfumo—was born in 1945.

Thomas was three months old when black railway workers carried out the first labor strike in Rhodesia. African trade unions were setting the stage for the nationalist struggle that would shape his life, though, for now, the boy remained with his grandparents on Tribal Trust Lands because his father had paid "a little lobola, but not enough." Lobola—*roora* in Shona—was the payment a woman's father demanded from the family of a young man who sought to marry her. Whatever the currency—cash, cattle, or goods—lobola was always substantial, and a real obstacle to marriage. Rhodesian missionaries tended to lump this tradition together with other heathen practices to be eliminated through church indoctrination. But a few black churchmen defended lobola as both moral and healthy for society.[31] In earlier times, it would likely have been unacceptable for Janet Chinhamo to become pregnant before securing the required payment.[32] Had she done so, her suitor would have been the one laboring on the Munhumumwe farm, working to repay his debt. Instead, in a changing world, Tapfumaneyi "went for good," leaving his son to assume the burden.

In their pre-Rhodesian pastoral, the Shona had lived famously long lives, so it is mysterious that their population remained so low, fewer than 900,000 on the plateau at the close of the nineteenth century. Beach thinks lobola largely accounts for this low figure; families of would-be Shona brides generally demanded more than most suitors could pay. A 1904 census of a Shona village found that nearly half of the adult men had remained single and childless, presumably because marriage was beyond their means. Ndebele families too demanded lobola, but with their larger herds—by one count, 170,000 to the Shona's 11,600—cattle wealth greased the wheels of population growth. Beach imagines "large herds leading to more bride-prices being paid, more brides, more children, more men, more raiders and thus even more cattle to swell the original herd."[33]

If Beach is right, population figures offer a stark gauge of Rhodesian acculturation efforts as well, for the Shona population on the plateau increased *tenfold* between 1890, when the Pioneers arrived, and Zimbabwean independence in 1980. That meant more children attending schools and churches that estranged them from their past, more youths of working age hankering to leave the village for the city, more Christian converts teaching their children that their African ways were inferior and backward, and more children born in urban townships, dependent on the Rhodesian state and removed from their ancestral ways. The speed and severity of social breakdown for urbanized Africans in Rhodesia were breathtaking. Those with the most exposure to Rhodesian authority became strangers in their own land.

Despite this, even today, no matter what upheaval roils in towns and townships, village life on the Zimbabwean plateau shows remarkable tenacity. Throughout the twentieth century, there was—and still is—a good deal of movement and exchange between rural and urban domains, especially for adults. But for young Michael Munhumumwe, the relative separateness of his rural home proved a blessing.[34] Despite his social limbo, he had spent his first ten years among Shona people who did not attend Christian churches and had never set foot in a colonial schoolroom. His early boyhood shielded him from Rhodesia's harshest realities and nurtured in him a kernel of African identity that would become the core of his personality and art.

Thomas recalled Janet as a fine singer and dancer, "especially after a few drinks." During bira ceremonies, where the mbira was mostly played, youngsters like Michael were forbidden entry. "We would go outside, form a circle, and start singing our own songs," he recalled. "These people were natural composers. We used to have ngoma [drums], and two people would go inside the circle and start dancing. This is how I fell in love with the sound of drums."[35]

Hamundidi and Kufera Munhumumwe never discussed politics. There was no radio in their house. They were stern authority figures who instilled in their charges paramount respect for tradition and duty. Because his grandparents attended *mapira* (mbira ceremonies), Michael came to view the mbira with reverence.[36] This instrument, this slab of hard wood—the *gwariva*—with iron prongs clamped to it, could be jammed into a big gourd, a *deze*, and played to produce a sound that was lulling, mysterious, hypnotic—a sound with the power to summon ancestor spirits to enter living people and speak wisdom from beyond the grave. Though barred from attending ceremonies, young Michael was steeped in the culture of the bira. This seductive musical ritual, so central in his childhood household, made a link with the precolonial past, and because of this, the boy felt his ancient roots more strongly than many of his generation.

Inevitably, the cataclysms rankling Shona society came to intrude on Michael Munhumumwe's pastoral boyhood. Sometime in the early 1950s, Janet married a car mechanic named John Kashesha Mapfumo, and the couple moved into the Salisbury township of Mabvuku. They had children of their own and visited the homestead in Marondera regularly, but Michael remained on the farm, increasingly at odds with his elderly minders. "My grandparents loved me very much," he recalled, "but when they started forcing me to go to school, I began to rebel as I thought that going to school would upset my whole life. That was very childish thinking, I must say, but you know when you are a kid you don't see any purpose of going to school at all. I wanted to go back to my parents, but my mother insisted that I stay with my granny until I was ten years old."[37]

In 1954, Michael began attending a Methodist church school in nearby Chihota. His grandparents felt social pressure to educate him, but as peasant farmers, they and their neighbors also needed children to work, especially during plowing and harvest times. The solution was to wake the children early enough that they could complete their chores before school. They were roused at 2:00 AM in order to herd, plow, and do other "dirty jobs" in the dark before returning to the house at 6:00 to wash and dress for school. This grueling regimen fueled Michael's rebellion, and after a year, Janet at last reclaimed her firstborn son.

He came to the city and, using the identification papers of one of Janet's young brothers, enrolled in school. The name on those papers was Thomas, and this is how Michael Munhumumwe became Thomas Mapfumo. Janet and John Mapfumo ran a strict, churchgoing household, far removed from cattle herds, harvests, and bira ceremonies. Despite the difficulties of adjustment, Thomas recalled his mother and stepfather with affection. John Mapfumo was "a good man, a straightforward man, a man who loved every one of us children." Thomas's daughter Chiedza recalled that their entire family also came to adore John, "an amazing man . . . very affectionate and very loving." Thomas soon came to think of John as "my true father, the man who looked after me, sent me to school and taught me good manners, to work hard and live with other kids." At the time, John earned just ten pounds a month, barely enough to feed, clothe, and educate five children.

John was a handsome fellow who remained lean and fit into old age. The son of a Shona mother and a white European father, he passionately rejected any distinction between the races. "It's in the Bible," he said. "Look it up." Born in 1922, a self-described "rascal" as a boy, John recalled his youthful years as a horse trainer and aspiring jockey. "Race horse, not summer horse," he said.

"This one doesn't pull a carriage. It was kept only for racing and making money out of it. That was my job." John never amounted to much as a jockey, and he later switched from training horses to repairing cars, the only jobs he held in his life. His church work meant most to him, and he proudly recollected how Thomas and his half sister Tabeth had been star singers in the Christian Marching Church choir.

When Thomas turned to rock 'n' roll as a teenager, John was chagrined. "Because," he recalled, "while I could never criticize the European, Tommy was [not like them]. European guys making music, they could control themselves nicely, but not an African. I said he's going to be full of himself. I didn't like it." John spoke of loose women, drinking, and drugs, all the familiar reasons not to let your son become a rock 'n' roll musician. The profession was synonymous with what the Shona called a *rombe*, a worthless degenerate.

Janet also discouraged her son's musical ventures, though both parents later came around. "In Mabvuku," she recalled, "that's when Thomas started making guitars out of empty tins. He drilled a hole in it and started making sounds. Then he was playing drums in church. At first, I was angry with him because he was playing these guitars. I was saying, 'This is not a good thing. You are doing bad stuff. Stop it.' Later on, I discovered that my son was talented in music. Then I was happy. Mmmmm. I was very happy before the liberation war. My son was a rock 'n' roll star." Janet also recalled the fear she later felt, during the war, when Thomas began to compose and sing political songs. "I thought my son is going to die," she said. "My son is going to be in exile." She said she tried to discourage him, but he didn't listen. He was "off with his music."

The poet Musa Zimunya, a close friend of Thomas's over the years, believed that Janet was "always, always very influential in Thomas's life, his spiritual guide, and a terror to anyone who would interfere with his business." Thomas, somewhat more mildly, also portrayed his mother as a teacher and mentor. "When it comes to cultural things," he recalled, "she is very much in the forefront, always out there consulting traditional healers about the well-being of the family." Janet understood that Thomas, unlike her other children, had a Shona African father. Tapfumaneyi was no longer a part of her life, but he would remain important to her eldest son's spiritual well-being. The Mapfumos' Christian household would always have to accommodate this stubborn fact of Shona religion, where the paternal line is everything.

As an old woman, Janet would return to the life she had known as a child, in a homestead amid rocky outcroppings and maize fields, thirty minutes' walk from the nearest road. Even before John died in 1999, Janet had taken up with a widowed farmer. The city had always been a place of necessity for her, somewhere to work, find a husband, and raise children. Once these things were done, she yearned for the land. Like Thomas, she remained forever marked by her rural beginnings, though for him, return could never be so easy. It would come mostly through acts of imagination and the transcendent communion of music.

2 / Singing Shona

> The Beatles, international finance groups, and colonial freedom
> agitators are all agents of a Communist plot to achieve world
> domination.
>
> HARVEY WARD, DIRECTOR GENERAL,
> RHODESIAN BROADCASTING CORPORATION

Southern Rhodesia took pride in its African townships, grids of tidy cement-block houses built along well-ordered streets. Salisbury townships like Mbare, Highfield, and Mabvuku were conceived as discrete African neighborhoods within the larger metropolis. But by the time Thomas came to Mabvuku in 1954, rural migrants looking for work inundated such places, and conditions were deteriorating. Thomas was surprised to find "a lot of people suffering" in the city. On his grandparents' land, everyone had been fed, and he had felt "free." Now he lived among people scurrying for cars and buses to travel busy roadways to schools, shopping centers, churches, and beer halls under the vigilant eyes of policemen and soldiers—all bewildering fascinations to a ten-year-old boy who had never seen a house with electric lighting or listened to a radio.

John and Janet were leaders in the Christian Marching Church, a breakaway faction from the Soldiers of God, and the Salvation Army before that. The church's charismatic leader, Bishop Katsande, had twice hived off with his followers in search of "a pure black church, an African church." The Christian Marching Church accommodated African beliefs within its Christian cosmology. Its members sang hymns and read the Bible during services, while at home or in their rural areas, some still placated their ancestors in ceremonies with mbira and millet beer.

Thomas had a new family. He had met his four half siblings—Tabeth, Edith, William, and Lancelot—during their visits to the farm. Now he was among them. The three brothers all described life in the Mapfumo household using the same summary adjective: "strict." William recalled that there was no time to go around the neighborhood and play with other children. "We were always going to church," he said. "In the morning, we would go to Sunday school. Nobody was allowed to drink tea beforehand. Tea was something very special in our house." Thomas had arrived rough-edged and farm-raised, not above a fistfight or other "things that you regret at the end of the day." John and Janet were determined to reshape him into a godly boy who obeyed his elders.

"Brother Thomas had always some arguments with the parents," recalled William. "One time, we were asked to go and buy some firewood, me and him. So we passed by a certain house where we saw a banjo near the doorstep. He asked me to take that banjo, so I picked it and we took it home. Then the owners followed us and reported to our father, 'Your sons have taken my banjo.' By that time, Brother Thomas was singing and playing the banjo while we were doing the backing vocals. I still remember the song we were playing, 'Ndaona Gudo [I Have Seen a Baboon].'" The baboon is a notorious trickster, often a bully in Shona folktales, but also confident and resourceful, raiding crops and picking up scorpions to munch along its way. Thomas would one day be known by the praise name Mukanya—literally "One Who Swaggers"—referring to the largest, most dominant male baboon. The name Mukanya denotes a subgroup of Thomas's paternal family totem, Soko, a general term for monkey. But already, this particular Soko—the baboon with its strutting bravado and cunning—was inspiring the boy's character.

Thomas was around twelve when he made his own "banjo"—an oil tin, a stick, and some wires was all it took—and began composing songs with his brothers in the bathroom outside the family home. For Lancelot, the youngest, this was proof enough of musical genius, though William recalled, "It was just a pastime. We didn't know he was going to take a long journey into music." John and Janet worried about the company their children kept and, during school holidays, took all six of them to the farm in Marondera. If the boys stayed in town they might fall in with "gangsters." Soon they would have still bigger worries.

In the early 1950s, England had reluctantly sanctioned the formation of the Federation of Rhodesia and Nyasaland—today's Zimbabwe, Zambia, and Malawi combined. The Federation briefly opened a window of hope that conditions might improve for Southern Rhodesian blacks. But as London had feared, Salisbury hard-liners dominated the new Federation Parliament, defeating a motion to end racial discrimination in public places and squelching efforts to reform labor and land laws.[1] Instead of easing, life for Africans worsened.

Schoolbooks the young Mapfumos would have read hawked the cheerfully blinkered propaganda of white rulers. African children studied English, French, and Latin, not Shona or Ndebele. The history they learned began with missionaries and dwelled lovingly on Rhodes, who stood beside Vasco da Gama and Columbus, pillars of courageous virtue. "I am sure you have all heard of that great man Cecil Rhodes!" reads a schoolbook called *How We Made Rhodesia*.[2] Older doings on "the dark continent" intruded only in sorry contrast to the sagas of European visionaries. Images of naked villagers, "savages," made the African past look naive and chaotic, ripe for "civilizing" by Rhodes and his benevolent minions. "The African loves laughter," read a 1969 tourist guide published by the Ministry of Information. "His needs are few and simple and when he has satisfied them, he is inclined to sit back. . . . How then should we deal with this man? We should remember his background and treat him with patience and courtesy. Loss of temper when things go wrong helps no one."[3]

Rhodesia oppressed with a velvet touch, and music was one of its tools. The Federation introduced centralized radio broadcasting in 1948 as a way to shape thought and opinion.[4] A government pamphlet of the era argued that education might take two or three generations to produce a "comparatively civilized African people," whereas broadcasting could "reach the masses" and speed African "enlightenment."[5] The Central African Broadcasting Service (CABS) out of Lusaka began creating Shona programs in 1954. When CABS was replaced by the Federation Broadcasting Corporation (FBC) four years later, operations moved to Salisbury.

"I personally remember the new exciting songs coming up in the fifties," recalled Musa Zimunya. "They were songs about the white folks, about the Federation. One says, 'Mother and Father, look what we are doing now. We are leaning on each other with the whites.' Meaning to say that we are *one* with the whites, with the Federation. That's what they were selling." The music's traditional *jiti* beat was the hook for Musa, but the idea of living well, like white folks, also appealed. "One of the most desperate problems for colonized peoples is the desire to be accepted by the colonizer," he said. "So when we learned English, we learned it *well* so that they would recognize us as human beings. Others who spoke only Shona were just monkeys."[6] Lest anyone wonder what happened when Africans took charge, there was the Belgian Congo not far away. Musa recalled mobile cinemas bringing black Rhodesians terrifying images from the Congo war of the early 1960s: "headless men, soldiers with bayonets" and "bloated bodies infested with flies."

Urban youths were inundated with propaganda at schools, churches, and social groups. But only radio could reach the African "masses," so it had to be especially alluring. To that end, Federation broadcasters deployed a war chest of popular music emanating from South Africa, the Congo, England, and the United States. Sitting by the family radio, Thomas became familiar with Miriam Makeba, the Manhattan Brothers, the City Jazz 9, and the Swingsters from South Africa; Franco, Rochereau, Grand Kalle, and Johnny Bokelo from Congo; then Frank Sinatra, Bing Crosby, Otis Redding, Fats Domino, Bill Haley and the Comets, Little Richard, Elvis Presley, and later the Beatles, Rolling Stones, Chicago Transit Authority, Blood Sweat and Tears, Jethro Tull, and, of course, Jimi Hendrix. "I thought all this music was just fantastic," said Thomas, recalling long hours spent listening and singing along.

Thomas also attended live concerts at Municipality Hall in Mbare, starting in the late 1950s when Rhodesia's version of "township jazz" was at its peak in Salisbury. Groups in South Africa had been retrofitting popular American jazz songs with African lyrics for decades. Mimicry had led to innovation, and now a distinctly African jazz sound was emerging, rooted in the American tradition but increasingly a genre—or set of genres—with its own identity.[7] The South African variety was originally dubbed *marabi*, or just *rabi*, and championed by Johannesburg acts like the Merry Blackbirds, the Jazz Revelers, and the Pitch Black Follies. Rhodesia's Ndebele population in Bulawayo, ever attuned to their ancestral home in the south, began producing local jazz acts in the 1930s, and by the time this music reached the Salisbury townships, competition was keen among groups like Bantu Actors, De Black Evening Follies, Dorothy Masuka, the Golden Rhythm Crooners, Cool Fours, Capital City Dixies, City Quads, and Epworth Theatrical Strutters.

Jazz conveyed unspoken subversion because it emulated America, where blacks were seen as free and self-respecting. The lyrics did not have to be political, although songs did occasionally run afoul of the Rhodesian censors. The City Quads' "When Will the Day of Freedom Come?," a reworking of an American spiritual, was banned from radio for its suspected double meaning. For the most part, Rhodesian jazz was an exuberant mishmash of vaudeville, minstrelsy, and South Africa's township follies.[8] "It was imitation music," recalled Musa Zimunya, "but the bands were polished. Right now, there's not a single band in Zimbabwe that could perform in such a gripping fashion."

Rhodesia's brief jazz age found expression in the magazine *African Parade*. "*Parade* was all about the up-and-coming black urbanites," recalled Musa, "and you couldn't talk about those without music." Writers mixed in sensational stories of the occult and cautious profiles of African nationalist leaders, but *Parade* was mostly about "the beauties of Harare," sublimely distilled in the local jazz scene. "They didn't cover rural music," said Musa, "because ideally, the Africans were running away from the primitive music. The culture of the colonials was cultivating a new sensibility, a new image of the African—what you saw, what you heard, what you ate. Of course, it turned out that was all very difficult to change. I mean sadza [cornmeal porridge, the traditional staple food of Zimbabweans] is still there today."[9]

Enraptured with his new milieu, Thomas obsessively parroted everything he heard at concerts and on the radio. John and Janet accepted his enthusiastic hymn singing and playing of the "church drum" at Sunday evening prayers. But they were furious when he slipped away from church to meet up with other musicians at a nearby youth center to do "the rock 'n' roll thing." Lancelot Mapfumo recalled, "Coming from evening prayers, me and Brother William could sneak through and find some holes in the canvas curtains and see Brother Thomas on the stage singing."

"He was brilliant," said William, "even as a young boy. I didn't hear him singing African songs. He was into rock 'n' roll and jazz. Elvis Presley was his favorite."

Lancelot remembered calling to their parents, "'Hey, come and see. There's your kid. He didn't want to go for the prayers. He is there. He is singing!' They were always pissed off, because they were leaders. So as a leader, you must show by example to the rest of the people in the church that your family is doing one thing."

Thomas attended Donnybrook School in Mabvuku. Just twenty-five cents paid for "all the necessary books," everything but the obligatory uniform, which was also cheap: khaki shorts, dark green jersey, black shoes, gray socks, a black blazer, and a green tie. "You looked so nice," he recalled. "You didn't look like you were a thug." At Donnybrook, Thomas palled around with "very naughty boys." They used to cut class, munch on carrots pilfered from a nearby garden, and make their way out to the Ruwa Golf Club to find day work as caddies. "We would go in the morning to school," recalled Thomas, "and then in the afternoon, we were nowhere to be seen. The golfers were told, 'Whenever you are coming from the city, you must pick up the caddies from Mabvuku.' We used to ride in some posh American cars—Chevrolet, Oldsmobile, Ford Galaxy. So, one beautiful car comes. 'Are you going to Ruwa?' 'Oh! Yes, sir. Yes, sir.' And we were scrambling for the door."

At first, this was just a way to "have some few pennies in your pocket" and buy sweets during recess. But Thomas became fascinated with golf, the stylish outfits and shoes, the clean surrounds, and, ultimately, the game itself, with its premium on concentration, discipline, and style. "I nearly became a very good golfer," said Thomas with a chuckle. He would continue to watch the sport on television with deepening fascination throughout his life. The white managers at Ruwa didn't ask why these young boys weren't in school. Each golfer would take the next caddy in line. The pay was twenty-five cents a day, with an optional five-cent tip. Pros like Bobby Locke, Nick Price, and Gary Player from South Africa had their favorite caddies. For the rest, it was the luck of the draw. The worst, recalled Thomas, were the "Boer farmers." If one barked in Afrikaans, "Have you got good eyes? Will you be able to see the ball?" you just knew the guy would be a disaster on the links, his golf balls "always in the *shatini* [bushes], hitting against trees."[10] One lunkish farmer joined the hunt for his lost ball and nearly stepped on a black mamba, the most dangerous of local snakes. "I pulled him back," said Thomas, laughing at the memory. "Then the mamba started going into the hole, running away, and this guy grabbed it by the tail. He wanted to pull it out, this farmer. Some of these guys were bad, man. They couldn't even buy you a drink. After nine holes, they would just leave you, just let you *die*." Thomas recalls these golfers more vividly and joyfully than he does any of his schoolteachers. He may have learned more from them as well—particularly how to make a strong impression with snappy dress and confident moves.

Thomas's musical activities in church and school soon made him visible in the community, and in 1960, a vocal quartet called the Zutu Brothers recruited him to sing rock 'n' roll songs in their shows.[11] Rhodesia's jazz bands were losing ground, forced to hire young people like Thomas to sing popular rock covers. "We were just a small group," Thomas recalled. "Sometimes we would use only a guitar. For the bass, we would put a hole in a crate, put a string in that hole and make a knot. Then we would tie the string onto a broomstick and use that to tune the notes. We would use one amplifier for the guitar and the singer—nothing else. Just put up a show."

Thomas's mother, Janet, lost a daughter in childbirth in 1958 and almost died. She was sick for much of the next year and a grave concern to all. After she had recovered in 1960, the family moved from Mabvuku to Mbare, exchanging houses with another prominent family in the Christian Marching Church. Mbare was close to the city center, so Thomas had to traverse the townships on his way to and from nighttime rehearsals with the Zutu Brothers in Mabvuku. Sometimes he would stay the night and return by bus in the morning. Once, at sunrise, he came upon a crowd in Mbare gathering around the corpse of a young man who had been murdered during the night. The victim was about fifteen, Thomas's age, and the image haunted him.

In the spring of 1961, Thomas completed Standard 6 (primary school) at Chitsere School in Mbare, the last formal education he would receive. This put him at the same educational level as roughly 40 percent of black Rhodesians at the time.[12] "Freedom came at last," he recalled triumphantly. "Even though I was seventeen when I left school, I thought I was old enough to do my own thing."[13]

A musician friend had followed a popular trend by moving north to Lusaka, Zambia. With the territories united under the Federation, such movement was easy, so bands from Bulawayo and Salisbury crossed the Zambezi River taking their music north, where there was less competition. "Groups started disappearing from the scene," recalled Thomas. "The Broadway Quartet, City Quads, Golden Rhythm Crooners—most of them went out of the country. They went to Zambia and ended up joining the liberation struggle. The situation was changing. Youngsters were coming up with their own groups, rock 'n' roll groups. Jazz was old-fashioned music now to the young generation." Thomas's friend wrote a letter to John Mapfumo asking him to let Thomas join him in Lusaka, where he would enroll in secondary school. Thomas's parents agreed, but during a year in Lusaka, Thomas mostly spent his days alone in the house while his friend worked for a transport company. Zambia was on the eve of independence, and blacks there enjoyed freedoms Thomas had never known. Still, as an outsider, with no job, no money, and few connections, he could not pursue his dream of becoming a singer and returned to Mbare discouraged.

Thomas got his first break at a rock 'n' roll competition staged at Stoddard Hall in 1961. He approached a group of white musicians called Bob Cyclones and persuaded them to back him on Elvis's "Mess of Blues." On stage at last, Thomas dug deep, channeling the King's deep croon and swagger.

I got a mess of blues
Whoops there goes a teardrop
Rollin' down my face
If you cry when you're in love
It sure ain't no disgrace

Thomas did not win the contest, but when his picture appeared in the *Rhodesia Herald*, a group of talented age-mates invited him to join them. The Cosmic Four Dots had a name worthy of the psychedelic era to come. They were just singers with no instruments or players to back them. "Go and see Mr. Mattaka," a friend advised them. Kenneth Mattaka was a music educator and father figure to young musicians in Mbare. He had grown up in Malawi and been taught by Scottish missionaries before coming to Rhodesia to work as a mine manager in Kadoma. Mattaka had moved to Mbare in the 1930s and created a multiethnic choir called Expensive Bantu, later the Bantu Actors, a group whose refinement and class had electrified Salisbury.[14] In 1943, a faction split off to form the sensationally popular De Black Evening Follies, beloved for their smart stage show and their loose-limbed front man Sonny Sondo, probably the greatest singer and dancer of his day. By the time Thomas met Kenneth Mattaka, Sondo had died tragically at thirty-four in a mining town in Zambia, stoned by a mob after his car struck a child.

In 1962, Mattaka was maintaining the Bantu Actors as well as his own Mattaka Family Revue. He ran an informal music school out of his home in the Beatrice Cottages district of Mbare. Mattaka allowed the Cosmic Four Dots to use his equipment and rehearse there. His son Edison—a prodigy, especially on piano—joined the group. "This boy was a genius," Thomas recalled. "He is the one who actually taught me about timing, how to come in singing when the song started. Before I had just sung in a haphazard fashion."

The Cosmic Four Dots began doing shows in Mbare. The group toured the farm circuit as part of the Mattaka Family's traveling show. The singer called Freddy was also a composer, and he and Thomas began making up songs together. "We were actually trying to sing in Shona," said Thomas. "But the beat wasn't African. We hadn't found our identity." Thomas adored the Capital City Dixies, who played "carnival music" and painted their bodies for the stage in imitation of Caribbean parade bands and the coon carnivals of South Africa.[15] Jazz songs in Shona, vaudeville and calypso shtick, rock 'n' roll shenanigans—"groups were mixing everything." Born of this milieu, the Cosmic Four Dots began turning up at the FBC radio studio to record songs that would occasionally air on national radio into the 1980s. The Dots folded in 1964, and Edison Mattaka died while still a teenager, a victim, Thomas believed, of witchcraft rooted in jealousy of so much talent in one so young.

Thomas's parents had no appreciation of the Mattaka Family's musical legacy, but they were starting to see upsides to their son's artistic bent. The first time Thomas entered a contest at the Skyline Motel, "he took number one," recalled brother William. "I don't know how much he was paid. But when he brought it home, he showed our father and said, 'Look at this money I made.' Yeah, our father loved it. That's when he began to know that one day his son might be rich through music."

Around this time, Thomas learned that his biological father, Tapfumaneyi Mupariwa, was tending fields on a farm in Beatrice, south of the city. Thomas had thought often about this man, so important to his spiritual line, yet someone he had never met. "It's a thing that kept me worried all the time," he recalled. "I had to look for him and see what kind of man he was." Janet had never said much about Tapfumaneyi. Thomas knew simply that he was a musician who sang and played guitar in the "full-C," open-tuning style known then as *painera*, what Joshua Dube called "African country music." As a young man, Tapfumaneyi had played in bars and beer halls for tips, but he had never achieved the success of other acoustic guitarists like Ngwaru Mapundu, George Sibanda, or Pamidze Benhura, who all recorded singles in the 1950s and 1960s.

Thomas borrowed his mother's bicycle, and he and Freddie of the Cosmic Four Dots rode out to Beatrice, where they were met by "an old lady." Tapfumaneyi's wife knew who Thomas was and told them to wait until her husband came home for lunch. Tapfumaneyi did not recognize his son, but he cried when Thomas introduced himself. "That afternoon," recalled Thomas, "he went into the forest and brought us some Guinea fowls, *hanga*. He was a very good hunter. The meat was cooked, and we ate hanga in the evening. Then the next morning, me and Freddy left to come back to Harare. I assured my father that I was going to pay him a lot of visits. He was very much impressed."

At home in Mbare, Thomas answered to, and loved, his strict but kindly Bible-quoting stepfather. But when he prayed at night, Thomas returned to the traditional practice he had learned from his grandparents and his mother, something like passing messages down a chain, ancestor by ancestor, to reach at last the ears of God. "The first person in that chain is your father," explained Thomas, adding a favorite phrase: "Your parents are the gods you can see." From this point on, Thomas's prayers would always begin with Tapfumaneyi Mupariwa of the Makore clan of Dande. By all accounts, Thomas's embrace of his true father did not create disharmony at home. But it did distinguish the young man from his half siblings in a fundamental way, one that would resonate throughout their lives together.

Independence fever blazed through Africa in the early 1960s. In the Federation's northern territories, churches became forums for nationalists and labor unions whose movements proved unstoppable.[16] Malawi was the first to break away. In 1963, President Hastings Banda came to power, and he ruled for the next thirty years.[17] Kenneth Kaunda took the helm in Zambia a year later. Southern Rhodesia, as Thomas's country became known, was left isolated and volatile. Methodist minister Ndabaninge Sithole emerged as the intellectual father of the Rhodesian nationalist movement, though he was soon overshadowed by a sharp-elbowed Ndebele man, the economist and labor leader Joshua Nkomo, who rose as the face of the Zimbabwe African People's Union (ZAPU).

In the Zvimba Native Reserve, the man who would one day overshadow Nkomo remained all but unknown for the time being. Robert Gabriel Mugabe was born in 1924 in a Jesuit-run village called Kutama. His harrowing boyhood foretold the man he would become—unsentimental, clear-eyed, quiet, intelligent, and, when need be, ruthless. An authoritarian Frenchman named Father Loubiere lorded over Kutama, banning spirit mediums from the town, enforcing strict Jesuit practice and education, brooking no dissent. Mugabe's father—a Malawian and a mysterious figure of whom he has rarely spoken—ran afoul of Loubiere, who then forced the family to move out of the village. Mugabe and his five siblings had to walk several kilometers through the elephant grass to attend school in the village. The family's remoteness led directly to the deaths of Robert's two elder brothers from illnesses that might have been treated in town. Mugabe's father abandoned the family in shame, and young Robert buried himself in his studies. He was twenty when his father returned from another life in Bulawayo, saddled the family with three more children, and promptly died, leaving twenty-something Robert in charge of a large brood.

Mugabe eschewed politics while studying on scholarship at Fort Hare University in South Africa.[18] Studious and solitary, he graduated in 1952 to work as a government-paid teacher, first in Rhodesia and then in Zambia. It was only after returning from a two-year teaching stint in Ghana, where he experienced the dawn of Kwame Nkrumah's pan-Africanist regime and met his future wife, Sally Hayfron, that Mugabe emerged as a nationalist.[19] In May 1960, a year of political awakening, he addressed a gathering of more than a thousand at Zvimba, making his first mark among the future leaders of the independence movement. Two months later, violence tore through the streets of Salisbury and Bulawayo.

The Rhodesians were not the British in India; peaceful measures would not move them. Instead, stone throwing, school burning, and sabotage prevailed. Nationalists recruited citizens aggressively. There would be knocks on township doors before rallies. Anyone who dared stay away risked having a petrol bomb tossed into his bedroom. Some felt that village chiefs, not politicians, should lead the movement because, as one put it, "politics is a filthy, dirty, stinking game." In Rhodesia, that game was just beginning.

The Zimbabwe African National Union (ZANU) was created in 1963, with Ndabaninge Sithole at the helm and Mugabe as one of his deputies. Sithole took pains to distinguish ZANU from ZAPU on philosophical grounds, but many saw it simply as a Shona challenge to the Ndebele party. More than a century after the Ndebele had first surged northward, an era of ethnic politics was dawning, and unrest was spreading fast. Prime Minister Winston Field of the Rhodesian Front was determined to crush dissent, and life in the townships became "hell on earth." Thomas experienced it firsthand:

> There was a lot of stone throwing, and a lot of petrol bombs. They burned people in this country. Barbed wire was put around Highfield and Mbare so that people were not going to escape from the law. A truck would come with a loudspeaker and start shouting to the people to come out of their houses and make a line in the street. Then they could bring in a lorry full of policemen who would start inspecting the line, looking at people's faces. If he thinks he might have seen you somewhere, he could just grab your hand and say, "Have you ever seen my face somewhere else?" And you would say, "Ah, no I don't recognize you." And he would say, "You don't recognize me, but I recognize *you*. I saw you throwing stones. So follow me." If you follow him, you were sent to detention—no trial. Just like that.

White Rhodesians were steeling themselves for a political showdown with England, which had now surrendered nearly all its African territory. Paradoxically, on the cultural front, London was becoming the new locus of "cool." Blacks and whites alike were mad about the Merseyside sound of the Kinks, Hollies, Rolling Stones, and Beatles. "So we actually crossed the floor again," recalled Thomas, construing the Atlantic Ocean as a global dance floor. Township "copyright" rock bands—the Chicago Drifters, the Echoes, the Springfields—now covered the Beatles and Stones as well as Elvis and Otis.

"The Springfields were playing at the Beatrice Blue Bar in Mbare," recalled Thomas, "so we went there, me and the Cosmic Four Dots, to listen to this group play." The Springfields' lead singer was in jail for throwing stones that night, so the group was playing instrumentals.[20] One of the Four Dots' musicians approached the bandstand and suggested that Thomas sing a number. Thomas shimmied onto the stage, shifted his hips Elvis-wise, and sang "I've Got a Dirty, Dirty Feeling," an exercise in bravado in which he promises to drag his runaway girl home and "chain you to the wall." Apparently, Thomas pulled it off; the Springfields offered him a job as a singer and trap drummer.

"Springfields was a good band," recalled brother William, "a well-disciplined band, and very smart on stage." Thomas began to be noticed. Hilton Mambo—a future singer, engineer, and broadcaster—remembered the band playing Friday afternoon gigs for underage kids in Mbare's Stoddard Hall, the township's top venue. "We even had Cliff Richard at Stoddard Hall," said Mambo. Thomas was moving up.

In those days, a viable band needed to ally with a bar or beer hall that would provide equipment, practice space, and a steady gig. For the Springfields, this was Rambanai Bar in Mbare, "a dangerous place," as Thomas recalled. "In the middle of the music, people are murdering each other. One guy got stabbed and he just died there. He was lying on the floor for two hours before the police came. During the concert!" *Rambanai* means roughly "breaking up" or "divorce," and the joke was if you took your wife there the two of you were apt to leave separately. On one occasion, Thomas recalled a "thug" waiting outside after the show and literally stealing a musician's girlfriend. "Girl, you are not going anywhere," said the assailant. "I am taking you home." The musicians could do nothing to stop him.

In those days, brother William was too young to enter a nightclub himself, so he and a friend used to show up in the afternoon before a gig and be paid twenty-five cents each to "clean the instruments." Then they'd stick around outside to hear the music. One night after the bar had closed, the police set up a barbed wire cordon around the neighborhood. According to William, it went up as if by magic, "without anyone hearing." In the morning, "you couldn't go away from your house." The police ordered everyone to leave their homes and line up on the street. Thomas recalled wearing a Mod jacket:

> I had this shiny jacket with no collar. You remember those jackets that the Beatles used to wear? Mine was silver. So this short policeman came over and said, "Why are you putting on this shiny thing in the morning?" I said, "Because I am a musician." And he said, "You! You are a disgrace." [*Laughs*] I never answered him. My savior was a certain police sergeant, a black guy. He actually came to my rescue. He said, "You should leave this youngster alone. He's only a musician. I have attended his shows at Rambanai. He's not a politician." They cleared me and I went home. I got lucky.

Even if they were not "politicians," musicians were used for political ends, both by the government and by the nationalists. The Springfields used to play

"Teen Time" concerts, fundraisers for ZAPU, still a legal entity at the time. "They did not book halls," Thomas recalled, "just open the doors without even paying. People were actually forced to attend those shows, teens, even grown-ups. Everybody had to come. It was a duty. That was not wrong. That was right, because the party had no money."

With new bands forming all the time, good players were always being wooed from one act to another. But once the Springfields recruited future Blacks Unlimited bass man Allan Mwale, the band's lineup held for five years. Barely five feet tall, Allan was already solid on bass, and uniquely experienced, when he joined the Springfields in 1967. A few years earlier, he had run into trouble in a band sponsored by ZANU's youth wing. "There was war between ZAPU and ZANU then," recalled Allan. "My parents' house was stoned three times by ZAPU people." Allan had escaped to Zambia and spent two years playing music up near the Congolese border. The bars in Kitwe catered to copper miners, many of them Congolese, and there Allan learned to play what the locals called *rumba*, that unique fusion of Cuban and Central African music that swept out of Kinshasa to become the most popular dance sound in Africa starting in the 1950s.

When Allan joined Thomas in the Springfields, Salisbury was awash in rumba, rock 'n' roll, and simmering rebellion. Winston Field had turned his government over to Ian Douglas Smith, a steely, razor-sharp man who had lived the Rhodesian dream on his farm in Selukwe, until World War II intervened. Smith had joined the British Royal Air Force and fought in Italy and France, surviving a plane crash that left part of his face paralyzed and expressionless. He had returned to cofound the hard-line Rhodesian Front. Once prime minister, he quickly declared a state of emergency in Highfield and arrested as much of the nationalist leadership as he could, including Nkomo, Sithole, and Mugabe. Mugabe was sentenced to one year for making subversive remarks, but he would remain in Hwa Hwa Detention Camp for eleven. In November 1965, Smith extended his state of emergency to the entire country and, days later, made the defining move of his career when he announced the Unilateral Declaration of Independence (UDI) from England.[21]

White Rhodesians were no longer fighting to preserve a European territory; they were defending their "homeland." Policemen were forced to swear allegiance to Smith's rebel government. Riot squads—half white, half black—were trained, armed, and deployed around the country. Nationalist radio broadcasts out of Zambia, meanwhile, encouraged blacks to organize and place petrol bombs in factories, schools, and government facilities, and also to sabotage farms by poisoning livestock, cutting fences and telephone lines, and burning crops. People did such things, but lacking the support of an organized guerrilla force, their actions did little more than galvanize the regime. Infiltrators from Smith's Special Branch attended rural "beer-drinks" and undid these haphazard plots from within.[22] But the game changed in April 1966 when a faction of ZAPU guerrillas out of Zambia and African National Council (ANC) fighters were attacked and killed by British South Africa Police in the northern town of Chinhoyi. Scarcely reported at the time, this bloody clash—the Battle of Chinhoyi—became the first real firefight in the war to free Zimbabwe.

The Springfields were tops in the townships that year and were recording songs for the Rhodesia Broadcasting Corporation (RBC). They scored a hit with a song called "Shungu Dzinondibaya." Unusual for its Shona lyrics, this became the first Thomas Mapfumo performance to be pressed to vinyl. Thomas had picked the song up from Charles D-Ray Tiger, a comedian with the Capital City Dixies.

I'm troubled in my heart
I used to own butcheries
I owned stores, my friends
I had cattle, my friends
I had sheep, my friends
Today I have nothing; surely I've nothing

Thomas recalled, "Charles D-Ray Tiger sang this song like it was a comedy, and I said, 'This guy is making a joke out of this song.' But it was a very good song. This was a rich man and all of a sudden he lost everything." Thomas sang a more poignant version with the Springfields for RBC in 1967, and somehow it became a record. "One day, I was going to the shops and I heard my voice in this record bar. I went in and there was my name on this record. Until today I don't know who sold that record and got the money."

The Springfields' recorded output—much of it for radio only—exists almost exclusively in Zimbabwe's National Archives. There, you can hear Thomas howling out covers of Elvis and Ray Charles. But among all the rock 'n' roll, rumba, and African jazz numbers are also a set of so-called traditional adaptations, including "Shungu Dzinondibaya." Dance bands like the City Slickers and the Hot Shots had been working up urban takes on African folk melodies since at least the 1950s. The Springfields also did a rendition of the Shona song "Chemutengure," set to a jazzy swing beat.[23] Thomas noted that this traditional song was well known at the time, even found in children's school books. But behind its playful ridiculing of a donkey cart driver lies a deeper critique of a system in which blacks were forced to labor for whites.

"Shungu Dzinondibaya" is not a traditional song, though on the Springfields' version, the drummer plays an mbira-like, eighth-note triplet pattern on his hi-hat—a new sound, and one that would one day pervade Rhodesia's popular music.[24]

Musicians were not yet profiting from recordings. The music business was still about live shows, so it was grim news when the Springfields learned that their manager, Lazarus Gambura, had been skimming their earnings at Rambanai. "My wages with the Springfields were two pounds a week," Thomas figured. "After about six months, the district manager of the municipality beer gardens, a Mr. William Bell, asked me how much we were getting paid as musicians." Bell heard the figure and "went mad." The city council was paying Gambura *a hundred* pounds a week, and apparently he had been pocketing most of it. The musicians rebelled, bursting in on a show by another of Gambura's bands and seizing as much of the manager's gear as they could carry away.

Thomas recalled the fracas with characteristic glee. "There was chaos at Rambanai that night!" A police investigation showed that Bell too had been stealing city council funds, intended to pay musicians. And it got worse. Bell's cousin was the city councilman in charge of municipality bars, and a friend of the magistrate presiding over the case. The court convicted Bell but let him off with a suspended sentence, while the Springfields lost their job at Rambanai and received nothing. Thomas was appalled at the injustice, reflecting later, "I think that this is where my whole revolutionary attitude began."[25]

In 1967, the Mutanga Nightclub in Highfield became Salisbury's first real African music venue.[26] Mutanga gave local acts a chance to showcase their talent, not simply placate bar clientele. Newspapers took note, and musicians from all over town began to congregate there. In the past, music lovers had favored the downtown El Morocco Room, which later became Job's Nitespot. Nationalists socialized there, including ZANU founder Ndabaninge Sithole, whose office was nearby. But the El Morocco tucked the band in a corner while the bar and pool tables kept much of the crowd in an adjacent room. Worse, it closed at 10:30 PM, when a curfew sent blacks scattering into the townships. "Mutanga stayed open until 4:30, sometimes 6:00 AM," recalled bass player David Ndoro. "Of course, there was no transportation home at that hour. We used to sleep at the bus stop." It was worth the trouble, said Ndoro, for at Mutanga, musicians long abused by corrupt middlemen like Gambura and Bell could negotiate their own deals with management. For the first time, township bands had an incentive to develop an audience.

Musa Zimunya described Mutanga as a big room shaped like a cross with an enclosed glass atrium at the center and a bandstand at the far end. Lancelot Mapfumo remembered the small connecting spaces, like the "dark room," where lovers could mingle by candlelight. Musicians from the biggest South African groups, like Mahlathini and the Mahotella Queens, would turn up at Mutanga after their stadium performances had finished. Clearly the place to be, Mutanga became the new home of the Springfields, who negotiated for 80 percent of the door, rather than a flat fee. "That was a mistake on Mutanga's part," recalled Thomas. "Every night we collected over 200 pounds. I personally would go home with 25 pounds. I tell you, I was stupid during that time. I played with money like nobody's business."[27]

The Springfields' star attraction was an irascible saxophonist named Isaac Banda. "I was nothing then," said Thomas, "just someone who comes to sing when the star of the show is resting." Banda became jealous of the popular rumba outfit the Lipopo Jazz Band and accused it of stealing the Springfields' jobs. One night, he snapped and assaulted one of the Lipopo guys. Expelled from Mutanga for "unruly behavior," the Springfields moved to Bulawayo, where they wound up playing at Marisha Cocktail Bar. Managed by a Mr. Zvambila, Marisha had a proper stage and drew a consistent crowd of township dwellers willing to pay to hear good music. Once again, Banda's hot temper roiled the waters. During one show, Zvambila noticed that Banda's colored girlfriend looked lonely, so he bought her a drink. Banda exploded, tossing his saxophone aside and lunging across the dance floor to seize Zvambila by the collar and punch him.

Zvambila held his powder. The Springfields were one of the hottest draws in Bulawayo, and he was not going to let a black eye stand in the way of commerce. But after six months, Mutanga was begging the band to come back to Salisbury, at double what Marisha was paying. "We decided to pack our things and leave," said Thomas. "We were just bored with everything." Zvambila intercepted them at the train station and forced Banda to sign papers acknowledging that the Springfields had broken their contract. Thomas and other band members were later detained in Salisbury until a court could secure Zvambila's money. Mutanga paid, happy to retrieve his top band.

But the Springfields soon soured on the deal at Mutanga too, and Banda and others split off to form one of Rhodesia's first successful recording acts, the Great Sounds. This combo launched its career with a song that Thomas had helped create, "Anopenga Anewaya (He's Crazy)." Thomas had simply composed Shona words to a well-known song by the popular Congolese bandleader, Franco. Thomas always said the Great Sounds "stole" this song from the Springfields. "But we never complained," he added, "because we had so much music." Still, this was a lesson in creative opportunism. Franco, Thomas, and the Springfields might all claim credit for "Anopenga Anewaya," but the financial reward went to the band that made it a hit record, the Great Sounds.

With the Springfields diminished, Thomas locked horns with Mutanga over money. He left the band and stayed home for a while, dejected, once again a worry to his family. Thomas went back to Mutanga on his own, trying his luck with this band and that. It was during this hiatus that he first teamed up with guitarist Joshua Hlomayi Dube.[28] Still a teenager at the time, Dube was that rare African musician whose family had actually encouraged him. With a Carlton "box guitar" his father had given him, Dube started out in Kwekwe, where he befriended the young Jonah Sithole, destined to become the *other* most famous Mapfumo guitarist. Kwekwe was an easy stop for bands moving back and forth between Salisbury and Bulawayo. A good player here might get noticed and swept off to a better gig. Dube's break came in 1969 when comedian-musician Safirio Madzikatire brought him to Salisbury, to the Mutanga Nightclub, and landed him a gig with a top rumba outfit, the Lipopo Jazz Band.

A year or so earlier, the Springfields had passed through Kwekwe, and Dube had been impressed by a jaunty young rock 'n' roller named Thomas Mapfumo. On his first visit to Mutanga, Dube recognized Thomas, then marking time with the Mutanga house band and drinking heavily. Dube had little feel for the Lipopo Jazz Band's rumba, but he played well, and Oscar Mutanga, the owner's son, asked him to join the club's stable of musicians. The act was billed as the Mutanga Modern Band, but Dube remembered it as nothing more than a shifting pool of players who came and went according to Oscar Mutanga's whims. Dube sensed that Thomas and the others didn't like "someone from outside Harare" in their group, but here, Mutanga was calling the shots.

Thomas had begun writing songs in Shona and was noticing that they often got a better response than well-known cover songs. After a decade in the business—it was now 1971—Thomas was bored by the emptiness of imitation, and the feeling of drift ran deeper than mere music. "We were missing something," he said, "our own identity. We people of Zimbabwe were lost." Growing ranks of nationalists agreed. They wondered "why musicians had the luxury to stage shows while others were taking to the bush to fight."[29] Few musicians in Salisbury's beer halls were interested in composing songs, let alone political songs. "Everything the radio played was foreign," said Thomas. "People were colonized. They never believed in themselves. They thought the white man was untouchable, like a god to African people."

This was not simply about race. Thomas has always credited white liberals like former prime minister Garfield Todd with sparking a new awareness among his peers. "*They* told [us], 'This is your country. Do not be cheated.' This actually woke up the African, because he had heard it from a white guy." Thomas cherished the memory of bira ceremonies on the land, the enchantment of drumming and singing while elders communed with ancestral spirits. He understood that such things had been devalued or forgotten by many of his urban peers. But not all of them. On the airwaves and in hidden corners of the townships, indigenous music was quietly gaining a foothold in Salisbury.

Since the 1950s, the national radio had been working traditional music into its programming, even bringing musicians to radio studios to play on the air. These broadcasts were aimed at attracting older rural listeners, with the idea that they would then become attuned to the government's social and political messages. But some radio programmers were genuinely interested in traditional culture. Singer, guitarist, and composer Alick Nkhata had started in radio under the Federation and had traveled through rural areas around Salisbury, encouraging local players to rehearse and record.[30] Nkhata's urgings must have puzzled musicians who had long been told that their traditional arts—especially mbira—were evil and ungodly. Now the government wanted them to perform on national radio? Nkhata found in one formerly musical village that "people do not drink beer anymore," and that since the coming of Seventh-Day Adventists, they instead gave tea parties and sang hymns.[31] Church suppression of African musical culture in Southern Rhodesia was a reality. But traditional music had not disappeared; it had simply gone underground.

Mbira musician Tute Chigamba saw it bubbling up in Salisbury in the 1960s. "On a Friday or Saturday," he said, "you could walk at night and find a bira—people dancing, ululating, playing *hosho* [gourd rattle]. In at least ten or fifteen houses, you could find people playing mbira." The sound of mbira flowing onto the streets of Highfield and Mbare signaled a new pride in rural ways that fit well with the rising tide of nationalism.[32] So much of what Rhodesians had done to strengthen their position with Africans later worked against them. Education efforts produced a black elite and, with it, the nationalist leadership. Repressive laws and brutality subdued misbehavior but also radicalized citizens. Now the RBC was using traditional music to help sell a Rhodesian worldview, and that very music was reacquainting Africans with their disgraced heritage.

Nkhata believed that traditions in Southern Rhodesia were in fact under threat, even vanishing. This was perhaps exaggerated but not altogether wrong. It grew out of his experiences in the field with legendary musical documentarian Hugh Tracey, then of Roodepoort, South Africa.[33] Throughout southern, central, and eastern Africa, Tracey had recorded music that was being eradi-cated by war, migration, natural disaster, and acculturation. He was an amateur scholar, an entrepreneur, and an unlikely evangelist for African traditions. Tracey's sons Andrew and Paul grew up playing African music in the heyday of apartheid, and they did so in a stage revue called *Wait a Minim*, which opened in Johannesburg before moving on to a two-year run in London and then almost a year on Broadway in 1966. While Ian Smith was rallying white Rhodesia to ensconce his racist worldview in a permanent state, two white boys from South Africa were playing Shona mbira music in the theaters of London and New York—and nobody called it "world music" then.[34]

The cultural knowledge of African broadcasters and educators was not always deep or firsthand. Many were, in Thomas Turino's word, "cosmopoli-tans," "more likely to be distanced from indigenous lifestyles," on account of growing up in middle-class urban settings.[35] Broadcasters in the 1950s and 1960s were no doubt attracted to mbira music because it sounded beautiful but also because it fit the perception of figures like Tracey and Nkhata that traditional culture was "dying out" and needed to be rescued.[36] Educated in mission schools, these cosmopolitans had long since distanced themselves from ancestral ways. Now, for Turino, they became "culture brokers," people empowered to decide which things from the past should be embraced and which rejected. Middle-class publications like *African Parade* and *Bantu Mir-ror* amplified this reeducated worldview, as in a 1959 review of a traditional dance concert in which "antics of ancient days" are transformed, and presum-ably legitimized, by the introduction of "modern stage craft."[37]

At the Kwanangoma College of Music, founded in Bulawayo in 1961 to preserve and teach both Western and indigenous music, students learned to be competent in a variety of ethnic arts, not to excel at any one in particular. There was no effort to catalog and preserve musical genres, let alone delve into their spiritual dimensions. Kwanangoma prided itself on innovation; for ex-ample, developing concert-tuned wooden-slatted marimbas and placing them in "schools, restaurants, nightclubs and tourist spots" around the country. Marimba ensembles entertained and taught, giving the appearance of "tradi-tion," even though marimbas had scarcely been played on the Zimbabwean plateau prior to the 1960s.[38]

At exactly this time, new regimes in West Africa were actively promoting their own revivals and fusions of indigenous music. Governments funded all sorts of bands and demanded that they create modern music rooted in local culture. In Guinea, Sekou Toure's cultural initiatives produced some of the most resonant African popular music of the era, probably his greatest legacy.

What was going on in Rhodesia paled by comparison. The most powerful music in Rhodesia, the sounds likely to raise hairs on the backs of young African necks, did not come from the Kwanangoma school, but from musicians educated in the oral tradition, sometimes living in urban ghettos like Mbare, and quite unsupported by the state.

Mbare in the 1960s was a carnival of musical impulses. Aside from mbira, there was the popular Jerusarema dance, its Christian-sounding name a ruse to mislead missionaries. There were village drummers accompanying informal jiti songs. On Sundays, churchgoers belted out Africanized hymns, and as afternoon turned to evening, all manner of music played in beer halls, under shade trees, and in backyards throughout the township. At night, venues like Stoddard Hall reverberated with African jazz, and always, everywhere, radios blared rumba and rock 'n' roll.

Poet and scholar Musa Zimunya moved to Salisbury to attend high school in 1971. His mother was the half sister of Thomas's maternal grandfather, and this is how Musa came to visit the Mapfumo household in Mbare. "Thomas drank beer and smoked cigarettes," recalled Musa. "He was very shy. I remember he had sort of elusive eyes. You thought you were talking to him, and then he wasn't there. You weren't reaching him at all. He was always like that." Musa would later write about Thomas during this period, describing him as "a drifter": "As he wanders and drifts, Mapfumo begins to reflect on the music of his times and slowly becomes disenchanted with the unthinking culture of imitation of transient western pop styles with their emphasis on instant pleasure. He is horrified by the moral decadence of heavy rock music and its spiritually destructive ambience. The suicide death of Jimi Hendrix, the pop icon of the hippy era, was the final nail in the coffin."[39]

"He is right," Thomas agreed, years later. "When Jimi Hendrix died, well, I just felt that was the end of that type of music. From that time, I thought heavy metal was just no good. It was music for drug addicts. I started hating rock 'n' roll."

Not long after Hendrix died, a musician named Daram Karanga approached Thomas with a proposition. "He said he had been to a copper mine," Thomas recalled, "Mhangura mine, and they wanted a band to be formed there. He was looking for musicians, so he came to me and we discussed. Mhangura is way out of town, out in the *shatini*, in the *bhundu*! I had to consider that I was leaving town to go and live in the bush." Thomas joined reluctantly. "I was not employed," he recalled. "And I was not going to be a menace to my mother and father. I had to move on like the man I was."

By all accounts this new band was talented and diverse enough to appeal to the ethnically mixed mining community. Karanga was from Zambia, guitarist/ singer Elisha Josam from Malawi, and Joshua Dube, recruited from Mutanga to play guitar, had Mozambican ancestry on one side. The mine boss, Mr. Walker, required that the musicians work during the day and rehearse and perform at night. The story goes that when Thomas and Josam found work at the local chicken run, Walker exclaimed, "Hallelujah!" That sounded like a band name to the musicians, but Walker wasn't satisfied, and said, "Why don't you call yourselves Hallelujah Chicken Run Band"?

The Hallelujah Chicken Run Band was expected to perform hits of the day, and they did it well. "Elisha was in his own class," recalled Thomas. "He could sing most of these American tunes by people like Marvin Gaye. The problem was he was a drunkard, and when he got drunk, he could start trouble. Sometimes, he would just stop playing in the middle of a song—pack up his guitar and amplifier and put it away in the storeroom." Thomas was again reduced to imitating foreign singers and working behind an erratic front man. Beyond that, life at the mine was dull: "We used to spend the whole day playing cards and teaching children how to play golf." Now Thomas missed both his peaceful rural childhood and the teeming crush of Mbare.

One day at rehearsal, Dube began picking out a traditional Shona song on his guitar. It was a tune his father had played on mbira, and it had crept into the boy's guitar repertoire. Itinerant guitar musicians had been performing fingerpicked renditions of mbira songs for years, perhaps as far back as the 1930s when South African workers first brought Western instruments to Rhodesia.[40] But these songs had mostly been ignored by urban dance bands of the 1960s. As Dube played, Thomas stood listening, transfixed. The piece Joshua was playing was "Karigamombe," typically the first song taught to a young mbira player. It uses the most familiar harmonic pattern found in Shona mbira music, a succession of four phrases that cycle over and over. Thinking like a guitarist, Dube had mapped out chord changes for each of the four phrases:

C	F	Am
Dm	F	Am
C	Em	G
C	Em	Am

The "Karigamombe" progression has a puzzle-like symmetry.[41] In Dube's formulation, it begins on a C chord but doesn't end there, hence its circular, unresolved feeling. No two phrases are the same, but all are similar. The first phrases *end* with the same two chords, and the last ones *begin* with the same two chords, so that one can hear the cycle either as two long phrases or four short ones. Of course, exactly where an mbira player begins and ends can vary, mystifying the Western ear, as if the song had been playing since the moment it was created and the player simply joined in for a time.

The rhythm of an mbira song is also unique. A phrase consists of twelve eighth-note beats. The hosho marks *four* main beats in each phrase, but Dube's chord progression has just *three* chords per phrase. So the rattle is playing four groups of three beats, while the harmony may fall into three groups of four beats—the same twelve beats, but two different feelings. The rhythms of a 4/4 triplet shuffle and a 3/4 waltz meld and merge as the piece unfolds, and this ambiguous meter, combined with the melancholy restlessness of the harmony, creates a sound found nowhere else—the sound that caught the ears of Hugh Tracey, Alick Nkhata, American ethnomusicologists Paul Berliner and Tom Turino, and even Ian Smith, who once allowed that mbira music was "lovely."

"So I was playing this instrumental mbira song on guitar," recalled Dube. "Thomas was there, and he said to me, 'Look, I think we can do that song together. I can sing that song.' I said, 'Okay, come and sing.'" The song would become the Hallelujah Chicken Run Band single "Ngoma Yarira (The Drums Are Sounding)."[42] Elisha Josam etched out Dube's chord progression on guitar, and Robert Nekati followed the harmony on bass while Dube moved to a staccato lead guitar line. On drums, Thomas took up the hosho rhythm on hi-hat, and the lead vocal was a throaty cry reminiscent of an mbira singer at a ceremony. The adaptation felt good. *Everything* felt good, and that very night, late in 1972 or early 1973, the band debuted their new song for the miners. "They went mad," said Dube. "And that's how Thomas started doing mbira music."[43]

3 / When the Spirit Comes

I had an uncle on my father's side who would play mbira after
drinking. He would start out slowly and quietly, very introspec-
tive. But as he picked up emotion, he would become animated,
even aggressive, until he'd crash the deze [gourd]—actually break
it—and he would cry at the end of it all. They'd say it was because
he had reconnected with the ancestors, and the world of the
living became an obstruction, an impediment to full sublimation
of his spirit and emotion. Because he was flesh, he could not be
free of flesh. Hence the violence.

MUSA ZIMUNYA

Mbira players are made, not born. Sometimes they are touched by spirits and
become suddenly gifted. Families known for their mbira musicians exist, but
children are never ordained by birth to eke out their livings at bira ceremonies;
they are not like the griots of West Africa with their professionally signifying
surnames. Ask an mbira player how he or she learned, and you may hear a
tale of magic. Stella Chiweshe and Beauler Dyoko speak of transformational
illnesses that opened a door to the spirit world, and dreams in which they
heard songs that sprung readily from their fingers when they awoke. To this
day, Stella says she sleeps with her mbira close at hand so that music passed
from the spirits in sleep will not elude her in the fog of waking.

Beauler said her awakening came when she rejected a philandering husband and fell mysteriously ill. She began dreaming about her late father playing
mbira, and this worried her Catholic mother. Beauler obeyed the messages
in her dreams. She left home and went to Guruve, in Dande. She stayed there

for nine months in the care of traditional healers, *n'angas*,[1] and, once cured, returned home to a mother who had given her up for dead. Her mother performed a divination and soon found herself speaking with a familiar spirit. "The spirit was her husband," Beauler recalled. "Now, my mother said I must play mbira. She was happy." Beauler's mother traded a cup of salt for an mbira, and soon the young woman played her first song, "Nhemamusasa," singing words given to her in a dream by her late father. The family brewed beer to thank the spirit. By the mid-1960s, Beauler was performing at ceremonies and recording songs for Rhodesia state radio, the RBC.

Tute Chigamba, a serene elderly man of the mbira, reported a childhood gift, an ability to hear mbira songs and play them effortlessly, without instruction. When Chigamba was a boy, an old man in Murehwa wanted money to teach him, so much per song. Chigamba refused, and working on his own, he mastered five songs in his first week. When he returned, the old man was angry. "Oh! You have been lying to me when you said you didn't play mbira before."

When Hakurotwi Mude was a boy in Mhondoro in the early 1940s, he had problems at school, "traditional problems." He often felt ill in the classroom and asked the teacher to excuse him. "My dogs would be sitting outside," Mude recalled, "and on the way home, we would go hunting. The moment I got home, I would be fit. Eventually I decided maybe school wasn't for me." Mude moved to the capital to work and began to play mbira. He sang magnificently and eventually became a *svikiro* (spirit medium). Mude named his group Mhuri Yekwa Rwizi after his uncle, a Rwizi chief. In high demand for recordings and ceremonies, Mude's group attracted some of the best mbira musicians in the city.

Mbira playing is a high art. It demands mastery of a repertoire rich with variations and opportunities for improvisation. Personal expression comes only within an understanding of the music's precise rhythmic and melodic language. An outsider wishing to understand, or learn to play, mbira music confronts an intellectual and technical challenge—especially if one is unused to music rooted in polyphony and polyrhythm. Given Zimbabwe's harsh experience with Western colonialism, and the profound spiritual origins of this music, it's easy to see why an mbira player might hesitate to share his or her art freely with a European or an American. Of course, many have. But through those experiences, some players have developed a habit of obfuscation, even "slinging the bull," as one longtime student of mbira once put it.[2]

Stella Chiweshe, one of the most successful mbira performers on the international stage, is known to give lyrically mystifying interviews to Western journalists. "When preparing myself to go on stage," Stella once said, first of all, I refrain from talking. Then I start to listen to sounds. The sound of the mbira for me represents water. It flows over the boundary of our thinking as human beings. As soon as I hold the mbira, my playing is taken into something that I cannot control. I cannot stop, and I am thinking, "Which song is this? Which song is this?" I am just playing and singing what I'm seeing in my vision at that time. It's not like an old song that you keep on playing, like eating stale food. Everything is fresh. It's like I am being driven.

Such alluring conundrums, along with the music's inherent complexities, might lead a person not raised with this tradition to imagine that the mbira player's art is actually *based* on misdirection and disguise. In a concert setting, the audience sees only a large gourd (deze) into which the player's busy hands vanish. The deze amplifies the mbira's sound but also rounds out its naturally clear tones. A person watching three players might be hard-pressed to discern who is playing what. Waltz time and shuffle rub together, jostling and commingling in a polyrhythmic matrix. Beads or bottle caps fixed to a metal bar on the mbira, and around the edges of the deze, vibrate in response to each note played. The "buzzing" they produce is essential to the aesthetic—as much as distortion is to rock guitar. To a Western ear, that buzzing may seem yet another distraction, obscuring the actual music.[3] But the adept player clearly hears, through all of this, the individual parts and their interrelationships.

Mbira players view the career of Thomas Mapfumo with a mix of gratitude and suspicion—gratitude for uplifting and defending their traditions, suspicion for entering the spiritual realm with neither credentials nor purely spiritual intent. Thomas does not play mbira and has never claimed occult powers, yet some believe that spirits speak through him. "His spirit does not give him songs through dreams," Beauler Dyoko asserted, "but through daydreaming. He can get a song on the stage. You can ask him, 'How did you play that song?' and he won't know. He will have forgotten, because the spirit came while he was on stage."

"Thomas is clever enough," observed Chigamba, with a note of derision. "He went to the ancestral spirits, and he paid for that permission to play the pieces any time. Each and every year, he has to go there to see the ancestral spirits, to say, 'Thank you very much. You have done a lot. You are guiding me, and my pieces are doing well.' And from there, they bless him again and give him more powers. He knows what he is doing."

Most mbira musicians I have interviewed praise Thomas's work. Typical was one who called him "the only man who has managed to play mbira with modern instruments to my liking." Musicians who emulate Thomas's approach are often rebuked for combining songs inappropriately, changing their proper names, and confusing the spirits by playing them under the wrong circumstances.

Many guitarists in Zimbabwe play mbira songs, though few merit the approval of mbira musicians. Jonah Sithole is the consistent exception. Sithole never played mbira himself, but he took the spiritual aspect of the music seriously and drew his lines directly from mbira performances. He performed with understated dignity, standing straight and still, all his energies directed into his hands. None of the talented guitarists who have passed through the Blacks Unlimited over the years—including his closest match, Joshua Dube—has ever challenged Sithole's stature as the gold standard for mbira guitar. "But I can tell you this," declared mbira player and maker Chris Mhlanga, "you will *never* play in a bira ceremony with a guitar."

Thomas and his coterie of musicians have succeeded in commingling a world of beer halls, rock 'n' roll bands, journalists, poets, and politicians with the more shrouded realm of bira ceremonies, spirit mediums, and ancestors. Over the years, a few mbira players have attempted to move in the other direction, lured from their spiritual enclave by the enticement of popular acclaim. Among the most resourceful of these was Thomas's contemporary Ephat Mujuru.

Ephat was born in 1950 in Mujuru village in Manicaland, not far from the border with Mozambique. He was raised by his grandfather, Muchatera, a spirit medium and superb mbira player. "He played very clearly," said Ephat of Muchatera, "slowly. He could play so much that when you would listen, you would go way back, far away. He could create in my imagination a place that I never saw." Ephat's absorption in his grandfather's mystical arts dominated his childhood. He dedicated himself to mbira and showed such talent that he played his first ceremony at age ten. Ephat's family even played at gatherings organized by Thomas Mapfumo's traditionally minded relatives. The two young musicians met very early on, though they never became close friends.

Ephat's life of music and spirituality collided with Rhodesian realities when he enrolled at Saint Peter's Catholic School in Rusape. White teachers looked down on village culture. Ephat recalled, "They would preach against anything like mbira, anything that sounded African. They would make sure that if people kept the traditions, their children suffered. One of the headmasters was very much against me because of what was happening in my village." Enraged by this attitude, his grandfather Muchatera rescued Ephat from the Catholics and sent him away to study in Salisbury. "It was 1962," recalled Ephat:

That was the big explosion, because that's when our first African nation-alism started, and people wanted to know, "What has happened to our history?" People began to have the pride of their music. You would go to Mbare and be surprised to see so many people holding biras. There was a time that the government was trying to ban the mbira, because it was very powerful.[4] I remember we were playing at a particular place, and the police came and said, "No. No playing here." But we didn't stop. The more they said it, the more we played, because we were not afraid of anything. After that, they kind of ignored it, because even the police began to be interested. They could also take off their uniforms and come for the dancing. "You know, I am a policeman. But I like the music!"

Ephat left school at eighteen and took a clerking job in an accounting office where people were "very colonial." He recalled, "They recognized my talent, but tried to discourage me. Then they told me that there was a limitation of work." He lost his job and struggled in an alien urban world, full of "so much hate." Ephat sought refuge among mbira musicians. He traveled to Seke, a rural area south of Salisbury, to learn from a great player named Bandambira. He traveled to Masvingo, near Great Zimbabwe, to spend time with mbira player and builder Simon Mashoko. Ephat recalled playing with Mashoko in surrounding villages for people husking corn, and Mashoko instructing him in the art of singing mbira songs. Ephat became enraptured by the Shona language these older mbira singers used, a tongue full of oblique references and archaic phrases—what he called "deep Shona." Back in Salisbury, Ephat came under the tutelage of his uncle, Hakurotwi Mude, who was by then playing mbira and singing at ceremonies in Highfield and Mbare. In 1972, following the lead of "Uncle Mude,"[5] Ephat formed his first group, Mhuri Yekwa Mujuru, and began composing and arranging pieces on his own.

Around the time Thomas began to adapt Shona music in the Hallelujah Chicken Run Band, Ephat was invited to perform on national radio. He re-called performing an arcane song called "Guruuswa," which asks, "How can I cross the river?" A Shona poet, David Kabaji, asked to be part of the recording, and, as Ephat and his musicians began to play, the poet added improvised lines about starvation and suffering. He spoke about "our people" being "bombed in Chinhoyi," a clear reference to the seminal battle there in 1966. The song was soon banned from radio play, an early badge of honor for Ephat, who then invited this poet to record with him.

Much later, after the war and independence, Ephat was one of the country's most established and well-known mbira players. Working out of the Zimbabwe College of Music, he used to escort foreign visitors to hear mbira music at the Bandambira family compound in Seke. They would gather inside a large mud-and-pole hut, its floor just packed earth with a fire pit at the center. On tall wooden shelves, pots, plates, clay urns, and enamel bowls sat on display like artwork. The thatched roof had no opening at its peak, and smoke settled there, its resins seeping into the charred thatch. The musicians would arrange themselves in a tight group against the wall, three mbira players seated beside Bandambira's widow, who cradled a baby in her arms while boys to either side wielded large, loud hosho rattles.

This was how I first saw mbira music performed, and how I met Ephat. Intrigued, I accepted his offer of a deeper experience, one where we would "greet the spirit." In January 1988, Ephat escorted me and three other Westerners to his Uncle Mude's house in Highfield. The cement-block homes on Hakurotwi Mude's rutted dirt street stood close together. They were well made and tidy, though a little dilapidated by years of relative poverty. There was a good deal of peeling paint and the odd boarded-up window. Some of the yards were nappy with overgrown weeds. Mude's front room had been cleared of everything but a few wooden chairs, a bench, and a white Frigidaire, against which mbira players leaned as they played, seated on a straw mat. The concrete floor was swept clean. When we arrived, petitioners, as well as mbira and hosho players, were gathering. For all its humility, this modest room was becoming a sacred space, deep in the heart of the township.

Ephat's wife, Emely, arrived with children—a new baby, four-year-old Sylvester, and six-year-old Elizabeth, who wore a lavender dress with a white lace collar. Elizabeth rushed forward to hug her father and then began to dance, swinging one leg forward, and then the other, producing a dull slap each time her bare foot landed firmly on the concrete floor. Sylvester stood in the corner, hairless, holding his hands over his ears and pulling them away in rhythm, smiling at the effect. Emely emerged from the kitchen, dancing too, and ululating with a fluttering hand placed before her mouth, the baby swaddled to her back. Most of the fifteen or so people gathered were dressed in subdued colors—gray, brown, black, and dull green—but Emely wore a bright blue blouse and skirt, an orange kerchief around her head, and two necklaces of white beads. Her smiling and ululating seemed to electrify Ephat, who stood in the doorway, his eyes afire with anticipation.

Two boys hovered in the kitchen doorway playing hosho. Each held two hosho. Their left hands snapped forward to punch out what seemed the basic beat (1, 2, 3, 4), while their right hands rolled to the side in answer—*and-ah, and-ah, and-ah, and-ah.*[6] Beneath the hosho's cracking triplets, the three mbira inside gourds produced a dense, metallic texture—ambient and audible but difficult for me to discern as any particular melody. With some ten dancers crowding together in that small space, the smell of sweat mingled with other vague odors: food cooked some hours ago, gas, and a large urn of "seven-days" millet beer, about to be served.

A stout man in a white shirt and gray slacks appeared in the kitchen doorway. Mude surveyed the scene. His grave face and bloodshot eyes seemed at odds with the mirth before him. He took his place next to the mbira players. Ephat told us, his guests, that photography and recording were okay, "except when the spirit comes."

The mbira players rotated, and Ephat joined them on the floor. Mude began to sing, quietly at first, humming along with the mbira. He called to the kitchen for beer, and a man carried in a large clay urn containing the essential brew. Seven-days beer is milky, frothy, tart, and fizzy from fermentation and is served at room temperature. A man with a ladle filled a large enameled tin cup, which was passed around the room. Some sipped, others guzzled. One man drained the full cup in a single gulp, then passed it back to the server. When beer spilled on the floor, Mude snapped his fingers and a small boy appeared with a tub of black dirt to sprinkle over the spill. The beer-serving man trampled the moist dirt, and the boy returned with a grass brush and pan to collect it.

The music intensified—mbira players reached for a white powder to ward off blistering on their thumbs and fingers. Without warning Mude opened his mouth and released a hornlike blast that overpowered even the hosho before undulating into soft unison with the lead mbira. Mude's singing continued that way, sometimes tearing forth in waves of broken, yodeling melody—the style called *huro*—then quieting down with gentle rhythmic *mahon'era*, vocal riffs so soft they were sometimes hard to make out over the music. A woman ululated, her tongue racing back and forth across her upper palate. Barefoot dancers slapped their heels into the concrete, thudding out familiar counterrhythms, traditional rhythmic phrases heard often in Shona music. Each successive song drew the participants closer together, and we edged toward collective ecstasy.

Mude's sporadic cries and melodious murmurs recalled Thomas's singing, and the dancers crowded into that small space moved in ways similar to the fans at Thomas's beer hall gigs—their chests forward, shoulders back, knees rising high in the air. Suddenly, a young woman began to jitter. She fell to her hands and knees and, with her whole body shaking, crawled slowly backward toward the kitchen doorway. The music crested. Mude stopped singing, his clouded eyes fixed on the woman. The spirit had come, and what came next was unlike anything seen at a Blacks Unlimited show.

Everyone sat down. The hosho stopped, and the mbira dwindled to near silence. People began to clap in slow, soft unison, their cupped hands coming together like mirror images—greeting the spirit. Another clay urn filled with millet beer was brought in, and the white cup continued to circulate. Mude had drunk none of the beer, but now he had his shirt off, and he sat perfectly still, emitting low, guttural sounds, almost growling. One of the dancers put a black cloth over the medium's head, covering it and reaching down to the floor. His head hidden, Mude slapped his upper arm against his bare side, this sudden movement a sign of possession. A young man brought him a bowl of water, and Mude let the cloth slip away as he reached for it. He lifted the water to his lips, drank, then spat out suddenly, spraying people near him, including the trousers of a white-haired man. Was this a scold? A blessing? I couldn't tell, but I was riveted. One door leading to an adjacent room had mostly remained closed. Now a man emerged through it with a long wooden ladle for the water, and also a cloth sack, which he handed to the white-haired man, who now assisted Mude in his role as spirit medium. The white-haired man reached in and pulled out garments with which to dress the quivering woman, first a black ostrich-feather headdress, then a black-and-white robe, and finally a short wooden staff.

The woman slid forward toward Mude, who handed her a wooden snuff flask. She poured fine, brown *bute* (powdered tobacco) into the palm of her hand, took a pinch in her fingers, and snorted it, feeding her closed-eyed rapture. Mude ladled water from the bowl onto his bare back. There was no music now, just a potent silence, broken occasionally by soft pulsing hand claps. Mude began to converse with the woman—hushed monotone utterances separated by lengthy pauses. The woman reached into her gown for a leather scabbard and produced a twelve-inch carving knife. She caressed it, then placed its point against her chest and released a low, birdlike whistle. The knife did not penetrate, but she held it there for a long time before suddenly withdrawing it and laughing. The closed door opened, and a boy appeared with a small drum.

Mosquitoes moved in the dank, still air, but when one of the foreign visitors opened a bottle of insect repellant, Ephat flashed a startled glare. "The perfume!" he whispered. "Not now. The spirit is greeting you." Spirits, especially ancient ones, eschew Western things, and odors are especially offensive to them. Our presence was tolerated, but there were limits. Mude intoned words in a deep, quiet voice, his eyes still trained on the possessed woman, who appeared to be sleeping. One mbira player leaned close to another, playing almost inaudibly, apparently teaching him a song. "This is the discussion," Ephat whispered. "Now, the spirit is saying that we should take off our shoes." There was a shuffling in the room as some thirty people obeyed, adding a new edge to the room's sweaty bouquet.

It was 2:00 AM, and the musicians had been silent for more than an hour. Now, as the mbira began gingerly to sound again, a man came forward and handed Mude a coin, which he tossed into an empty wooden bowl. The white-haired man removed the coin and replaced it with a two-dollar bill. A few others added to the pot. Emely stood up, the baby again swaddled to her back and sleeping. She took Elizabeth by the hand, and as the hosho players went into action, they began to dance. Soon the boy with his drum started playing, and as dancers filled the floor again, Mude sang, piercing the air with high notes. Ephat took over the drum, beating out Shona rhythmic patterns. There was no real groove to his playing; that was the work of the hosho rattles. Rather, his drumming was like speech, little rhythmic arguments, separated by pauses and mirrored in his expressions and gestures—wide eyes, a stiffened neck, a shake of the head, and gruff exclamations: "Heh, heeey!"

Standing in the kitchen doorway with arms swinging, Emely released a siren-like ululation, and the ceremony reached its pitch. The possessed woman exited to the kitchen followed by the white-haired man. She returned in her street clothes and began dancing, her lively fluid movement affirming her release from possession. Younger musicians came forward to play the mbira. Women approached Mude to ask for snuff. One hoarded hers in a small vial she stowed between her breasts. During the next song Mude gestured the dancers away, clearing the floor for himself. The spirit medium danced in a series of poses and sudden hops, jagged movements scarcely related to the music. His black shawl tied around his waist and a metal spear in his hand, he looked downward as he moved. Everybody watched, but no one reacted. The dance seemed not so much a performance as a sign that the ceremony had reached its end.

It was just past 3:00 AM when Ephat circulated among the musicians, handing each of them a two-dollar bill from the wooden bowl while everyone sat around drinking warm Coca-Cola. The drumming boy said, "Tonight we stop early. If it is a pungwe, we go from 6:00 PM to 8:00 AM.[7] Tonight, there were just two spirits. Sometimes there are so many. Sometimes, *everyone* gets possessed." This lad probably meant that all the mediums present got possessed, but the message was clear: we foreign visitors had merely tasted the full experience of a bira ceremony. As the sky began to lighten, Mude's son drove us back to the city in an old Peugeot 404 with a bumper sticker that read "I Survived Catholic School."

This was *dandaro*, a social gathering, not a full-fledged bira. A more serious ceremony might be held in response to a problem—sickness, drought, or unexplained death. On such an occasion, music would be chosen to attract the svikiro's particular spirit. And it is less likely, though not impossible, that any foreign visitors would be present.

A svikiro, or medium, is not the same as a n'anga, or traditional healer, though their worlds overlap. Some mediums are proficient in healing arts, and some healers can become possessed by spirits. All over Harare, hand-painted signs read "Surgery/Chiremba," a confluence of British English and Shona. A Shona dictionary translates *chiremba* as "doctor," but not exactly in the British sense. Within these clinics, tucked between tailor shops and beauty salons, medical nurses work side by side with n'angas, all certified by the Zimbabwe National Traditional Healers Association (ZINATHA). At the chiremba, the n'anga would begin with herbal remedies, but if he deems it necessary, he might arrange a bira with a svikiro, seven-days beer, mbira musicians, and all the accoutrements needed to enlist the help of a spirit.

There are various sorts of Shona spirits. The *vadzimu*, as in *mbira dza-vadzimu*, are family ancestors who have passed away and gained knowledge of the future and insight into the causes of illness.[8] "Ancestors make the perfect parents," one scholar wrote, adding, "Human life is greatly enhanced by the ending of it."[9] Then there are *mashave*, roving souls who can travel great distances and are useful in healing. A *shave* that a family relies upon generation after generation can be adopted by the clan, becoming a *mudzimu*, the singular of *vadzimu*. On the other hand, a mudzimu who is never called upon may abandon its earthly relatives to become a shave.[10] And of course, there are evil spirits, *ngozi* and *varoyi*, witches who can possess you at will and "ride you through the night."

The *mhondoro* are ancestors for an entire clan or chieftaincy; the word literally means lion, for when a chief dies, he is believed to turn into a lion cub and slip off into the bush. A claim of mediumship for a mhondoro spirit requires rigorous scrutiny before it is accepted by the community. A mhondoro corresponds to a spirit province representing the actual land that a chief conquered or controlled during his lifetime.[11] In theory, Mashonaland can be divided into many such provinces, each with a single medium for its mhondoro, although in recent times things have rarely worked out so neatly. Sometimes, no medium arises to claim a spirit. Sometimes, the community rejects a claim, especially when it involves a highly revered mhondoro, such as those associated with Shona origins, or with fateful fights against the Ndebele, and later the Rhodesians. Topping the list of mhondoro are three names: Kaguvi, Nehanda, and Chaminuka. These figures are inseparable from this region's history, for they play a crucial role in the psychology of the 1890s Shona rebellion and the 1970s liberation war. Kaguvi and Nehanda have already been mentioned in this context. Chaminuka poses his own special set of complications.

British adventurer Frederick Selous—the man who guided Rhodes's Pioneers—provides an early written account of Chaminuka in his book *A Hunter's Wanderings in Africa* (1881).[12] Selous describes the murder of Chaminuka's spirit medium, Pasipamire, at the hands of Ndebele warriors loyal to their last king, Lobengula. "I am too old to run," Selous has Pasipamire saying, "but bid my son, who is young and swift of foot, creep away in the bushes while there is yet time, and carry the news to my people." The medium dies, but the people of his village, Chitungwiza—the same Chitungwiza that sprawls with music, life, and poverty south of Harare today—escape harm.

The story of Pasipamire's death is one of the most enduring tales of the Shona past. The "radical missionary" Arthur Shearly Cripps called Chaminuka "the man whom God taught," in his 1928 account. Here, the first British scouts are making inroads on the Zimbabwe plateau, the Ndebele still terrorize Mashonaland, and Pasipamire is a godlike figure deemed the "owner of the land."[13] It takes a full Ndebele army to defeat him, and even then, spears cannot actually kill Pasipamire, Chaminuka's medium. The final deed must be performed by a prepubescent boy.[14]

Mediumship is complicated and, where mhondoro are involved, often controversial. "There is no medium for Nehanda alive today," Thomas said once, and his view is typical. The mbira player Tute Chigamba follows these matters closely, and in 1998 he began to hear about a supposed medium for Nehanda who had turned up in Chipinge. The proof hinged on the woman's knowledge about where Nehanda had buried a pot of water. "They went there together," Chigamba reported, "and the woman said, 'Okay, you dig there.' And then they dug there, and they found the pot with the water inside. She said, 'I left you this.' So people believe that. Well, it's what they do. They take advantage. There is one Ambuya Nehanda in Mazoe area, and there's one in Zambezi Valley." His skepticism was unmistakable.

In the early days of Rhodesia, Shona spirituality was terra incognita for whites in general, including scholars and intellectuals. When a woman surfaced in 1903 claiming to be the new medium for Chaminuka, the administration sent a spy to eavesdrop on her. While possessed by her spirit, the woman proclaimed, "I am Chaminuka. I know everything. I am all-powerful. I caused the downfall of Barozwi and the Matabele and I will cause the white man to leave the country. Nothing is impossible to me." Jailed and interrogated, the woman committed suicide in detention.[15]

About twenty years later, the government sought to discredit a medium named Reresayi, the next to claim Chaminuka as her spirit. Reresayi was well-spoken and intelligent, and deemed dangerous because she professed to be "the government in charge of rain" and argued that people should pay tribute to *her* rather than to the thieving white government. Then, in 1934, a young man from Chiduku Reserve in Makoni also proclaimed himself the medium of Chaminuka. This claimant did not interfere with local tax collection as Reresayi had but instead engaged with white authority figures. In fact, he served as a crucial informant to influential authors—first, to a scholar of tropical diseases and herbal remedies, Michael Gelfand, then to Rhodesian historian Donald Abraham, and later on to the American ethnomusicologist Paul Berliner. Gelfand and Abraham, in particular, published groundbreaking works in advance of the liberation war. Historian Terence Ranger writes that much of the information in these books was incorrect, but Rhodesians had paid so little attention to African culture that these writings assumed outsized authority, providing all who read them with a radically oversimplified map of Shona culture and history.

The young medium from Makoni who spoke with Gelfand and Abraham, and thus whispered into the void of history, was Ephat's grandfather, Muchatera Mujuru. His words would echo loudly but, in the end would have unintentionally tragic consequences. Asked about this family connection with Zimbabwe's liberation struggle, Ephat became reticent. "There are things that even history should not know," he said. "There are things that should just be forgotten."

But Muchatera Mujuru has not been forgotten. Based largely on his information, Gelfand's 1959 book, according to Ranger, establishes Chaminuka as "the great messenger" between all Shona people and God, or Mwari. Complex regional and clan distinctions fall away in Gelfand's account, replaced by a friendly hierarchy wherein all Shona people are united under the watchful eye of a super ancestor spirit, Chaminuka. Ranger reports that Gelfand's book "was greeted with delight by most of those interested in the African past of Zimbabwe."[16] The book at last made Shona culture comprehensible to readers who had few other ways of approaching the subject, because they were either whites who had little contact with Africans or else Christianized Africans who had lost touch with their spiritual history. However flawed, Gelfand's picture of a monolithic Shona society, history, and cosmology suited an era in which Africans were laying aside old differences as they prepared to take on the Rhodesians.[17]

The success of Gelfand's book in Rhodesia helped Muchatera bolster his claim on the mediumship of Chaminuka and cast himself as an invincible figure. Ranger argues that this was Muchatera's ultimate objective, for, despite what he had told Gelfand, authorities in Makoni had rejected his claim to be possessed by Chaminuka. Through Gelfand, Muchatera promoted not only the mhondoro Chaminuka but himself as well.

Muchatera's stock rose higher still in 1963 when a historian of even greater stature than Gelfand, Donald Abraham, delivered, and later published (1966), a lecture on mhondoro cults in Shona political history. With Muchatera as his main source, Abraham revisits the history of the Rozvi Empire, giving Chaminuka the starring role. Abraham elaborates on Gelfand's claim that Chaminuka's spirit had impregnated the mother of the first Rozvi king, Mutota. This disputed claim made Chaminuka the father not only of the Shona religion but also of Shona politics. Little surprise that Rhodesian government strategists in the emerging independence war would come to see Muchatera as a potential pressure point for influencing black Rhodesians.

A decade later, as the war raged, Muchatera, now an old man, bent the ear of one more white scholar, Paul Berliner, whose rich book *The Soul of Mbira* (1978), with accompanying Nonesuch Explorer recordings, introduced Shona music and culture to the world. Brought to Muchatera by his grandson Ephat, Berliner pursued the old medium as a source on mbira music, not history as such. But along the way, Muchatera told Berliner a magical origin story for the mbira itself, once again giving key credit to Chaminuka—now effectively the father of Shona culture as well as religion and politics. Berliner presents this origin account as one among many, and he implicitly questions its veracity. He writes tactfully that Muchatera's "following in eastern Zimbabwe believe him to be the medium for the ancient Shona spirit Chaminuka," hardly an endorsement.[18] Still, for Ranger, Muchatera had now proven himself a "virtuoso informant," using the vehicle of white scholars to enhance his own claim to be medium for the most powerful of all Shona spirits.[19]

Chaminuka and Pasipamire pervade the fiction, poetry, song lyrics, and political oratory of the liberation struggle. Neither Gelfand nor Abraham sympathized with the African nationalists, though they inadvertently helped them. Gelfand was naive enough to think that promoting traditional life—including the activities of spirit mediums—would ensure the loyalty of Africans, whom he perceived as "law-abiding, polite, kind and considerate."[20] Abraham further buoyed the nationalist cause by proclaiming the historical existence of a Shona "state" whose "moral cement" had come from "Mwari [God] and his lieutenant Chaminuka."²¹ Nationalists could now argue that they were restoring order, not upsetting it. By most accounts, no overarching Shona polity ever existed. Indeed, there is not even a word for "state" in the Shona lexicon.

Muchatera was a self-serving and fanciful historian, but Ranger concludes, "It is hard to deny him the title of the single greatest influence on the Shona cultural revival."²² What is certain is that Shona culture was in revival. The vibrant, musical atmosphere Ephat Mujuru and Tute Chigamba experienced in Mbare in the early 1960s, and attributed to "our African nationalists," did indeed take place amid Chaminuka mania. Bira ceremonies and *dandanda* drumming and dance parties, the brewing of beer, and the dicta of spirit mediums were becoming means to "keep the spirits uprising, and give powers to the fighters."²³ No surprise, then, that military leaders on both sides worked hard to enlist the support of Shona spirit mediums, including Muchatera—as it turned out for him, an unfortunate by-product of his carefully orchestrated celebrity.

This battle for the loyalty of mediums was particularly intense in the far northern province of Dande, where Thomas Mapfumo's father was born, where Beauler Dyoko traveled to be healed by n'angas, and where bold guerrilla raids on white farms sparked all-out war in Rhodesia in 1972. Deep in Mashonaland, beyond the ragged northeast edge of the Zimbabwe plateau, Dande had survived the colonial ordeal buffered by its inhospitable climate and terrain. Now it became the scene of intense fighting between guerrillas and government forces. The region's deep valleys are hot and dry, covered with blade-sharp grasses and contorted trees. Anthropologist David Lan writes that most Zimbabweans regarded it as "a place of wild animals and backward people, drunkards and witches, left behind by modern times centuries ago."²⁴ What better place to hide and train a guerrilla army!

Traditionally, Dande's people lived in the valleys to be near rivers, but their minds were forever on the plateau above, where the ancestors came from and the climate was moist and mild. In the valleys, there were no cattle to support life. Salt, found along the riverbanks, was the main item of commerce from the sixteenth to the twentieth century. Spirit mediums were preoccupied with manipulating the rain clouds that lingered at the rim of the plateau, for the surest measure of their power was the ability to make rain in the gnarled and dry lowlands.

Dande is home to the Korekore people, who claim the great Nehanda among their local mhondoro spirits. This is why ZANU guerrilla commander Mayor Urimbo traveled there in 1971 to meet a frail old woman believed to be Nehanda's medium. Urimbo described his fateful meeting to David Lan.

She was very old. She never bathed and ate only twice a week. Her food had to be ground with a mortar and pestle. She hated all European things. We told her: "We are the children of Zimbabwe, we want to liberate Zimbabwe." She was very much interested. She knew very much about war and the regulation of war. She said: "This forest is very, very difficult for you to penetrate," but she gave us directions. She told us what kind of food to eat, which routes to take, what part of the forest we were not allowed to stay in or sleep in, where we were not allowed to fight. She said we were forbidden to go with girls and she taught us how to interpret many signs in the forest, which would allow us to live safely and know when our enemy was near.[25]

Urimbo's fighters looked after Nehanda's medium, carrying her to Zambia on a stretcher when it became too dangerous for her to stay home. Leaders in ZANU also won the allegiance of other Dande mediums, who helped direct convoys of porters carrying weapons from the Mozambique border and empowered guerrillas to read nature's signs. Two eagles fighting meant bomber planes were coming. A tortoise in the path meant the route was safe. A snake was a warning to turn back. A pinch of bute (medium's snuff) brushed across a forehead could shield a man from bullets, and there are stories of mediums teaching guerrillas to vanish in thin air.[26]

Many guerrillas came from missionized Christian backgrounds, so it was by no means clear that they would win the support of mediums in this forbidding environment. These august figures in their black robes, rejecting Western clothing and technology, even soap, even Coca-Cola, were a force unto themselves. Unlike n'angas, healers who could charge money for their services, spirit mediums were of necessity poor so as to remain incorruptible. Mediums revered water and reviled blood. What sympathy would they have for warriors armed with guns and machetes? And if they were to choose sides in the war, which way would they go? In 1973, the Rhodesians conducted a national survey of spirit mediums and found some willing to condemn the guerrillas for the shedding of blood.[27] But most mediums ultimately backed the guerrillas. Lan writes that they were guided by one overriding truth: "The single most important duty of the spirit mediums is to protect the land. From the grave, from the depths of the forest, from the body of a lion or of their mediums, the *mhondoro* control in perpetuity the land they conquered during their lives. Under the rule of the whites their land had lost its fertility. Sacred places had been fenced off and ruled out of bounds. The guerrillas offered land as renewed fertility and as restored tradition. They offered a Zimbabwe returned to its original and rightful owners."[28]

Spirit mediums made onerous demands on the guerrillas, including that they refrain from sexual activity. To the extent this was followed it was a hardship, and it became part of a culture of discipline among them. Even Christian fighters came to respect the mediums and follow their advice. The influence of Dande's mediums became lore in the cities, adding fuel to the traditional revival.

This was the context in which Thomas Mapfumo's music would soon resonate widely. But even as Thomas was fashioning "Ngoma Yarira (The Drums Are Sounding)," his first militant song, rooted in mbira tradition, Shona spirituality was already finding its way into another kind of "chimurenga song," namely, propaganda music used by guerrillas to recruit supporters. In 1972, union man turned ZANU "political instructor" Dickson Chingaira—aka Comrade Chinx—began changing the lyrics of popular hymns, school sing-alongs, drinking songs, and recreational *jiti* and *shangara* numbers born of village parties, for political purposes. "I love Jesus" became "I want war."[29] Mbira music was also a source for Chinx. "Nhemamusasa," an mbira song about making a shelter from a tree, became "chimurenga" or even "sabiedhu," submachine gun. Familiar melodies made the songs easy to learn; militant lyrics made them exciting to sing. During the war, Chinx organized impromptu choruses to sing chimurenga songs on ZANU's Voice of Zimbabwe broadcasts out of Maputo, Mozambique. A Rhodesian air serviceman recalled coming across "Africans in the bush, sitting around a radio, singing."[30]

As much as the Rhodesians tried to co-opt African culture, they could not compete on this level. Addressing the nation in 1973, Ian Smith said of the "terrorist" guerrillas, "They found a few witchdoctors of doubtful character and of little substance, and succeeded in bribing them to their side. . . . I'm sure I do not have to inform you how easy it is to mislead these simple gullible people who still believe in witchcraft and the throwing of bones."[31]

Muchatera Mujuru had persuaded influential people that he was Chaminuka's medium and had made friends in high places, including the government, in the process. But his conflict with the chiefs in his hometown, Mutota, only intensified. Traditionally, Lan writes, "the chiefs of the past . . . select and install the chiefs of the present."[32] This happened through the vehicle of the spirit medium, through whom the chiefs of the past spoke to the living. The Rhodesians had interfered with this practice, sidelining the spiritual selection process and appointing chiefs they imagined they could control. This inevitably set up conflicts between traditional and political authority. If a local chief recognized a medium, especially for a great spirit like Chaminuka, he effectively surrendered power, and perhaps displeased his governmental benefactors. In 1962, a chief named Zambe publicly declared Muchatera's claim to be Chaminuka's medium bogus. Zambe summoned Muchatera to a private meeting at which he said, "You don't pay your respects to me. I am not interested in you and I do not accept you as a medium."[33]

Subsequently, Muchatera became known for socializing with the white district commissioner over tea. He was said to prefer buns over *sadza*, and to hang photographs of whites in his *banya*, his ceremonial dwelling. Key figures in ZAPU and ZANU concluded that Muchatera's loyalties lay with the white government. Guerrilla leaders claimed that the medium had even flown in a helicopter over Dande, dropping leaflets that read "I Chaminuka condemn the terrorists."[34]

In January 1977, a group of ZANU guerrillas marched into Muchatera's compound and shot him dead in broad daylight. They blew up his banya with a rocket and forced the people there to bury him without ceremony. Muchatera's murderers wanted no one to wonder whether security forces, or local chiefs, or even Ndebele carrying an old grudge against Chaminuka, might have been responsible. They arranged a meeting with the Catholic Justice and Peace Commission and explained that Muchatera had been killed because he was being used by the Rhodesian government. For Ephat, the guerrillas' targeting and killing of his grandfather—the man who had raised him and taught him to love mbira—was unbearable. *"There are things that even history should not know. There are things that should just be forgotten."*

4 / Songs for the Book of History

I didn't know Mugabe. I didn't know what ZANU was. No one
came to me and told me how to join the guerrilla war. It was out
of these songs. [Mapfumo] was sort of telling us, "You belong
somewhere. You people must work toward something. That
makes you Zimbabwean. That makes you black."
ELIAS MUDZURI

From its founding in 1891, the *Rhodesia Herald*—later just the *Herald*—was
always a government mouthpiece. Flashes of journalistic independence aside,
the paper's mission has been to serve rulers, whether Rhodes, Smith, or Mugabe. In 1971, *Herald* stories still referred to the "Rhodesian independence
dispute," reflecting Smith's belief that he could negotiate an end to African
nationalism. Smith unveiled his Anglo-Rhodesian Agreement that year, telling
the *Herald*, "I am a very happy man." The settlement made minor concessions
to nationalists in return for recognition by England. Black nationalists joined
white hard-liners in dismissing it as a sellout, and when the accord failed four
months later, Smith was bitter. He lashed out, punishing enemies on the left
by imposing racial restrictions on public drinking, swimming, and university
housing. Smith now faced a hard truth: preserving the country his forefathers
had built would demand the blood of its sons and daughters. This was war,
but winnable, as Smith's people saw it: "the best counter-insurgency force in
the world" versus a bunch of "garden boys."[1]

   In June 1972, a coalfield explosion at Hwange (then Wankie) killed 390
Africans and 36 whites.[2] The nation was still reeling from this tragedy when
guerrillas armed with AK-47s mounted a dawn attack on the Altena farm near

Mount Darwin, then slipped back to their bases in Mozambique, unaccosted. Rhodesian forces had swiftly crushed the demonstrations, strikes, and riots of the past. Altena signaled a new kind of resistance—bold, violent, well coordinated, and informed by intelligence.

The year 1973 brought robust rains, economic vigor, and the creation of "protected villages," razor-wired encampments intended to starve the guerrillas by denying them contact with civilians.[3] The collateral result—half a million disease-ridden captives—would one day be a national scandal. For now, *Rhodesia Herald* headlines touted Operation Hurricane, Smith's military campaign against the camps in Zambia and Mozambique. Casualties were chronicled in a routine way, intermingled with news about petty crime, road accidents, beauty pageants, soccer matches, and debates about the unsightliness of curbside garbage collection. For the most part, Rhodesian town dwellers, four-fifths of the white population, could still ignore the war that would soon upend their lives.

Few places in Rhodesia were farther removed from the action than the Mhangura copper mine where Thomas Mapfumo and the Hallelujah Chicken Run Band plied their trade that year. Front man Elisha Josam later complained that Thomas never seemed proud of the band and gave it short shrift in interviews. "He's probably right," Thomas agreed, mostly recalling the tedium of the band's routine at the mine. And yet, it was here, in this artificial world, that Thomas and Joshua Dube dipped into the sacred mbira realm and created "Ngoma Yarira," a landmark in Zimbabwean music history.

The song's significance was far from obvious at the time. The musicians knew its percussive guitar lines and African melodies excited the miners, but there was no reason to think this enthusiasm would translate to the country's urban centers. Even Thomas put more faith in the band's Afro-rock repertoire—a brassy, jazz-infused sound reflecting the influence of the contemporary Ghanaian band Osibisa. Thomas told *African Parade* he wanted to play the saxophone like Stan Getz and predicted, amusingly, "Fifty years from now, jazz will still be popular when pop is not."[4]

In Salisbury, the Teal Recording Company was beginning to press vinyl discs of local music. Along with South Africa's Gallo Records, Teal had kept a branch office in Bulawayo since the mid-1960s. Gallo's Rhodesian productions had ventured beyond township jazz acts and rock 'n' roll cover bands to include guitar outfits singing in Shona, starting with the Green Arrows and the Great Sounds. But Teal had focused more on the lucrative foreign music market, picking up licensing rights for RCA Victor just in time to ride the Elvis wave. This success inspired British tycoon Tiny Roland to buy up a controlling share, making Teal part of Lonrho, one of the biggest mining conglomerates in southern Africa. As one Teal manager recalled, "Lonrho knew nothing about music," so, with cash on hand and little supervision, Teal's A&R (artists and repertoire) man, Tony Rivet, started looking for producers and artists to create records for Rhodesia's African market.

In the summer of 1974, Teal held a nationwide talent competition at the Skyline Motel, and Hallelujah Chicken Run Band competed alongside top acts like Harare Mambos, Safirio Madzikatire, Eye Q, and OK Success, most of whom played rumba variants. "We were very confident," recalled Thomas, "because we had something different to offer. It was their first time to hear Afro-rock being sung in Shona, and people went wild. We won the contest— the first prize." Crispen Matema, the best producer Rivet had recruited, was in the audience that day and knew instantly he had found an act for Teal's new Afro Soul imprint. He drove to Mhangura to meet the band and arrange a recording session. A Teal driver brought the musicians to Mbare at night, and the next morning they entered an eight-track studio called Advertising Promotion Limited, on the eleventh floor of Robinson House in downtown Salisbury. The studio allowed for no overdubbing, and there were few retakes. By Thomas's count, the band tracked seven singles that day, including "Ngoma Yarira," which was credited to "Thomas and Joshua [Dube]," a shared acknowledgment that would reoccur rarely in Thomas's canon.

Thomas was frankly surprised when this mbira adaptation outsold the other songs. "We were playing a lot of variety," he recalled, "but the people picked 'Ngoma Yarira.'" Listening today, you can hear the essential Mapfumo sound coming together in this crisp two-minute recording. Drums are scarcely audible, but the lilting, hosho-like, 12/8 sizzle of the hi-hat is there, and the two electric guitars—played damped, with a little flesh rolled over the end of the strings on the picking side—are backed by a leaping bass line that drives the rhythm with the tight mesh of mbira music. Dube's guitar line has more punch and clarity than the soft, round-toned mbira it imitates, but the source is unmistakable. The song's vocal alternates between a strong, raspy melody sung by Robert Nekati, and soft, wavering chants sung by Thomas—between them echoing the high huro and the low mahon'era vocals of a bira ceremony. This was not the first time a modern band had adapted Shona traditional music, but it was the time that mattered. "This actually made me change *my* mind," recalled Thomas. "From there, I really knew what the people wanted."

Teal sales rep Emmanuel Vori was just eighteen and fresh out of school when "Ngoma Yarira" came in the door. Vori vividly recalled the moment when Shona speakers at Teal first heard it. The title translates "The Drums Are

Sounding," and the song's sparse lyrics include the line "Boys, let me get killed." Vori said that for the "guys in the library" the sounding of drums coupled with a willingness to die could mean only one thing: "It's war. We are going to war. That's what the song is all about." Thomas confirmed that "Ngoma Yarira" was "a war song," but, intriguingly, his cocomposer, Joshua Dube, looked past the political message, construing the song simply as a reworking of an mbira standard—nothing more.[5] Dube provided the basis for the song's music, while Thomas composed the lyrics; this likely explains their divergent memories of the song. The B-side of "Ngoma Yarira," "Murembo (Elephant's Tusk)," also builds on a traditional Shona melody and has political overtones. Amid oblique references to a "hornless cow, . . . the entanglement of snakes in the veldt," and "the buzz of bees," comes the refrain "Vana vapera hondo yauya" (All the children have perished. The war has come).[6] Thomas has called this pair of songs the first "chimurenga single," explicitly linking its intent to the liberation struggle, and, he insisted, "people knew exactly what it was talking about."

"The war had arrived," recalled Musa Zimunya. "'Murembo' says, 'Look out, here comes trouble. Here comes conflict. Because of human misbehavior, we're always in conflict like snakes.' It was banned off the air in Rhodesia. They picked it right out."[7] During the war years, even the white managers at Teal— far from attuned to Shona idioms—suspected that the success of Thomas's songs had something to do with the conflict. One recalled Thomas's "gift for producing music that had two meanings." Public perceptions were shaped by race, culture, language, class, and, in the Cold War setting, education. Some blacks went to school in South Africa and returned with a pro-Western outlook; others studied in the Soviet Union and came back as quasi communists. In this balkanized world, it was hard to predict how a song would be heard. "Thomas's single would come out," the Teal manager recalled, "and the Rhodesian Broadcast Corporation would play it a few times, and then somebody would point out to them the way people in the townships were interpreting the song. Then they would ban it."[8]

Thomas knew he was tapping into incendiary emotions. "We lived in darkness," he recalled. "We were always at each other's throats. Each time I saw a white man, I saw him like an enemy, and he thought I was his enemy." In a *Parade* interview from 1975, Thomas dwells on the *sound* of the music.[9] To acknowledge any political agenda would have spoiled his game. Nevertheless, well-attuned listeners now began looking for messages in Thomas's songs and, soon, in those of other singers. The moment when the tide of Rhodesia's popular music culture began its gradual shift from passive imitation to engagement came in 1974 with "Ngoma Yarira" and "Murembo."

"We threw all that other music in the dustbin," recalled Thomas, who now boasted to *Parade* that his band's new African sound would outlast "Pop, Soul and Motown." This idea surely intrigued the magazine's cosmopolitan editors, but Thomas was out on a limb. Foreign music would rule Rhodesian airwaves and dance floors for years to come. The most important thing "Ngoma Yarira" had changed so far was Thomas himself. Had he lacked the passion and determination to take his idea to the wilderness and master it, this single would have been as Dube remembered it—just another traditional adaptation, albeit a successful one.

Effectively "owned" by the Mhangura mine in early 1975, the Hallelujah Chicken Run Band was performing up to thirty hours a week and earning ten Rhodesian dollars per hour, plus proceeds from day jobs—better money than most of the Africans at the mine. This inequity raised eyebrows among other entertainers at the mine. "The compound manager didn't like the band," recalled Dube. "Even the footballers were jealous."

"We had a book," recalled Thomas, "and if we played for so many hours, we would write down the number, and be paid for those hours. But we ended up not being paid. So I went to this store in Harare where we used to buy things on account, and got a lot of LPs and things. I sold those things because I was trying to recover my money. That was a stupid thing to do, and I got myself into trouble. The police were after me."[10]

Thomas was arrested in Salisbury and brought to court to face charges for abusing his mine account. Released on bail, he slipped away to the home of a girlfriend, a singer in Kadoma, and then an uncle's house in Bulawayo. The police caught up with him there, sitting outside with the uncle's family, listening to mbira music. After a few days at Gray's Inn Jail, Thomas was transferred back to Salisbury and the courtroom, and, with the help of a lawyer, he made a good case. The magistrate did not jail him but insisted he repay the mine R$900. Teal picked up the bill. According to Emmanuel Vori, the record company was eager to do it, as the arrangement freed Thomas from his contract with the mine. Thomas could now tour the country and promote his own records. But first he needed a new band, and that would take some doing.

Thomas's biological father had died after a sudden illness in 1973. The old man's brother Jeremiah had not known where to find Thomas, and by the time word reached Mhangura, Tapfumaneyi Mupariwa had already been buried. Thomas had endured this shock alone, part of the confusion and numbness of his life at the mine. Now, two years later, he returned to his mother and stepfather and spent a few weeks sitting around practicing his saxophone. Once again, Musa Zimunya, a distant relative, found him there. The University of Rhodesia, where Musa was studying, had become a hotbed of nationalist activity. Whites had taken to calling it "the little Kremlin on the hill,"[11] and there were frequent demonstrations and police actions on campus. "I was a radical youth at the university," recalled Musa, then preparing to leave the country and study in London. "Somebody had picked up the information that they were going to raid us at the university. They said if you have relatives in town, go and put up with them for the weekend. So I put up at Thomas Mapfumo's place."

Musa felt a creative kinship with Thomas. "I could understand what he was doing," he recalled, "because I was trying to do the same thing with my poetry—interpret the situation. I knew that he was sympathetic, but Thomas then, he didn't have many words. He would follow things, but I don't think his political views were that organized. There was nothing in his shyness to suggest that he was militant." Musa still perceived Thomas as haunted by "despair and aimlessness," more personal than political. Thomas had fathered his first child in 1970, out of wedlock. Now, five years later, Musa recalled "a woman who came to the house with a baby" and a troublesome "row" within the family. "I remember," he said, "in all the discussions, even over this woman, Thomas was quiet, and it was left with the mother." Musa said Thomas was absorbed in the challenge of making an artistic statement, something that would differentiate him. "I remember he had his saxophone in his hand one day, and I said to him, 'Why are you learning the saxophone?' He said, 'Because everybody is so good with guitar. Everybody is trying to play like Jimi Hendrix. Nobody plays the saxophone.'"

Thomas started hanging out at Jamaica Inn, twenty kilometers out of town on the Mutare Road, an out-of-the-way bar where married guys took their girlfriends. The white manager, Mr. Wilson, was a fan of Thomas's who had once driven to Mhangura to try to convince him to leave the mine. Now that Thomas was free, Wilson wanted him to form a band. Jamaica Inn had a good track record with music. In 1974, the South African "saxophone-jive" star and Gallo Records producer West Nkosi had come to Salisbury scouting for talent and had discovered Zexie Manatsa and the Green Arrows there.[12] Now Nkosi was paving Zexie's path to stardom. The first single they produced together, "Chipo Chiroorwa," featured wah-wah guitar and sold more than twenty-five thousand copies to become Rhodesia's first gold record. With the Green Arrows off and running, Thomas cobbled together a nameless group to take their place at Jamaica Inn. But nothing serious happened until the day Jonah Sithole walked through the door.

Sithole was a soft-spoken young man with a friendly face and dark, penetrating eyes. His quiet intensity was something you felt instantly, and he played guitar with the force of a loaded truck rolling down a mountain road. "I admired Jonah straightaway," recalled Thomas. "His playing just touched me, and I said to myself, 'This man is good, good enough to play chimurenga music.'" Of course, in 1975, "chimurenga music" was not a known genre, at least not outside those clandestine pungwes where guerrillas led villagers in militant sing-alongs until sunrise. All that was a world away from the nightclubs where Thomas and Sithole now began their episodic courtship.

Sithole was born in 1952 and grew up next to the Shabani asbestos mine, not far from Great Zimbabwe. He picked up guitar from his older brother and, after being "chucked away from school" in Bulawayo, made his way north looking for opportunities in music, first in Kwekwe, where he palled around with Joshua Dube, then in Salisbury, where he distinguished himself as a rumba guitarist in the Lipopo Jazz Band. When that band's Congolese players were deported in 1974, Sithole floundered again. He halfheartedly joined Pepsi Combo, a pop and soul band out of Mutare, and that's when he stopped by Jamaica Inn and met Thomas. "We met just by chance," recalled Sithole. "I had my group. I was looking for work. Thomas was there with his saxophone. He had no group and we had no kit. So we teamed up."

They formed a band called Black Spirits—a name Oliver Mtukudzi would later adopt—and just two months later, they were wooed away by a better offer in town. The wooing came from Solomon Tawengwa, who would one day be elected mayor of Harare. At the time, Tawengwa had just opened a new hotel and bar in Highfield called Mushandira Pamwe, "working together." Thomas recalled Tawengwa as an ally of local musicians, and Mushandira Pamwe would be a fixture of the city's music scene for decades. The place was a box of a building with a central glass column around which stairs wound up to a large hall with a raised stage at the far end. Floods of beer, sweat, and blood would grace its vinyl dance floor over the years, leaving it worn and grimy by the 1990s. But in 1975, the place seemed modern, even glamorous, "in a class of its own," recalled William Mapfumo, Thomas's half brother. It had modern toilets and an elevator to the hotel rooms. Musa Zimunya remembered it as "beautiful—singularly the most exquisite showplace in town." Musa was awed by the red curtains surrounding the performers and the luminous power of stage lights, all conjuring an enchanted world of late-night music jams, drinking, and dancing, a world he longed for but had little access to as a university student. The last rides to the campus in Mount Pleasant left Highfield just after sunset, and if you missed them, you were stranded until morning.

The Black Spirits played three months at Mushandira Pamwe. Sithole deeply admired Thomas's Afro-rock style, which reminded him of Fela Kuti's Nigerian Afrobeat sound, "really African." With guidance from Thomas, Sithole now began playing what he called "chimurenga guitar," lifting lines from mbira pieces and other traditional sources. Thomas remembers the Black Spirits as a cover band that mixed tunes by the Blue Notes and the O'Jays with the odd Shona song. The band never recorded. Sithole recalled, "Some old friends of Thomas's muscled in, so there was no peace anymore. I had to pack my bags with some other guys, and go back to Mutare."

Mutare is Zimbabwe's fourth-largest city, with around 170,000 people and located one hundred miles east of Harare, nestled among the mountains of Manicaland in a scenic, bowl-like valley. Once a haven for gold and diamond prospectors, Mutare now drew both Thomas and Sithole away from the hubbub of the capital. They would spend much of the next two years there, out of the limelight and free to experiment. Two months after Sithole abandoned the Black Spirits, Thomas showed up in Mutare with a group of musicians that included his uncle Marshall Munhumumwe on drums and guitarist Leonard "Pickett" Chiyangwa, who had grown up playing traditional Shona music.[13]

Thomas and his musicians found an abundance of tranquillity at the Nyamanindi Hotel in an outlying Mutare hamlet called Basilbridge. Owner George Nyamanindi wanted music but had little to offer in return. "It was real country life," Thomas recalled with a laugh. "We used to go and wash our clothes by the river, and get firewood from the forest to do our cooking. Sometimes, we would just wait for a bus coming from the city to bring some people to play for." The band soon moved to a nightclub in Zimunya, closer to Mutare. It turned out the owner there, Mr. Murape, was already in negotiation with Sithole. Sithole recalled:

> That's how we met for the second time. But this old man was a crook as well, you know? These exploiters! Within two months nothing was doing, so I told the guys, "Hey, I think we have got a program now to go and invade Harare and get some jobs." Thomas said no. He didn't think the time was right, and I said, "Well, what are we going to live on? This old man is skinning us alive." So I told them, "Okay guys, I'm going back to Harare." And I came back and played with the Great Sounds from 1975 into early '76.

"Jonah was always a problem," said Thomas, recalling the guitarist's fickleness during this period. Neither Thomas nor Sithole could name all the musicians who came and went from Murape's nightclub. Among them was a drummer named Danny, best remembered for his eventual death by electrocution while attempting to steal copper wire from high-voltage power lines in Highfield. A particularly strong lineup Thomas and Sithole assembled in their Mutare laboratory became the first to use the name Blacks Unlimited. They had wanted to call the band Blackmen Unlimited, but Murape insisted on the shorter take.

The money was abysmal, seven Rhodesian dollars a week for Thomas and less for the others. Thomas and Sithole both dismissed this chaotic era as a preamble to the start of their real career together a year later. Nevertheless, the original formation of Blacks Unlimited did record four great singles.[14] These energetic, freewheeling numbers are mostly in minor keys and feature bluesy bent notes in Thomas's vocal. Thomas's dalliances in Afro-rock, American pop and soul, rumba, and Shona music all color the sound. On "Imhere," his voice breaks like Wilson Pickett's, just before the song shifts to a racing Shona beat. The best remembered of these songs is "Yarira ne Hosho (Play the Hosho),"[15] a take on the traditional song "Baya Wabaya," revved up with what Musa Zimunya termed a "jerky rock beat." "Yarira ne Hosho" outsold anything Thomas had recorded. But the real action went down at the band's live shows in Mutare.

Geoffrey Nyarota—destined to become one of Zimbabwe's best political journalists and editors—was a young teacher at Regina Shelley Mission School at the time. He lived in Nyazura, near the Mozambique border, and made weekend trips to Mutare to "spend Saturday evening listening to Thomas Mapfumo and his band." Nyarota had first heard Thomas sing at an aunt's wedding reception in Mbare in 1964. Just thirteen at the time, Nyarota had helped the Springfields set up, feeding an extension cord through the window of his aunt's "matchbox house" and plugging it into a light socket to power the amplifiers. The band had played hits of the day, with a young woman singing Millie Small's "My Boy Lollipop" and a gangly kid belting out the Beatles' "I Feel Fine." Twelve years later, that kid had acquired charisma. "I could see that Thomas was feeling successful," recalled Nyarota, "as if he was conscious that he was a big man. And he had a following. Guys used to drive all the way from Harare just to listen to him." Nyarota also noted Sithole's unusual guitar style. "You listened to that guitar," he said, "and what you heard was the sound of the mbira. This was a new genre of music, different from anything we had listened to."

Nyarota had been a devotee of the Lorenzo Marques Top 20 out of Mozambique (LM Radio), an international hit parade of Rolling Stones, Jethro Tull, Thin Lizzy, Deep Purple, Black Sabbath, and Jimi Hendrix.[16] "When I was in primary school," recalled Nyarota, "if there was a program of mbira music on the radio, I would switch it off. That was music for *old* people." Nyarota was vaguely aware of the traditional music revival going on in Mbare in the 1960s, but his ear was tuned to rock, soul, rumba, and *mbaqanga* music from South Africa. "These were the popular music styles of the day," he insisted. "Mbira was not. So for Thomas to go off on this tangent was very brave."

The Zimbabwe African National Liberation Army (ZANLA), which was ZANU's military wing, had begun to move freely across the border to and from the camps in Mozambique. That country had undergone a sea change in 1974 when Portugal—worn down by fighting insurgencies in three African countries, under strong international pressure, and unsettled by a military coup back home—had abruptly granted independence and left. Samora Machel, Mozambique's new president, had closed the official border with Rhodesia and declared open support for ZANLA. White Rhodesians felt the sting of being denied access to Beira's beaches, wine, and prawns, but that was the least of it.[17] Mozambique was becoming the deadliest front in a deepening armed conflict.

"Up to 1976," recalled Nyarota, "the war was something that we heard about from a distance. It was in the northeastern districts of the country, Mutoko and Mount Darwin. But after '76, it moved to include Manicaland. Our school was seven kilometers from the border with Mozambique, and this was the route for loads of youngsters crossing the border from the interior, from as far away as Salisbury. Our school became a very popular port of call for ZANLA."

In Salisbury, William Mapfumo recalled people disappearing from the street, going to war. "You could see somebody you knew very well," he said, "and then you don't see him anymore. He's not dead. That's when we knew, 'Ah, he went to Mozambique. He made it.'" On the way, many making this journey stopped by the club in Zimunya and took succor in the sound of Thomas crying out with the wail of a bira ceremony, and Sithole summoning mbira melodies from his guitar.

Manicaland was on its way to becoming a "liberated zone," and for the first time, Geoffrey Nyarota believed victory was possible. The songs he heard in Mutare fed this feeling. Strangely, this literary man did not perceive political statements in Thomas's lyrics. For him, the *music* was the message. It was "preparing us for a future where our own identity would be paramount," recalled Nyarota. "Mapfumo was spearheading this process, bringing the village to the nightclub, and making mbira music, which had always been there in the back of our minds, a popular genre. He made *me* dance to this music, which I had never done."

Late in 1976, Nyarota was driving out of Nyazura when he encountered a group of ZANLA guerrillas heading into town. On his return, he heard shots and explosions. The downtown police station was under attack. On his twenty-sixth birthday, Nyarota was arrested. The police resented this young mission schoolteacher with his fancy car and assumed he must have had a role in the police station assault. Nyarota was held for twenty-one days, beaten, and tortured, but he never revealed that he had in fact seen the guerrillas coming, a confession that would likely have cost him his life. Eight months later, ZANLA held a pungwe in the mission school's dining hall. Rhodesian soldiers heard the singing and attacked, leaving two ZANLA men and a number of children dead. The school was closed the next day, and Nyarota's teaching career ended. He returned to Salisbury to begin a new life as a trainee journalist, becoming the first black reporter to write for the *Rhodesia Herald*.

The Blacks Unlimited had been renting equipment from a Salisbury businessman whose wartime alias, or "chimurenga name," was, to Thomas's great amusement, James Bond. When Thomas hit town, he returned the gear, and among the young musicians he found rehearsing at Bond's place was Oliver Mtukudzi, a young singer with a gospel background and a forceful, husky voice. "Oliver Mtukudzi was *discovered* by James Bond," Thomas liked to say. Oliver was trying to break into the pop scene, working on a song in English that Thomas recalled as "Red for Stop, Green for Go." Thomas said, "After I listened to this guy, I said to him, 'Ah, man, you have got a beautiful voice, but the music you are trying to pursue is not your kind of music.' I was trying to sort of convince him. I had a Shona tune that I used to sing myself called 'Rova Ngoma Mutarava [Beat the Drum].' So I gave him the tune, and he recorded it. It did very well on the local scene."[18] Oliver gratefully confirmed that it was Thomas who had encouraged him to sing "in our own mother tongue." For a few months after that initial meeting, the two singers toured the country together backed by a group called Wagon Wheels. Thomas was now finished with singing covers, and he used the tour to present his own growing repertoire of songs in Shona. Oliver recalled, "Each time I would hear him doing those songs, I would say, 'This is us. This is what we are supposed to be.'"[19]

Guitarist Leonard "Pickett" Chiyangwa had joined a group called the Acid Band, playing at Machipisa—formerly Mutanga—Nightclub. Thomas used to drop in on them, and he observed the Acid Band gradually shifting from rumba to a more indigenous sound. Pickett had listened to itinerant street guitarists rendering traditional folk songs, including mbira songs, on guitar. Now he used that in a band setting. The Acid Band's leader and bass man, Charles Makokowa, had a natural feel for the distinctive, after-the-beat feel of mbira bass lines, and the second guitarist, James Chimombe, a future star in his own right, was working with Pickett to arrange interlocking guitar parts. These musicians were playing "the real thing" as Thomas heard it, and he proposed to Charles that they rehearse and record a few of his songs.

Thomas had a night gig with the Pied Pipers at Mushandira Pamwe, but he spent his afternoons with the Acid Band, the group that would record his next single for Crispen Matema's Afro Soul label. Thomas had written a song called "Pamuromo Chete (It's Only Talk)," a response to Ian Smith's signature declaration: "I don't believe in majority rule ever in Rhodesia . . . not in 1,000 years." Geoffrey Nyarota remembered this song well from Mutare, though, again, he said that if Thomas was talking back to Smith, "he never explained that to us." In those days Thomas rarely "explained" his songs to anyone, but even without the context, the lyrics to "Pamuromo Chete" are provocative. They evoke the plight of refugees who have run away from the war and been forced to dwell amid filth in urban marketplaces. The song "sold like hotcakes," said Thomas. It became his first gold record, topping the local charts and remaining in play there for more than ten weeks. After "Pamuromo Chete," the Acid Band was voted Best Band of 1977.[20]

Thomas was now the Acid Band's official lead singer, and they started touring the country and drawing big crowds. "The records had done the job," Thomas recalled. "We were now earning at least 1000 Rhodesian pounds per performance."[21]

Teal had established an efficient recording and distribution operation that would remain in business—later as Gramma Records—through war, independence, drought, scandal, economic collapse, and foreign competition. Sadly, the original company had no concept of archiving and record keeping, so the master tapes for much of its pre-independence music have been lost. Gramma could not provide definitive release dates for any singles prior to 1979, but between 1977 and about May 1978, Thomas Mapfumo and the Acid Band released ten or twelve singles and an album called *Hokoyo* (Watch Out). These recordings established Thomas as a mainstay of black culture in Rhodesia.

After "Pamuromo Chete" came "Pfumvu Pa Ruzevha (Hardship in the Reserves)," a "very hard song," in Thomas's estimate.[22] Its lyrics lay out a compendium of suffering experienced by rural people during the war:

They have a hard life in the rural areas
That's why I am now a pauper . . .

Did you know that granny is dead?
Did you know that mummy is dead?
Did you know that your brother is dead?
Did you know that there are no rains?
Did you know that our plot of land was taken? . . .

Have you seen the hardships in the rural areas?
The hardships at home?

"Pfumvu Pa Ruzevha" does not point fingers, although the line about land being "taken" had to worry attentive authorities. Some of Thomas's songs had been banned, though for the most part he could still fly under the censorship radar. Rhodesian culture minders may even have thought that the hardships he was enumerating could be blamed on the guerrillas. Thomas was sensitizing a distracted urban public to the dark events unfolding in the countryside, and once again, music counted as much as words. With the mournful lyricism of mbira, channeled through simple guitar work—strummed chords and Pickett's prickly lead melody—"Pfumvu Pa Ruzevha" lured urban people into a rural frame of mind, bringing them face-to-face with the anguish of relatives on the land.

Guerrilla fighters, some of whom now found themselves relying on spirit mediums for their very lives, were also vulnerable to the power of a song like "Pfumvu Pa Ruzevha." Even mbira musicians, who had never paid much heed to popular singers, now responded to this new alloy of spiritual and social reality. One mbira musician, Chris Mhlanga, said Thomas was "seriously arousing the spirit" with such songs, "much more than he thought he was doing," and another, Cosmas Magaya, said that hearing Thomas's songs was enough to inspire a person to "go and join the liberation struggle."

Thomas kept changing his public image. At the Skyline band contest in 1974 he had fronted the Hallelujah Chicken Run Band gripping a wooden staff, a loincloth around his waist and an elaborate metal necklace drooped over his bare chest. Geoffrey Nyarota recalled him sporting a "Carnaby Street look" a year later in Mutare—bell-bottom trousers, a colorful shirt, and platform shoes. But with the Acid Band, Thomas turned away from London chic and adopted the air of a spirit medium in a long black robe and wielding a ceremonial ax. This was effective artifice. Stella Chiweshe, like Mhlanga, said she believed Thomas had tapped into powers he himself did not understand. Her effort to assimilate Thomas within her own formulation of mbira spirituality is provocative, perhaps questionable, but fascinating:

I liked when he was wearing his robe. And his stick. I liked it very much. During those years when he was first singing, his voice was like food for the soul. When he was singing, his song was coming out at the same time as that action he was singing about, and then when it happens, the song is there. What people should know about Thomas Mapfumo is that he *is* a spirit medium. You know, people who are mediums are not treated like any other people, because they are not straightforward themselves. When it comes to being with them, you don't always know who you are talking to.

Acid Band singles kept coming. There was "Tozvireva Kupiko (Where Shall We Tell Our Story?)," a lament about the way the world was turning a "deaf ear" to the plight of "our people." "Chiiko Chinotinetsa (What Is It That Troubles Us?)" called for unity in the face of adversity, and the flip side, "Chaive Chinyakare (It Was the Tradition)," mourned the decline of indigenous culture. "Ours was a sad story," recalled Thomas. "This country is a holy place, but our culture was stolen away from us. We were being taught how to live like an Englishman, talk like an Englishman, read like an Englishman." Another popular Acid Band single, "Chiruzevha Chapera (Rural Life Is Gone)," focused on the way the war itself was threatening traditional life on the land. Thomas believed the deadly droughts of 1976 and 1977 may have been caused by disruptions in spiritual life. "In this land there were no rains," said Thomas. "Maybe that was because so much blood was being shed. People were kept in keeps [pens], guarded like animals. People were running away from home, running away from the soldiers, coming into towns, so there was no more life in the communal lands."

Thomas projected a vivid personality through his performances. Mischievousness, humor, and moral outrage all come through as he croons in melodiously rich baritone on "Pamuromo Chete" and finesses the nuances of mbira vocal techniques on "Pfumvu Pa Ruzevha." Thomas worked at mbira singing, maneuvering to get his hands on the few available recordings, so he could study them. Hakurotwi Mude—Ephat Mujuru's spirit medium uncle—recalled:

> One day, Mapfumo was playing at this Chikwana shopping center in Chitungwiza. Thomas came to me, and I talked to him. I had an LP record and I left it with him to keep for me. When I came back, Thomas told me that it had been stolen. I was very disappointed because I think he must have kept it. I think he used my recording to start his imitation of my singing. At that time, he wasn't singing the way I sing. But from that time on, I could see that he had changed, and he was singing just like me.

Thomas did not recall this incident, but he acknowledged Mude's influence on his singing style. "Pfumo Rinobva Mudziva (The Spear That Originates in the River Pool)," with its mysterious warnings about river spirits, has Thomas crying out until his voice breaks, then settling into a hum that lingers in the back of his throat—pure huro and mahon'era, with the imprint of Mude's robust take on these vocal styles. Sometimes Thomas would reinterpret known mbira songs with new lyrics, as he had with "Ngoma Yarira," and as mbira composers themselves have always done. The most powerful Acid Band singles marshal these techniques to animate war scenarios. "Ndoziva Ripizano (Which Way Should I Choose?)" is a version of the mbira song "Bukatiende (Wake Up, Let's Go)," originally a rallying cry for hunters. Shifting the context from hunters to hunted, Thomas portrays the confusion of villagers preyed upon by guerrillas and soldiers, each demanding loyalty and punishing betrayal. Rural people caught between ZANLA, Zimbabwe People's Revolutionary Army (ZIPRA), Selous Scouts (named for the intrepid explorer Frederick Selous), Rhodesian army regulars, and other contingents surely understood the agonizing portent of Thomas's question.

The Rhodesians had trained the mostly black Selous Scouts to undermine the liberation fighters using devious maneuvers.[23] Scouts learned to sing chimurenga songs; they shucked uniforms off the corpses of dead guerrillas and infiltrated villages; they earned the trust of guerrillas and their young helpers, the *mujibas*; they gave away radios and record players equipped with homing devices. Scouts would brutally flog a presumed "sellout," then leave him behind as a spy. They could "flip" a captured guerrilla within twenty-four hours and use him to gain access to secret plans and places. When these methods failed, they could also kidnap, torture, and kill.[24]

The *Herald* reported government actions using sterile statistics but dwelled morbidly on "terrorist" violence and black-on-black barbarity. A *Herald* headline from 1975 reads "Terror Gang Enforce Cannibalism in Village: Wife Made to Eat Flesh of Her Husband." The front-page spread includes a grotesque photograph of the husband in a hospital bed, his face and hands bandaged.[25] Reports like this made news around the world, though it was impossible to know the truth behind them.

Any action—even singing—could be spun by either side. Thomas Turino writes, "One [war veteran] said that because Mapfumo's lyrics were ambiguous, they could be used by either side, and that he should have been more explicit if he didn't wish to be misused."[26] More typical, though, is the account of novelist Alexander Kanengoni, who had left home to join the comrades in Mozambique. Kanengoni recalled sitting around a table at the guerrilla camp and hearing Jonah Sithole's single "Sabhuku" (1977) for the first time: "There was silence, absolute silence as we listened to that song. It was magical. There was the electric guitar now playing the mbira. And the story is about the situation in the rural areas where the war was raging. There was no doubt in my mind, and I suppose in everyone's mind, that a new direction had been set as far as our music was concerned."

"Sabhuku" played for Kanengoni as a dramatization of village life during the war. The *sabhuku* is the village headman, and in the song, he interrupts a beer party, warning people to finish up their drinks and get moving. Sithole explained his song as a cautionary tale about witchcraft, but for Kanengoni and his cohorts, witchery became a metaphor for government collusion, and the beer party was being interrupted by an armed attack. Thomas's songs, often more direct than "Sabhuku," also left room for interpretation, but Kanengoni said his comrades found them profoundly "meaningful," especially in the way they reinforced the "spiritual dimension of the war." It made all the difference that these artists couched their words in mbira melodies. "Thomas could have put these same words in rumba," Musa Zimunya observed, "and they wouldn't have mattered one bit."

Late in 1977, a squad of guerrillas invited Thomas and representatives of the Acid Band to visit their camp near Mount Wedza, a place where spirit mediums gathered, and guerrillas hid.[27] Thomas recalled:

We had to be careful in the way we were going to meet these people. We were always being watched. We parked our car at one of the houses in the village; then we walked by foot, right into the forest. It was on a hill where we actually found these people waiting for us. They welcomed us, the top brass of that group. There was one tall guy who was wearing a black cowboy hat and everything black—he called himself Jimi Hendrix. There were others who were like watchdogs, posted out there. They were changing position each time, watching both sides. Well, we started talking about music and the war. After a while, some women came with food from the village—sadza, meat, crates of beer. [The guerrillas] told us about how they crossed over from Mozambique, and how they were now all over Rhodesia. They were confident that they were winning, and they thanked us for supporting them through our music. They actually wanted a guitar, and we had that guitar with us, so we gave them a lot of records and the guitar. We shook hands with them. Nobody ever knew that we met those people.

These guerrillas advised the band not to travel with vehicle convoys as they moved about the country, because these convoys would now be targets. The band had always assumed there was safety in numbers, so this advice was a tangible benefit from what was probably Thomas's riskiest action of the war. He and his party would have faced imprisonment, torture, even death had they been caught making contact with guerrillas. Finding treason in song lyrics was, by contrast, a subtle matter, complicated by language, culture, and deliberate obfuscation by African interpreters. Emmanuel Vori said the Teal librarians understood the songs right away, but being "our guys," they tried to shield Thomas from scrutiny, sitting on songs as long as possible before passing them on to managers who would give them to the censor board. "Unfortunately," said Vori, "the librarians were at the bottom end of the ladder. They could not get the music on the radio. [Eventually], everything done by Thomas was censored."

The Acid Band did record straightforward traditional songs like "Shumba (The Lion)" and even the odd love song like "Tombi Wa Chena (Lady, You Are Looking Smart)." But mostly, Acid Band songs tantalize with suggestion and innuendo—"Zeve Zeve (A Whisper)," with its line "Don't speak out loud," also "Usatambe Nenyoka (Don't Play with a Snake)," "Tonga Nyaya Dzino Netsa (To Judge Troubling Issues)," "Mwana Asina Baba (Fatherless Child)," and "Teererai Mitemo (Listen to the Laws)," a taunt that the government was violating its own laws.[28] Thomas's fans now identified him with the struggle and gave him a title to prove it—Tafirenyika, meaning "we die for our country."

The song that unleashed the flood was "Tumirai Vana Kuhondo (Send the Children to War)." With rousing, beer-hall swagger, this traditional grinding song had become a call to arms. Geoffrey Nyarota—who had thus far missed the politics in Thomas's lyrics—finally understood. "It was explicit," said Nyarota. "You could call it incitement." The true picture is actually less clear. This song tells parents to send their children to war, but it does not specify a side. Even this late, some blacks still joined the Rhodesian army. Could Thomas be singing for *them*? That was the defense Tony Rivet used when Teal received yet another visit from government censors. "Thomas's music!" Rivet recalled: "Whew! If you knew what the words were like before—we had to change some of the words . . . so the songs would be acceptable to the government. I remember they came along to me one time and said, the *terrs* are getting all the tribes-people to sing the *gook* songs. The one they really didn't like was 'Tumirai Vana Kuhondo.' I told them it was a bloody RAR [Rhodesian Army Rifles] marching song, an old military marching song."[29]

Thomas denied ever changing his lyrics for anyone, but he backed Rivet up on the source of "Tumirai Vana Kuhondo." He said, "Government soldiers used to sing this song whilst marching. We were sort of mocking them, while encouraging our boys to come and have a good fighting year."[30] Twenty-seven years later, Nyarota still believed "Tumirai Vana Kuhondo" was "Thomas's composition." In reality, the original Rhodesian lyrics remained; all the Acid Band had changed was the musical accompaniment and the singer.

Thomas's chimurenga singles were being produced in a milieu where the business of music seemed to trump the passions of war. One might speculate that Rivet and his white colleagues in some way sympathized with the sentiments behind the music. After all, they'd been conscripted into the Rhodesian army, serving regular six-week tours of duty. Rivet used to show up at Acid Band recording sessions in his Rhodesian army uniform. However they felt inside, Teal's white managers took advantage of this chance to mingle with the enemy on neutral ground though, culturally, they were worlds apart. While Thomas and his musicians retired to township hovels and listened to mbira songs and Bob Marley, these folks returned to English-style homes where classical music and white pop played on stereos built into cabinets and side tables. Rhodesian military men delighted at Warren Zevon's mercenary burlesque set in the deep, dark Congo, "Roland the Headless Thompson Gunner":

> His comrades fought beside him—Van Owen and the rest
> But of all the Thompson gunners Roland was the best
> So the CIA decided they wanted Roland dead
> That son-of-a-bitch Van Owen blew off Roland's head
> Roland the headless Thompson gunner

On weekends Rivet and his mates would gather around the *braai* (barbecue), drink heavily, and sing patriotic songs, especially "Rhodesians Never Die," a durable anthem composed and recorded in 1973 by Clem Tholet, Ian Smith's son-in-law:

> We're all Rhodesians
> And we'll fight through thick and thin
> We'll keep our land a free land,
> Stop the enemy coming in,
> We'll keep them north of the Zambezi
> Till that river's running dry,
> And this mighty land will prosper
> For Rhodesians never die.

Thomas now referred openly to his songs as "chimurenga music." "You had to give it a word," recalled a Teal manager, "and that was the local term for it. We didn't call it that. I mean there is no way we would have recorded something that was *obviously* chimurenga, like 'Let's go out and kill 20 white farmers.'" As long as the songs kept to a modest level of subterfuge, Rivet and his colleagues simply overlooked their "chimurenga impact."

During 1977 and 1978, government officials flat out demanded that Teal censor its recordings and stop releasing chimurenga songs. "That's not our job," Teal managers protested. "You can ban the record with the greatest of pleasure, but we have to produce it in order for you to ban it. We can't do it any other way." Teal set up an on-site rehearsal room so musicians would not waste time in the studio. The company provided petty cash to each bandleader on the morning of a session, so players would not show up hungry. "I know it sounds pretty crackpot," the manager recalled, "but that's the way it worked. 'Here's the practice room. Here's your food. Now get on with it.'"

When records were banned, Teal arranged live concerts in the townships, providing instruments, PA systems, and security. Sometimes money went missing and equipment was damaged or stolen. Thomas sold enough records to be worth the trouble but, this manager recalled, "he was extraordinarily difficult to deal with. If he wanted the studio, we would book it for him, and we had to book it at four o'clock in the afternoon. There was no way he could sing if it was daylight. And we would have to make sure that there was plenty of *dagga*, or marijuana, and a couple of bottles of brandy for the band as well."

When records were ready for market, Teal dispatched mobile disco trucks manned by DJs spinning vinyl and sales reps moving product. These flash parties rolled through the townships spreading the word and doing business. "And of course," recalled Emmanuel Vori, "Thomas was always on the road performing live. It just spread like wildfire. The people knew what they wanted, and once the guys in the record bars ordered the records, they never stopped playing them."

Sometimes there was tension at live shows. On the morning after an Acid Band concert in Chiredzi, Thomas was arrested by black policemen. He was hauled into the station in town and charged with singing incitement. "I saw a lot of these former guerrillas," he recalled, "some with limbs missing, no legs, no hands. These people were brought to me as an example. If I insist on playing this music, I was going to end up like them."

Hokoyo is the only full album of songs Thomas recorded before independence, and one of the first by any local artist. The session once again went down in Crispen Matema's Robinson House studio. Twenty-seven-year-old Hilton Mambo, then Rhodesia's first black recording engineer, assisted. Mambo recalled:

Tommy was right there, man. He was not a miracle. No. He was in the right place at the right time—but he had the vision. He knew exactly what he was doing. He used to structure his lyrics so that even the black policemen wouldn't quite know what the hell he was talking about. "Hokoyo" was

like, "Watch out! We're coming. Hey. Be careful, man. We're getting there."
That kind of thing. If you're a Shona-speaking person, you know what the
brother is saying. But Tommy is like that. He has always been very socially
conscious, aware of what's happening. Tommy grew up in the ghetto and
he knows what we all went through—when a guy can't afford to buy a
loaf of bread. He can go back and talk about the way we used to live in
the olden days before the white man came, the stuff we were told by our
grandmothers and grandfathers. It's a gift.

The lyrics to the song "Hokoyo" bristle with street punk bravado: "Look at
the knife / I have the knife / and I have the ax / So watch out / Don't underestimate me." Riding over a sunny saxophone riff, Thomas's vocal comes across
more playful than threatening, part of the song's sonic fig leaf. *Hokoyo* has the
arc of a unified creation, with interconnecting themes of warning and prayer,
and thoughtful variation among musical styles—mbira, Afro-rock, *jiti*, and
strains of jazz and township pop emanating from South Africa. *Hokoyo* set a
high creative bar for Thomas's would-be rivals.

Now in demand everywhere, the Acid Band needed to pull together an
organization capable of arranging tours and operating as a business. Charles
was the band's ostensible leader, and Crispen Matema its manager, but as the
star singer and composer, Thomas wielded new influence, and now, for the
first time, he turned to his family for help, recruiting his brother Lancelot to
be the band treasurer. Lancelot worked in a leather shop in Mbare, making
belts, handbags, and jackets. When "Brother Thomas" came to him saying
the band was heading to Bulawayo and needed someone to collect money at
the door, Lancelot recalled resisting. Thomas said, "No, man, that's peanuts
you are getting. There is no money here. We should go together to Bulawayo."

In Bulawayo, Thomas met his future wife, Vena Sibanda Dangarembwa.[31]
Vena was the daughter of a pharmacist, Dennis Dangarembwa and his wife,
Molly. According to Vena, who was born in 1962, "My name was supposed
to be Verna, but the people at the district office made a mistake, and they put
Vena." Her parents, four sisters, and a brother—and everyone else since—have
honored this bureaucratic typo.

Thomas remembered meeting Vena for the first time at the Happy Valley
Hotel when he and Charles spotted two girls obviously in love with the music.
They arranged to be introduced after the show. "Charlie had a Peugeot 404,"
recalled Thomas, "and these girls asked us to take them back home to Mzilikazi. Well, the two of us spoke, and I actually promised her that I was going
to write her some letters when I got back to Salisbury. We communicated a

lot and became very good friends." As wholesome as this sounds, Thomas was already married at the time to a woman named Agnes Kurwakumire. The two never had children, and soon after Thomas met Vena, he divorced Agnes.

"I loved Thomas's music," recalled Vena, although her memory of that first encounter differed slightly from his:

I was very young then, doing my Form 3 [about age seventeen], and my brother invited me to go and see [Thomas] at the McDonald Hall in Mzilikazi. That's where he saw me, and he asked this other woman to come and talk to me. He wanted to see me, but I respected my brother so much that I didn't see him. I don't know how he managed to search for my parents' house, but as I was coming from school one day, my sister-in-law was outside and Thomas's car was parked by our gate. She was saying, "Hurry up, hurry up. Come and see Thomas!" because everyone else at home loved him. So I came rushing. I just spoke to him for a few minutes. Then we had a date. He said, "Come and see me tomorrow." We met and had a drink, then that's when I started knowing him.

During these years, Thomas and his musicians enjoyed a ritual of late-night drinking at Mushandira Pamwe. Everyone would bring his beer, Bols, gin, whiskey, or Chateau brandy and sit around a table, imbibing the night's earnings. Thomas favored "half brandy and milk," and by his own account, he could handle a lot of it. But one night, he recalled, "I got up from that table, I left Mushandira Pamwe, I sat in my car, and I just thought: What kind of a life are you trying to live?"

Thomas's friends didn't believe him the next day when he told them he was through with alcohol, but he never returned to that table. In the *Hokoyo* sessions that year, he recorded a version of the traditional song "Hwa Hwa (Beer)," based on a record by the mbira group Yekwa Chiboora. This song would remain a pillar in Thomas's repertoire, evolving through a series of arrangements. Decades later, he would introduce it from the stage, saying, "I have stopped drinking beer because one day when I was drunk, I beat up my mother-in-law." That line is straight out of the Yekwa Chiboora recording, though fans could easily mistake it for autobiography. A twinkle in his eye, Thomas generally left them to wonder. As to the coincidence of his alcohol epiphany and the first recording of "Hwa Hwa," Thomas was clear: "no connection." The true catalyst for his sobriety was perhaps his budding romance with Vena. "I remember telling him," Vena recalled, "that if he continued that kind of drinking, then I don't think we will get together."

By the time the Acid Band released *Hokoyo*, Jonah Sithole had returned from Mutare with his own group, the Storm. Both bands were now successful enough to tour the country, and after a chance encounter with Sithole, Thomas got to thinking. He was impatient with lead guitarist Pickett, who was "not improving." Thomas set his sights on Sithole, who "never went wrong with his notes" and "was determined to play good music." Thomas proposed that they combine the best musicians from the two bands and form "a much stronger group." Sithole replied, "Well, we are used to working together. We can't seem to part. So we might as well make the best of it. I agreed, and we merged as the Blacks Unlimited. Ah, it was solid now."[32]

The decision to revert to the name Thomas and Sithole had used in Mutare signaled a reset for both musicians and, on the surface, a pact between equals. At first, Sithole handled the band's money and was responsible for paying musicians. The Acid Band's Charles Makokowa maintained his role as chief in the new band. "We all recognized him as the bandleader," said Thomas. But whatever title or responsibilities any musician held, the Blacks Unlimited would, in reality, be Thomas's band, the first and only band he would ever lead. Twenty years later nearly every member of that 1978 lineup would be dead. That band's recorded work would all be credited to "Thomas Mapfumo and Blacks Unlimited." From here on, said Thomas, "my name was written in the book of history." A rough road lay ahead, but Thomas's drifting days were over.

5 / Bishop and Pawn

I heard that music from the sky . . . from a plane . . . Shona
music through those horn speakers. They were playing Thomas
Mapfumo's music, to sort of attract people. And then one of the
commentators who was in the plane shouted out, "If you keep on
fighting, you are fighting for nothing."
LEONARD SIMBARASHE, POLITICAL DETAINEE,
CHIKURUBI PRISON

Our enemy was not the white man, but an oppressor and
exploiter, whether he was black or white. . . . There were quite a
number of blacks . . . sell-outs . . . who were killed by the people.
TOM HAMA, ZANLA POLITICAL COMMISSIONER

The Blacks Unlimited picked up where the Acid Band left off, moving feet
from the dance floor to the battlefield. By 1976, Teal's 45 rpm records were
finding their way into the hands of guerrillas and shortwave radio broadcasters
in Zambia and Mozambique, as well as expatriates in Tanzania and England.
Thomas was now a player in the struggle, and his success was earning him
new friends and enemies. He would later recall the war's denouement and the
nationalists' victory lap as the most difficult period in his career, a time when
his reputation was nearly destroyed. Ironically, Thomas's brush with disgrace
was brought on by a man he had long admired, the country's first elected black
leader, Methodist bishop Abel Tendekai Muzorewa.

Muzorewa was born in 1925 in Mutare, the eldest of nine children in a
peasant family. His paternal ancestors, the Makonde clan, had fought the

Portuguese from the mountains, and his parents were among the region's first converts to Christianity. Muzorewa writes in his 1978 autobiography that his greatest fear as a child was of the baboons that harassed him on his way to school. He used to carry an unloaded gun on his shoulder to frighten them, but the animals saw through his ruse when the gun never fired a shot.[1] In Muzorewa's writing, this anecdote foreshadows, and helps justify, his eventual transformation from pastoral pacifist to reluctant warrior.

Evangelist teachers inspired Muzorewa as a boy. During "revival week" before Easter, young Abel answered the reverend's call for students to come forward and "meet Christ in a new way." They went out to the base of the mountain to pray at dawn, and there on sacred Shona land, he experienced his epiphany, accepting Jesus Christ as his savior. Muzorewa delighted in sharing faith, as when he converted a Mozambican boy who had never heard of Jesus. He was ordained a minister in 1953 and worked in the Rusape area until he became a church elder four years later. At an African National Congress forum in 1957, Muzorewa was appalled to hear future Rhodesian Front leader Winston Field declare, "I do not believe that an African will go to heaven." When a white Anglican bishop was the only one to challenge Field, Muzorewa writes, "I wondered how soon we African Christians would rise up to join in that struggle for justice."[2]

Muzorewa studied for six years in the United States in the late 1950s and early 1960s. In Fayette, Missouri, he and his family were the lone blacks among an enclave of white intellectuals in the still-segregated South. Whites walked out of church when the Muzorewas entered. Friends apologized that they could not bring the minister home to meet their families. Despite these affronts, Muzorewa found America progressive. People held racist views, but the *state* stood for equality. When he returned to Rhodesia—"the valley of dry bones," he called it—Central Intelligence Organization (CIO) interrogations and heavy-handed surveillance awaited.[3]

Muzorewa was back at the mission in Mutare when he became the first black bishop of the Rhodesian Methodist Church. The post allowed him to travel to Zambia, Angola, Ghana, and Liberia, to see for himself the promises and perils of African independence. Meanwhile, freed from British oversight by his declaration of independence, Ian Smith worked to fortify Rhodesia. But when he enacted the racist Land Tenure Act (1969) restricting church activity in black areas, religious leaders rebelled. Smith met with them for what was officially a "cordial and constructive" encounter. Muzorewa recalled "a head-on clash." Smith banned the bishop from visiting Tribal Trust Lands, home to three-fourths of the country's blacks—effectively, his flock.[4]

Two months after locking horns with Smith, Muzorewa joined the nationalists. One observer said the bishop was "pitch-forked into active politics," though he describes a more graceful transition. The nationalists needed someone outside their squabbling ranks to unify the new African National Council (ANC).[5] As ANC leader, the stalwart preacher of nonviolence would represent fighters, politicians, "terrorists," and spirit mediums. Muzorewa prayed for three weeks before accepting history's call. His first challenge was to thwart Smith's Anglo-Rhodesian Agreement (1971), an anemic effort to legitimize the Rhodesian claims on the country in British eyes. Muzorewa toured the country, consulted with the exile community in London, and argued before international bodies that Smith's plan would not "decolonize" but "recolonize" Rhodesia. Muzorewa predicted a "holocaust" if the accord passed, and he won credit as a prominent shepherd of its ultimate defeat.

Thomas recalled his family's satisfaction with the "tremendous job" the bishop did in blocking Smith's plan. With nationalist leaders "locked up," Muzorewa was "the only man who had a voice." He was "a man of the cloth, preaching to the people." Thomas was still singing rock 'n' roll with the Springfields at the time, still drinking, smoking cigarettes, and sporting bell-bottom trousers. Things were tense at home. But then as ever, Thomas respected his parents' religious life, and Muzorewa, coming from the church and taking up the cause of freedom, awed black Christian Rhodesians, including all the members of Thomas's Christian Marching Church family.

Muzorewa began to address large crowds, both black and white. He championed a peaceful resolution to the conflict, seducing the center while riling hard-liners on all sides. Church leaders objected to the bishop's politicking and banned him from speaking in Salisbury's Anglican cathedral. But history was on Muzorewa's side. Rhodesia's independent neighbors were pressuring nationalist factions to work as a unified force, and they chose Muzorewa in 1974 to spearhead a new Declaration of Unity. Briefly, the bishop felt himself "the tallest man in the world."[6]

Robert Mugabe had spent just over a decade in Hwa Hwa Penitentiary by then. He had earned degrees in law and administration through correspondence with London. (His proudly touted "degrees in violence" still lay ahead.) Upon release in 1974, Mugabe headed for the seat of ZANU power in Lusaka. He received a brusque reception from Zambian president Kenneth Kaunda, who was determined to keep ZANU under Ndabaninge Sithole and the talented young barrister Herbert Chitepo.[7] Muzorewa too made a pilgrimage to Lusaka that spring to meet with Chitepo and bring ZANU into the ANC fold. On the chilly March morning when Muzorewa and Chitepo were to talk,

Chitepo switched on the ignition of his Volkswagen and was burned to ashes by the resulting blast. Suspicion lingered that Mugabe had arranged Chitepo's death; the crime was never solved, but in its wake, an angry President Kaunda dispatched the entire ZANU leadership to Mozambique, which would remain the guerrilla command center for the duration of the war.

Mugabe soon made the journey to Maputo in the company of Edgar Tekere, a close ZANU ally at the time.[8] There is some evidence that Smith directed border guards not to stop them, perhaps believing that their radicalism would destabilize the liberation forces. If this is true, writes Heidi Holland, "one could speculate that it was Ian Smith who gave Mugabe his biggest break in politics" because in Maputo, quite suddenly, Mugabe emerged as the de facto spokesman for all the guerrilla fighters. "Automatically, we heard he was the leader of ZANLA," said Thomas, recalling the surprise of people in Salisbury who followed events through the grapevine. Just how Mugabe attained so much power so quickly is a puzzle. Tekere would later describe him as a man with no guiding philosophy and claim that ZANU men in Maputo had "corrupted" Mugabe, regaling him with power that soon went to his head. Thomas doubted Mugabe had simply been anointed. "This guy was too ambitious," Thomas insisted, "from the beginning."[9]

Muzorewa's house had been firebombed in 1974, forcing him to flee Rhodesia for eighteen months. In exile, the bishop concluded that talking with Smith was pointless, yet the two met one last time at opposite ends of a railcar, hovering on a bridge over the thundering waters of Victoria Falls so that he and Nkomo could remain technically in Zambia, and Smith in Rhodesia. Balancing the demands of an increasingly bloody fight against the credo of "Thou shalt not kill," Muzorewa arrived at his notion of "righteous violence"—a personal philosophy that modified the Bible, Gandhi, and Martin Luther King by allowing a resort to arms if "the intensity of the provocation" proved sufficient.[10]

Smith, too, was revising strategy. After the Victoria Falls meeting, the prime minister continued to talk secretly with Nkomo but became so unnerved by the Ndebele leader's rhinoceros-steady fixation on power that he resolved to stop him, whatever the cost. In September 1976, Smith shocked the nation by announcing that Rhodesia would see majority rule within two years. This was a stunning reversal from his "not in 1,000 years" rhetoric, just months behind him—"only talk" after all, as Thomas had sung in "Pamuromo Chete." Smith grudgingly decided it was better to midwife majority rule on his own terms than be washed away by it. A kingmaker—no longer a king himself—Smith sought the most pliable possible successor, the gentle Bishop Muzorewa.

Smith lured Muzorewa back to Rhodesia with an invitation to participate in yet another set of constitutional talks, this time in Geneva. For all the bishop knew, he might have faced arrest, angry protest, or an assassin's bullet when he stepped off the plane in Salisbury, so he was more than gratified to be greeted by 500,000 supporters in Highfield, many of them shouting the ANC slogan, "Heavy! Heavy!"

The Geneva talks of 1976 lasted two months and produced no break-throughs.[11] Afterward, war spread freely through the country. The so-called protected villages—mass prisons, really—multiplied, sabotaging traditional agriculture and poisoning the morale of soldiers. A Woolworths in Salisbury was bombed. Church leaders began openly defending the guerrillas, and whites could no longer escape the effects of war because the national economy was collapsing around them. Chronicling the fall of white Rhodesia, Peter Godwin and Ian Hancock write, "School-leavers were forced to grow up very quickly, honorable men shot defenseless peasants, bank clerks drowned their fears in bars and night clubs, the lonely wives of serving men found solace in furtive encounters outside the marital bed, and more families shed tears and sent death notices to the press."[12] Eighteen thousand whites left Rhodesia in just one year. On their way out, some sold their properties to blacks of means, like ZANU's Ndabaninge Sithole, who became the first black homeowner in his Salisbury neighborhood, Houghton Park.

Smith's regime had become toxic. Jimmy Carter's envoys—Cyrus Vance and Andrew Young—refused to coddle him as Henry Kissinger had. During 1977, a total of 3,046 people of all races were killed in Rhodesia. This was nearly half the number who had died during the entire conflict to date, and somewhere amid all those deaths, the will of white Rhodesians to defend their "homeland" flagged. In August 1977, a traumatized white electorate awarded "Good Old Smithy" his biggest electoral win, knowing that he would now move toward majority rule. Smith summoned Muzorewa to his office and agreed to an election on the basis of one man, one vote. Muzorewa was ec-static. "Allow us to enter, Mr. Smith," he proclaimed with naive triumphalism, "we have come to take our country."

Smith and Muzorewa hammered out the details of a negotiated peace they called the "internal settlement." The plan established a transitional government led by Smith, Muzorewa, Sithole, and one Chief Jeremiah Chirau, a small-time Mashonaland official financed by the Smith regime.[13] Smith claimed this coa-lition represented 85 percent of all Rhodesians, though few outside his circle believed it. When the United States' Vance and Young visited Salisbury to push for all-party talks, police stood by as Chirau's supporters pelted them with rotten tomatoes. Carnivalesque tactics could not hide the fact that this government would enjoy no more international support than had the previous one.

The new regime presided over a national fantasy, changing the name of the country to Zimbabwe-Rhodesia and banning from broadcast all mention of the Patriotic Front, ZANU, ZAPU, ZIPRA, ZANLA—in short, any political entity not on the planned April 1979 ballot.[14] Meanwhile, the government imposed near martial law and engaged in the bloodiest warfare ever to unfold on the Zimbabwe plateau. The guerrillas now had heat-seeking ground-to-air missiles and used one to bring down a civilian airliner—Air Rhodesia Flight 825—shortly after its takeoff from Victoria Falls.[15] Rhodesian forces responded with merciless attacks on guerrilla camps across the Zambian and Mozambican borders.[16] The year 1978 claimed another twenty-six hundred lives.

This was the chaotic environment in which the Acid Band produced its incendiary run of Thomas Mapfumo singles. Up to this point the white regime had done little more than ban these songs from airplay. Now the thinking changed. A popular figure like Thomas, if handled correctly, might present an opportunity to sway black opinion toward the Smith-Muzorewa plan. This would not be easy. Thomas's song "Hokoyo (Watch Out)" played as a defiant response to the internal settlement. "So watch out," sang Thomas. "Don't underestimate me. I am also armed." Muzorewa supporters—and there were still many—also danced to "Hokoyo."[17] But if Thomas himself felt any glimmer of hope for Muzorewa as a leader, his songs do not reflect it. One of the first releases from the newly formed Blacks Unlimited in the fall of 1978 was the immensely popular "Africa." The song assumes the voice of a young colonial adventurer heading out to the dark continent, "where there's milk and honey . . . where there's easy money . . . the land of lotus eaters." The song ends with the boy's grandfather saying, "If you want to go, go, my grandson. Others went [but] they came back lazy. . . . Others went [but] they ran away from the war." The message was that colonial adventurers fail while indigenous people triumph.[18]

The mournful "Kuyaura (Tribulation)" offered stronger fare. Its 12/8 beat is slow and heavy, and Jonah Sithole and Pickett Chiyangwa interweave muted guitar lines that echo mbira tonalities but trace a rock-simple two-chord vamp (Dm/Am). Thomas's vocal leaps and dives with hints of mbira singing, though the song's descending refrain is sharp and catchy enough to have been uttered by Bob Dylan or Bob Marley around the same time. The song dwells on the "suffering of the homeless" and "the poor" and lists family members who have died after being displaced by war. "Kuyaura" finds Thomas in full spirit medium drag, intoning the names of the dead and invoking "guardian spirits," even varoyi, to lend their "evil powers," and "traditional herbalists," to "give us their charms . . . to combat our enemy." The song's stormy trance culminates in oblique questions—"Where are the old women to bite our ears? Where are the old men to prick the leaf?"—and this ominous prediction: "We will bathe in blood."[19] Thomas is calling on forces of flesh and spirit to finish the work of war—the precise opposite of the Smith-Muzorewa message. In composing "Kuyaura," Thomas was so unconcerned about censorship that he openly acknowledged the banned Patriotic Front, singing, "Where is Mr. Chitepo to lead us?," a brazen salute to ZANU's murdered chief, fast acquiring martyr status.[20]

The only way Rhodesians could hear such songs on radio was to tune in Radio Mozambique's Voice of Zimbabwe broadcasts out of Maputo, especially the weekly "Chimurenga Requests" program in which music, including Thomas's singles, served as filler between militant speeches and newscasts from the Mozambican front.[21] Thomas had first heard these programs while living in Highfield in the early 1970s, with his paternal uncle Jeremiah Makore. Thomas and Acid Band leader Charles Makokowa had lived in adjacent rooms there, Charles with his family. The two musicians used to huddle together around Jeremiah's shortwave. They had heard Robert Mugabe delivering screeds laced with Marxist rhetoric about "the masses." Thomas had recognized the voice of his boyhood friend Webster Shamu reading the newscast. He and Shamu had been together in the old neighborhood in Mabvuku. Shamu had gone on to become a DJ on RBC, but after leaving to cover the Ali-Foreman "rumble in the jungle" in Kinshasa in 1974, he had slipped off to Maputo and resurfaced with a "chimurenga name"—Charles Ndlovu—and a key role on Voice of Zimbabwe.

Naturally, these rebel broadcasts did not escape the notice of Rhodesian authorities. One night at a Blacks Unlimited show in Chegutu, the band's driver got into a fight with a man who turned out to be armed. Black policemen descended on the skirmish, creating a scene that drove the fans from the hall, and the band—confused and panicked—ran from the stage without switching off their amplifiers. The wail of guitar feedback echoed through the empty hall as policemen burst into the dressing room to confront Thomas. "Cops," recalled Thomas, "black cops came in with their guns. They said, 'Mapfumo, you are the one. You are singing politics. We want to shoot you right now.' I said, 'You want to shoot me? For what? What did I do? *You* were fighting by the door. I don't know what you were fighting for. So where do I come in?'"

One of the doormen ran to a nearby police station, and ironically, white policemen showed up in a Land Rover to end the standoff. "They saw these black officers with their guns," recalled Thomas, "and they *klapped* them. They took away their guns. That's how it ended. Everyone started coming back to the hall, and the show went on." This incident underscores the confusion of this time, as order and discipline, even racially based power relationships, were breaking down in the dying days of the Smith regime.

The Blacks Unlimited were an exceptionally tight combo. "We didn't have keyboards," recalled Jonah Sithole. "We didn't have mbiras. We just played guitars and a few horns, which meant that nobody could be found wanting." The players had become skilled at arranging mbira songs for guitars playing interlocked, single-line melodies. Charles Makokowa had developed a trademark bass style, lagging behind the beat, echoing the *kutsinhira*, the secondary mbira part, which interlocks with the lead part (*kushaura*) by placing important bass notes on the second beat of the triplet rather than the first. Thomas took special pride in his brass section. He wanted a sound with the force and bluster he admired in jazz-rock bands like Chicago Transit Authority and Blood Sweat and Tears. At the same time, he insisted that the horn breaks have an "African feel," so he composed his own lines and sang them to the players. Nothing was written down. If parts were forgotten or changed before the next rehearsal, or if Thomas was still dissatisfied—and he often was—he would simply start again. Only the strongest music made it to the stage and the studio.

The Teal Records production team underwent a shake-up around that time when Crispen Matema, champion of the Hallelujah Chicken Run Band and the Acid Band, was replaced with a producer from Bulawayo, Abnil Mapfumo, no relation to Thomas. A manager recalled that Matema had "lost his touch," but Thomas traced the problem to a personal rivalry between the two black producers. Thomas disagreed with the change, thinking Matema the better musician, but he accepted it. Rhodesian producers, after all, were not artistic visionaries—no Phil Specters or Barry Gordys these guys. The white players were manufacturing product they could understand only superficially; the African producers understood more, but they also had a job to complete. If musicians knew what they were doing, the producer's job was little more than to make sure guitars were in tune and work got done on time. Thomas would be marked by this no-nonsense approach to recording. He might fuss over a song's tempo, change the key to get a stronger vocal performance, or scrap a song that wasn't working, but his main goal was always to get songs on tape fast and to start composing new ones.

Even without airplay, Thomas's records were selling in 1978, and for the first time in his life he had enough money to rent his own house, in the Waterfalls district of Salisbury. "It was a leap forward," recalled Geoffrey Nyarota. "Waterfalls was an area for poor whites, so that's where we started. As the poor whites were moving out the moneyed blacks were moving in, and Thomas was one of the first." The achievement was that much more remarkable for an entertainer, a person of low status. "Thomas had broken away from that stereotype," said Nyarota. The *Rhodesia Herald* sent Nyarota to interview the country's most successful black singer—about his good fortune, not his music. Nyarota had heard a militant message in "Tumirai Vana Kuhondo," but as he put it, "One swallow does not a summer make." Nyarota did not ask Thomas about the country's rapidly shifting politics.

Nyarota was then an aspiring journalist in the capital. He worked long hours and spent his nights fraternizing at the press club and after-hours nightspots. He listened mostly to foreign pop cassettes in his car and never heard the Voice of Zimbabwe on shortwave, rarely even the RBC's African Service. He never attended Teal's mobile disco parties in the townships, let alone Acid Band or Blacks Unlimited concerts. "I don't want to appear more revolutionary than I was," Nyarota explained, scrupulously avoiding what he called his generation's tendency to "embellish their revolutionary credentials" years later. The fact is, one could easily live in Salisbury in the late 1970s—even as a working journalist—and have no idea that Thomas's, or anyone's, music was being banned.

A very different newspaper story appeared in the *Herald* on January 22, 1979, under the headline "Let There Be Peace—The Song of Today." It opens, "The suffering and disintegration of tribal life as a result of the war have been two main themes in African music in Rhodesia in recent years." The writer focuses on "traditionalists" Thomas Mapfumo and Oliver Mtukudzi and reports that "the cry for peace and for an end to suffering" is the overriding concern for both composers. Comments attributed to Thomas make up the bulk of the short article, including the following:

> Our music reveals our recognition that as singers we have a special role to play in portraying the situation in which we find ourselves. . . . in a situation as explosive as ours there can be no music which is not in some way political, in some way a protest. . . . The music is a positive re-establishment of the authentic African culture, a reassertion of African values. We are groping implicitly through the imagination towards a new order. As we move into the future, we should not forget our great traditions of oral literature, for it is on the heritage of the past that the music and literature of the future will be based.[22]

It is difficult to imagine Thomas uttering a phrase like "groping implicitly through the imagination"—even if translated from Shona—but language aside, the ideas ring true. Thomas admits he is a protest singer but bases his protest in culture rather than politics. His remarks are like his songs, ambiguous, laced with a sly wink and a nod. There is no mention of struggle or "chimurenga," yet if you wonder who is behind this fight to reassert African values, the answer is clear: the guerrillas and their spirit medium mentors. The *Herald* headline tries to spin Thomas as a peacenik, but the words they attribute to him speak of "protest" and assert "a new order." Coincidence or not, he was detained for questioning shortly after this article ran.

The last single the Blacks Unlimited released before Thomas's arrest was "Kwa Gutu Ndakenda Nani," which asks, "How did I come to be here in Gutu . . . in Murehwa . . . in Bindura?"—all sites of guerrilla activity. The answer is, "The chimurenga brought me." This, said Thomas, was one of the songs that "brought me a lot of trouble."[23] Brian Cader had taken a job designing record jackets for Teal. He recalled Tony Rivet's arrest and interrogation by intelligence agents shortly after "Kwa Gutu" was released. Accused of disseminating banned music, Rivet held his ground, arguing that his company had a right to sell the music it produced. His questioners pressed him to admit the music was political. Rivet shot back, "No. I'm a white man. I just understand the *rhythm* of these people's music, and it is a throbbing, thriving rhythm, so we can't deprive them of it." Teal's lawyers managed to rescue Rivet after a day or two behind bars.

As for Thomas, over the years, he has recounted the story of his 1979 detention many times, and with great consistency. What follows is a composite of three accounts, from 1981, 1991, and 1998:

One day, we were out at Teal Records doing our rehearsals. It was on a Thursday. After practice, I went home. That's when I saw this message from the CID, the Special Branch. They wanted to see me. Well, my heart just went boom. I was shocked. I had a very small car, a Morris Minor. I had just bought that car two weeks before my arrest. So we went to Mbizi police station the next morning, me and Charles and Sekuru Jira. Charles was driving the Morris Minor because I had no license myself. At the station, there was this plainclothes policeman, very big. We went into his office and he gave me some forms to sign. I never read them, but I knew exactly that this was trouble. After I signed, he read a statement to me: "You are under detention. We are locking you up." I said, "No problem. You can lock me up." I told my uncle and Charlie that they should go back home and tell my parents and my brothers that I was arrested. Then I was taken to Southerton police station, a much bigger complex. I was put into a cell. Well, it wasn't very good in that cell. The blankets were dirty, and there was a bad smell. I stayed there from Friday, Saturday, Sunday, Monday. . . .

They kept trying to interview me about my music, and I kept saying it was our traditional music, and there was nothing wrong with it. The guys I spoke to were black. They understood the words. Well, I just told them those were the words and I wasn't going to change them. On Tuesday, they decided to move me to Chikurubi Prison, a real detention camp, right in the farms. I was put in cell number 7. There was this big white man, the superintendent of the jail. Each morning, he would pass by me and say, "How are you, musician?" Every time he wanted to talk to me. He didn't know my music. I think he just loved music. He decided that I should have a haircut. I had very long hair. My hair was cut short.

I had friends who were working as prison warders. They used to bring me things, cigarettes, even tea from their homes. Because they had known me through my music, they were very friendly to me. There was one warder who was a young brother to one of the famous footballers in the Zimbabwe Saints Football Club, playing in the premier leagues. He could ask his wife to cook something better and bring it from his house. Sometimes he even brought me something to smoke.

One day I was taken out—handcuffed—for interrogation with a certain Special Branch man. I still remember the only question he asked me was, "Are you the chimurenga singer?" I said, "What are you talking about?" He said, "You know what I'm talking about. You sing about chimurenga and supporting terrorists. You support Mugabe, so that's why you are being detained." I tried to tell him, "I believe what I sing is our own African traditional music."

For three months, they were sending a lot of different types of policemen to ask me questions about the music. They thought maybe I was going to say my music was political, but I never said that. I wasn't afraid. This was my culture and I was just going to live it. I'm an African. They brought a lot of records. Some of those records were not even mine. There were records by Zexie Manatsa and the Green Arrows, but they made a pile and said all that was my music. I said, "You must be joking." They even came with translations—such bad translations!—of my records.

Some of them wanted to scare me, wanted me to just disappear. It was a dangerous game. My mother and my sisters came to see me. They actually had heard I was no longer at the prison. I was taken away somewhere where they would not able to see me anymore. These were just rumors. But I had become famous with the people. Even people overseas had heard about me, so they were a bit afraid to put me down. Well, as you know, I live by the spirits. I think my ancestors must have actually just protected me from these people. They wanted to kill me, but that didn't happen. I'm still here.[24]

When Jira returned to the family with the news that Thomas was being held, everyone was stunned. No one had seen this coming. "Not at all," said William Mapfumo. "We never thought [Thomas's songs] could land him in trouble." Lancelot recalled, "That was one of the worst moments in our family life." After two weeks, black officers within the police force told the family that Thomas was being held at Chikurubi Prison, grim news. Later, when they were granted short weekend visits, family members were reassured to find that Thomas was not suffering. "The other prisoners had khaki shorts and khaki shirts," recalled Lancelot, "but him, he wasn't like a criminal prisoner. He had these long trousers and a brown jersey, the uniform we used to see messengers wearing."

The duration of Thomas's detention has never been precisely established. Just a year after the jailing, he sat for a long interview with Julie Frederikse and explained that he was held on a "30-day detention order," which his warders expected to be renewed. When after two additional weeks there was no new order, they released him, making his total time behind bars just over six weeks.[25] Lancelot roughly confirmed this, calling the detention "a month and some days." When Thomas told his story to Fred Zindi for his book *Roots Rocking in Zimbabwe* (1985), he said he was locked up for three months, and that is the figure he has stuck with ever since, though when pressed in 2004, he said, "*about* three months." Whatever its length, Thomas's detention paled in comparison with the treacherous terms of his release on March 30, 1979. Here are recollections shared with me by Thomas and various band members.

Thomas: It wasn't just a release like that. They had other ideas. They wanted to use me. Bishop Muzorewa was now in the internal settlement. He was talking to Smith and he wanted to form his own government. When they released me, the police told me to report the very next morning to Muzorewa's office, that if I didn't report to the UANC [United African National Council, Muzorewa's party] offices, I would be arrested again. When I showed up there, those UANC people told me I had to go and play with my band at their rally in Bulawayo. I knew that was the start of trouble. I couldn't refuse, because my every move was being watched. I had to say, "Ah, yes, with pleasure, we can play for you." But we didn't go there willingly; we were forced to go and play. We were even collected from our houses by some of these security men from the UANC.[26]

They released me on Friday. Muzorewa was going to speak in Bulawayo on Sunday. It was a very difficult decision to make. The first thing I did was to meet my own people, before I met the band. And then in the evening, I met the band, and I told them that we were actually going to Bulawayo to play at Bishop Muzorewa's rally. The band didn't like that. Some were saying we were going to be labeled sellouts.

Lancelot Mapfumo: Muzorewa used to preach a lot about politics. At the beginning, everybody loved him in Zimbabwe. Every man in the street was thinking that Muzorewa was working hand in hand with ZANU. But now there came this point where the guerrillas were in Mozambique, and Muzorewa had joined hands with Smith. Muzorewa is the one who signed on for the Rhodesian soldiers to go and bomb these guys in Mozambique.

Everson Chibamu (Blacks Unlimited trumpeter): That time, Muzorewa was becoming very unpopular with the people. They were trying to use Thomas's music. Pickett didn't want to go to Bulawayo. Everyone in the band didn't want to go to Bulawayo. The situation was bad.

Joshua Dube: Most of the musicians didn't like Muzorewa, especially Jonah Sithole. He was against that. Because Jonah had been a member of ZANU when it was Ndabaninge Sithole's party. Even Charles was a ZANU member. He didn't like Muzorewa. It was dangerous playing for Muzorewa at that time. Very dangerous.

Thomas: These guys, they feared the guerrillas. Every one of us, including myself. Because we thought we were going to have some really bad repercussions. Well, I told these guys that, really, we had to go there and play. Otherwise, we will be in bigger problems. They will come after us. I had to convince them that we were just a group of musicians. We were not armed. We had to safeguard our lives.

Everson: We went there by force. [On Saturday night], we were playing a show in Tafara. From that show, they said, "There's no one who is going home. We are going to Bulawayo straight."

Thomas does not portray himself as especially brave or heroic in this circumstance. He acknowledges that he could have refused to play the rally, been rearrested, and the "book of history" would have told a different story. At the same time, there was a certain logic, not just intimidation, behind Thomas's decision. "It wasn't only fear," he explained:

> We wanted to go and sing our Zimbabwe revolutionary songs for the people. To me, that was very important. I wanted people to know that the war was not over. There were still fighters out there. [The internal settlement] wasn't a good solution. We all knew that. So we went there to Bulawayo. We played at this rally. We played our revolutionary songs. People there were asking questions. Why were we still singing that type of music? And I told them they knew very well that I was in detention. I didn't have time to compose music to suit their situation. Well, they swallowed that. We just thought everything was going to be rosy. But that was not it. What made the situation look very nasty was the next morning in the *Herald* when there was a picture of me and Bishop Muzorewa standing side by side to make it look like I was supporting him. A lot of people got confused. There were some jealous so-and-so's. They knew very well that the Blacks Unlimited was the only band that actually fought for freedom, and some of these people didn't like that. They were creating stories. We played for Bishop Muzorewa. We had sold out. But we never changed. We kept singing our revolutionary music until the war was won and the guerrillas came home.

On Monday, April 2, 1979, the *Herald* featured the UANC "youth rally" as its top story under the headline "Bishop Urges a Ceasefire, Terror Bosses 'Want Dictator.'" Muzorewa pulled no punches that day, declaring, "Our war with Ian Smith is over," and that those who continued the fight must no longer be called freedom fighters but "downright terrorists" conducting a "shameful war for a person rather than Zimbabwe." Warning that his foes would deliver a "lousy dictator," the bishop said, "Those people have become hopeless and senseless murderers whom the people's militias must fight tooth and nail. Those who die now—whether they be boys still in the bush or the dirty *mujibas*—are dying for nothing." The police estimated 25,000 attendees at the rally; the UANC claimed the number was 50,000; either way, this was far less than the 500,000 Muzorewa had drawn in Salisbury in 1977, a clear sign that the public was abandoning him.[27]

The *Herald* photograph itself is less incriminating than Thomas recalled.[28] It shows Muzorewa in his white skullcap, festooned in feathers and colorful fabric, dancing for the camera, stretching out his arms to all but obscure any view of the musicians behind him. It is difficult to make Thomas out at all, but he is named in the caption and in the text. Although songs like "Pfumvu Pa Ruzevha," "Pamuromo Chete," and "Kuyaura" may well have been unsettling for campaign officials to hear, they go unmentioned in the *Herald* report, where Thomas's music is characterized only as "traditional"—just as he had told the police. The story itself did the real damage because it linked Thomas with Muzorewa's most outrageous rhetoric—calling the brave boys who helped the guerrillas, the *mujibas*, "dirty," letting Smith off the hook, adapting his language of "terrorism," and insulting the fighters as they endured hellish conditions in the bush. For Thomas Mapfumo and the Blacks Unlimited, the rally at Barbourfields Stadium was a disaster.

Looking at a photocopy of that *Herald* story twenty-six years later, Bishop Muzorewa was hard-pressed to recall this exact rally or the music that was played there. He seemed placid, serene, perfectly open, but in the context of a bishops' conference in Washington, DC, in 2005, he plainly found it difficult to reconstruct this, among all the tumultuous moments of that fateful year, 1979. Muzorewa studied the photograph through heavy reading glasses and laughed a little nervously at the sight. "I have forgotten a lot of things," he said. "But, of course, it's a fact. It is here in black-and-white." Regaining his poise, Muzorewa pointed out that he had never been a fan of radio or television, let alone popular music, and knew little about Thomas beyond the fact he was "a famous singer." He did not recall meeting Thomas in his office but said it could have happened. As to the music selected for his campaign rallies, that was all arranged by the party's central committee. "There would be people who would deal with the culture, and history, our traditions and so forth," Muzorewa explained. "That would definitely not be my business. In fact, I would come to a stage and find out who is performing when I got there. I was just one of the entertained people, not the entertainer."

"That is a lie," said Thomas on hearing this. "I was coming out of prison, and he knew that. It's not a thing he would forget."

Muzorewa went further, saying he "wanted to believe" that Thomas had participated in that rally in the spirit of hope and victory. "I wish I would remember the songs that they sang," he mused. "But I wouldn't be surprised if they had something to do with celebration of freedom, or the coming of freedom."

Hardly. Thomas may even have sung his late-1978 single "Zuva Guru (The Big Day)," in which he implicitly pooh-poohs the coming election, saying that the *real* big day will come when the war is won. Muzorewa claimed ignorance of Thomas's musical advocacy of traditional culture, spirit religion, or war politics, during the struggle or since. He allowed that over the years he had "heard" the story about Thomas's detention and had wondered what really happened that day. He went so far as to speculate that Thomas might have made the story up in order to "vindicate himself with the guerrillas." If Muzorewa's people had made a deal with government jailers, he assumed it must have been orchestrated by the Special Branch, who were "not quite under the grips of the executive."[29]

Vena Dangarembwa, Thomas's future wife, attended Muzorewa's Bulawayo rally. Vena had grown up trained to step off the sidewalk onto the street to let a white person pass. She understood that the war was about her future. But growing up in the heart of Matabeleland with a Shona father and an Ndebele mother, she also knew and feared divisions within the movement, especially the ethnic tension festering within the ZANU-ZAPU divide. "That's why my dad had to change our surname from Dangarembwa to Sibanda," she recalled. "He wanted to appear like an Ndebele." Vena had been corresponding with Thomas up to the time of his arrest. She had felt helpless when he was seized, but as a schoolgirl under her parents' custody and far from the capital, she could do nothing about it. "It was quite touching to see him there," she recalled, "free and singing, and people loved his music. At that time I don't think I thought about the rally as such. I was just happy to see *him*."

There is doubt as to how many UANC rallies the Blacks Unlimited played. In later interviews, Thomas insisted there was only one, but he spoke to both Frederikse and Zindi in the 1980s about "rallies."[30] He told Frederikse that the band was asked to do more UANC shows and said they would do so only if paid. In the next breath, he spoke about ongoing intimidation, in particular a relative in the army who warned him that the Selous Scouts planned to kill him. Joshua Dube, who began playing guitar with the Blacks Unlimited around this time, remembered UANC and security people visiting Thomas at his Waterfalls house in the run-up to the vote. "Thomas was playing most of the gigs for Muzorewa," claimed Dube. "I remember one day we played here in Harare, and the next day we went to Gweru, playing for Muzorewa." Everson Chibamu too recalled "some other gigs." "That went on for some time," he said, "those campaigning or fund-raising shows. There were orders from UANC and the Special Branch." Muzorewa himself thought he had shared the stage with Thomas only once, though the band could have played rallies where he was not present. In any case, there cannot have been many such events because the voting began just eighteen days after the Bulawayo rally.[31]

More damning than any rally appearance was the appropriation by Muzorewa's campaign of the Blacks Unlimited song "Bhutsu Mutandarika," a jocular, *shangara*-style tune that talks about "oversized boots." The song is an artifact from the days of forced labor in Rhodesia when miners were issued one-size-fits-all rubber boots. The Blacks Unlimited version exudes optimism with bright guitar interplay, a bantering brass section refrain, and a break in which Thomas whistles like a herd boy corralling his cattle. Helicopters dispatched by Muzorewa's campaign flew over the bush where guerrillas lay in hiding, loudspeakers blasting "Bhutsu Mutandarika" while a friendly voice and a hail of flyers bade the fighters to lay down their arms and vote. Thomas's old friend and booster Webster Shamu witnessed the response of fighters in Mozambique when they heard about this. "People call you a sellout," Shamu would later tell Thomas. "Some people thought I was in that helicopter myself," said Thomas. "I think that was their motive. They really painted me. They painted me bad. They painted me black."

When the election came—April 17 through 21, 1979—67 percent of the eligible population cast ballots, and 64 percent of those went for Muzorewa's UANC.[32] The United Nations quickly passed a resolution declaring the vote "illegal," essentially exposing it as a ruse to entrench white rule under the guise of democracy. Nevertheless, as victor, Muzorewa could boast greater electoral popularity than either Jimmy Carter or Margaret Thatcher, both of whom would decline to recognize his government.[33] As Muzorewa prepared to assume power, the *Herald* did its best to impart confidence in the new regime. It mourned the broken spirits of fighters returning from the bush and puffed about the "new team at the top" and the bishop's "historic trek to independence." Smith stepped aside as gracefully as he could, telling the paper he had "no regrets," though slipping in that he would have preferred a slower, more "evolutionary" process than the one he was "forced into." The forcing continued. Almost nine hundred people died fighting in May. The feared Selous Scouts seemed to be losing their edge, resorting to desperate attacks, and repeatedly failing in their mission to decapitate the guerrillas by assassinating Nkomo. All the arcane, no-holds-barred trickery, all the bombing and raiding, all those dead Rhodesian boys, and even the co-opting of the fighters' favorite singer, Thomas Mapfumo, had failed to turn the tide.

The *Herald* ran an update on popular music, citing the parallel rise of foreign disco and the "modern traditional" music championed by Thomas Mapfumo and Oliver Mtukudzi. The spread features photos of smiling DJs (two black, one white) and of Thomas looking confident and happy in mod white, side-buttoned trousers with a heavy chain around his neck—more Sly Stone than Hakurotwi Mude. Thomas and Oliver are credited with becoming popular because they were "giving the people what they want," an obvious echo of a Muzorewa campaign slogan. As DJ Wellington Mbofana predicts, "Very soon we are going to have an international black star."[34] Thomas and Oliver are his candidates, and poster boys for a happy new nation.

While the *Herald* cheerled, rumor and innuendo about Thomas filtered though the townships. Former Blacks Unlimited stalwarts stopped coming to shows, and bookings dwindled. Meanwhile, Thomas's song "Chikonzero (The Reason)" reached the top ten in July with lyrics pleading for the dawn of Zimbabwe: "Everyone is crying for it. This is the reason people have endured hardships, climbed mountains, lived in exile, slept in caves, and walked long distances in the bush." Lest anyone question Thomas's continued solidarity with the guerrillas, "Tichakunda (We Shall Overcome)," his first postdetention production, sought to remove doubt:

Knock, knock, knock,
Come in, sir.
This is Harare
The famous Harare
Our lives are a round of poverty
Our houses are like fowl runs,
We sleep like rats . . .
But we shall win in the end.
The oppressors shall be defeated.
They shall confess.[35]

This song tapped into public dissatisfaction with a new government that was unable to improve living conditions. Prices stayed high; fuel remained rationed; international sanctions continued. In Maputo, voz broadcasters now denounced Thomas. Meanwhile, others, particularly in the expatriate community, were still excitedly discovering his music. Musa Zimunya followed events from England, where he was a student. To him, it meant everything that Thomas stuck with his militant message. "As far as Muzorewa was concerned," Musa recalled, "[Thomas] was like Ananse the Spider or like Br'er Rabbit. He is one thing to you and another to himself. Muzorewa didn't understand that there was nothing changed in the presentation of these songs. So what difference would it make to Thomas if the UANC tried to hijack his music? It didn't make any difference as long as he was out of jail."

In August 1979, the Blacks Unlimited performed at Salisbury's premier pop culture event that summer, the wedding of fellow singer Zexie Manatsa. Manatsa's nuptial bash drew sixty thousand paying celebrants to Rufaro Stadium, and it began with the couple entering the stadium while Thomas sang "Africa."[36] Muzorewa, the new president, had foolishly scheduled a public speech that day and blamed the wedding concert for the low turnout he received. A headline ran: "Zexie's Wedding Spoils Muzorewa's Rally."[37]

The next day, Muzorewa's cabinet announced it was dropping the word "Rhodesia" from the country's name. "It Will Be Zimbabwe," blared the *Sunday Mail*. The government was scrambling to remain relevant. But days earlier, it had been forced to agree to "all-party" constitutional talks, effectively signing its own death warrant. Thus began the better-known history of Zimbabwe's birth: the combative Lancaster House talks in London that December, the year-end cease-fire, the dramatic repatriation of Nkomo and Mugabe, and ultimately Mugabe's election in February 1980. This breathtaking succession of events would leave blacks and whites alike drained and dizzy. When it was over, Thomas would go out of his way to proclaim his allegiance to Robert Mugabe, the only time he would do so for a politician. His expressions of fealty are understandable, given the circumstances. Beneath them, misgivings lingered.

Decades later, when his regard for Mugabe had ebbed substantially, Thomas allowed that he had always harbored reservations about the guerrilla leader's seeming love of violence and his philosophical slant.[38] "Mugabe used to say he was a Marxist," recalled Thomas. "Well, I myself never liked Marxism or Leninism because I had read very bad things about such people. I didn't like Russia at all. A lot of our people were being fooled." Once in power himself, Mugabe would champion a strong central government and state control of industry, and many of his policies would curtail individual rights. His model for leadership was not so much Marx or Lenin but Stalin—a dubious hero for a young man like Thomas who loved jazz, Elvis, and traditional Shona religion.

As for Muzorewa, Thomas continued to admire his church roots and advocacy of Western-style democracy, even as he condemned the bishop's betrayal of the struggle. At the Lancaster House talks in London, Muzorewa proved out of his league, unable to hold sway against steely Patriotic Front negotiators backed by a guerrilla army. An exasperated Smith reviled Muzorewa as "wet putty" in the hands of British negotiators. When the shape of the new constitution emerged, the bishop yielded to history, accepting the agreement "in the name of justice, honesty and fair play." Smith, sidelined by this process, was so bitter that he told the *London Spectator* that Muzorewa was "the most inept politician—no, man—I've ever met."[39]

Robert Mugabe radiated inevitability at Lancaster House. The white Rhodesians in Muzorewa's delegation, dazzled by the sight of wealthy Arabs walking in the streets, were like farm boys gone to the city, forever upstaged by the relative glamour of the Patriotic Front representatives whose agenda was so much simpler and less compromised. Back home the war raged on, providing a powerful incentive to keep Mugabe and Nkomo at the table at all costs. The CIO reportedly stalked them in the streets of London. Mugabe nearly walked away from the proceedings when the British ringmaster, Lord Carrington, laid out an ultimatum calling for an immediate cease-fire. Mugabe's response—that Carrington could "go to Hell"—made headlines in the *Herald* and made Carrington retreat. With that, the deal was done.

Mugabe was white Rhodesia's worst nightmare, and this had to appeal to blacks. His hard line in London yielded true independence and majority rule at last, and wherever you stood, the achievement was immense. It had taken many blows to dismantle the stubborn Rhodesian state, and Muzorewa had certainly played his part. But it was Mugabe who delivered the coup de grâce and emerged as the erudite, charismatic guerrilla statesman. Muzorewa became a footnote in history, remembered by few outside the country and hated by many within it. Significantly, the issue of land reform was left until the end and not fully resolved at Lancaster House. The agreement calls for a ten-year grace period followed by land transfers and compensation from England, but details are vague. For all his confidence and bluster, Mugabe privately feared that he had been tricked, just like Lobengula with the Rudd Concession a century earlier.[40]

When the Lancaster House deal was done, and a cease-fire at last declared in December 1979, eighty-two ZANLA and ZIPRA commanders flew to Salisbury from Zambia and Mozambique, beckoning their followers to gather up arms and move toward sixteen designated "assembly points." There was pandemonium as tens of thousands poured out of the townships and stormed the airport to greet their liberators.[41]

On December 31, 1979—the last day of the decade—Mugabe's political party, ZANU, held its first public rally in Zimbabwe, even though the man himself had yet to emerge from his Mozambican lair. The event began with spirit mediums parading in silence before the gathered thousands. The crowd that day waved clenched fists and chanted: "Down with Muzorewa! Down with Smith! Down with sellouts and oppressors!" It was now, as the fighters streamed across the borders—wounded, scarred, haggard, and haunted—that the true price of Thomas's association with Bishop Muzorewa would be exacted. Thomas instinctively withdrew into his work, composing, recording, and performing amid storms of criticism. He did not argue or defend himself. He just kept making songs, confident that, in the end, they would redeem him.

"I don't think Thomas was ever a firebrand," reflected Musa Zimunya:

Once in a while, you get these people who symbolize the cultural vision of a community. Walt Whitman was not such a wonderful politician, but he was a great poet. You could say the same thing about Mark Twain, maybe even Norman Mailer. Thomas Mapfumo isn't Norman Mailer, and he isn't Mark Twain. But he was a welcome arrival on the scene, someone who had an integrated vision of the necessity for *cultural* revolution within the political revolution . . . and he himself, more or less single-handedly, made it a *respectable* revolution. I'm not saying that Oliver [Mtukudzi] didn't play his part, or [Zexie Manatsa and] the Green Arrows. They certainly played their part, but they didn't have quite the same—I wouldn't call it bitterness, or anger—but *passion*.

With his passion intact and his reputation in tatters, Thomas braced himself for a new round of elections in 1980.

6 / Agony of Victory

They are sitting in the Sun
Their heads are all white with age
Their faces are gloomy with sorrow
But why Mama and Papa yet we are free . . .
Yes we are in Free Zimbabwe but our hearts are in pain . . .
The old man drags himself
He takes the mbira and starts playing
He sings the song, Yes the song of longing
A name in the song he mentions Tichatonga my Son
The name brings tears to his face
I listen! that name is mine
Yet they don't remember me
FROM "EVE OF FREEDOM" BY AMON MATIKA

Three rallies in January 1980 foretold the fate of Zimbabwe's first presidential election. Bishop Muzorewa gathered thousands and warned that both ZANU and ZAPU politicians were "fascists" who would nationalize industry and squelch democracy under a one-party regime. A week later, ZAPU's Joshua Nkomo flew in from Zambia, his Puma helicopter alighting amid a crowd that police put at 120,000 (the party called it 300,000). Nkomo criticized no one. He spoke Shona, Ndebele, and English, stressing "unity" and reconciliation. Two weeks later, Robert Mugabe swept in from Mozambique for the biggest rally the country had seen. The police estimate was 150,000 (ZANU's, 1.6 million). An aerial photograph of the Highfield event carpeted the *Herald*'s front page edge to edge with a speckling of pinpoint heads. Mugabe—barely heard above chanting and singing—belittled his rivals, promising victory and a better life for Zimbabweans. He made a spiritual appeal, pledging not to ban churches—as some had predicted—but also not to condemn those who chose to honor vadzimu spirits rather than Jesus Christ.

Somewhere amid the ocean of humanity enveloping the stages at Mugabe's rally, the Blacks Unlimited performed. Thomas barely recalled the music, only the chaotic milieu, the excitement of finally seeing the man behind the guerrilla war, and the irritation of ZANU officials who were "not very happy to see us playing there" because they had "forgotten what we did during the struggle."

Political parties were busy corralling popular musicians. Zexie Manatsa and the Green Arrows became a ZANU band through the machinations of Webster Shamu, who had returned from Mozambique with Mugabe's entourage. The party supplied Zexie and his musicians with guerrilla uniforms to wear on stage. Throughout a brief, kinetic campaign, Shamu accompanied the Green Arrows around the country, touting their valor and patriotism. Shamu had once boosted Thomas's songs on his Voice of Zimbabwe radio program, but at the war's end, the broadcaster had turned against him, excoriating Thomas for playing at the Muzorewa rally. "Webster Shamu was now very much against us," Thomas recalled bitterly. "He tried to make Zexie a hero, to put him in my place." Thomas confronted Shamu in Chegutu, where both the Green Arrows and the Blacks Unlimited had shows. "I told him there was no band who did what we did during the struggle. We risked our own lives. We went out there to meet the guerrillas in Wedza. They were trying to hijack the whole story."[1]

The election began on February 28, 1980. Under the eyes of 565 bobbies from London and legions of international observers, some 2.6 million people voted—as much as 90 percent of the eligible population—and the result was decisive:

Mugabe's ZANU-PF: 63 percent, for 57 seats
Nkomo's PF-ZAPU: 24 percent, for 20 seats
Muzorewa's UANC: 8.3 percent, for 3 seats

Observers declared this a "free and fair" vote, a crushing verdict for Muzorewa. The bishop had wept upon hearing Ian Smith urge voters to support Nkomo—anything to stop Mugabe. Muzorewa had complained about every aspect of the campaign, including its inevitable result. Now his voice would fall silent while Mugabe and his wife, Sally, were seen everywhere, always in the company of real and symbolic roosters, the totem animal of the ZANU-PF party. White Rhodesians faced the reality that not just "garden boys" and "nannies" but avowed, militant Marxists and people who took guidance from ancestor spirits would now rule the land.

No Blacks Unlimited songs from the election period refer to the controversy engulfing Thomas's career.[2] Over time, the music of the Muzorewa interregnum, like its politics, would be forgotten as a wave of existential change washed over Zimbabwe. But for the Blacks Unlimited this remained "a very trying time." Hard feelings about the Muzorewa rally still lingered among fans, especially in the cities. "Every month," recalled Thomas's manager at the time, Thompson Kachingwe, "we went out of Salisbury because we didn't have good support in town. Sometimes we did sixteen shows, nonstop." Even then, earnings were meager, far less than the band had known before Thomas's detention.

Muzorewa aside, Thomas and his band were specifically unwelcome in Bulawayo due to an incident that had occurred there in 1979. The band had played a show in town and afterward retired to their customary *shebeen* (speakeasy), in fact, the apartment of "a sister" named Sarah. Black Rhodesian soldiers also frequented Sarah's shebeen, and on this particular night the band's drummer Jonasy had led the way, bursting into the second-floor apartment to find a room full of uniformed men. These soldiers, who had attended Thomas's concert, recognized Jonasy as a member of the Blacks Unlimited. Thomas said the soldiers resented musicians who had money to spend when they did not. One might also imagine serious tensions between a band of musicians singing for the guerrillas, and a group of drunk soldiers whose job it was to defeat those guerrillas. Whatever the motive, the soldiers set upon Jonasy straightaway. Sarah's waitress flung open the window and shouted to the street where Thomas was standing by his car with the two doormen—the boxer Kilimanjaro, and a young nephew of Jonah Sithole's named Shumba. Shumba picked up the wrought iron rod that Thomas used to dance with on the stage, and he and Kilimanjaro headed up to the shebeen. "They forced the door open," Thomas recalled, "and started assaulting these soldiers. Jonah's nephew had that wrought iron and he hit this guy several times by the head. These guys were beaten to nothing by our people."

The man assaulted with Thomas's iron staff died on arrival at hospital. The doorman, Shumba, confessed and was jailed for six months. A trial ensued, and according to Thomas, the victim's father testified *against* his own son, characterizing him as a worthless troublemaker. The judge declared the killing a mob action and ruled it unfair to blame a single person.[3] Shumba (who was Shona) went free, but many in Bulawayo would not soon forget this dubious application of justice. The victim may have been a Rhodesian soldier, but he was also a local Ndebele, for some, a more important identity.

A year later, as the April independence celebration approached, expatriates were streaming back to Salisbury from their refuges in Tanzania, Mozambique, Zambia, and England. They found a city in delirium. Where bombs and curfews had once rendered public places ghostly, brass bands and pop groups entertained merry crowds in parks and squares by day, and in hotels and beer halls by night. Those returning knew little about Thomas's detention, the Muzorewa rally, let alone the Bulawayo killing. In London, Musa Zimunya and his friends had danced to Thomas's records like "ecstatic initiates."[4] Returning now to a fellowship at the University of Zimbabwe, Musa immediately sought "spiritual contact"—a Mapfumo show at the downtown Elizabeth Hotel.

"In England," Musa recalled,

I had seen B. B. King, Eric Clapton, and British jazz musicians, and I'd always admired how it was like you just had to push a button and the performance came right on cue. Only a few years before, Thomas had looked like a pretender, getting too old before he had achieved anything. And now to come back to find that he had his own combo—and boy, it was the *punchiest* thing I'd ever known. Everything is glowing in this instant. If I had taken a photograph, it would still be glowing. They were wearing all white and bell-bottoms, like the Commodores. They looked young, trim, clean, smart—like Thomas Mapfumo would want it to be.

Mugabe had unveiled the country's new flag: red, green, and gold stripes with a core of black and a fish eagle—*hungwe*—emblazoned over a red star. He had sounded a message of peace and brotherhood and invited all to forgive and forget in a new Zimbabwe. The centerpiece of the transition was to be a ceremony at Rufaro Stadium on April 17, when the Union Jack would be lowered for the last time as an official flag in Africa. Robert Mugabe would be seen with his vanquished rival, Joshua Nkomo. Thomas Mapfumo, Oliver Mtukudzi, Zexie Manatsa, and other local acts would play alongside the king of Jamaican reggae, Bob Marley. Some forty thousand old Rhodesians and new Zimbabweans would come together, stalwarts of the old regime in black tie and guerrillas in camouflage and fatigues. England's Prince Charles, India's Indira Gandhi, and Australia's Malcolm Fraser would attend, alongside leaders from young African nations—Alhaji Shehu Shagari of Nigeria, Kenneth Kaunda of Zambia, Seretse Khama of Botswana, and, the darling of them all, Samora Machel of Mozambique, without whose help this day might never have come.

In 1980, Salisbury looked like few cities in Africa. Its downtown was a neat cluster of high-rise office towers, elegant hotels, and shopping establishments. Its wide paved streets were clean and orderly, filled with British, American, German, and Japanese cars, but mostly the Peugeot station wagons used as public transport and known as "ETS"—emergency taxis. Buses moved in and out of the central transport hub, taking black workers to and from their homes in high-density suburbs. Schoolchildren, white and black, wore tunics and uniforms, and even the poorest workers typically managed a Western-style shirt and a pair of trousers, or a plain blouse and dress. There were none of the street vendors, pushcarts, fruit stalls, dashikis, or colorful African fabric wraps that would have been commonplace in cities as nearby as Beira or Maputo. The Rhodesians had spent eighty years shaping a population of Africans who would yearn to participate in English ways. That legacy lingered on the city's streets at this knife's-edge moment of change, not only in clothing, cars, and architecture but also in deeply conflicted hearts and minds. Rhodes's Pioneers had named the city Salisbury after a British prime minister. Zimbabweans would call it Harare, after the Ne Harawa, a Zezuru clan.[5]

On the night before the Rufaro celebration, Thomas performed at the Queens Hotel: "8:00 PM till late," the hand-pressed posters read. The Blacks Unlimited had been writing new songs, including one called "Nyarai (Be Ashamed)." The title sounds scolding—and it is—but the music of "Nyarai" exudes chest-thumping joy, starting with a bright guitar riff from Jonah Sithole. The guitar's timbre is taut and feisty, slightly damped to suggest mbira, fraught with pent-up emotion. A single crack from the high tom-tom extends into a tumbling drum fill. A tambourine shimmers, and the ensemble kicks in with sizzling hi-hat, an eruption of bass, and an elastic second guitar line that dodges its way through Sithole's lead. Thomas comes in booming, exultant in Shona:

> We are celebrating the birth of Zimbabwe!
> Zimbabwe is for us all. . . .
> Congratulations, comrades . . . who fought the Chimurenga war
> To liberate Zimbabwe. . . .
> All ancestral spirits adore the liberators

Then, out of the blue, Thomas raises the specter of "rebels" who don't want to be ruled by others. His pitch rising, he sings:

> What sort of people are you?
> Why are you not ashamed when you have been defeated?

Be ashamed. Be ashamed
Be ashamed when you have been defeated

As he attacks this refrain, Thomas's voice seems to race ahead, and the band wobbles to keep pace, nearly spinning out of time as the snare drum rolls, the bass lunges, and the brass section blares out a victory fanfare. Thomas ends by shouting:

Viva Zimbabwe!
Viva Africa!
Viva Prime Minister Robert Gabriel Mugabe!
Viva povo!

The Portuguese words are a nod to the Mozambicans. The effusion of praise for Mugabe, so rare in Thomas's repertoire, seems almost conspicuous. Thomas insisted his celebration of Mugabe in "Nyarai" was heartfelt at the time. "Mugabe was a freedom fighter," he declared. "We all thought he was a savior, a messiah." But "Nyarai" has a taunting edge that sets it apart from other celebratory anthems Zimbabwe's musicians churned out that spring. Who exactly should "be ashamed"? Is it Smith and the Rhodesians? Is it Muzorewa and those who sold out in the internal settlement? Is it those who opposed Mugabe in the election, particularly Joshua Nkomo and his Ndebele followers in Matabeleland?

Ndebele discontent was a worry. Mugabe had achieved a commanding electoral win, but local election results showed a lopsided victory for Nkomo and ZAPU in Matabeleland. Joshua Nkomo accepted a place in Mugabe's government, but this uneasy arrangement would not last long.[6] Shona and Ndebele guerrillas had clashed during the campaign, and ethnic violence would continue beyond independence, prompting Mugabe to extend Ian Smith's state of emergency, six months at a time, for the next ten years.

Thomas acknowledged that "Nyarai" was "sung for the people of Matabeleland," adding, "When ZANU-PF won, ZAPU wouldn't accept an invitation to join the government, so we composed that tune. It was bringing the people together, making them see reality, that unity was essential. It doesn't mean we hated people from Matabeleland. They are our people. We had to politicize them, teach them what unity is all about." Everson felt that Thomas's song "Nyarai" had generated more lasting ill will in Ndebele Zimbabwe than even the shebeen killing. Emmanuel Vori agreed, noting that Thomas's rhetoric about "unity"—even as it echoed Nkomo's own campaign message—had an irksome ring coming from a Shona singer. "They didn't take kindly to that," said Vori. "You've got to understand the history of the Zimbabwean people. We are proud of our tribes. One tribe will always want to dominate the other. That will never, ever stop."

Vori's language is loose here. The Shona are in no way a "tribe." Their identity is constructed from a set of clans living on the Zimbabwe plateau. Shona and Ndebele people are not immediately distinguishable. Some Shona—like Thomas and his brothers—have distinctive faces: high cheekbones, full lips, and towering foreheads—features beautifully captured in modern Shona stone sculptures. Family names are indicative, and language can be a clue, especially for Sindebele speakers not secure in Shona. But there has been a lot of intermarriage. Walking down a Zimbabwean street today, one would be hard-pressed to identify the ethnicity of many passersby. The Shona-Ndebele tension Vori and others cite remains a factor in Zimbabwean social and political life, though not a dominant one.[7]

On the morning of April 17, a DJ for the newly named Zimbabwe Broadcasting Corporation (ZBC) played "Nyarai" back-to-back with Bob Marley's song "Zimbabwe," which celebrates the fighters' willingness to "mash it up."[8] Marley's song, like so many of Thomas's, recognized that victory had come not through patience and nonviolence but through bloodshed: an estimated thirty thousand people had died during Zimbabwe's seven-year conflict. For this DJ, Thomas singing "Send the Children to War" was no different than Marley singing "Get Up, Stand Up." The singers were equals and peers, musical comrades in a global struggle against the vestiges of British colonialism.

The outside world saw a different picture. Marley had become an international superstar, a symbol of Pan-Africanism, and leader of a cultural movement that was changing popular music worldwide. Thomas Mapfumo was virtually unknown outside Zimbabwe and its enclaves abroad. The two singers were almost the same age—Marley thirty-six and Mapfumo thirty-five—but whereas Thomas's greatest achievements lay ahead, Marley was nearing his end. The aching, bandaged toe he had wishfully dismissed as a soccer injury was, in fact, cancerous. He had sealed his fate by rejecting a doctor's advice that he have it cut off, declaring, "Rasta no abide amputation." The king of reggae would give his last concert less than six months later and would die in just over a year.

Bob Marley and the Wailers flew into Harare the day before the independence ceremony, unannounced. Their flight coincided with the well-publicized arrival of Prince Charles, and while crowds massed to the prince and his entourage, Marley's people slipped away scarcely noticed. Dera Tomkins, the daughter of a Boston church activist, was in Harare for the celebration and accompanied the Wailers' entourage during the hectic days that followed. From the airport, she reported, their first stop was Rufaro Stadium, where a rehearsal was under way for the ceremony. Marley, with his wife, Rita, two of their sons, and the Wailers band, stood near the stage and watched a column of three hundred ZANLA fighters march into the stadium, singing. Marley teared up. It was his first time seeing an African revolutionary army, the sort he celebrated in his songs, parading before him in the flesh and filling the air with proud chimurenga songs.[9]

This was a spectacle, and a history, that fit Marley's notions about Africa. He had visited the continent once before, and the experience had been disillusioning. As a Rastafarian, he believed that Haile Selassie, the former emperor of Ethiopia, was God—the literal Light of the World, the King of Kings incarnate. In Ethiopia in 1978, Marley had mingled with a population that viewed Selassie as a mere man, and a corrupt one at that. This earthly deity had been buried in an unmarked grave and denied public remembrance by the government that succeeded him. Marley's most intimate biographer, Timothy White, writes that this experience had left the singer "severely shaken."[10] Marley had somewhat impulsively accepted Edgar Tekere's invitation to perform at the independence ceremony in Zimbabwe. After failing to persuade Chris Blackwell to fund the trip, he eventually paid for everything himself, bringing PA equipment and records and pins to give away as gifts.[11] Marley wanted to interact with ordinary people as much as possible.

If Zimbabwe affirmed Marley's Afrocentric political outlook, it likely dimmed his view of African hospitality. Drunken soldiers accompanied his entourage to have tea with Robert Mugabe, where the Jamaicans were unimpressed by a menu of cucumber sandwiches and lemonade. Marley nevertheless obliged the president's family by sitting at the piano and performing "No Woman, No Cry." The musicians dined at Job's Nitespot, where they were served pork appetizers, swiftly removed once the hosts learned pork was taboo for Rastafarians. While Thomas was starting his independence eve show at the Queens Hotel just blocks away, Nitespot owner Job Kadengu—a secondhand car dealer turned ZANU insider—hastily arranged to house Marley's inner circle at a posh suburban home, twenty miles out of town.[12] The arrangement was a tight fit that left the musicians cut off from the life of the city, and without ganja to smoke. Marley's handlers kept him out of mischief. One history of white Rhodesia notes, "[Marley's] 'type' was considered a threat to the country's innocence and the Chief Superintendent intended to arrest him for the slightest hint of a transgression."[13]

The independence ceremony at Rufaro was organized by ZANU and, like the ceremonies of the nationalist struggle, it consisted mostly of music: church choirs, traditional ensembles, military bands, a troop of "Hindoo dancers" and their accompanists, chimurenga choirs, guitar bands, and, of course, popular singers like Comrade Chinx, Zexie Manatsa, Oliver Mtukudzi, and Thomas Mapfumo.[14]

Thomas and his musicians arrived at 8:00 PM, as instructed, but there was no schedule to follow. The organizers called performers to the stage as they saw fit, and the Blacks Unlimited waited. Oliver Mtukudzi (Tuku) earned the prime slot, just before Marley's performance and the official ceremony. Tuku had emerged on his own now, a soulful troubadour whose confident tenor voice had helped soothe a nation at war. The long-standing debate as to whether Tuku or Mukanya (Thomas's totem) loomed largest had begun, and for the moment, Tuku was on top. In this setting, though, neither singer could hold a candle to Bob Marley.

Thomas had been in awe of "Brother Bob" since 1977, when he had walked into a record bar and bought a copy of *Exodus*.[15] Sinatra's swing, Elvis's swagger, and Wilson Pickett's soul had all worked their spells on Thomas, as had the Congo's rumba, the Afro-rock of Osibisa, and melodious jazz from Stan Getz in New York and Dollar Brand in Cape Town. But Marley cut to the bone. For a people battling to reclaim stolen land and identity, no foreign music had ever sounded this good.

We know where we're going, and we know where we've been
We live in Babylon, we're going to the promised land

From the moment Marley shouted the words "Viva Zimbabwe!" through the biggest PA system Harare had ever heard, the atmosphere turned electric. He eased in with a feel-good number, "Positive Vibration," and then dug deep with "Dem Belly Full"—"A hungry man is an angry man!" As the band lit into "Roots Rock Reggae," it became clear that the sound was reaching far beyond the lucky thousands inside the stadium.

Marley's performance had been publicized only a day earlier. Some in the surrounding neighborhoods were probably caught unaware when they heard his singular voice bellowing from Rufaro. People who had been unable to secure passes had been collecting outside the grounds. Now, ignited by the music, hundreds, maybe thousands, began approaching the gates, ignoring police warnings as they scrambled to enter the stadium. After years of quashing public demonstrations, the police responded instinctively, firing round after round of tear gas to drive back the advancing mob. The wind lofted noxious fumes into the stadium, and soon there was the spectacle of cabinet ministers, members of Parliament, and foreign dignitaries coughing, weeping, and burying their faces in handkerchiefs. Down on the field, Dera Tomkins grabbed a ZANU cloth banner and wrapped her head in it to quell the burning in her eyes. Marley seemed the last to notice, closing his eyes as if in trance, and forging on until at last he was overwhelmed and left the stage. "Think," recalled the Wailers' Aston "Family Man" Barrett, "from where I was born, I have to come all the way to Africa to experience tear gas."[16]

After forty minutes the gas fumes cleared and the band returned briefly to the stage, minus the singing I-Threes, who had retreated to Job's house with Marley's sons. Marley sang "War" and the inevitable "Zimbabwe," but his heart had gone out of the performance. Blending English, Portuguese, and even a word of Shona, Marley put on a brave face, saluted the crowd, and exited. In the aftermath of near disaster, more heads of state entered the stadium to witness the exchange of flags,[17] and the crowd reacted to each new arrival, cheering especially loudly for the African presidents. Formations of the Rhodesian army and the various guerrilla factions marched in together. Historian Thomas Parkenham recalled watching the guerrillas in jungle fatigues running "laps of honor like sportsmen . . . a strangely innocent way to end a seven-year 'bush war.'"[18] Roars of adulation broke out when Prime Minister Robert Mugabe rolled into the stadium in a white Mercedes with motorcycle escorts and cadres of bodyguards, ten of them running "American style" next to his car. A band played "God Bless Africa," as Mugabe slowly circled the stadium field.

Prince Charles stood at the rostrum minutes before midnight, and the Rhodesian Signal Corps band broke into the royal salute as the Union Jack descended. A blue spotlight shone on the new flag of Zimbabwe that rose to replace it, and the sight of that colorful banner triggered pandemonium in the stands. With each blast of the ceremonial twenty-one-gun salute that followed, the shouting, ululating, singing, and dancing intensified, spreading to the crowd outside the stadium and throughout the city, and swelling again as the sonic boom of a single low-flying jet plane shattered the air like cannon fire. Robert Mugabe lit the Independence Flame, which would be carried to nearby Salisbury Kopje to burn eternally.

Most of those present in Rufaro were young enough to experience this moment as the successful end of their long liberation struggle—cause for celebration, to be sure. But the oldest witnesses, black and white, must have experienced an even greater awe. It had been less than ninety years since the first twenty-one-gun salute had echoed off these low hills. On September 13, 1890, when Lieutenant Tyndale-Biscoe had hoisted the Union Jack up the tallest tree he could find, guns had heralded the start of an altogether different history—hopeful in its own way, but doomed. The very oldest Shona within earshot of Rufaro in 1980 had been children when the Pioneers arrived. They had seen everything: occupation, oppression, forced labor, propaganda, Christianity, protest, war, and now, what seemed a final victory. "Nyarara Kuchema (Do Not Cry)," Thomas counseled in a song prepared for the occasion, "Things will be okay." The lyric acknowledges pain within the nation's triumph, for everyone who had survived this struggle had wounds to heal.

Mugabe took his oath of office sometime after midnight. He too seemed to grasp the need for healing as he tried to put aside the darkness of war with gentle, generous words. "If yesterday," declared Mugabe, "I fought you as an enemy, today you have become a friend with the same national interest, loyalty, rights and duties as myself. If yesterday you hated me, today you cannot avoid the love that binds you to me and me to you."[19] Mugabe had genuine affection for Lord and Lady Soames, and he let the whites closest to him know he would need their help in order to govern. "I don't know anything about governing a country," one recalled him saying, "and none of my people do either."[20]

Watching the ceremony from the stands in Rufaro, Thomas Parkenham witnessed a turning point bigger than the history of one nation. He believed Zimbabwe would show the way for others around the continent, because "its new African rulers were quite as well educated as the men they replaced."[21] Now that proposition would be tested.

After the ceremony, a joyful chaos reigned. Bob Marley and the Wailers were strangely abandoned. Job and the other hosts hurried off to private parties and balls. Geoffrey Nyarota was among a contingent that flocked to Job's Nitespot on the rumor that Marley and his band would be there. In fact, the Jamaicans had been left to the mercy of Thompson Kachingwe, not the best chauffeur, as he knew neither the directions to the band house nor how to operate the manual transmission truck in which the musicians were traveling. As the Jamaicans entered the traffic jam that was Harare, local bands began entertaining a dwindling cohort of ragtag revelers in Rufaro Stadium.

Thomas was steaming. "They kept saying, 'You are going to play very soon,'" he recalled. "Can you imagine? We went in there at eight o'clock. We thought each time we were going to hear our name being called out, but they kept us waiting until every head of state and every important Jack and Jill had gone home. We were being treated like a group of kids who wouldn't fight for the struggle." Only as the African sky began to brighten at the horizon were Thomas Mapfumo and the Blacks Unlimited at last called to perform the final set of the independence celebration at Rufaro. "Well, we were not above it," Thomas recalled with bemused pride: "We were not angered, because we played for the guerrillas, the real people who fought for our freedom, and the *mujibas*, the youth who gave moral support to the freedom fighters." That's the image that would linger for Thomas: morning sun, music, and dust rising from the feet of "poor people and fighters dancing with their AKs. To us, that was victory."

The Blacks Unlimited unveiled a new song that day, "Kwaedza mu Zimbabwe (It Has Dawned in Zimbabwe)," a boisterous romp that once again names the new prime minister—"Comrade Mugabe, Father, we thank you"—and singles out ZANU as champions of the liberation struggle. As the band struck up the tune, Thomas unleashed a throaty rooster crow, evoking ZANU's totem animal and heralding the first morning in Zimbabwe.

Hakurotwi Mude (PHOTO: PAUL BERLINER)

Muchatera Mujuru with his ceremonial assistant (PHOTO: PAUL BERLINER)

Thomas Mapfumo, circa 1975 (PHOTO: BESTER KANYAMA)

Thomas Mapfumo performing in cape, circa 1975 (PHOTO: BESTER KANYAMA)

Thomas Mapfumo live in Harare in 1984 (PHOTO: BESTER KANYAMA)

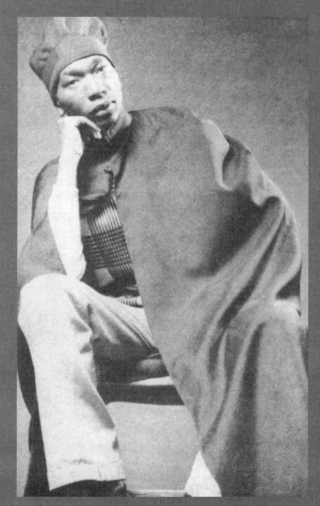
Thomas Mapfumo, circa 1977 (PHOTO: JIMMY SALANI)

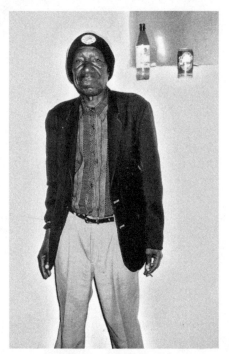

Sekuru Jira in Zimbabwe
(PHOTO: BROOKS BARNETT)

Thomas with his mother, Janet (right), and Aunt Chipo, Janet's sister (left), at home in Harare, 1998

October 1985 cover of *Folk Roots*, the first cover in the UK magazine's history to feature an African musician

Thomas Mapfumo performing in the United Kingdom in 1985
(PHOTO: IAN ANDERSON / FROOTS)

KEY GUITARISTS

Joshua Dube,
Harare, 1998

Joshua Dube,
Harare, 1993

Jonah Sithole, Harare, 1993

Jonah Sithole and
Chartwell Dutiro, 1988

Emmanuel Jera and Joshua Dube at the Zimbabwe College of Music in 1993

Ashton "Sugar" Chiweshe,
Harare, 1993

Ephraim Karimaura, SOB's in New York City, 1989

Gilbert Zvamaida,
World Financial Center
in New York, 2012

Vena, unidentified, Tapfumaneyi, Chiedza, and Thomas, at home in Harare, 1993

Ephat Mujuru, Boston, 1991

Kudzai, Ephat, and Tendai, reunited in Atlanta, Georgia, 1989

Mbira maker and player Chris
Mhlanga in his workshop in
Harare, 1998

Bishop Abel Muzorewa,
Washington, DC, 2005

Thompson Kachingwe,
Harare, 1998

Musa Zimunya, Harare, 1998

Sungura star John
Chibadura (with guitar
and hat), Harare, 1993

Oliver Mtukudzi at
Mushandira Pamwe
Hotel in Harare, 1993

Chris Bolton at the mixing board

Bob Coen and Saki Mafundikwa

Joshua Dube, Everson Chibamu, Gibson Blathewick, and Willard Karanga
in Harare, 1998

Thomas Mapfumo at Central Park Summerstage, 1992
(PHOTO © 1992 JACK VARTOOGIAN / FRONTROWPHOTOS)

Thomas Mapfumo, Harare, 1998

II ZIMBABWE

7 / Snakes in the Forest

When the mamba strikes
the word spreads like fire and venom
from mouth to mouth and soul to soul . . .
until slowly the old man becomes all men
all women all children turning tar-black
from shin to brow, crow-black

MUSA ZIMUNYA

While Zimbabweans basked in peace at the end of 1980, the Blacks Unlimited remained "abandoned" by local fans. Embittered by neglect, Thomas protested to the *Herald* that he and his band had "never changed sides" and declared, "This government is ours because we struggled for it."[1] But doubt lingered, and it would take time, new music, and new ideas for Thomas to regain his standing. Thompson Kachingwe, still the band manager despite a rough year, turned to an old friend who had fought in Mozambique using the chimurenga name Chairman Mao. When Mao had accompanied ZANU to the Geneva talks, Kachingwe had bought him dress suits at Milton Fisher so he would look like a gentleman on Swiss streets. Now his friend was at Mugabe's side, and Kachingwe sought his advice. "We are not angry with Thomas," Mao reassured him, and said he would prove it.

Soon afterward, Thomas was invited to perform at the first prime minister's luncheon, a lavish affair held in the City Sports Stadium. William Mapfumo remembered the event's extravagance more than its politics. "There was game meat," he said. "You could find the whole kudu being roasted." For Kachingwe, the luncheon's payoff came when Thomas sang "Chitima Cherusununguko

(Freedom Train)," a new Blacks Unlimited song that once again named Mugabe. "The prime minister stood and danced," said Kachingwe. "It was real touching, and this was on TV. From that day all our shows were full houses."

Thomas, too, recalled Mugabe dancing to his song, though he doubted this had brought the public around. What did that, he said, was the Blacks Unlimited's fidelity to singing about the struggle, and the creative vigor of their musical innovations. The *Sunday Mail* began gushing about the band's "new style," a meld of traditional, Western, and Zairian (Congolese) elements that left listeners "completely knocked out." And, of course, any time Thomas was heard singing Mugabe's name from a radio or a concert stage, it chipped away at the perception that he had ever seriously backed Muzorewa's campaign.

Thomas's music was now heard everywhere, along with that of Oliver Mtukudzi, Zexie Manatsa, Safirio Madzikatire, and an ever-burgeoning crop of newcomers. Teal changed its name to Gramma Records and set about building a catalog of local releases. Gramma's white managers were wary of the new government, but peace and sanction-free commerce put money in peoples' pockets, and record sales, especially of Zimbabwean music, soared. Days before Christmas 1980, Gramma released *The Best of Thomas Mapfumo*, the country's first "greatest hits" album, and the initial pressing sold out immediately.[2] The lead track "Chauya Chiruzevha (Rural Life Is Back)" was an exuberant update of the Acid Band single "Chiruzevha Chapera (Rural Life Is Gone)" (1978).

> Old women fry vegetables . . .
> Old men fell timberwood . . .
> Girls roast maize kernels [popcorn] . . .
> Rural life is back and really back

Commonplace images take on a miraculous hue when filtered through blistering guitar work, a brass section in overdrive, and Thomas's gleeful bantering and crooning.[3] The "best of" record put wind in Thomas's sails. The *Herald* raved, celebrating Thomas as the only local musician to produce seven gold records in two years (1977–78) and concluding that "he can honestly be called the father of modern Shona traditional music." The Blacks Unlimited seized the momentum, returning to the studio to produce their first complete LP—and a standout in the entire Mapfumo canon—*Gwindingwi Rine Shumba*, released in April 1981. Shumba, the lion Thomas sings about in the title track, evokes mhondoro spirits—the ultimate authors of victory—but also the guerrillas themselves. During the war, this song had played as subversive protest. Now it trumpeted patriotic nostalgia.[4]

"Shumba" also raised the bar for guitar-band mbira adaptations. Jonah Sithole and Pickett Chiyangwa interweave their flat-picked melodies with Charles's burbling bass, while Thomas barks out his vocal in staccato cross-rhythm. Together, they limn the sonic architecture of mbira with economy and style. The album also hotwires other popular and traditional sounds—village ngoma songs and cantering 12/8 boogie with warm, three-chord harmony. The Blacks Unlimited brass section was special.[5] The players rarely improvised, but together they pounced like leopards. Choirs singing chimurenga songs during the war had been known for their mighty attack, "almost shouting," as Thomas heard it. "That's how our horn section comes in," he said, "like an African choir."

In the old-school, rock 'n' rolly "Rita," Thomas sings of "a housewife" returning after the war. Poets of the era lauded figures like Rita for their heroic reclamation of life—farming, tending herds, cooking, raising children, rebuilding a shattered world. Steven Chifunyise had just returned from exile in Zambia when *Gwindingwi Rine Shumba* appeared. He would soon join Mugabe's government and ultimately rise to become minister of sports, recreation and culture. A scholar and playwright himself, Chifunyise was fascinated by Thomas's cultural references. One lyric talks about *magobo*, a Shona word for the Rhodesian practice of uprooting trees to clear virgin land. "It's the hardest part of farming," said Chifunyise. "It's sweat. It's hot sun. And then you burn it and you come away black with smoke." As nearby as Zambia, magobo never existed. "You can't simply think Mapfumo is singing for the entire world," noted Chifunyise. "Other people wouldn't have that history. He was singing for his people."

The artwork on *Gwindingwi Rine Shumba* gave the public a first glimpse of Thomas's budding dreadlocks. If this was a nod to Bob Marley, as many assumed, the jacket cover also expresses homegrown themes. The band sits, mostly shirtless, before a mud-and-grass hut, taking a break from work and passing around a cup of seven-days beer. Thomas stands aloof in the background, at the edge of a cornfield, his body sheathed in the black cloak of a medium. On the back cover he appears in portrait, eyes glazed, wearing a smart goatee and sports jacket, with a small cross hung around his neck—a stoned, mystic, Shona, Christian dandy.

Popular music in Zimbabwe was blossoming. Wartime exiles living in Kenya, Tanzania, Zambia, and Mozambique were returning home with new songs in their heads and new dances in their legs and feet. East African rumba was sometimes called *sungura*, Swahili for "rabbit," and a reference to the skittering dance steps the music inspired. The giddy sungura songs would not become commonplace in Zimbabwe.[6] Thomas criticized the music as "stolen from Tanzania," and many urbanites and intellectuals complained of its shallowness, frivolity, and irrelevance to local traditions.[7] But this exuberant music has remained the top-selling genre in Zimbabwe from its rise in the early 1980s right up to the present.

Sungura was in its infancy when *Gwindingwi Rine Shumba* appeared, showcasing the polish and energy of the Blacks Unlimited at the height of Jonah Sithole's tenure. Thomas would not produce another album for almost two years, but his band was now once again ascendant on the live circuit, delivering some of the era's most electrifying performances. "Everyone used to love Jonah," recalled one fan. "'Ah, give us Jonah, Jonah. Jonah.'" Given his personal celebrity, Sithole surprised few when he left the Blacks Unlimited near the end of 1981 to form his own band, Deep Horizon. "I liked Jonah as a guitarist," recalled Thomas. "I didn't like him as a singer. But there was nothing like a power struggle between the two of us. When he came to tell me, 'I would like to leave and do my own thing,' I said, 'Well, good luck, brother. If you fail, you can always come back to the band. We can still work together.'"

The Blacks Unlimited's home base was the downtown Queens Garden Hotel, where, on a Sunday, Thomas could keep the open-air courtyard packed from early afternoon until midnight. Kachingwe handled the money and paid musicians according to established percentages—by his account, 20 percent for himself, 40 percent for Thomas, the rest for the band. Gramma paid band members with individual royalty checks in those days, and for the first—and only—time in the band's history, most Blacks Unlimited members drove their own cars.

Having seen the band through hard times, Kachingwe nevertheless cut expenses any way he could. On the road, the musicians and crew carried cooking pots and bought food in shops rather than restaurants. "We'd stop at a lay-by," recalled Kachingwe, "put up a fire, and cook." During a trip to Botswana, Thomas spied three guinea hens crossing before them. "Food is in the road!" he bellowed, instructing the driver to aim for the birds. The driver obliged, yielding an excellent meal but shattering the truck's windshield. This inconvenience was a small price to pay for a hilarious story Thomas would not tire of telling.

In the flush of renewed success, Thomas married Vena Dambarengwa. "My family didn't want me to live with him," Vena recalled. "But I loved him as a human being, and I was trying to prove to my family that I could handle it." The couple wed in an Anglican church ceremony. They moved into a small apartment on Albarn Court, in the Avenues, an upscale Harare neighborhood lined with leafy, flowering jacaranda trees. In 1984, Vena gave birth to a boy. The newlyweds decided to give their firstborn a name from Vena's side, Taipei. This was a gesture aimed at fostering harmony between the marrying families. But the child's relentless crying led Thomas's mother, Janet, to a spiritual, ancestral explanation—the sort that might emerge from a bira ceremony. Janet came to believe that Thomas's biological father, Tapfumaneyi, wanted the boy to have *his* name. The family accepted this idea, and once he was given the name Tapfumaneyi, the boy stopped crying. Later on, family and friends would simply call him Tai, which works for both his original and his actual name.

Parenting was a new world for Thomas, a responsibility he embraced with enthusiasm and pride. By day, he was now a "family man," moving about town with wife and baby. By night, he remained a rock star, commanding the stage in hotel gardens and urban beer halls until dawn.

There was turnover in the band in the early 1980s, but Thomas was a top name now, able to attract talented musicians whenever he needed them. To replace Sithole, he leaned on his old lead player from the Hallelujah Chicken Run Band, Joshua Dube.[8] "We must work together," Thomas told Dube, as if their collaboration were preordained. In 1982, Thomas had recruited one of the best drummers he would ever work with, Sabastian Mbata, the heartbeat of the Blacks Unlimited for the next twelve years. Saba was a "ghetto boy" from Mbare, "very confident," Thomas recalled. He drank too much and became violent on occasion, but from the first audition, Saba showed chops and drive rare in a Harare drummer. "We had to accommodate him," said Thomas. On the eve of a sixteen-city tour, guitarist Pickett also quit, forcing Thomas to tap an unproven young player named Emmanuel Jera. Manu, as they called him, was an unlikely choice, a devotee of Santana, George Benson, Earl Klugh, and Mark Knopfler—not of Shona tradition—but willing to learn from Dube.

The Blacks Unlimited recorded six singles in 1981 and 1982, including a classic mbira adaptation, "Pidigori." This song celebrates the departure, perhaps death, of a bad man. There's a bitter edge to the lyric, but the music is deep and ebullient, the stuff of many ecstatic Blacks Unlimited stage jams to come. Dube's mbira guitar style is more florid and technically demanding than Sithole's. Where Sithole masterfully pares mbira melodies down to their lyrical essence, Dube is more apt to sketch the detailed architecture of an mbira part, leaping between low and high notes in accompaniments and surging forth with bursts of high-pitched melody on solos. On this recording, Manu at first feathers in the mbira-esque counterrhythms to Dube's lead, and then the two converge in a joyous crescendo. Charles's heavy bass line, with its pregnant pauses and thunderous downbeat, would become a template for other Blacks Unlimited songs and a litmus test for future bass players seeking to join the band.

As 1983 began, Thomas prepared to record a new LP. Manu recalled him "looking worried" as the young guitarist tried out parts, hoping to assert himself creatively. "Thomas is a serious person," said Manu. "You rehearsed from morning until about five o'clock every day. Every time you see him, it was, 'Get your guitar.' And no jokes. If he is not happy with what you are playing, he tells you then and there." After studying Manu's ideas, Thomas reportedly said he played "like a white guy." The young player took this as praise, though Thomas was most likely ribbing him. As attentive as he was to his music, Thomas was rarely beyond humor. And in later years, he would take some pleasure in recalling Manu's own seriousness, which, as we shall see, could become troublesome.

In February, the "father of modern Shona traditional music" told the *Herald* that record producers were "killing our music" by turning to rumba and sungura. Thomas conceded that his own band sometimes experimented with foreign music styles, but that local tradition would always be its mainstay. He vowed to produce fresh music that would "show the people how sweet *Zimbabwean* music is."[9]

Then tragedy struck. Charles had spent a day celebrating after receiving his royalty check at Gramma. Flush with cash and drunk on beer, he had fallen asleep at the wheel while driving through Mbare, and his car had veered into a yard and killed a five-year-old boy. He was sentenced to six months in jail, a tough blow for Thomas, as Charles was not only key to the band's new sound but also Thomas's closest friend. So Thomas needed a new bass man, and Manu suggested Washington Kavhai, a young player living meagerly on eight dollars a week at the time. Thomas was skeptical when Washington turned up in shabby clothes. "Here in Zimbabwe," recalled Manu, "people judge you for your dressing." But when Thomas heard the young man's limber bass style, he thought again. At last the band entered the studio, and in a single day recorded enough songs for two LPs.

In May 1983, Thomas released *Ndangariro*. The title refers to a preoccupying recollection, and the weight of war is palpable in the songs, the best of them dark, driving, and concerned not so much with the liberation conflict's memory as with its aftermath. Thomas appears alone on the cover, once again in a village setting, seated on a rock with a round house and a wooden wagon, a "scotch cart," in the background. His lengthening dreads are bundled into a woolen hat—an African hairstyle presented Rasta-style, at once evoking local tradition and foreign revolutionary chic—and he sports a goatee and side-burns, also a black tank top jersey, black leather pants, and blue leather shoes that glisten in the sun as he stares down the camera. For all the paradoxes in its presentation, *Ndangariro* delivered clear and potent messages, most notably in the song "Nyoka Musango (Snake in the Forest)," a stormy guitar jam overlaid with militant chanting. Amid a cyclic trance of ominous foreboding, the song says, "There are snakes in the forest. So they must be eliminated. The snakes must be eliminated."

"These are the dissidents," explained Thomas, "fighting against their own people." Thomas later revised this explanation, limiting his targets in "Nyoka Musango" to South African infiltrators, who were trying to undermine the new Zimbabwean regime. But in the early 1980s, the word "dissident" was code for Ndebele resisters. The Ndebele leader Joshua Nkomo had not stayed long in the ZANU government, and when he quit, Mugabe had vilified him as a "cobra in the house." While Thomas was preparing the songs on *Ndangariro*, Nkomo fled house arrest in Bulawayo and slipped away to Botswana, a "hunted fugitive," and a broken man at sixty-six.[10] "I still remember the time when Joshua Nkomo was the only leader recognized in this country," recalled Thomas. "Everyone was behind him. He came from Matabeleland, and we never did anything to disrupt his plans, because we saw him as a good leader. But people can change like the wind. We became convinced that the leadership of Comrade Nkomo was not straightforward."

There were no doubt snakes in Zimbabwe's forest after independence. If they included a few Ndebele dissidents out to overthrow the new government, those numbers would have been small, hardly a credible threat. Stories never-theless circulated that Nkomo had held forces back during the war, saving them for a planned coup should Mugabe win the election. Meanwhile, on the ground, Shona and Ndebele soldiers were commingled at assembly points and even in military housing. In 1981, tension flared tragically at Entumbane, a base near Bulawayo, when Shona and Ndebele former fighters turned on one another as they ate in the mess hall. Details about this incident remain clouded as a government report on the melee was never made public. But more than three hundred died at Entumbane, and, afterward, hard-core ex-ZIPRA fighters organized a loose command structure and tried to launch an Nde-bele guerrilla insurgency in Matabeleland and the Midlands. These insurgents probably numbered no more than four hundred men, and it is doubtful they ever answered to Nkomo or the ZAPU leadership.

Then there were the South African snakes Thomas identified. Keen to wreak havoc in the region's black-ruled states, South Africa dispatched proxies to stoke civil war for two decades in Mozambique, and nearly three in Angola. The plan to destabilize Zimbabwe relied on stoking Shona-Ndebele tension through Operation Drama, a deployment of a hundred or so South African "Super ZAPU" agents who moved into Matabeleland to commit atrocities and radicalize the Ndebele. Ex-ZIPRA fighters were suspicious of the Super ZAPU, though they too committed atrocities, including rape. Neither group found much support among ordinary Ndebele, and neither posed a serious challenge to the government. But this did not stop Mugabe from releasing snakes of his own.

The operation was called Gukurahundi, literally "the rain that washes away the chaff before the spring rains." Gukurahundi began with swift brutality in 1983, and by the time it ended in 1987, it had taken the lives of some twenty thousand Ndebele civilians. Most of them were killed by the notorious Fifth Brigade, an elite corps of ZANLA war veterans and a few white Rhodesians whose mission was to "combat malcontents." North Korea's Kim Il Sung dispatched one hundred of his specialists to Zimbabwe to train this ruthless force, which answered directly to Mugabe.[11] In early 1983, the Fifth Brigade murdered thousands of civilians and razed hundreds of homesteads.[12] The government engineered a news blackout in Matabeleland, barring access to journalists, and the trickle of information that did emerge was conveniently—and believably—dismissed as South African propaganda.

In 1984, Mugabe halted food aid to 400,000 people on the heels of a three-year drought, and many Ndebele starved to death.[13] A decade later, mass graves would be found throughout Matabeleland, including mineshafts choked with dried bones and shredded clothing. Confronted with awful evidence, the government would conduct a long "investigation" and, once again, not release its findings. Independent researchers concluded that tens of thousands were "tortured, beaten, raped or imprisoned." Not only was any hint of Ndebele rebellion crushed but, within a few years, the political leadership of ZAPU was "detained, harassed, beaten, killed or forced into exile."[14]

Joshua Nkomo believed Mugabe's objective was to crush political opposition and create a one-party state, "in keeping with African tradition."[15] Nkomo eventually acquiesced to this reality when he merged ZAPU into ZANU-PF as part of the Unity Accord of 1987. Thomas believed the Ndebele leader's fighting stance finally withered when ZANU soldiers gathered enough Ndebele corpses to fill a train car and summoned Nkomo to survey them. "When Nkomo looked at these dead bodies," Thomas claimed, "he even cried, and that made him change his mind."[16] This was unity, Mugabe style.

There has never been a Truth and Reconciliation Commission in Zimbabwe, not to air the horrors of building Rhodesia, nor the Smith era, the liberation war, the ravages of the Fifth Brigade, or anything since. Somehow, collectively, the society has preferred to bury its depravities, to mask them with narratives of bravery and sacrifice, anything to avoid the nation quietly locking eyes with the innocent victims of slaughter and torture, let alone slaughterers and torturers. Thomas never intended "Nyoka Musango" to be the sound track to a massacre. Like most Zimbabweans at the time, he had little idea one was even happening, and he was duly outraged when the facts about Gukura- hundi did emerge. Nevertheless, this mesmerizing call to arms broke on the Zimbabwean airwaves just as the Fifth Brigade swept into Matabeleland. *The snakes must be eliminated.*

What most people remember about *Ndangariro* is its writhing energy, music as exciting as anything the Blacks Unlimited had produced. "It had a funky feel," recalled Emmanuel Jera. "And that album promoted Thomas in Europe." Zimbabwean vinyl had long circulated informally in London. In 1981 a South African expatriate named Jumbo Van Renen was perusing the bins at Rough Trade Records when he came across an imported copy of *Gwindingwi Rine Shumba*. Van Renen loved this record and immediately recognized its uniqueness. He soon quit his job at Virgin to start his own company, Earthworks, to release African music in the United Kingdom. Van Renen dealt with a pair of white Kenyan businessmen—the Andrews broth- ers—who licensed him master tapes from African labels. "There was a lot of intermeshing between Kenya and Zimbabwe and South Africa in those days," Van Renen recalled, "dodgy apartheid-busting business." The Andrews broth- ers demanded a hefty cut of sales, 18 to 20 percent, but required no advance, so Van Renen could go to market with minimal investment. In 1981, he licensed *The Best of Thomas Mapfumo* and *Gwindingwi Rine Shumba*, releases that became Thomas's calling cards to the world.

Van Renen understood that Thomas's story could sell records. He renamed the "best of" release *The Chimurenga Singles* and provided lyric translations and a brief, mostly accurate account of Thomas's career on the back sleeve cover. The gist was that despite Rhodesian trickery, Thomas had wooed the masses because he was "young enough to be a revolutionary, and yet had a mature voice that demanded respect."[17] Van Renen followed up with *Ndan- gariro*, this time without notes. No point in complicating a clear narrative with subplots about restless support musicians and counterrevolutionaries.

Back in Harare, Thomas was staging a newly dynamic live show with car- nivalesque shenanigans, including a fire-eating act by Willard "Masantula" Sarutawa.[18] The Blacks Unlimited rehearsed and printed concert posters on

Harare's Pioneer Street, in a space rented from one of Thomas's relatives. Sekura Jira now supervised the doormen and equipment, collected money and paid musicians, printed posters, and, as ever, prepared ganja—known in Shona as *mbanje* or *fodya*.[19] Masantula recalled Jira as a "hard person" who did things his way and refused to share smoke without Thomas's explicit okay. When Jira came up with "shit dope," he would toss it out among the neighbor's banana trees, seeds and all. Masantula recounted a tense incident when the neighbor, a white man, noticed hemp plants sprouting on his land and called the police: "We just saw cops coming and said, 'Hide, hide, hide!' Everyone was shivering." The officers surprised the band by entering through the back door. Jira concealed a fat spliff under a pile of posters. Thomas picks up the story, savoring the memory of yet another close call with authority:

These guys came and said, "So, you are growing ganja here."

We said, "No, we are not growing ganja. Who said that? Where did you pick these from?"

"From outside in the yard."

"So? It's not ours."

They were searching everybody, and finally one guy searched under the posters, and he found this big thing there. And he says, "Oh! Oh, we got it! We got it."

I said, "What is it? It's not mine. He found it on the table. Nobody was holding it. Nobody was having it in his own pocket."

But they said, "Oh, no. We have to go to the police station." So we went there to the police station, and this guy wanted to start to search us again.

I said, "We have been searched already. And you want to keep on searching?"

"Oh, Mapfumo! You argue too much."

The police went to Thomas's apartment, which Vena, forewarned, had cleansed of evidence. "I smoke, my friend," Thomas told the policemen, "but I don't have it here." At Lancelot's house, a poster of Bob Marley puffing up a cloud of smoke tantalized the searchers, but they missed the stash rolled up inside a bolt of cloth under the bed. Looking back, Thomas held no grudge. The cops were just "doing their job," and he did not fear them. For one thing, his ancestors were looking after him, and besides, cops were smokers too. "Most of them used to come backstage to smoke with us," Thomas recalled. "They would always show up and say, 'Where is Mukanya?'" Such was Thomas's cat-and-mouse routine with the Zimbabwean police in the early years of Zimbabwe.

After Charles was released from prison, Thomas sought a way to keep both him and Washington in the band. This is how Charles and Lancelot began studying piano with composer Keith Goddard at the Zimbabwe College of Music. Goddard was an ally, versed both in Western classical traditions and in a number of forms of Zimbabwean indigenous music. Keen to advance his sound in every way he could, Thomas sought to bring knowledge of music theory and Western training into his mix. He sized Goddard up as "a very good teacher." Goddard, for his part, struggled with Lancelot, "more of a drummer than a pianist," he recalled, with stiff fingers and poor eyesight that made reading music difficult. Charles, on the other hand, was a natural who advanced quickly. It would take some years, but Charles's postprison music studies would one day bring new ideas to the band, including ways to render mbira music on keyboards rather than guitars.

Late in 1983, Thomas released *Mabasa*, his second album that year. The songs are as strong as those on *Ndangariro* but sunnier, focused on building the nation rather than rooting out malcontents.[20] *Mabasa* means "work," and the title track is a propulsive braid of pointillist guitar lines driving home a proletarian message: "Everyone is working for the good of Zimbabwe." The record jacket plays on this theme with musicians posing as workers—Dube washing a teapot, Washington sporting a tire iron, and Lancelot with a waiter's jacket pulled over his leopard-patterned shirt.

Mabasa makes history with the song "Chemera Chaunoda (Cry for the One You Want)," the first Blacks Unlimited song to use actual mbira.[21] This was an experiment, created in the studio. The song was buried on the album's B-side and attracted no special notice, but, like Charles's lessons with Goddard, it planted a seed that would bloom magnificently in the future.

A Christmas Day *Sunday Mail* headline reads, "1983—Definitely Mapfumo's Year." The article offers a flattering synopsis of Thomas's career, including his "90 days" in detention and no mention of Muzorewa. A month later, when a small British monthly, *Afro Heat*, named *Ndangariro* "record of the month," the *Sunday Mail* crowed: "Mapfumo record voted top LP in Britain." Readers of this article might have imagined a Zimbabwean music invasion under way in the United Kingdom, with Thomas leading the charge. In March, however, adulation from Zimbabwe's government-controlled press gave way to jarringly different news: "Mapfumo Group Splits Up."

The *Herald* reported that Thomas's musicians had abandoned him en masse because he was unfairly claiming "the lion's share of the group's income." Rebellious musicians had absconded with instruments and equipment, taken up the name African Herb, and signed a contract with the Queens Garden Hotel. In the *Sunday Mail*, Thomas blamed financial mismanagement by the now-fired Thompson Kachingwe and accused the departed musicians of stealing Z$8,000 worth of equipment that belonged to him. "He had Thompson and me arrested," recalled Dube, indignant years later at having spent two nights behind bars. A magistrate returned the equipment to Thomas but imposed no sanction on the rebels. "Thomas, you are a thief!" a bitter Dube recalled telling his old boss. "That's why Thomas doesn't like me much, because I told him the truth." Unfortunately for Dube and the rebels, African Herb failed to win fans and soon disbanded, proving once again that Thomas, not his band, was the real draw for the paying public.

"It's a social thing in this country," broadcaster Hilton Mambo observed. "Thomas is the leader. The boys always think the leader is making too much. But what the boys overlook is that *he* is the guy who attracts the people. Without that guy, *there's no band.*"[22]

Thomas now asked his brother William to manage the band. William had spent nine years working as a laborer for Biddulphs Removals, whose main activity was transporting furniture to South Africa for white people "running away" from black rule. William's wife, Sylvia, tried to convince him not to give up a coming ten-year bonus and the security of a reliable job. Thomas prevailed. William had a good ear for musical talent, and over the years, he would be responsible for recruiting important band members, particularly guitarists. The band's musicians mostly remembered him as a heavy. "He came on very strong," recalled trumpeter Everson Chibamu. "He wanted to push around everyone." Other players recalled William as "mean," officious, and uninterested in their problems. Thomas has steadfastly resisted these characterizations, insisting that William was "not a bad guy" and "never treated anyone badly." But it seems clear that William's presence in the band's authority structure made room for Thomas to create, and to enjoy easy, joking interactions with his musicians, while others laid down the law.

As ever, the Blacks Unlimited rebuilt. Thomas tapped a guitar team he had used in Mutare in 1976: Pickett and Lucky Mupawaenda. Shepherd Munyama took over on bass, and, after Thomas lured back his departed brass section, the band got to work, returning to the studio to record *Mr Music*.[23] This album was released in August 1984, an impressive recovery, though it does not match the musicianship of its predecessors. After all, the African Herb rebellion had cost Thomas A-list players. *Mr Music* is significant not so much for its sound—although it too includes one song, "Kufa Kwangu (The Day I Die)," with mbira in the mix—as for the way it signals a telling shift of message for the poet champion of the liberation struggle. Since independence, Thomas had been enthusiastically vocal in support of Mugabe and his policies, and he had reaped rewards for this support. The previous spring, the Blacks Unlimited had been invited to perform at the ZANU-PF party congress in Borrowdale Park, and Thomas had composed a song for the occasion. Released as the lead track on *Mr Music*, "Congress" plays out with fairy-tale whimsy, listing animals coming to the great congress. But some listeners, including Musa Zimunya, detected a note of satire. "He's starting to tease them," said Musa. "He sings, 'Even hare, even baboon. Let him come out. Even snake. Let him come out.' And they were *dancing* to it. Some probably wondered, but the insiders were too drunk with their own power to worry."

"When these people came back from war," recalled Thomas, "they were like little gods. They wanted to be worshipped. 'Did you go to Mozambique? Were you in Chinhoyi? No? Then you have got nothing to say. Don't talk to me.' This is how the country was defrauded of a lot of money. Because people feared them. When you are in fear, someone can do almost anything to you."

Mr Music was not a big seller, but Thomas was a cat with lives to spare. For the moment, he was yielding ground to Oliver Mtukudzi, James Chimombe, and swelling ranks of sungura party bands.[24] Zimbabweans were drifting away from war nostalgia and the mbira-driven spirit crusade. Better to make love and party. Meanwhile, in Europe, the buzz over chimurenga music, while hardly an "invasion," was reaching critical mass. The mbira player Stella Chiweshe had married a German named Peter Reich. Reich was a journalist who would later form the Piranha world music record label, along with Florian Hetze and Christoph Borkowsky. After a visit to Zimbabwe, they recommended Thomas and his band for a government-sponsored tour of German cities. Borkowsky asked his friend Jumbo Van Renen to set up concerts in London. Thomas's London debut—scheduled for the Hundred Club, where Bob Marley had played—quickly became "the hottest gig in town." The Germans found a sponsor for an Amsterdam concert at the Melkweg nightclub, and the itinerary for Thomas's first tour beyond African soil was set.

On the eve of departure in the fall of 1984, the *Sunday Mail* in Harare ran a letter lamenting the fact that Thomas's London debut would happen at such a small venue. "Given adequate publicity and record-company backing," the writer complained, "Mapfumo is quite eligible for bigger London venues like the Hammersmith Odeon where Nigeria's King Sunny Adé made his debut early last year." This anonymous analyst notes that reggae had been the "music of the '80s in Western Europe," and that artists from Nigeria, South Africa—why not Zimbabwe?—were now poised for international glory. The letter concludes: "Unless protagonists for [African music's] marketing, that is, Island and Virgin record companies, are willing to invest not only in promoting records but also backing live tour performances as well, our predictions may well be proven dismally wrong."

Before Thomas had boarded his first airplane, a local Harare wag had foretold the tragic arc of African music marketing in the West: the pipe dream of repeating reggae's success, the danger of poorly funded promoters, the hesitancy of record labels to underwrite tours, and the way those promoters and labels would be blamed when big dreams failed to come true. Thomas too knew the stakes were high for this tour. He told the Zimbabwe press it would be "the greatest challenge we will ever deal with."

The band arrived in West Berlin on November 5 and rehearsed for a few days at International, a dilapidated nightclub where—in its heyday—black American GIs had hooked up with German girls amid a Cold War milieu of soul music and premium beer. The Zimbabweans showed up with neither instruments nor enough clothes to face the German winter. Borkowsky recalled loaning Thomas his Zobel fur coat and never seeing it again. When Thomas fell asleep one evening with a burning hashish spliff in his hand, Borkowsky said he nearly lost his house as well. Thomas's wife flew in a couple of days later, unannounced. Then Temba, the trumpet player, fell so ill he had to be hospitalized and left behind in Berlin. All this kept the Germans on edge, but when the band made its European debut in a scarcely publicized practice gig in Berlin, there were no regrets.

Ten musicians took the stage in Germany, with Lucky and Pickett—wearing his trademark feather headdress—both on guitar, and Charles now on keyboards. The two brass players also sang, played percussion, and danced in snappy, choreographed routines with Thomas.[25] A video of the band's set that night shows Thomas darting about the stage and bantering with the crowd. His condemnation of alcohol while introducing "Hwa Hwa" brings an awkward silence, but the German crowd rallies when Thomas proclaims himself "a man of peace." Thomas is dressed casually in beltless, faded jeans and a snug-fitting sweatshirt—this while Pickett dons his feathers and loincloth and others wear loose dashikis. The musicians' appearance is haphazard, but their guitar-spiked grooves blaze relentlessly, and the spectacle of Thomas joining hands with two limber-limbed Shona dancers as they hoist knees and shimmy in easy synchrony—left, right, left, right—offers a rare glimpse of Thomas as showman rather than sage. Thomas would later display Miles-like disregard for stagecraft, but in his first European gig, he maintained the aesthetic of the Rhodesian jazz age, and Elvis-era rock 'n' roll—domains in which a front man is expected to *move*.

Van Renen brought the band to London "on a wing and a prayer," borrowing money from a bank to cover expenses. Fans that were turned away from the sold-out Hundred Club show massed to an overflow gig at the Forum in North London a week later. More than a thousand people attended that show, and Lucky recalled a venue "so packed that you could hardly walk inside." Afterward, the musicians basked in the novelty of having white British admirers. As the band began its shift from the edgy militancy of snakes in the forest to the creeping parody of snakes at the ZANU party congress, these fans, unable to understand the Shona lyrics, heard only the most mysteriously beautiful African music they had ever encountered.

Thomas Brooman, then in the early years of establishing the organization World of Music and Dance (WOMAD), booked a Friday night show at the Western Star Domino Club in Bristol. The musicians arrived in two vans, and as they were mounting the stage for the sound check, they discovered that rhythm guitarist Pickett had not come in either vehicle. There was no time to fetch him from London. On hand as a roady was London multi-instrumentalist Lu Edmonds, a Mapfumo fan who had internalized the music on *Gwindingwi Rine Shumba*. Edmonds picked up a guitar and began playing the opening lines of "Mhondoro." "Jaws dropped," he recalled. "Charlie the bassist frog-marched me to Thomas and said, 'Do that again.' After some discussion in fast Shona, Thomas nodded, and the show went on. Lucky started every song with my line. I would shadow it, and when I nodded to him, he would leap into his part and the weaving began."

Brooman recalled Thomas climbing the short flight of stairs from the small dressing room to the stage, "preceded by billows of smoke" and then "tottering" from one side to the other. Brooman, at the far end of the stage, said he physically turned Thomas around and propelled him back toward the microphone. Once there, Thomas anchored himself, took charge, and was "fabulous." Brooman never forgot the audience's collective realization that "there was a real star in the house that night."

Thomas was grateful to Van Renen for bringing him to the United Kingdom, clearly fertile ground for his music. But the artist was beginning to see that record companies, starting with Gramma, had been stacking the deck against him all along.[26] Van Renen knew the Kenyans he had been dealing with were exploiters, and that his current distribution company, Serengeti, was run by a "dreadful . . . old colonial system guy" named Mike Wells. "If I gave one hundred pounds to Mike Wells," Van Renen speculated, "then fifty pounds would go to Gramma, and by the time it gets to Thomas, it would be, 'No, we already gave you that last year to buy clothes. There's nothing left.'" As plans got under way for a second European tour, Van Renen suggested they use the opportunity to produce a new Blacks Unlimited album in England, applying a fairer business structure.[27]

Around that time, a Zimbabwean in London sent a cogent letter to the *Herald* arguing that the Zimbabwean government should use Thomas as a goodwill ambassador to counteract the country's negative image in the UK press. The writer points out that BBC DJ John Peel often played Mapfumo songs on his national broadcasts, that musicians from other African countries were gaining popularity in England. He concludes, "The Zimbabwean Government would be well advised to consider helping Thomas Mapfumo to tour Britain, to promote one of the most exciting elements of Zimbabwean culture."

This was a moment of opportunity. *If* Thomas had fielded a manager capable of negotiating with Gramma and Earthworks—or another foreign label—and *if* Zimbabwean government insiders had promoted musicians as part of a public relations strategy rather than figuring out new ways to tax them, and *if* Thomas had formalized his business arrangements to ensure that key members of his organization were fairly paid and remained loyal, Thomas would surely have known greater success in the 1980s. As it was, William—Thomas's half brother—improvised the role of manager, lacking the skills needed to shape an artist's international career; the government—busy crushing political opposition and securing its grip on the country's resources—ignored opportunities on the cultural front; and Thomas's musicians continued to leave his band in mostly futile searches for greener pastures.[28]

Charles Makokowa had been at Thomas's side since the Acid Band, and under Keith Goddard's tutelage, he was now emerging as the Blacks Unlimited's first keyboardist. But misfortune dogged him. The band played an afternoon Christmas party in an armed forces compound that year. When the show ended, soldiers, drunk and reveling, demanded more. They put such pressure on Thomas that he actually returned the band's fee, $Z400. Still not satisfied, the soldiers closed the gate, ordered the musicians out of the bus, and began beating them. Charles took the worst of it. A rifle butt blow to the gut damaged his liver, an injury that would afflict him for the rest of his life.[29]

The band had returned from Germany with a pair of conga drums. Singer Tobias Arakete had been opening Thomas's Harare shows, singing reggae numbers in English and playing these congas with the band. A "good musician" and a "cool guy," Arakete had fans, and Thomas decided to bring him to London to be part of the new recording. Lancelot Mapfumo, however, noticed Arakete was more comfortable playing percussion on reggae, rumba, or rock than on Zimbabwean grooves. "Now me," recalled Lancelot, "I had grown up going to the rural areas. Each time there was a ceremony for the elders,

I used to peek through the window just trying to see the guy who was playing the ngoma. I knew how to play this drum. So, I felt I had a duty." Lancelot continued his piano studies with Goddard, but his keyboard playing would never surpass his impact as the tall fellow hunched over congas at stage left, gravely slapping out angular ngoma rhythms.

In July 1985, the band returned to Europe for a seven-nation tour, arranged out of London by Rikki Stein, who had worked with Nigerian Afrobeat legend Fela Kuti. On the eve of the band's departure came news that Blacks Unlimited fans had long awaited: Jonah Sithole would return as lead guitarist. This development meant that Sithole's Deep Horizon—like African Herb—had failed, a bitter pill for the guitarist. His wife, Gladys, urged him to swallow his pride. "Just go and play," Gladys told him. "Mukanya wants to play with you. Why can't you just join him?" Sithole's return was harder still for Pickett, who was permanently cut from its lineup after ten years. For the first time, Thomas added two women—Terry Mhuriro and Priscilla Masarira—whose singing and traditional Shona dancing added feminine charm and left Thomas free simply to sing.

After shows throughout Europe, the band huddled in London to record. Van Renen arranged to work at Addis Ababa Studio on Harrow Road. The band was efficient, though Van Renen was disappointed that Thomas seemed to lack ambition in the studio, that he was "not really a producer." Van Renen had imagined that the freedom to work without time pressure in a modern facility would unleash hidden creative energies. Instead, he said, "They just came and played, the same way they've always done. There's an engineer and everybody plays, and when it all sounds good, you record. There's no mystery to it."

The resulting album, *Chimurenga for Justice*, includes a strong shot of reggae, thanks to the participation of players from the London-based band Misty in Roots. The song "Mugarandega (The Loner)" is a throwback thematically, evoking the liberation war as seen through the eyes of a man preparing to join the guerrillas. The man is private, secretive, a "loner," ready to slip across the border and return fighting. Tobias Arakete toasts like a Jamaican, "Mr. Thomas, a true man African. . . . You know, I love Mr. Thomas." Arakete even raps about how, under the Smith regime, "them a put him in jail . . . because he was singing culture, culture for the motherland."

"Mugarandega" was released in Zimbabwe as an extended-play single and became Thomas's biggest hit in years. It triggered a sharp debate about the band's pursuit of reggae. One Chitungwiza fan wrote to the *Sunday Mail* in November 1986, begging Thomas to "turn to reggae" and accusing him of going "too far back culturally" in his earlier work, on which he was "singing ancient culture that doesn't reach the modern world's fancy." The writer ridicules Thomas's "hoi-hois" and "ho-iho-honde-ndeha-ha-has" as stuff that "only old beer drinkers would like to imitate" while "staggering home" from the bar. Another similar letter calls "Mugarandega" the best work done by any local artist, at last a Zimbabwean export that "can be heard all over the world."

Others regretted the new emphasis on reggae. Van Renen, for one, did not consider *Chimurenga for Justice* "a very good album." In Zimbabwe, the album sold less than the advance single had. Many found it hard to reconcile Thomas's embrace of reggae—a foreign sound—with his frequent denunciations of sungura singers. "Don't dictate to our singers," scolded one *Herald* letter writer. Whether it was fan pressure, taste, or a realization that championship of African culture—the pillar of Thomas's musical identity—could not be squared with a shift to reggae, Thomas demurred. Of "Mugarandega" he said, "We were just experimenting, to see what a chimurenga song sounded like in a reggae rhythm. Reggae is a music that we love, but we are not for reggae. We are for chimurenga, our Zimbabwean beat." In the same 1988 interview, Thomas distances himself from the Rastafarian worldview as well, rejecting it as naive from an African perspective. "I love God," he says. "I was created by God and I am his servant. I am not for a man like Haile Selassie. I am for the *real* God, and no other gods shall I kneel to. I-a-man no pray to another human being, because I am human, and I do so many sins."

During the 1985 tour, Lucky and the two singer-dancers all began romantic liaisons and left the fold to marry and settle in England. Van Renen, overextended financially and unhappy with the album he had sponsored, parted ways with Thomas. "I had a good relationship with him," Van Renen recalled, "but when a person is not particularly sympathetic and they are demanding vast quantities of ganja and hashish when you haven't got a whole lot of money, you start to get a little resentful. So by the time we finished that album, I just said to them, 'Good luck, but this is more than I can deal with.'" Van Renen took a job at Island Records and turned Earthworks over to Trevor Herman, who rebuilt the label on the strength of the electrifying *Indestructible Beat of Soweto* CD series.[30]

Through this messy process, Thomas was nevertheless winning hearts and minds in Europe. In a few short years, he had transcended Zimbabwe with all its intrigues and limitations. In October 1985, he became the first African musician to appear on the cover of the increasingly influential *Folk Roots* magazine. "Our folkie readers were completely bewildered," editor Ian Anderson recalled. African music was entering the *Folk Roots* purview from many directions, but Anderson believed that Thomas's sound in particular would move his readers. Youssou N'Dour's *mbalax* pop from Senegal was daunting rhythmically, actually intimidating to dancers. Fela Kuti was making waves, but essentially playing funk. Other acts—like South Africa's sunny Mahotella Queens—were almost too upbeat. "The thing with Thomas," recalled Anderson, "was he wasn't that obvious." With mystic allure and a distinctive, lulling sound, Thomas had become a standout figure in the early days of international African music.

When Anderson learned that Thomas's 1985 tour would include a gig at Bracknell, England, just down the road from the magazine's office, he said, "Wild horses couldn't have kept me away." Thomas performed in overalls, kneeling on the stage in a paradoxical display of bravado and reverence. David Ambrose reviewed the concert for the September issue of *Folk Roots*, calling the music "quite simply the best folk/rock I've ever heard." Anderson wrote the magazine's landmark cover story on Thomas the next month, reinforcing the "folk/rock" theme.[31] In the piece, Thomas unfolds his impressive history and evokes a vision of Zimbabwe far from the brutalities of guerrilla warfare and political squabbles that had dominated the UK media for decades. In one charming touch, Thomas praises the "all-African church" his parents led, full of African music and dancing. This notion so pleased Pete Seeger that the self-described "old pagan" cited it in his Appleseeds column for *Sing Out!* magazine.[32] The lion of the liberation struggle had now earned the gentle embrace of the West's most serene and sagacious folk music patriarch.

8 / Corruption

When I see my old teacher, Herbert Murewa, the minister of
finance, I keep asking him, "Why the hell didn't you guys open up
this bloody country in 1980?" Instead of this socialism crap. 1980,
you put your roots down. You check it out. 1981, you put your
people in place. 1982, open the fucking place! You want to invest
in this country? You are from America? Okay! You take yours;
you leave us ours. We could have been laughing.

HILTON MAMBO

In 1986, a Mabvuku resident calling himself EXTREMIST TM FAN wrote to the
Sunday Mail to complain that fame had spoiled Thomas Mapfumo. At a recent
show, police had had to quell an angry crowd dissatisfied with the band's
"excessive, unwarranted breaks and the singing of old, mediocre tunes." The
charge was that international exposure had made Thomas complacent. "Once
our musicians are showered with praise," wrote EXTREMIST, "they think they
are demi-gods." Before the year's end, Tobias Arakete, riding high on his star
turn on "Mugarandega," would sever ties with the Blacks Unlimited and strike
out on his own. He would drift into obscurity and die a one-hit wonder a few
years later. Some predicted a similar unraveling for Thomas. One Gramma
Records veteran left Zimbabwe for South Africa that year, convinced that
chimurenga music was over. "Everyone had moved on," he said.

In interviews at the time, Thomas sounded anything but complacent. He
was all about causes—the fight against apartheid, the South African regime's
pernicious agents stoking civil war throughout the region, and, in liberated
Zimbabwe, the plight of local musicians struggling to create a viable busi-

ness environment. The Mugabe government had erected barriers to success, funding musicians only during political campaigns, meanwhile levying steep "luxury" taxes on the tools of their trade. Record company contracts were out of step with international norms. Nightclub owners remained free to abuse and underpay musicians. Thomas led a chorus of artistic voices calling for legislative reforms. Government officials said they would listen, but only to a union that reflected the artistic community as a whole. Thomas mocked this evasion. Zimbabwe's musicians' union had always been, and would remain, stymied by "big-headed fellows" more interested in building personal fiefdoms than solving problems. Zimbabwe's musicians and the government were at a stalemate.

For Thomas, the root of the problem was state-run radio, which he felt violated Mugabe's socialist principles by promoting a two-tiered society. Wealthy folks in low-density suburbs sent their children to European schools and listened to foreign music on Radio 3. Poor folks in the ghetto scraped by as ever, praying to their ancestors, and satisfying themselves with stigmatized local music on Radio 2. Thomas said, "Our children will think that Radio 3 is better because this is where they get American styles. Even their tone of speaking. I've got my own tone, *like an African*, and my own accent, *like an African*. This is what God gave me. I don't want to speak like an Englishman." Disc jockeys were chosen for their clean English diction; this favored those who were most assimilated and least in touch with local music. To anoint such people as tastemakers was, for Thomas, cultural suicide.

As South Africa edged toward civil war, Thomas criticized popular singers there as well for jettisoning township music in favor of disco and bubblegum. "Forget about singing American music," he told them. "It is very interesting to hear a black man singing funky music. But when we are in a war situation, we don't need love songs. What sort of people are we? Are we free? Or are we being led by our noses?" Ironically, Thomas's favorite young South African singer was a white man, Johnny Clegg, who championed a hybrid, Zulu rock sound. If Thomas's attitude struck Zimbabweans as antiquated, it must have seemed incomprehensible in South Africa, where ethnic divisions and sophisticated media pretty much precluded the possibility of a popular roots guru in the Mapfumo mold. Thomas stood against a tide of cultural change, and he relished the position.

Since independence, Chartwell Dutiro, an mbira player from a village near Bindura, had played saxophone in the Prison Band, a brass ensemble that had performed in protected villages during the dying days of Rhodesia, and on the streets of Harare at independence. Chartwell had completed a correspondence course with the Royal School of Music in England, learning to read and write musical notation and mastering the basics of theory—all while continuing to play mbira as he had since his boyhood in Bindura. Through a soldier friend, Chartwell managed to meet Jonah Sithole, and then Thomas, who instantly sized him up as an asset and moved to add him to the band. Thomas unexpectedly produced an airplane ticket to Europe, which allowed Chartwell to waive his requirement to give the Prison Band three months' notice. Chartwell quit overnight, but leaving his government job also meant losing the housing that came with it. Thomas solved this problem as well, offering a bed in his own home, a gesture he had never made to any musician except Charles. If Charles had been like a "brother," Chartwell now became something of a son, living with Thomas and his family for the next four years.

Chartwell moved deeply into the Blacks Unlimited fold. Jonah Sithole was chilly toward Emmanuel Jera, who returned to the band around this time, but he nurtured Chartwell, sharing insights about the music, such as when a guitarist must start with an upstroke or downstroke in order to lock his part into a song's rhythmic structure. In his calm, quiet way, Chartwell studied all aspects of the band's operation, including its business.

On the eve of his third European tour in 1986, Thomas took the band into the studio to record a twelve-inch "maxi-single." "Kariba" is a love song about a young man who travels town to town across Zimbabwe to reach his impossibly beautiful girlfriend on the shores of Lake Kariba. This northern reservoir was the fruit of a massive dam project along the Zambezi River in the 1950s. Building Lake Kariba had displaced thousands of Tonga people—who would long grieve their loss—and created a vacation destination beloved by generations of moneyed Rhodesians, Zambians, and Zimbabweans. The lyrics of "Kariba" evoke this idyllic resort, no doubt cherished by the Radio 3 crowd, while its music veers back into Shona tradition with an ambling shangara beat and guttural vocal refrains. Charles plays a prominent keyboard hook, adding a new veneer to the band's roots sound. Perfectly calibrated, the song garnered strong press reviews to become a Blacks Unlimited classic. Still, Thomas complained, out-of-touch DJs mostly let the record "gather dust" while they filled the airwaves with Western fare, "some of which doesn't even qualify to be called music."

"Kariba" was the first title released by Thomas's own production entity, Chimurenga Music. Gramma would no longer be the band's all-powerful producer and label, only its distributor. Thomas envisioned Chimurenga Music as an emerging commercial force that would one day have its own studio and stable of artists. Musa Zimunya got involved, translating song lyrics so that

English speakers would understand their significance, and writing copy for the *Chimurenga Fan Club Newsletter* to be circulated among members of an international fan club. Meanwhile, promoter Rikki Stein telephoned from London to say he was arranging for the band to travel on to the United States after the European concerts—a first for any Zimbabwean band.

"Then in Europe," Emmanual Jera (Manu) recalled sourly, "the same thing again: mismanagement." The band's initial payment came a week late and fell short of promises made in Harare. At the Musiques Metisses Festival in Angouleme, France, Manu observed Mory Kante of Guinea fronting an aggressive, West African pop ensemble. Kante had recently scored a hit on the French music charts with an adaptation of the traditional song "Yeke Yeke." This supercharged music thrilled the guitarist and made him feel that Thomas needed to make a stronger fusion with modernity, an opinion he shared freely. As good a musician as he was, Manu's displeasure with everything made him a difficult tour companion, to say the least.

"Sometimes you could think he was crazy," recalled Thomas, tickled years later at recalling Manu's escapades on this tour. As the band boarded a train in London, the guitarist was drunk, and Zimbabwean DJ Mike Mhundwa—traveling with the band—scolded him for mishandling a guitar they had borrowed from Misty in Roots. Manu became incensed. "Can *you* play?" Thomas recalled him asking Mhundwa. "Then, just like that, he dropped the guitar down, picked up his bag, and got out of the train. In the middle of London! The train went WOOOOOO," said Thomas, heaving with laughter. Manu wound up at the Zimbabwean embassy, and the promoter had to buy him an air ticket to Holland. "So on the plane," Thomas recalled, "he got drunk again. He stood up from his seat and started threatening the rest of the passengers. 'You people! Enjoying yourselves, eh? While people in South Africa are suffering.'" As challenging as the financial aspects of touring were, the cultural and personal ones could prove equally vexing, however hilarious in retrospect.

After a festival gig in Germany, the band returned to London to discover that there were no UK dates booked, and no American ones either. The musicians were stranded with no program, pinching pennies and crashing with members of Misty in Roots. Thomas made an urgent plea to Gordon Muir, a graphic designer from Hawick who had begun managing the Bhundu Boys, then beginning their steep rise to international fame. This band's sunny amalgam of mbira grooves, village songs, rumba, and South African jive skillfully bridged the past and future of Zimbabwean music. Their concise, well-crafted sound featured tuneful vocal harmonies and taut guitar play that inspired comparisons with the Beatles. Muir had brought the Bhundus from Zimbabwe to Scotland and was putting them up and booking them in local bars. But one Zimbabwean band was all he could handle, and he had to turn Thomas down.

Rikki Stein tried to bail out the Blacks Unlimited's London hiatus by arranging a New York press trip for Thomas and Mike Mhundwa. The two made a stop in Kingston, Jamaica, where Mhundwa was hoping to book Gregory Isaacs for a Harare concert. The high point of their Jamaican sojourn was a ritualistic ganja-smoking encounter with "the Professor," a Rasta spiritual figure in Isaacs's circle. Thomas was entranced by the scene at the Professor's compound, with dreadlocked children running around and burly Rastas smoking from an enormous, clay chalice. "Three puffs," Thomas recalled. "One, two, three. Then big clouds of smoke, and then the *coughing*. I thought this guy was dying!" Naturally Thomas partook, though he said it nearly killed him. As for New York, Thomas did a few radio interviews, but he and Mhundwa were stuck in a Catholic guesthouse, smoking bad ganja with a towel placed along the bottom of the door. This experience was demoralizing. Stein had promised American shows, but now the Bhundu Boys would play the United States before Thomas—more bitter medicine. The Blacks Unlimited returned to Harare dispirited and nearly broke, and with no representatives in Europe. For all their high hopes, it would be two years before they would travel abroad again.

With "Kariba" soaring on the charts, and an audience starved for live Mapfumo shows, the band kept busy. But Thomas knew the ground was shifting in Zimbabwe. He had heard the complaints of EXTREMIST TM FAN. He understood that the Bhundu Boys were stealing headlines, and the band Devera Ngwena was outselling him two to one.[1] Meanwhile, John Chibadura's rowdy sungura was becoming the staple sound of Harare's beer halls. The Blacks Unlimited needed to turn the tables. Working closely with Chartwell and Jonah Sithole at the start of 1987, Thomas devised music for a timely new recording, *Zimbabwe Mozambique*.[2] Brilliantly counterflow, this was a concept album focused on a serious matter: the civil war reaching its bloody crescendo just across Zimbabwe's eastern border.

Mozambique's president Samora Machel—Zimbabwe's most loyal ally during the liberation war—had died in a plane crash in October 1986. Even if an accident—and not the South African plot many assumed—this was a tragedy for the region and was deeply felt in Zimbabwe. *Zimbabwe Mozambique* tapped into wrenching emotions, beginning with its cover art: the two nations' flags, black-and-white images of Mugabe and Machel, Black Power fists, and an assortment of hand-drawn African design elements. Citing Mozambique's role in the struggle, Thomas called the album a gesture of "sheer love" and sought to place himself on a higher moral plane than other Zimbabwean musicians. "We are for the freedom of people," he said in one interview. "That is what we stand for. We would like money to make our families survive. But we mustn't be mistaken. We are not a commercial group. We stand as fighters."

Zimbabwe Mozambique's title song begins with a warm, lilting vamp heard by some as an evocation of Lusophone music. Its melodious vocals give way to guitar and brass passages in an unusual, evolving structure. Midway through the song's nearly ten minutes, a blustery saxophone riff from Chartwell signals a shift to a fast, minor-key, Korekore groove with prayer-like vocals that reprieve the spiritual force of Thomas's war-era hits. Musa Zimunya heard this as "a total song . . . breathtaking. It just opens up the heart, and opens the mind." One might also hear the piece as beginning in a quasi-reggae mode, then turning decisively to Shona tradition, as if signaling Thomas's return to indigenous form after the experimentation of *Chimurenga for Justice*. Either way, fans were riveted.[3]

The song "Zimbabwe/Mozambique" conveys tacit endorsement of the Mugabe regime, portraying it as a partner on the side of good in the Mozambican war. "This is the government we were fighting for," Thomas said in an interview about the album. "This man is our president. We believe in him and his working ways, and how much effort he has put into the whole southern Africa situation. He is the kind of leader we would like to follow." Mugabe's early record on health and education had been promising, although his minister of health would stumble badly with the emergence of AIDS, allowing the country's blood supply to become contaminated with HIV, a development that resulted in unnecessary deaths. But land resettlement had advanced between 1980 and 1986, slowly and systematically. Filmmaker Simon Bright worked in Mugabe's Department of Agriculture. Though he would later become a fierce Mugabe critic, Bright calls ZANU's early agricultural program "one of the finest examples of land resettlement in Africa." But seven years after independence, all this was beginning to falter in the face of economic woes and a creeping culture of corruption in ZANU ranks.

Tucked among the songs on *Zimbabwe Mozambique* is "Nhamo (Trouble)," which speaks of suffering in Zimbabwe: "Since I was born, *nhamo*, problems, you have been with me," Thomas sings. "I thought I had left you behind, but to my surprise, you are still with me." At the time, Thomas denied that the government was to blame for these "problems," but he later allowed that "Nhamo" had been a veiled protest, saying, "I could foresee that we were headed in the wrong direction." This may be revisionism on Thomas's part. The truth is Thomas was not yet ready to point fingers or assign blame, but a reevaluation of Mugabe was beginning to surface amid the congratulatory swell of *Zimbabwe Mozambique*.

The Black Unlimited's burgeoning musical creativity owed much to the deepening bond between Thomas and Chartwell. Other mbira players had recorded and performed with the band, but Chartwell brought new purpose to the task, addressing troublesome issues of tuning and amplification that would pave the way for mbira to become central in the Mapfumo stage sound. Regarding tuning, mbira groups often use individualized variants on traditional tuning regimens, often involving notes not found in the tempered, Western scale. Playing mbira alongside guitars, keyboards, and horns meant standardizing each mbira's tuning to match some combination of notes found on a piano. Ultimately, Thomas would require his mbira players to play music far outside the instrument's old repertoire. This expansion of the mbira's potential use in popular music is a major legacy of the Blacks Unlimited, and one that would inspire many imitators within Zimbabwe and, eventually, around the world.

"Thomas changed my way of thinking about music," Chartwell recalled, recognizing the value of the opportunity Thomas had given him. "As a boy, I wanted to be out there playing with bands, but I never grew up in a township, like Harare. It's not like Thomas—he's one of the ghetto boys who grew up with Youth Clubs where they would go to a hall and play guitar and just hang out like jazz musicians. I had none of that experience." But Chartwell understood mbira music deeply, making him a crucial collaborator during this rich new phase in Thomas's musical development.

In 1987, Thomas bought his first home, a spacious ranch house in the once all-white neighborhood of Mabelreign. Behind a security fence with a remote-controlled sliding gate, the house on 20 Dorchester Road had a veranda and swimming pool, a car port, separate servant's quarters, and a living room big enough for a crowd to gather around a centrally located television set, where Thomas would nightly air his favorite entertainments: soccer, professional wrestling, and American horror films. Foreign visitors might be puzzled by the middle-class conventionality of Thomas's home. It seemed at odds with the gritty, roots vibe of his art. For Thomas, this was the Zimbabwean dream: country boy makes good in the city. Sekuru Jira stayed in the servant's quarters when he came to town for weekend gigs. Chartwell moved into the main house with Thomas, Vena, three-year-old Tapfumaneyi, and newborn daughter Chiedza.

Chartwell sensed jealousy from others in the band, even from Thomas's wife, who then worked as a paralegal secretary preparing titles and mortgage bonds. In the end, though, Chartwell's gentle nature, winning smile, and keen sensitivities helped him keep the peace on all fronts, and for a time, familial solidarity prevailed in the Blacks Unlimited.

The names of two young filmmakers, Bob Coen and Amy Merz, top the "special thanks" list on *Zimbabwe Mozambique*. Bob had lived in Rhodesia as a boy, the son of Egyptian Jews who had fled during the Suez Crisis, first to Paris, and then to Salisbury. During the 1970s, Bob's father had produced educational materials for Rhodesian blacks. Bob recalled tuning in Voice of Zimbabwe on a shortwave radio and listening to Webster Shamu's *Chimurenga Requests* program with songs by Thomas Mapfumo and Zexie Manatsa, interspersed with slogans like *pamberi nehondo* (forward with war), which Bob learned to repeat, shocking the blacks who worked in his father's office. Bob was eighteen when his father dropped dead from a heart attack; two years later, at the height of the war, he moved to New York to pursue film. Amy was a student in one of Bob's video classes, and the two fell in love and married quickly. They moved back to Zimbabwe in 1985 and began work on a documentary about Mozambique. While casting about for music, they struck gold in the form of Thomas's stormy traditional adaptation "Guruve," the B-side of his hit "Kariba." In lieu of cash, they offered to create a video for Thomas in exchange for the use of "Guruve." So began a mutual seduction.

In the early years of MTV, Zimbabwean television was airing locally produced music videos, and Bob and Amy's offer had obvious appeal to a cinema buff like Thomas. The filming, for a single called "Ngoma Yekwedu (Our Music)," took place in Chihota, near where Thomas had spent his rural boyhood. It was a loosely conceived scenario showing the village greeting the band, a boy herding cows in a field as Thomas once had, and the musicians in their new green camouflage uniforms dancing around a fire, lit by car headlights, lip-synching the words while Chartwell simulated brass lines by blowing on a kudu horn.

Bob and Amy were being drawn into the vacuum created by Thomas's lapsed management. "There was nothing happening," recalled Bob. "He was just playing local gigs." Thomas and the band rehearsed ten kilometers out of town at the Red Lantern Hotel. In the dining room where the musicians met, the stucco ceiling was peeling in thick slabs. Its brown and cream walls had a worn, greasy hue. They recorded their ideas using a cheap, pink plastic boom box. It struck Bob as near criminal that the cultural hero of the liberation struggle was reduced to such paucity. Yet every weekend came the incomparable experience of a room full of Mapfumo fans stamping out Shona rhythms as the beer hall floor heaved beneath them.

Thomas received promising attention from America when Sean Barlow and I first visited him to do research for National Public Radio's newly launched *Afropop* program in January 1988. The Chimurenga Guru and his entourage arrived for an interview at the posh Bronte Hotel. Wearing a shiny black trench coat, Thomas parked his Ford Granada with its faux leopard skin roof and seat covers.[4] He strolled past trimmed hedges into the lobby, where he raised eyebrows among the hotel's mostly white clientele. Sealed into a room so he could smoke freely—a requirement for the interview—Thomas told his story at length, peppering his account with the occasional "I and I" and "I a man," hangovers from his recent Jamaican visit. The *Afropop* encounter bore fruit when Sean Barlow recommended Thomas to New York's Dance Theater Workshop, which set up the Blacks Unlimited's first U.S. tour for fall 1989.

Meanwhile, one-party rule became official in Zimbabwe. Eight years after his triumphant return from Mozambique, Mugabe assumed the role of president as well as prime minister, completing his systematic consolidation of power. The Blacks Unlimited took in the news at their weekly business meeting in the Queens Hotel. The musicians viewed the ZANU-ZAPU accord favorably, as the resolution of a perilous conflict, a bullet dodged. None spoke of the violence it had taken to turn Joshua Nkomo into, by his own account, "a china ornament sitting in the showcase."[5] None seemed to question the wisdom of giving Mugabe and his party such power. An official at Gramma Records was more skeptical, calling the Unity Accord "the annihilation of the Ndebele people," and asking not to be quoted lest he be "locked up."

In *Afropop*'s Bronte Hotel interview, Sean asked Thomas whether he felt free to criticize the government in his songs. "You sing about what you want in this country," Thomas asserted, adding, "I don't see why you cannot sing about corruption within the government, just because they're leaders." This, the world would soon know, was no mere bravado.

The video for "Ngoma Yekwedu" became a hit on ZTV's weekly *Mvengemvenge* program, and Bob and Amy resolved to make a feature-length film about Thomas. The subsequent *Sunday Mail* headline, "Zimbabwe Story to Be Screened Abroad," proved premature. There was simply no way Bob and Amy could make a documentary film while also managing Thomas's career. A keen Mapfumo observer, Gramma's Brian Cader had high hopes for these American managers. He adored Thomas's art but considered the singer "his own worst enemy." Cader said Thomas's downfall was that he trusted no one—"not that I blame him," he added. Cader endorsed the idea of a "white guy" managing Thomas. "He may rip you off," he mused cynically, "but at least he'll give you something back."

Midway through 1988, a series of newspaper articles chronicled Thomas's legal troubles. A woman claiming he was the father of her child had won her case, requiring Thomas to pay Z$100 maintenance each month. When he failed to make payments, a new case arose, and the magistrate's reprimand of Thomas made for savory, if ephemeral, gossip.

Soon, a more consequential story seized headlines. Geoffrey Nyarota—the former schoolteacher who had attended the earliest Blacks Unlimited concerts in Mutare—was now the editor of Bulawayo's principal newspaper, the *Chronicle*. In the wake of the ZANU-ZAPU Unity Accord, tensions were easing in Matabeleland. Nyarota thought it time to flex journalistic muscle and pierce the silence surrounding evildoings by Mugabe's inner circle. The government had arranged for each minister to receive one Mercedes Benz directly from Willowvale Motor Vehicles. In theory, officials would use these cars to visit their districts. With foreign exchange currency drying up, new vehicles were scarce, and older ones were tough to service because shops rarely stocked spare parts. The automobile of choice among Mugabe's ministers—the "chefs"—was the Mercedes, which ran about Z$250,000—expensive, but a shrewd buy. With so many officials driving Mercedes, there would always be parts available.

Nyarota learned that ministers were exceeding the one-car limit. He began to investigate, and the more he dug, the more he found. Nyarota uncovered an "iceberg of corruption." One minister had acquired fourteen vehicles and sold them on the black market. A Toyota Cressida purchased in the morning for Z$30,000 was sold later the same day for Z$115,000. "So we investigated," recalled Nyarota, "and reported. This had never happened before." The *Chronicle* published a blow-by-blow account of the so-called Willowgate scandal, serialized over fifty-four days, and it rocked the nation. Mugabe feigned surprise and appointed a commission to look into the matter. Ministers were forced to resign. One of them, Maurice Nyagumbo, committed suicide by eating rat poison. In the scandal's wake, media of every sort felt emboldened, and for a time, press accounts of corruption flourished in Zimbabwe.

A crackdown against journalists ensued, and Nyarota was its first victim, transferred from the writing desk and made group public relations executive in Harare: "very high sounding, but signifying totally nothing." A year later, Nyarota became a columnist and editor for Zimbabwe's first independent newspaper, the *Financial Gazette*, once a scion of white Rhodesia, now black-run and fiercely ambitious. Nyarota sought out writers unafraid to challenge the government, and among his best finds was a young academic named Jonathan Moyo. Moyo's bristly columns won him national celebrity as a man of the people. No one could have imagined that this columnist would one day become the most determined political adversary that Geoffrey Nyarota, or Thomas Mapfumo, would ever face. But that in its time. Meanwhile, under pressure from the government, the *Financial Gazette* ultimately fired Nyarota, effectively ending his journalistic career and driving him into exile for six years.

Nyarota had made his mark in breaking the Willowgate scandal, and in December 1988, Thomas seized the moment, releasing a maxi-single that distilled two months of newspaper stories into one short, sweet refrain: "Corruption in the so-ci-e-ty."

> You can't get away with corruption
> Watch out my friend; they're going to get you
> You can't run away from justice
> Eight years of freedom
> I work so hard to make a living . . .
> Every day, like a slave . . .
>
> The big fish don't care about it
> Some women strip for a job . . .
> Everywhere there is corruption
> Everyone seems corrupt . . .
>
> Something for something, nothing for nothing
> Corruption in the society

Thomas sang these words in English over a gentle, R&B-cum-reggae beat that made scant reference to traditional music, though Louis Mhlanga's muted guitar line carries the faintest whiff of mbira.[6] Female backing singers taunt sassily, "Corruption, corruption, corruption." The song might have been dismissed as a general complaint, as it references everything from graft to prostitution, but the line "Eight years of freedom" is stubbornly specific. Slipped in almost at random, it leaves no doubt that the Mugabe regime is the ultimate subject. And when Thomas speaks in a confident near whisper, "I will give you something, that is, if you give me something in return," he captures the familiar essence of silken sleaze. Elias Mudzuri—who would one day become mayor of Harare in opposition to ZANU-PF—described what was no doubt a common reaction around this time. "I was in civil service," he recalled, "and I didn't even know. But when Mapfumo sang it, I started noticing."

"Corruption" caught Thomas's friends in the government off guard. Having built him up as a revolutionary hero and used his music and performances in ZANU political campaigns, it was not easy to turn on a dime and call him a traitor, though some wished to do just that. Webster Shamu (aka Charles Ndlovu) did not hesitate. "He didn't like this record," said Thomas. "Charles Ndlovu goes to see Mugabe. Mugabe thinks that Charles is a nice boy. But they got the message. Some of them were talking about it, even in the Parliament. 'You want to ban this record? For what? Tell us the reason. Because it's telling us to stop corruption?'"

Gramma's Emmanuel Vori recalled, "The authorities couldn't say, 'Don't play a black brother's record on the black-controlled station under a black government.' It would have been a sticky situation. But they just quietly told the guys, 'Don't play it,' and it was shelved." After ZBC was forced to deny accusations that it had banned "Corruption," DJs began to include the song again, if only to prove there was no censorship. Such double plays would now typify Zimbabwean media, teetering between its mission and its masters.

"Corruption" outsold every record Thomas had made since independence. Surprisingly, few musicians dared follow its lead. Solomon Sikuza, an Ndebele singer and friend of Thomas's, did a song called "Love and Scandal," but this hardly made a trend. Some writers proved braver. Novelist Alexander Kanengoni, a ZANU insider, had been writing articles critical of government corruption since the country's second general elections in 1985, though the *Herald* and other publications had generally refused to publish them. But a singer with Thomas's profile had the power to reach many more people and would be harder to silence. "Because my mind was already traveling along that direction," recalled Kanengoni, "I was with him. I thought it was long overdue."

Ethnomusicologist Thomas Turino once observed that it took far more courage for Thomas to challenge Mugabe than it had to take on Ian Smith a decade earlier. In the 1970s, the tide of history had spurred him on; now he faced a headwind of entrenched black power. For Thomas, there was no distinction. He often told interviewers that he was not on the side of any race, party, or politician, only "the people." Singing "Corruption" was not knifing revolutionary leaders in the back, simply holding them to their word. "They said they were going to look after poor people," he said, recalling the rhetoric of the government's first year. "There was going to be free education, free medical care. And is there any free education in this country? Any free medical care? When we supported the struggle, we all thought there was going to be some light at the end of the tunnel. Instead people in top posts are stealing money."[7]

After "Corruption," everything Thomas sang or said would be examined through a new lens, one from which the rosy hues of liberation victory and tribal loyalty had fallen by the wayside. Shortly before "Corruption," the *Herald* had commented on Thomas's "new look," declaring him "more hard-working," and his act "more polished by the day." But Thomas's decision to criticize the regime would gradually alter his relationship with state-controlled media. "Corruption" revived lingering suspicions about Thomas's loyalty to the regime, but now this looked like courage, not acquiescence to official pressure.

Dance Theater Workshop was proceeding with its plan to bring Thomas and the band to the United States in the fall of 1989. Buoyed by that news, and the buzz over "Corruption," Amy Merz flew to London, and then New York, in search of a record deal. Her target was Island Records, where Jumbo Van Renen now held sway. Jumbo told her that he still loved Thomas, and as long as there was reliable management, he was on board. Van Renen sent Amy to New York to meet A&R man Jerry Rappaport.[8] Jerry also loved the idea of signing Thomas but was unsure about Van Renen's commitment. "So I called up Jumbo and said, 'How do you feel about this?'" Rappaport recalled. "I needed to know that he would be able to work with Thomas. And Jumbo said, 'It's okay with me, except I can't sign him. *You've* got to do the deal.' Maybe I should have known right then and there."

Rappaport's was the quintessential story of a "world music" industry player. As a young man, he dreamed of becoming a DJ, until gatekeepers told him his strong New York accent would pose a serious obstacle to advancement. After a decade managing security for Barnes and Noble, Rappaport took a pay cut to become the blues buyer at Tower Records on West Fourth Street. He soon found himself in charge of Latin, reggae, gospel, country, and, in 1983, the new "international music" department. Rappaport's expertise and affection for African and Brazilian music grew, and he aspired to use that knowledge to recruit artists for a label. He knew Island Records was moving in this direction and managed to arrange an interview with Island chief Chris Blackwell. Rappaport waited five months for the phone to ring. In the interim, U2's *Joshua Tree* had gone gangbusters for Island, and Blackwell at last had the funds he needed to launch a global music imprint, Mango. Rappaport was hired to help in 1986 and proved his mettle promptly by recruiting Senegalese singer and bandleader Baaba Maal. Other prominent catches soon followed, including Benin's Angelique Kidjo. By the time Amy Merz walked through his door two years later, Rappaport was at the top of his game.

Though she had never represented an artist, Amy negotiated skillfully and returned to Harare with a contract for *six* Mapfumo albums on Mango. Van Renen blessed the deal, secure in the knowledge that he would not have to organize concerts or cater to the personal needs of musicians because, as he said, "There was *money* behind it this time." The prospect of an international record deal boosted the Blacks Unlimited's expectations. Jonah Sithole felt it was time to institute salaries and contracts for band members, and at first, Musa Zimunya recalled, "This looked to every one of us like a very reasonable thing." Thomas begged to differ, and an extended band palaver began.

The musicians had been recording a new album. But in mid-March 1989, Thomas abruptly went back to the studio and retracked some of the guitar, drum, and backing vocal parts. Amy now felt a personal stake in what was to be Thomas's first Mango release, and she was appalled to learn that Thomas had "wiped out" some of Sithole's guitar tracks and replaced them with work by a "rock 'n' roller" who "cannot play chimurenga music at all."[9] This rock 'n' roller was Ashton "Sugar" Chiweshe, a policeman whose tenure with the Blacks Unlimited went back to the time of Thomas's jailing. Thomas was impressed that Sugar had grown up playing mbira and knew Shona music. Still, Sugar's musical heroes were George Benson, Carlos Santana, and Mark Farmer of Grand Funk Railroad. He felt no allegiance to mbira guitar conventions, such as they were, and was interested in creating his own sound, ever a subject of controversy among the Blacks Unlimited faithful.

Bob and Amy were powerless to stem the impending feud between Thomas and Sithole, and now the band's mood was shifting. Musa recalled, "Suddenly, the other members, including Lancelot, were saying that Sithole can't be trusted. They said, 'Even when we go abroad, he has got a different vibe from everybody else.' And you know how it is with a band. If someone has a different vibe, it won't work. Sithole therefore is a bad influence. He is holding back." Sithole stood the band up for a big show in Chegutu. Dispatched to find him, William discovered the guitarist at home, watching television. The Mapfumo brothers' opposition to Sithole crystallized when their mother, Janet, weighed in with spiritual insights. Musa recalled, "The mother said, 'This Jonah Sithole has got a big evil spirit, and that evil spirit wants to destroy this band, and he won't rest until he has destroyed it.'"

The showdown came when Thomas demanded to know who else among the band wanted a contract. When nobody spoke, Sithole was alone. He would not go to America. Musa recalled that Sithole had regrets and tried to apologize. Others said the guitarist was pleased with the outcome. After two European tours, he doubted there was a pot of gold at the end of this rainbow. Bob and Amy solicited letters from Sean Barlow, me, and others, vainly urging Thomas to reinstate Jonah Sithole.[10] Not a chance. This palaver was over.

Sithole's departure drew little media attention in Zimbabwe. Riding high on "Corruption" and news of the U.S. tour, Thomas appeared on the *Mvenge-mvenge* television broadcast on the eve of the April 1989 independence celebrations. He expanded his attack on DJs, record companies, and the government for doing everything in their power to squelch the production of local music and promote foreign sounds. "One would have thought," Thomas told the interviewer, that "with the coming of independence things would even get better. But no, we are back to square one, the position we were in before our self-discovery. It's back to Western music for our radio stations and goodbye to our own music." The interviewer tried to put Thomas off stride with a question about his dreadlocks: Were they not a Jamaican import? Thomas was ready with a riff about how Bob Marley had introduced the hairstyle—which the Shona call *mhotsi*—to Jamaica "following his first marriage to a woman from Africa." Actually, Rastafarians had been wearing dreadlocks well before Marley, and it was Rita Marley—who is not from Africa—who helped nudge him toward the Rasta faith and the dreadlock look. But the essence of Thomas's statement—that dreads have long existed in Africa—was true, and the *Sunday Mail* thanked him for "educating the nation."[11]

The album the band had been working on, *Varombo Kuvarombo* (From the Poor to the Poor), came out in July 1989. With the blunt force of "Corruption" still ringing in the nation's ears, Thomas now sang about those neglected and persecuted by the regime. Two mbira songs convey the album's disgruntled essence, "Moyo Wangu (My Heart)," with its allusion to a "confrontation" that comes when exploited people say "enough is enough" and stand up to "those who do not practice what they preach," and "Muchadura (You Will Confess)," which burnishes Thomas's image as a man who "preaches the truth to the people" and so is "hated by those in power."

Also noteworthy is the song "Chigwindiri," which closes the curtain on the ZANU-ZAPU divide, implicitly celebrating the end of Ndebele resistance in Matabeleland. Zimbabwean scholar Alice Kwaramba detects derision in the song's reference to "outcast(s) without a home," but Thomas categorically rejected the notion that "Chigwindiri" tilts toward Shona or ZANU supremacy.[12] The shebeen killing in Bulawayo was ten years in the past, and with the Fifth Brigade in abeyance and the Unity Accord signed, the time was right for Ndebele people to reappraise Thomas and his music. "They actually found out that this band was *not* a ZANU-PF band," Thomas recalled. "That became clear to them when we recorded 'Corruption.' So then they started believing, 'These are real freedom fighters, not part and parcel of the government.'"

Guitarist Ephraim Karimaura debuts on *Varombo Kuvarombo*, as do the "Singing Daughters."[13] In fact, Tendai Ruzvidzo and Florence—whose last name is not remembered—were unrelated. Florence was a problem, for Thomas's interest in her went beyond music. Bob had recently escorted the band on a tour around the country with the Singing Daughters in the lineup. Suspicious, Vena had followed the band to Hwange and surprised Thomas and Florence in a hotel room. Bob recalled Thomas emerging from the scuffle with wounds on his face. Thomas continued to insist that Florence be included in the U.S. tour, and for months the band members, Bob, and, reluctantly, Amy all became parties to shielding Vena from this affair. But Vena was not fooled, and as Bob recalled, "They had some serious potshots over this girl."[14]

Tendai Ruzvidzo was the strongest and most naturally talented of all the Blacks Unlimited women over the years. She was raised a "church girl" in Murehwa by her Seventh-Day Adventist mother and stepfather. She defied them by clandestinely pursuing traditional music and dance and got her break when she joined the Zimbabwean National Dance Company under the direction of Ephat Mujuru, who later introduced her to Thomas. Ultimately, Florence was forced to leave the band, and Tendai recruited Kudzai Chiramuseni, also of the National Dance Company. With that, Thomas's first U.S. tour lineup was complete.

Island decided to add "Corruption" to the songs on *Varombo Kuvarombo* and to name the album after the famous single. The label had learned of a Zimbabwean graphic designer living in New York, someone with a genuine feeling for Thomas's music and the skills needed to create strong artwork for the release. This is how Thomas came to know Saki Mafundikwa, one of the most loyal friends he would have in his life. Saki first heard Thomas sing in the late 1960s with the Springfields. Ten years Thomas's junior, he'd had to stand outside, but the voice alone impressed a kid just discovering rock 'n' roll. Later, Saki followed the Acid Band as "a local act," inherently inferior to foreign rock gods like Thin Lizzy, Deep Purple, the Stones, and Nazareth. Then, in 1978, buzzed on beer from Mushandira Pamwe Hotel, Saki and his mates attended a rock festival at Gwanzura Stadium. Primed to watch Dr. Footswitch do his Hendrix impersonation alongside Salisbury's rock wannabes, the young men were instead blown away by Thomas, dressed in his black spirit medium cape and singing over taut Shona guitar lines. As Saki recalled, "A new era had begun."

Saki experienced the liberation war's endgame from the perspective of Indiana University. By the time he visited Harare again in 1981, his musical tastes had moved on to Bob Marley, Fela Kuti, and King Sunny Adé. He spotted Thomas driving through Harare in a sporty car, sprouting little dreads, and surrounded by his entourage, and saw a man with world stature: Zimbabwe's *own* Fela. Later, dreadlocked himself, married, and successful as a graphic artist in New York, Saki avidly collected Blacks Unlimited vinyl. He swooned over the song "Corruption," recalling, "I went home on holiday and that song was rocking the place. I mean *rocking*. Even my father was into it. What a wicked song!"

Saki approached the cover art for *Corruption* mindful of Lemi Ghariokwu's lauded work on Fela Kuti's Nigerian LPs—colorful images that merged social messages with a psychedelic aesthetic. Saki asked his brother to mail him news clippings from Harare, and he used them to create a montage featuring the faces of government ministers shamed during the Willowgate scandal. The mock-up pleased Island.[15] But in Harare, Thomas was uneasy about naming officials. "We won't be able to go home," he declared. Saki settled the matter by blocking out the ministers' eyes and changing their names to phony ones like Comrade Manyepo (Liar) and Comrade Greed. Saki's artwork helped introduce Thomas to Americans as a liberation war hero but no sap, a man forward-looking enough to chant down Babylon irrespective of race or revolutionary credentials.

9 / Big Daddy and the Zimbabwe Playboys

> The money gets siphoned away, and Thomas, more than anybody
> else, blows the money. He has no problem with that. It's like
> Woody Allen says about his thing with Soon-Yi: "The heart wants
> what it wants." That is the problem that you have when you deal
> with Thomas.
>
> TOM TERRELL

Chris Bolton was the son of a truck-driving father and a factory-working
mother in Hillington, near Heathrow Airport outside London. Chris traversed
worlds as a boy, attending grammar school with children from well-to-do
families, his uniform smart enough to elicit ridicule from neighbors and
shabby enough to get him sent home by school officials who thought him
"improperly dressed." He moved on to art school and came of age during the
1960s ska era, with its ethic of interracial synergy. Chris loved to hang out in
West End nightclubs "full of hookers and all-night music." He mortified his
mother when he brought home his first black girlfriend, already pregnant,
and soon to become, briefly, his first wife. He hated to cause his mother grief
but comforted himself with the notion that rebellion was Bolton family lore.
A grandfather had helped close down the High Street during labor unrest in
1926; an uncle had died in the Spanish Civil War; and Chris's father—less
racist than his mother—had championed the aspirations of England's downtrodden immigrants.

Forced to leave home at eighteen, Chris spent his days working in classical
libretti at EMI—awash in Beatles money at the time—and his nights as a DJ
renting out a PA system with his pal Bertie, a singer for the reggae band Misty

in Roots. Chris believed he was on the front lines of a culture war, fighting a rising tide of "fascism" in England. In the early Thatcher years, Chris and a few Misty in Roots musicians served jail time for obstructing a police raid on their studio amid the chaos of a race riot, and he burnished the tale as a badge of honor befitting a Bolton. Black girls, rebel music, and a clenched-fist response to racism all became prologue to Chris's prolonged encounter with Zimbabwe.

On April 17, 1980, as Zimbabweans celebrated independence in Rufaro Stadium, Chris attended the London celebration where Zimbabwean expatriates rubbed shoulders with punk rockers, West Indians, and the "rock against racism" crowd. "When the flag went down in Zimbabwe," he recalled, "the flag was going down in London." That rally was Chris's introduction to the voice and music of Thomas Mapfumo.

Misty in Roots had earned stripes with local Zimbabweans by playing benefits for the freedom fighters, particularly when a show was disrupted by a gang of skinheads. After independence, Misty was invited to perform in Zimbabwe, and Chris accompanied the musicians on a six-month visit there, during which they shared stages with the Blacks Unlimited. By the time the two bands reunited in London's Addis Ababa Studio to record *Chimurenga for Justice* in 1986, one Misty in Roots singer had gone so far as to buy a farm in Zimbabwe—later seized as a "white farm"—and Chris had begun making yearly trips there, importing badly needed PA gear and hiring himself out as a soundman.

One night, while working a show at Harare's Holiday Inn, Chris met a beautiful Ndebele woman named Anne and, after an electrifying romance, married her. This helped him become certified as a guest worker in Zimbabwe, and he soon went into business, earning a living doing sound for the country's top bands: the Blacks Unlimited, Devera Ngwena, the mixed-race band Ilanga, and even the fabulously successful Bhundu Boys.[1] Chris befriended Benny Miller, Thomas's pick to travel as the soundman for the upcoming American tour. As Chris helped Benny prepare, it became clear that Benny "really didn't fancy being on a tour." When Benny pulled out, Chartwell nominated Chris to step in. Chartwell admired Chris's unflappable demeanor—in part, the result of a steady diet of half-tobacco, half-ganja cigarettes. Underneath, Chris was built like a bull and ghetto tough, and now he too had fallen hard for Thomas's music. He leapt at the opportunity.

The tour's sponsors, Dance Theater Workshop and Island Records, had negotiated the entourage down from sixteen to twelve people, but it remained a large group, including the two female singers, William as manager, and Chris as soundman.[2] On later tours, Chris would have to road-manage and drive the bus in addition to doing sound. He would later remark that Thomas had the mixed fortune of "starting at the top" in America. Dance Theater Workshop had secured underwriting from the Rockefeller Foundation, and while this meant the Zimbabwean musicians would be treated like the grand international artists they were, it did not reflect the reality for African bands touring in America. "It was like a dream for us," recalled Island's Jerry Rappaport, "very serendipitous, because it was the first time I didn't have to sit there for weeks at a time trying to make numbers work that would never work."

Rappaport and Van Renen had signed Thomas on the understanding that he had reliable managers. In reality, Bob and Amy had taken on the job because it seemed "the cool thing to do," and because Thomas's agenda had dovetailed with their own. The two filmmakers had used archival footage from their Mozambique film to produce an impressive video for "Zimbabwe Mozambique," a landmark television event in Zimbabwe. But when Amy traveled to negotiate the Island deal, and Bob accompanied the band on a winter tour of Zimbabwe, their experiences diverged. Bob had assumed the role of Thomas's de facto chauffeur, sharing his morning spliff and moving through his complicated world with deepening obsession.

Bob thrived on the entrée Thomas provided to Harare's off-limits communities, worlds he had viewed with distanced fascination since childhood. He lived for those nights at Club Saratoga in Highfield, known as a "real thieves' hangout." At one show, someone told Bob that Thomas was "working with the gangs." Bob recalled, "Someone said to me, 'You know what Thomas has just said? He's sent the message out in the music that now is the time to pick the pockets. They are ripe for picking.' Then the thieves would go into action." This was something one heard, though I never found any evidence for it; and Thomas denied any such arrangement categorically. Nevertheless, Bob was intrigued, not repelled, by this well-worn riff from Harare's urban folklore. "I even got my wallet picked at that show," said Bob, with something like pride.

As Bob lived out a boyhood dream, money began to flow out of the family bank account, and there was trouble on the home front. Bob could not bring himself to ask Thomas for payment when every Monday he witnessed the band meetings at the Queens Hotel, ever "fraught with tension" as musicians' envelopes appeared containing "whatever Thomas felt like giving you," sometimes as little as Z$20 for a weekend's work. Only Jonah had dared speak up for the band, but after the failed contract palaver, he had abandoned the others to their fates. Bob sympathized with the musicians, but mostly he admired Thomas, who was "like a magician, keeping everything going in his own quiet way," Jira and William at his side, and the constant force of his mother, Janet, the mystic matriarch, in the background, felt but unseen. Bob had the impression that "everything Thomas did was for her."

On the eve of the U.S. tour, Thomas made his first pilgrimage to Guruve, ancestral home of his blood father, Tapfumaneyi Mupariwa, who had died more than fifteen years earlier. Thomas recalled, "I was actually told by a medium spirit that I should go and see where I come from. My people wanted to see me. They were not very happy about my staying away from home. So I just went there to introduce myself, and everybody was happy. They did all the traditional things like brewing beer. We took the band there, and people played music the whole night through because this was something special. That was the first time that I saw where I come from."

Bob accompanied Thomas and the band on the trip to Guruve, with everyone packed into a van for the three-hour drive. Masawu, a dried plum-like fruit, was in season, and upon arrival, the musicians bought kilos of them and began gorging themselves. Then, under a full moon, twelve young men appeared with enormous ngoma drums and began pounding out rhythms. Thomas vanished into the private cloister of a local spirit medium while Bob and the musicians smoked ganja, drank seven-days beer, and ate masawu as the drums played on through the moony night. "As dawn broke," Bob recalled, "we walked with the spirit medium down onto the paddock, and he picked out a little calf and slaughtered it. This thing had just had its throat cut and was still gurgling, and they cut off a piece of its rump and had a fire going, and we roasted this meat really quickly. Then we were sitting and eating this most amazing meat, while this thing was still dying next to us."[3]

Years later, when he worked as a CNN correspondent in war-ravaged Sierra Leone, Bob would meet a Canadian adventurer living amid a violent world of arms dealing, diamonds, and drugged-out teenagers. "Why do you do it?" Bob would ask, feeling instant empathy when the Canadian replied, "It's the *jaaaazz*." That's how it was for Bob with Thomas. It was the *jaaaazz*—long nights in Chitungwiza surrounded by grinning guys with beer bottles dangling from their fingertips, stomping out Shona rhythms while thieves prowled and musicians on stage wove an imaginary ladder to a world of spirits and ancestors; medicine show romps around a country convulsed with hidden traumas and unbridled enthusiasms, winding up on a leaf-green paddock eating fresh-killed beef from a spirit medium's knife at sunrise. Bob was not the first stranger to be seduced by Thomas's universe. He would not be the last. But well before the band boarded their plane for New York City in September 1989, Amy had laid out a stern ultimatum: Bob would have to choose between this life and his marriage. He chose marriage. Amy estimated at the time that the couple had invested $30,000 in Thomas's business affairs. Years later, Bob could not name a figure but conceded it was "a lot."

Once again, the Lion of Zimbabwe was looking for a manager, and this time the honor fell to a young man with roots in Georgia and North Carolina, and no experience with African music. Kenneth Kutsch had been working with temperamental bass wizard and jazz-rock phenomenon Jaco Pastorious. When Jaco died after a Florida drug and alcohol binge, Ken was crushed, ready to quit music and become a waiter. Then he heard the voice of Thomas Mapfumo, speaking in one of the first broadcasts of the *Afropop* public radio program. "I hadn't even heard the music," Ken recalled, "I just loved what he was saying. I called Sean Barlow and said, 'Who *is* this guy?'" Sean provided Thomas's number in Harare, and Ken promptly engaged Thomas in a half-hour conversation, by the end of which he had become the new manager for the Blacks Unlimited.

Right away, there was conflict. Ken thought Island was overinterpreting the record contract, claiming both recording royalties and publishing for the *Corruption* album—"double dipping," as he saw it.[4] Ken engaged a lawyer—Joseph Grier of Grubman, Indursky and Schindler—and confronted the label. Ken recalled that he and his label contact wound up shouting over the phone "like bullies in a sandbox." With the whole deal about to collapse, Island relented, and Grier set up Chimurenga Music as Thomas's publishing company. Kenny, as Thomas called him, seemed the ideal advocate—a clear-eyed, sharp-elbowed professional who knew his way around the business and was not bewitched by chimurenga music or partial to ganja. But Ken would have to work with Rappaport in New York and Van Renen in London, and both men already disliked him.

Ken contacted the Third World Agency, operating out of Sounds of Brazil (SOB's), a nightclub in Soho, New York, and a gateway venue for African acts seeking their fortunes in America. They set about booking additional dates for Thomas on the heels of the Dance Theater Workshop tour. Bob agreed to road-manage the band through that initial three-week run, and then, to save his marriage, he would pass the baton on to Ken. Ken had no intention of doing much traveling with the band, so he reached out to his friend Tom Terrell, the only black DJ at WHFS in Washington, DC, and asked him to handle the additional dates.[5] The timing was good. After seven years, Terrell had been squabbling with WHFS over money and was ready for a change. "I really had no idea what Thomas's music was about," recalled Terrell, "and Ken described him as 'like a reggae artist,' so he clearly didn't know that much either."

Zimbabwean music had enjoyed almost no exposure in the United

States—a handful of small releases and a few published reviews.[6] *Afropop* had introduced Thomas's music and story to a significant niche audience, a definite boon. Still, if Ken could liken Mapfumo to a reggae artist, and Robert Christgau could preview his SOB's debut in the *Village Voice* as "mbaqanga-inflected soukous," much work remained to be done.[7]

Dance Theater Workshop presented Thomas on a double bill with legendary Manding electric guitarist Sekou Diabaté and his Bembeya Band from Guinea.[8] Both acts were terrific on the stage, but their narratives and natures could hardly have diverged more sharply. The Guineans were French-speaking Muslim teetotalers whose careers had been shepherded by a government committed to using music as a means of unifying people. The Zimbabweans were beer-drinking, ganja-smoking, English-speaking Christian animists with a deep mistrust of government officials, white or black, who saw their own music as an act of spiritual and political defiance. Diabaté was a florid guitarist whose expansive, even hammy, electric guitar solos had earned him the sobriquet "Diamond Fingers." Soundman Chris Bolton heard him simply as the "world's loudest guitarist." Little warmth developed between the two bands, and many who saw these shows found one of the groups sublime, and the other bizarre or boring. Still, there was brilliance to the pairing, as it vividly displayed the paradoxical diversity of modern African music.

Corruption came out just in time for the tour, and it earned favorable reviews. Still, Jerry Rappaport knew that no amount of praise or tour support was likely to secure his bottom line, for the simple reason that records like this would not receive commercial radio play. "In the eighties," said Rappaport, "there was no way for the numbers to work on these records. Chris Blackwell basically decided that he believed in the music enough that he was going to back it. One of the beautiful things about working for Chris in A&R back then is you didn't make a record based on how many copies it was going to sell. You made a record based on whether *Chris* was going to like it."

The tour opened in a hall in Stamford, Connecticut, essentially a dry run. Upon arrival at the hotel, the Zimbabweans took their per diems and vanished into a mall across the street. Ken—who had only just met them—had to scramble to find everyone in time for the show. Next came two packed nights at SOB's. The musicians, looking dazed and exhilarated, filed into the dark, empty club on the afternoon of their New York debut. Ken followed with a box of T-shirts, handsomely sporting Saki Mafundikwa's *Corruption* artwork.[9] Chartwell greeted a few waiting journalists, eager to tell them about the new recording the band had been polishing back in Harare. Thomas played it cool, dressed in a trench coat and black fedora, sizing up the room, shaking hands, scanning for a target to ask the question that would punctuate so many encounters along the road: "Can you find me something, my brother?"

The show began with an instrumental during which Chartwell danced in a spirit medium's robe. Then amid the sharp plinking of electrified mbira, Thomas sauntered on stage, leaning a little oddly, his glassy eyes slow to connect with the cheering fans. The band launched into one of its unreleased songs, "Chamunorwa." Ephraim stood at the back, statuesque, forcefully picking out melody on his guitar. The snare drum cracked, and the band locked into its groove, mbira and guitar moving together in serene dialogue. Everson snapped out hosho (shaker) percussion to define the signature 12/8 lope of mbira music. He kept his eye on Thomas, who wandered the stage, waiting and listening for the longest time. When at last he sang, his voice filled the room with unexpected authority. Every eye now fixed on this mysterious, hunched man, veiled in uneven, ropy dreadlocks, crouching and singing as though summoning power from somewhere deep within the earth. Hair on necks stood up, for the sound was incomparably beautiful. Tendai and Kudzai stood to Thomas's left, swinging their arms and stepping in forthright unison, wailing out haunting responses to his subsonic calls. A *New York Times* reviewer called the show "luminous" and "hypnotic."[10]

Rappaport accompanied Chris Blackwell to the SOB's debut. The Island impresario turned to his A&R man midset and flashed a smile that said it all: no matter how much trouble this turns out to be, it's worth it. Rappaport adored the band, especially Chartwell, who had an easy way of traversing cultural realms, providing a reassuring bridge to the more inscrutable Thomas. Rappaport worried about Ken as band manager but tolerated him after assessing Brother William as "clueless." Chris Bolton impressed Rappaport as "a fucking madman," high praise in his book. As a teenager, Rappaport had hit the road with Howlin' Wolf, and Chris reminded him of his former self—in it for the *jaaaazz*. When the lawyer Joseph Grier attended the second SOB's show and looked over the band's tour itinerary, he could hardly believe its ambitiousness, as if "someone didn't realize how big the United States was."

Bob Coen recalled, "There were scary moments on that tour. There was a Kansas show where the ganja had run out." A planned three-week supply had vanished within days, despite Bob's effort to ration. "Well, forget it," he said. "The last joint was smoked at sound check. It's now the show, and Thomas is like, 'There's no ganja. There's no show. I can't go on.' And I'm like, 'Thomas, man, this is *Kansas!*'" Bob scanned the crowd for a longhair or Rasta willing to trade herb for a pass to the concert. Scarier than the ganja was the sex. "I bought a jumbo box of condoms for that tour," said Bob. "And I told them,

'You guys, feel free to take as many as you want.' And I tell you, not *one* condom was used in two months. And every show, there were groupies waiting. College girls!"

Thomas boasted that Ephraim was "better than Jonah Sithole," but the young guitarist still had tentative moments on stage. Every day in hotel rooms, Chartwell and Washington huddled around him, singing in his ear while he picked out lines on his unplugged electric. Meanwhile, Ken huddled in New York, working the phones. A booking agent Ken was wooing passed after seeing the San Francisco show. "It was just an off night," explained Ken. "Thomas is like the Grateful Dead. Some nights it totally fucking cooks, and then there are nights when it doesn't." That San Francisco show took place in October 1989, days before the worst earthquake to hit the Bay Area since 1906. The Zimbabweans were soon riveted by televised images of the devastated Bay Bridge, which they had recently crossed. By then, they were in Houston, and DJ Tom Terrell of Washington, DC, was taking over for an additional four weeks of shows—as far north as Vancouver, British Columbia, and down south to Atlanta.

At the handoff, Bob Coen gave Terrell one overriding piece of advice: resist buying ganja with all you've got. Marijuana was scarce and expensive that fall, and Bob had found that a $400 bag lasted the band only a couple of days. When this expense exhausted petty cash, Thomas would say, "Take it out of salary." Terrell knew right then that "there were going to be shortfalls." The band was tired. Two members were sick, and right away they faced a long, hot drive to San Diego for a gig at the SOMA collective, a holistic healing establishment. The "sisters" in charge there treated the musicians with natural remedies and vegetarian feasts. "Normally," recalled Terrell, "the rules were: chicken, chicken, chicken. And fish." But in this case, New Age hospitality hit the spot. Terrell had yet to actually *hear* the band perform, but at that San Diego show, he finally discovered what Thomas Mapfumo and the Blacks Unlimited were all about.

"I was mesmerized," he recalled,

so mesmerized I forgot to do what I was supposed to do, like give them water on stage, give them towels. Watching those two sisters dance reminded me of two teenage girls at home in the living room practicing routines all day and all night, and *laughing*. And Chartwell was the man, jumping between sax and mbira. Chartwell had a spark. He was like Mingus; his mbira playing was fucking strong. You felt like he could walk around that damn stage and you would still hear him in the hall. And Charles had this pixieish grin on his face. Every time he would play certain notes, it was like he had some private joke with himself. And Ephraim—killer guitar player. I felt this guy was going to be a big African guitar star.

The players' personalities came through in their performances. Drummer Kaya was an "irrepressible kid, just having a ball," and Washington on bass, quiet, still, and strong, "the smartest of them all." Washington neither drank nor smoked, and he stoically endured the resulting ridicule. He alone resisted the band's obsession with shopping at every opportunity and instead saved his money. Terrell spotted Everson as a drinker. "You just know," he said. "And it wasn't that he was drunk so much, but alcoholics have a certain thing. They never get rid of the alcohol. It makes their skin look waxy."

Terrell marveled at the rigidity of the band's social order: the "Sekurus" (uncles), Thomas, William, Lancelot, and Charles at the top, "off limits," and then Chartwell, Ephraim, and Chris Bolton. Everson was on the outs because of his drinking, though William—whom Terrell perceived as Thomas's "straw boss"—also drank, getting a pass because he was family. Washington and Kaya ranked low, though not as low as the "girls" who had "no rights," rarely spoke, and were sometimes forced to change in a bathroom or on the bus while the men took over the dressing room. "That pissed me off," recalled Terrell. "Thomas set rules for everything, where people sat, what they could do and when." Rules even governed the smoking of ganja. Thomas kept all the roaches and when there was nothing else left, these would be rolled into one final spliff, passed from Thomas first to Charles, then William, then Lancelot, and when it was mostly gone, the other musicians. "They were not going to sit and pass around in a big circle," said Terrell. "Oh no. And then, you've got to save that roach, and give it *back* to Thomas."

The driver Ken had hired demanded an end to smoking on the bus. Terrell recalled, "Thomas says, 'I must have my ganja.' And I tell him, 'But Thomas, this guy is pissed. Why don't you go back in the bus and close the door?' 'No, no. I want to sit up front. I want to have my ganja.' So this guy is threatening to pull over any minute." Things came to a head in Vancouver, British Columbia. As the bus pulled into town, Terrell spotted a mall. He stood in the middle of the aisle and bellowed out the line for which he would most be remembered: "*Attention shoppers!* There is a *mall* to the left." But Terrell's gift for generating hilarity went only so far. The Vancouver show sold out, but the venue broke contract and paid the band in less valuable Canadian currency. The next morning, the driver summoned the police to the hotel, demanded his pay, and quit on the spot. Terrell used the Canadian cash, avoiding arrest, but now he was forced to break a cardinal rule of road management: never drive. He and Chris, with his Zimbabwean driver's license, rented two vans, and the band headed south for Seattle in a blinding rainstorm. "I kept waking up sleeping," Terrell recalled. "I don't know why we weren't dead."

A large crowd had assembled at the Backstage nightclub in Seattle. Thomas had a local constituency of Shona music aficionados in the Pacific Northwest. Seattle was this community's nexus, the home of its artistic progenitor, Dumisani Maraire. Dumi, as his students called him, had trained on the smaller, secular mbira (*karimba*) at the Kwanangoma College in Bulawayo and had come to teach at the University of Washington in Seattle from 1968 to 1972, remaining in the area afterward.[11] Beginning with Dumi's first group, a succession of marimba ensembles performing Shona music had begun spreading with cultlike zeal from Seattle to Portland, Eugene, Santa Cruz, and beyond.[12] Dumi's extended musical clan made natural Blacks Unlimited fans. But the Seattle situation became awkward when the local promoter suggested that Dumi and his group open Thomas's show. Word came back that this was out of the question. It is not clear whether the decision was made by Thomas—he did not recall it—or by Ken, whose sister, coincidentally, performed in a marimba ensemble that had fallen into rivalry with Dumi's.

Terrell was puzzled to learn that Dumi was "not respected" among the Blacks Unlimited. The issue seemed to be that Dumi had "dumbed down" Shona music for foreign consumption. Dumi's Kwanangoma training had led him to present mbira as a musical art rather than a spiritual practice—a big difference from Thomas, who explicitly leveraged Shona religion as an aspect of his art, and Chartwell, who actually began his career playing mbira for a local spirit medium. It didn't help that Dumi had spent the hot years of the liberation war living in comfort in America—even releasing an album with the unfortunate title *Mbira Music of Southern Rhodesia*—while Thomas and his band had been embroiled in the fight to liberate Zimbabwe. In any case, the Seattle organizers and Dumi himself were chagrined when, instead of being received as an honored guest, the professor was refused a complimentary ticket to the show and not allowed backstage. Terrell, the road manager, recalled his discomfort at seeing Dumi standing in the club's cavernous entryway, waiting for a ticket.

The band flew to Chicago, where Shona-savvy American marimba players gave way to Zimbabwe expatriates starved for a taste of home. The Zimbabwean presence lifted the band's performance. Two nights in Chicago with good crowds, good food, friends bringing ganja, and no travel or hotel hassles—this was luxury. The only hitch came when, after the first gig, Terrell's sacrosanct four hours of sleep were interrupted by a telephone call from Thomas, complaining that his room was full of Zimbabweans who wouldn't leave. "Well," said Terrell, "you're Thomas Mapfumo. Tell them to leave."

"No, you don't understand," Thomas explained. "If I tell them to leave, it's an insult. *You* have to tell them to leave." When Terrell arrived in the role of bad cop, Thomas played the scene out, protesting the intrusion: "Tom, please. These are my friends. These are my people." As the last Zimbabwean left the room, Thomas gazed sorrowfully at Terrell and asked aloud, "What kind of man is this?" Funny stories and raucous laughter were more Thomas's style, but he could also manage deadpan.

Terrell's enduring memory of traveling with the Mapfumo entourage was the way that no matter how ugly or dire things became, the music the band played never lost its power to "kick away the gloom." It was a curative. The Blacks Unlimited delivered a triumphant show at Chicago's Cloister Club. Everything came together. Even Lancelot, whom Terrell perceived as the band's weak link, was on fire. "This night, he was Ray Baretto," recalled Terrell. "And this night, Ephraim got the shit right, totally sailed. He was taking long solos, just gone, way up. And Chartwell was egging him on, taking him out. I remember that gig to this day. It was incredible, incredible, incredible."

One reason the band sounded so good on tour was that Chris Bolton understood the subtle art of mixing Thomas's music. Over the next decade touring with the band, he would bail out countless rock engineers who unfailingly made a hash of the Blacks Unlimited's sound. "In the first place," recalled Chris, "they're going to put the bass drum up too loud—*whack, whack, whack.* That's it. That will kill the music to begin with. The way I mix it, I mix it down. If you can't hear something, I try to pull everything else down. Because it is never, *ever* meant to be loud music." The band's force lay not in any individual's performance but in the whole, and when its synergistic heat reached the truly transcendent heights Terrell witnessed in Chicago in 1989, it was often just because nothing else got in the way.

For a while, the good times rolled. A new bus driver piloted a school bus from Portland, Oregon, to Chicago and on to Champaign, Illinois, where the band spent three blessed days and nights. The Champaign visit went beyond midwestern hospitality. The promoter, Bob Diener, had arranged everything: bargain hotel rates, a public radio interview, an appearance in ethnomusicologist Tom Turino's class at the University of Illinois, nightly feasts catered by a Rastafarian chef, and all the ganja and beer the Zimbabweans desired.

This encounter with Bob Diener would have long-term ramifications. Bob was an unassuming record store owner with a hearty community spirit and a dogged nature. In years to come, Bob would embrace Thomas Mapfumo and Zimbabwe with missionary devotion. He would create his own record label, Zimbob, and release three Mapfumo CDs in the United States. He would visit and stay with Thomas in Harare, eventually buying a car and a house there. He would bring Manny Rettinger, an Albuquerque sound engineer and bandleader recruited to master Zimbob releases, to Zimbabwe. And Manny, in turn, would introduce Thomas to an independently wealthy rock and jazz drummer named Al Green, who would also start his own record company and release six more Mapfumo CDs between 1998 and 2003. In short, the next fourteen years of Thomas's international career were largely preordained in that first merry sojourn in Champaign, Illinois.

As the band pulled out of Champaign and headed south, the musicians were as happy and harmonious as Terrell would ever see them. Thomas began reminiscing about his old days singing cover songs with the Springfields in Mbare. Terrell recalled Charles spurring him on, saying, "'Thomas, do the Otis Redding. Call Otis! Call baby!' So we're going down the highway in this school bus, and in the middle of the aisle, Thomas starts singing 'I've Got Dreams to Remember.' In his thick accent, he's going, 'Baby, baby, baby, baby,' and he's *good*. He's doing the whole routine in the aisle, spinning around, dropping to his knees. He's *giving* it." After this, Terrell christened the band Big Daddy and the Zimbabwe Playboys, a name he thought captured who they *really* were. Whenever Thomas became peeved over some small thing, Terrell could cut the tension in a phrase: "Come on, Big Daddy. Chill out, Big Daddy." This animated, wiry black dude had a hold on these musicians. Terrell had only to bark out the phrase "Attention shoppers!" and all their Shona intrigues, roastings, and inside jokes would dissolve into perfect, even excited, focus. Here was a man who seemed capable of managing the Blacks Unlimited.

Thomas's next two dates, in Knoxville and Atlanta, were double bills with mbira maestro Ephat Mujuru, who was touring that fall as a solo act. It was an inspired pairing, though an awkward one for two artists who had never entirely embraced one another. "If George Washington were alive today," led the preview in the *Atlanta Journal Constitution*, "he'd probably be jamming with Zimbabwean star Thomas Mapfumo, a revolutionary musician who is not only first in war and peace, but first on the pop charts of his countrymen." The Variety Playhouse show in Atlanta culminated a full day of Zimbabwe-focused events, including a workshop by Ephat and a screening of a film by Gei Zantzinger and Andrew Tracey, which unnerved Ephat by closing with the brutal death of his grandfather, the spirit medium Muchatera.[13] *There are things even history should not know.*

Thomas generously told the *Constitution Journal* that performing with Ephat was a "special occasion" for him. Ephat missed no opportunity to note that his family had played mbira at Thomas's home when they were children, nor to take credit for having "given" Tendai and Kudzai to Thomas. The women positively glowed at the sight of their old mentor. On stage, Ephat's whimsical mbira sets created a perfect entrée to the trance magic of the Blacks Unlimited.[14] In his early American tours, Thomas always began the show with an mbira adaptation, sometimes with no guitar or bass, and then moved into his wide-ranging repertoire, bringing the set to a swinging, brassy crescendo with the women dancing their hearts out, and Ephraim's guitar piercing through with soulful, cycling melodies.

The tour hit Charleston in the ghostly aftermath of Hurricane Hugo. The hotel rooms smelled of mildewed carpet. Thomas kept requesting a change, but each room smelled as bad as the one before. When at last the manager asked, "And what the hell have you been smoking?" the musicians burst into laughter and said they would keep the room. The band moved on to the notorious Kilimanjaro Club in Washington, DC. Now Terrell was on home turf, and he had cause to be apprehensive about Kilimanjaro owner Raymond Paris, famous for bilking bands. At the show, Terrell stationed a friend at the door with a clicker, knowing he would have to fight for the guarantee. "When Raymond showed me his numbers," recalled Terrell, "I showed him mine." Terrell got his way, but the next morning, he discovered that Paris had not paid the hotel bill as required by contract. Terrell would take serious heat for his decision to settle the $900 bill using band funds, but with the bus double-parked on a busy street, the hotel threatening to call the cops, and Paris nowhere to be found, he had little choice but to pay up and roll north.

Outside New York, the band camped in a hotel on the Jersey side of the Lincoln Tunnel, and Terrell took stock of the tour's mounting deficit. In addition to ganja, shopping, added bus expenses, and Raymond Paris's expert rip-off, there was Thomas's insistence on telephoning Vena in Harare from his hotel room—very expensive. This time, Terrell instructed the hotel desk not to enable the telephones. Terrell was uneasy about this tactic. For all his frustrations, he viewed Thomas with awe. "This guy is a patriot," said Terrell. "He's a war hero who defied a government. He inspired hundreds of thousands of people. He's done greater things than I've ever done or probably will ever do. At the end of the day, I've got to give this guy leeway." That night in Jersey, leeway reached its limit. Terrell recalled:

I go to his room, and we get in this argument about the phone calls. Thomas is adamant. He just doesn't want to hear it. And finally, I say, "You know something?" I take the phone and throw it, not at him, but on the floor. "Fucking call whoever you want. I'm out of here. I'm tired of this bullshit."

And he says, "What?"

And so I get on the phone right there, while he's in the room, and I call my mother. "Ma, what's up? Ma, you know, I've been working with these people. Look, Ma, would you mind if I asked y'all, could you come and pick me up? Could you come tomorrow? I've had enough of this shit. I'm sorry, Ma. Sorry I'm cursing. But this is it. I've had enough."

Now, my mother talks kind of loud anyway. So I hold the phone away from my ear, and she says, "That's all right. We are cool. We will take care of you. Just leave them. Leave them right there." And Thomas can hear this.

And I say, "Okay, Ma. Thanks, Ma."

Then I say, "Thomas, I'll call Ken in the morning. He can arrange it, and the bus will take you in. I'm going the other way. I've had enough of you. I've had enough of your authoritarian plans. I'm the fucking tour manager. You don't listen to me. I'm out of here."

"Oh, Tom, you don't have to curse."

"Fuck if I don't."

So, I go back to my room, and one by one, all the members of the band are coming to my room, and telling me, "Thank you. Nobody has ever stood up to Thomas that way before. Thank you. Thank you. Thank you." It's weird. It's like a pilgrimage. The door closes, and the next one comes. Even Charles. He says, "Brother Thomas is difficult, but thank you. Brother Thomas needed to hear this." And then, finally, William comes to my room, and says, "Brother Thomas doesn't want you to leave. And he will not use the phone."

In New York, Island had arranged a photo shoot with Thomas, Burning Spear, and Brinsley Forde, lead singer of the reggae band Aswad. Chris Blackwell was there. He introduced himself to Terrell and thanked him for "the whole thing." A few months later Terrell was hired to work at Island, an unexpected reward for his service.

On balance, Ken Kutsch viewed Thomas's first American tour as an auspicious start. He was particularly proud of the pay structure he had arranged. Percentages were established in three tiers, for Thomas, then the Sekurus—William, Charles, and Chartwell—and then the other musicians. Thomas accepted and honored the deal, and for the first time, his musicians returned from a tour with real money for their families.

Chris Bolton was also pleased with this tour. He loved seeing an artist grow before his eyes, constantly getting new ideas about how to develop the music. Chris agreed with Thomas that too many of the African groups they met in their travels did not "show themselves as Africans." Cameroon's flamboyant Les Tetes Bruleés, with their body paint and hyperactive rhythms, epitomized the "silly" side of Afropop, something Thomas must avoid. "If you've got a platform," said Chris, "you try to use it, and be serious. I don't like all that, 'Put your hands in the air. Everybody say, "Ooo." Everybody say, "Aaah."' It devalues the audience and the artist, and I just think, 'Well, this is *Sesame Street* now.'" For his part, Thomas appreciated Chris's brutish charm. They shared a kind of urban underclass rebelliousness, something that transcended skin color and culture.

In his first interview back in Harare, Thomas gloried in the success of his North American concerts with their five-minute standing ovations and triple encores. He spoke of a "blitz," a "Chimurenga avalanche . . . sweeping the West," and said that *Corruption* had sold twelve thousand copies in the first two weeks. There was no mistaking the mood of pride many felt at Thomas's triumphs abroad. But in this *Sunday Mail* interview, Thomas did sound one sour note. He lamented that so few African Americans had attended the shows. "It's hard to believe but painfully true," he said. "Our fellow men treat our music with contempt and as inferior."[15] Thomas was not alone among African stars making a first foray to the United States and feeling disappointed that, for the most part, their audiences were white. Thomas's message should have appealed to black America amid the rising swell of hip-hop defiance. But its surround of African tradition and spirituality telegraphed something different: a celebration of ancient culture, the solidarity of insiders, not marginalized people. This, perhaps, remained a bridge too far for black America.

Days after the band's return, the Zimbabwean release of *Chamunorwa* hit the market and the *Sunday Mail* declared it "spellbinding . . . addictive." The reviewer said that when he first played the record in his house, it drew an audience of neighbors, and when it ended, "the crowd went haywire."

Chamunorwa, why do you fight?
In the newspapers you scandalize me
You have slapped the lion with your bare hands
You provoked me while I lay asleep

You may rule but as I speak now
Monsters are growing out of the land
You may rule but as I speak now
Thorns are growing out of this soil[16]

R. J. Smith commented in an earlier *Village Voice* piece that the lyrics on *The Chimurenga Singles* felt less like poetry and more like "the things worried families trapped by war might say to comfort each other."[17] The song "Chamunorwa" reveals a more sophisticated poetic mind, as well as ideas that cut deeper than mere charges of official corruption. Thomas offered little insight when interviewed about this song, reducing it to a bland, "let's-all-get-along" message. The words suggest something more portentous, and prescient—dark forces boiling up, unseen "monsters" and "thorns" creeping around the feet of rulers.

Chamunorwa is a near-perfect album. With its preponderance of mbira songs, it marks a new emphasis on the traditional side of Thomas's musical formula. These long, unhurried tracks are the first to approximate the spiritual power of the band's live performances of mbira repertoire. Thomas adapts the mbira song "Nhemamusasa" as "Chitima Nditakure (Train Carry Me)." He described the traditional lyric as reminiscent of blues, the sad saga of an old man going home, tired and broken:

Don't you know in four days I should be gone
O girl you don't know how much I loved you
But I am leaving you because your mother is deadly
She moves around with an owl in her basket
She has a black mamba that cooks meals
While another viper holds the torch
And now I am too old and weak for this dance
But once upon a time I could perform miracles
When I smacked a donkey it laughed[18]

Washington recalled, "Most of the songs on *Chamunorwa*—that's Chartwell. He did the arrangements. Thomas would just bring his voice." Chartwell was certainly a force in the band during this peak creative period, but along with his magnificent "voice," Thomas also brought an expanding vision of the music, as well as his ever more penetrating lyrics, melodic hooks, and brass section passages. Thomas plunged into new songwriting, creating what Chris Bolton called "an immense outpouring of music," significant portions of which were never recorded, or if they were, never released. Live shows were frequent and long, giving the band an edge over others in Harare—for Chris, the same edge the Beatles developed by playing marathon club dates in Hamburg. Chris recalled a band shackled by Thomas's "workaholic" obsession:

> It's power. Mukanya, the baboon. When he's making the music, he's like that. On stage, he wanders around like the big baboon. If they're not doing it right, he'll go up and tell them. And they have to play for so *long*. There's only a dog left, but still you've got to play. Sometimes the people who run the hall will say, "Look, we want to go home. We're not selling any more beer." Thomas will cuss them off and say, "Don't you switch the lights out. I'm not finished yet. It's not five o'clock!" No other band works that hard.

Though prolific and energized, Thomas had difficulty ensuring that the recording and mastering of his work matched the quality of the songs and performances. When he released a twelve-inch single called "The Game Is Over"—a political, English-language reggae rant—the *Sunday Mail* panned it as a halfhearted effort to reprise the success of "Corruption." Vivian Maravanyika, who had lauded *Chamunorwa*, wrote that "Thomas should desist from his habit of producing the records himself."[19] Island Records would go to considerable lengths to upgrade the sound and mix on *Chamunorwa* before releasing it internationally. And Thomas's subsequent Zimbabwean recordings would also suffer from technical shortcomings. In October 1990, Thomas released the immodestly titled *Chimurenga Masterpiece*.[20] Maravanyika praised the album's energy and inventiveness but again assailed its "pathetic" production. Thomas's angry response became news in itself; one fan wrote the *Sunday Mail* cautioning that pique did not become him: "A person of his caliber should not look worried."

Chimurenga Masterpiece is best remembered for the brass-driven dance song "Jojo," which tells the story of a "son of a patriot" and "lover of this land" who is manipulated by politicians and ultimately killed. "Politics is full of graves," sings Thomas, straining for high notes over a thrashing beat. Thomas explained in interviews that "Jojo" delivered a universal message about the world's dirtiest profession, but there is little doubt that this song was inspired by the ZANU-PF regime's long-standing penchant for thuggish intimidation. Thomas knew plenty of poorly educated patriotic young men who had been coaxed into party service and never heard from again. In the *Chimurenga Fan Club Newsletter*, Musa Zimunya wrote about women compelled to "bend down to their knees and weep" when they heard "Jojo." One explained that the song brought up "bitter memories of her brother whom she lost in clashes during the recent national elections."[21]

Thomas's shows lured even urbane audiences to dodgy township venues. "Ah, Mapfumo has got a rough crowd," said Radio 3 DJ Kudzi Marudza. "People take a taxi and tell it to wait, because if you take your car, by the end of the show, the radio is gone." Marudza repeated the urban myth that when Thomas shouted, "Put your hands in the air!" this was a signal to the tsotsis, and "the thieves are busy now." Township desperados needed no help from Thomas; they would work any crowd they could find; his just happened to be among the biggest. Chris Bolton recalled seeing the floor of Mushandira Pamwe littered with wallets at the end of the night.

In 1991, novelist and poet Chenjerai Hove wrote a rhapsodic New Year's Eve reflection on *Chimurenga Masterpiece*, extolling the way its songs reconnect listeners to the precolonial past. "The old men and women," wrote Hove, "listen to Mapfumo's voice and hear their long departed composers who tore the village apart with new passions, new dreams of other lands, new visions. . . . The national spirit of the soil comes back, in the rivers, rocks, hills and caves."[22] Sanctioned by journalists and intellectuals, Thomas could sing about corruption, scarcity, and even political violence with seeming impunity, but as songs like "Chamunorwa" and "Jojo" made increasingly clear, he was now on a collision course with the formidable Mugabe regime.

10 / Sporting Lions

There's no such thing as "making it." There's just more work.
LARRY GOLD, OWNER OF SOB'S

Mbira were not made to rock. They use idiosyncratic tuning systems, and their mode of amplification—the large, severed deze gourd—produces enough sound to fill a hut, not a concert hall. The Blacks Unlimited brought mbira to the stage with help from a craftsman named Chris Mhlanga, a manual laborer and copyright musician who took up mbira in the 1960s and soon began constructing instruments in his Highfield workshop. After independence, students and instructors at the Zimbabwe College of Music became interested in traditional music, and Keith Goddard tapped Mhlanga to provide mbira. When Goddard learned the Blacks Unlimited needed instruments for the stage, he suggested Thomas and Chartwell pay Mhlanga a visit. "That was an astonishment to me," recalled Mhlanga. "But I knew it could happen somehow, because whenever people deal with the culture, they end up here."

Mhlanga carved mbira soundboards from an indigenous tree known locally as *mubvamaropa* (blood wood), "not too hard, not too soft." For each instrument, he forged twenty-two iron keys—slender at the base and flanged on the playing end—expertly gauging thickness, length, and width to produce the correct pitch and a clear tone for each. He affixed the pressure bar, 7¼ inches across, loosely at first, to the top of the soundboard with four eyebolts, then inserted the twenty-two keys in three arrays, the two lower-pitched ones interleaved to the left, and the high-pitched one ascending scalewise to the right. He fine-tuned each note before clamping the pressure bar down to hold the keys firmly in place. He burnished the playing end of each key with sandpaper; the player's hands would do the rest. He drilled and sanded a hole on the lower right side for the player's smallest finger to stabilize the instrument, and attached a tin plate with bottle caps wired to its surface to create the mbira's signature buzz. And now, for the Blacks Unlimited, he placed a contact pickup on the back, seeking the sweet spot where notes would sound more or less evenly when plugged into a guitar amplifier. Future mbira makers would refine the electronics, embedding one or more pickups and a jack into the actual wood. But the essential design of an electric mbira was born in Mhlanga's humble Highfield workshop in Harare.

Ultimately, the Blacks Unlimited would use mbira in three different keys.[1] The players sat in a row at center stage, each with his own amplifier—usually a Roland JC10 Jazz Chorus—placed behind his chair. Although these amps produced plenty of sound, the players continued to wedge their instruments into deze gourds, presenting the look of a bira ceremony. "The sound had changed," recalled Thomas. "The guitar was no longer going to dominate. We actually had a rhythm section—those mbiras. When it's the guitarist's time to take his solo, he comes up a little bit, not very high like he used to do. And we are no longer muting the strings now. We are playing the real sound of the guitar, but well controlled so he is going to allow this rhythm section to flow."

Thomas had long ago sought spiritual permission to perform mbira songs on guitars. Now mbira themselves were taking their place alongside Western electronics, long viewed as anathema to traditional Shona life. "It's good. It's not so good," said mbira master Tute Chigamba. "Young people enjoy that, but for old people, it's a part of driving away our spirits again. Because the sound we hear from the guitars is so loud. Mbira sound is soft, and those spirits, they draw near." Chigamba worried about repertoire as well. With mbira improvising alongside guitars, traditional songs could morph and merge, confusing the spirits and muddling human memory of the past. Mhlanga understood these concerns, but they didn't worry him. Even as he fashioned mbira that could vie with the blare of an electric guitar, he knew that the realm of tradition was sacred. After all, it was he who pronounced: "You will *never* play in a bira ceremony with a guitar."

However, for a period in the early 1990s in Zimbabwe, a bloom of new bands followed Thomas's lead by playing mbira alongside guitars in nightclubs and beer halls—Vadzimba, Ndemera-Ites, Legal Lions, Sweet Melodies, Pio Macheka and the Black Ites, Beauler Dyoko and the Black Souls, Jonah Sithole's reconstructed Deep Horizon, and Ephat Mujuru's Spirit of the People. Traditionalists might object, but these electric mbira bands were doing their best to reach young Zimbabweans who might never attend a ceremony or visit a traditional healer.

On the way home from their first U.S. tour, the Blacks Unlimited stopped in London to play the Forum. At the show, Ken Kutsch met WOMAD festival director Thomas Brooman, who proposed booking Thomas for WOMAD's Music of the Frontline States tour the following summer. These were the flagging days of South African apartheid, and Brooman made a tour of southern Africa, signing up groups from Zambia, Botswana, Mozambique, and Angola. He visited Harare and experienced Thomas in his world. Brooman came away with an understanding that, beyond the stage, Thomas was "a politician . . . the leader of a community . . . an economic engine . . . a guy with huge responsibility." Thomas headlined a series of "Frontline" WOMAD festivals in Europe in 1990.

"It was like the summer of love in the UK that year," recalled Ken. "Everybody was doing Ecstasy." Thomas and the band befriended successful post-punk acts the Stone Roses and Happy Mondays. After hypnotizing the crowd at the Glastonbury Festival, the Zimbabweans were invited to perform at Spike Island, near Liverpool, and then were invited to Finland to play with the Stone Roses. Charles, overjoyed in the midst of this thirty-concert run, told Ken, "Every day feels like Christmas!"

Thomas was receiving the best fees of his career, as Ken recalled, US$8,500 for the most lucrative festival appearances. Brooman was pleased, though he worried that Thomas's managers were "a bit more keen than might have been entirely sensible." Ken and Chris Bolton acted as though they were representing a major rock act, and after that summer, Brooman sensed a chill among promoters in his network. "The thing about this business," said Brooman, "is that if you drive bargains too hard, to a place where it doesn't work for everybody, it isn't going to last. I think promoters felt nailed down to fees that were unrealistically high, and it created rather a heavy atmosphere around Thomas as an artist."

This charmed summer had its snags, including a bust at the Amsterdam airport—not for ganja but for pornography. Washington, the only sober male in the band, was caught with illicit videos. Worse than his treatment by the authorities, Ken recalled, was the tongue-lashing the bass man received from Thomas. In Germany, presenter Jean Trouillet was upset when Thomas tried to wrap his show up after just an hour. "I had to be very, very angry with him," recalled Trouillet. Thomas took it in stride, returning to the stage for two spellbinding hours. Trouillet recalled Kasper König, darling of the German contemporary art scene, standing stageside amazed. The band crossed the Atlantic for two Canadian shows. At a Toronto festival, they met Ry Cooder—then on his way to becoming a major player in crossover music for his Grammy-winning collaborations with Malian guitarist Ali Farka Toure and with the Buena Vista Social Club. Cooder became so engrossed in the Blacks Unlimited's sound that he sought them out personally, falling into conversation with Chartwell. Cooder floated the idea of working together in some way, but, to Ken's exasperation, Thomas showed little interest in pursuing it.

Jerry Rappaport had been unhappy with the recording quality of *Corruption* and had shipped fresh reels of two-inch tape stock to Harare to be used for the new material. "And what did I get back?" he recalled. "A master tape that had probably been recorded on fifteen times." What Rappaport didn't know was that *Chamunorwa* had already been tracked by the time his tape stock reached Harare. The big problem with the *Chamunorwa* recording was Thomas's vocal, which sounded murky and buried in the mix. To remedy this, Ken, Thomas, and Chris remained in London after the WOMAD tour and retracked all of Thomas's singing. Ken described a "bonding experience" at Island Studios, where Bob Marley had recorded, three "brothers" from different worlds sharing ideas as equals.[2] The reworked *Chamunorwa* wonderfully showcases Thomas's voice, its resonant low end enveloping the ear with warmth and portent.

Before leaving London, Thomas bought a used BMW he'd found in *Loot* magazine, and Ken inherited the task of shipping the car to Africa. A week earlier at Gatwick Airport, Ken had seen the band off, "over the moon" with their purchases of appliances, instruments, baby clothes—everything they could carry on an airplane. A BMW, however, struck Ken as an extravagance.

Back in Zimbabwe, Thomas set about upgrading his mbira section. He recruited seventeen-year-old Bezil Makombe of Seke, a rural area known for its musicians. This shy, scarcely educated young man had performed at biras since age eight and could improvise as well as any mbira player the Blacks Unlimited would ever know.[3] With two mbira in the lineup, Thomas began to experiment. He would open his set backed only by mbira and drums, creating a poignant air of ceremony before the full band hit.

In April 1991, Thomas set out on a three-month world tour, most of it booked by Chris Goldsmith of the Falk and Morrow Agency in Solana Beach, California. A rock and blues agent, Goldsmith had seen the band perform only on video and had hesitated at the sight of Thomas crouching by the monitors. "What kind of stage presence does this guy really have?" he wondered. Goldsmith went ahead, reassured that the song "Corruption" had been licensed for the Hollywood film *Bad Influence* with Rob Lowe, and that Island planned to release *Chamunorwa* in advance of the tour. As the shows began in California, Ken sat the band down to explain that if they were willing to make sacrifices—sharing hotel room beds, driving through the night on occasion—there would be more money in their pockets in the end. Ken had hired a dirt-cheap tour bus out of Louisiana, and it came with an easygoing bus driver whose drink of choice was beer mixed with tomato juice and who abided ganja smoking on his bus.[4]

Meanwhile, Polygram had bought Island Records and there was new pressure to show financial results for every artist. Rappaport recalled, "I knew radio was a waste of time. With the exception of NPR and some college radio, it was going to be all about press. Basically, we were making coffee-table records." Sales aside, touring an African band was impractical. It was always: Who can we cut? The horn section? The backup singers? "It wasn't a lot of fun," said Rappaport. "And it's a testament to Thomas that despite all the funkiness on the business side, everybody was still committed to the project."

Island loaned Thomas $15,000. "In the back of my mind," recalled Rappaport, "I always knew that we would not see all that money. But we didn't get *any* of it. They missed the first payment, and Ken didn't even call me. The next thing I know I get called into the office of the president of Island, and he turns to me and says, 'You want to tell me what's going on here?' He hands me a letter that Ken has written asking for my removal from anything to do with Thomas Mapfumo." While in New York for a show at SOB's, Thomas, William, and Ken sat down with Rappaport and his team at Island.[5] Rappaport told Ken he had crossed a line and wondered aloud whether the two could really work together. "It was dicey," said Rappaport. "Toward the end of the meeting, I looked over at Thomas and said, 'Thomas, what do you think?' And Thomas was *asleep*. He opened up his eyes and he looked at me and said, 'Jerry, whatever you want is what I want.'"

Ken too recalled this "Mexican standoff" at Island, though he reported Thomas's quote as: Whatever *Kenny* wants is what I want. "Because we were a great team," said Ken. "I can remember us having chats on the tour bus. It wasn't just a personal thing between me and Jerry. It was *us against them*." Instead of helping Thomas grapple with the realities of the music business, Ken was now feeding the fires of grandiosity, with predictable results. Soon, Blackwell announced that Island was dropping the band, a decision Thomas would later attribute to Ken's "pushing them around." Van Renen compared Ken to a religious fanatic, who "couldn't tell the difference between fantasy and reality. No matter how much you liked Thomas Mapfumo, you just didn't want to deal with Ken anymore. So we said, 'Okay, Ken. Go and make him a big star.'"[6] Van Renen insisted that artistic direction was not the issue. "We weren't trying to change the music," he said. "Blackwell just felt, 'We've got two great records from Thomas. Why do we need more of the same?' I couldn't really argue with that." Nor could Rappaport, though it pained him to let go of such "a special cat."

Thomas's predicament with Gramma in Harare was equally contentious. He was determined to escape Gramma's monopolistic stranglehold. Musa Zimunya managed production and distribution of Thomas's vinyl and cassette inventory, and he found accounting practices at Gramma infuriating. Musa recalled, "They were happy to be wearing their Cross belts and sitting behind those big, oak desks and talking blasé about, 'Well, you know, Thomas is not selling.' *Sneer, sneer.* We used to have such fights. Quarrels! You can't say it isn't accurate, because you don't know how many records they are pressing."

Gramma employees recalled doors closing up and down corridors whenever Thomas paid a visit. The most notorious dustup came when a new album, *Hondo*, was finished and ready for release. Thomas and his posse arrived and confronted a white distribution manager, accusing him of leaving Thomas's albums out of printing runs in a deliberate effort to "sabotage" his career. Chartwell said Thomas threatened the man, brandishing his briefcase as a weapon. Thomas remembered grabbing the terrified manager by the throat: "I wanted to *fight* him." When it was over, Thomas stormed out of the building and headed straight to the office of Dave Smith, owner of Zimbabwe's largest record retail chain, Music Express. Thomas proposed a complete bypass of Gramma and an exclusive distribution deal for *Hondo*, directly from artist to retailer.

Dave Smith had grown up in Rhodesia's white womb, perceiving black music as tuneless noise used to market home furnishings to Africans by the Nyore Nyore franchise. But after independence, Smith had fallen in love with "Nyore Nyore music," saying, "All you've got to do is *listen* to it." Smith built a chain of Music Express stores around the country. He set low prices and switched music sales from 80 percent international and 20 percent local in 1985, to the reverse seven years later.[7] Like Thomas, Smith blamed ZBC for promoting ignorant DJs at Radio 3, while placing any who actually cared about local music at Radio 2, "the *povo* station." The whole music industry was ruled by bureaucrats who considered music a "luxury." It was not, Smith insisted. No matter how expensive clothing and food became, sales of local cassettes and vinyl never faltered in Zimbabwe.

When Thomas "pitched up" in Smith's office, his eyes flashing with rage from his latest tangle with Gramma, Smith recalled, "I looked at this bloody fastball and said, 'Oh, *sheesh*, do I need this in my life?'" Smith told Thomas he could expect no more than 65 percent of the market penetration he'd seen with Gramma. Thomas accepted, viewing the deal as a stopgap while he built up his own distribution enterprise, the Chimurenga Music Company. Chartwell had high hopes for the Chimurenga label and hated the deal with Music Express. Smith struck him as "a *bumbaclot*" (toilet rag), drunk on his own power and incapable of securing the radio play it would take to make a record successful. Smith said he lost money on *Hondo* and conceded that the deal had not served Thomas well either. Thomas never regretted the decision. He had stood up to Gramma and would not be treated so shoddily there again.

The word *hondo* means "war."[8] The title song originated as an improvisation by the band's mbira players and grew through Thomas's customary process of listening and embellishment. In creating a song, Thomas typically begins by working with either a guitarist or an mbira player. As the initial idea emerges, other players join in, either improvising or playing parts Thomas gives them. If parts are improvised, they must meet Thomas's approval—and, as many a Blacks Unlimited veteran will tell you, many do not. As the band plays, Thomas goes from musician to musician, making changes to parts by singing what he wants to hear. In the case of "Hondo," the result of this process is one of the most serenely entrancing songs about war ever created. Thomas's lyrics portray wars as extensions of class struggle where "the poor get killed" and "the rich survive." If this irked some liberation war veterans, "Maiti Kurima Hamubvire (You Once Boasted You Were a Great Farmer)" offered a more pointed critique of the ZANU government, needling the regime on the sensitive subject of land:

How many years have gone by now, my lord
While we awaited the truth of your words?
How many months, respectable one
While we awaited the truth of your promises?
Yet you once boasted farming was easy . . .
Your sermon is just a lot of pipe dreams . . .[9]

More than a decade after the Lancaster House agreement, land reform had stalled. The "willing buyer, willing seller" approach would not transfer farmland from white to black ownership, hence Thomas's reference to a "pipe dream." Zimbabwe's red-hot debate about land lay ahead, but this song took a prescient stand: Mugabe's people were failing to deliver on the central aim of the liberation war.

Hondo marked a move away from the traditional mbira repertoire exploited so successfully on *Chamunorwa*.[10] From this point on, the band would more often use the mbira as a composing tool, creating songs with simplified harmonic structures, like "Hondo," which is built around an ingenious two-phrase (rather than four-phrase) cycle. The other songs on *Hondo* have nothing to do with mbira at all, instead featuring racing, 12/8 grooves, simple three-chord harmony, and thickening layers of vocal, brass, guitar, and keyboards.

The song from *Hondo* that attracted the most attention was "Mukondombera." The word translates as "holocaust" and is the Shona term for AIDS. Unchecked by official action—prevention, treatment, or even education—HIV had infected 25 percent of the country's adult population by the mid-1990s. Zimbabweans hesitate to discuss sex in public, so it is significant that Thomas was among the country's first popular singers to warn about AIDS.[11] His song calls the disease a "plague," from which "we are all perishing." Taking on his avatar as conscience of the clan, Thomas bids "fathers, brothers, and sisters" to "stop your mischief." His characterization of AIDS as a "punishment from God" smacks of evangelist cant, though it also echoes Thomas's familiar rhetoric about the price of abandoning ancestral spirits. In his *On the Beat* column for the *Sunday Mail Magazine*, Tinaye Garande swooned over *Hondo*, singling out "Mukondombera" as "frightening."

Zimbabwean prudery also shaded public opinion on foreign music, especially rumba. Congolese singer Kanda Bongo Man was the top-selling rumba artist in Africa and a superstar in Zimbabwe. Kanda's stage show featured two dancers who invited people on stage to engage in shank-shivering moves—to some observers, nothing short of simulated copulation. Tinaye Garande found such performances "repulsive" and writes in shock of women "jumping on the stage to show a leg" while their husbands cheered them on. "Small girls," continues Garande, "were shaking their small waists and boys gyrated vigorously and I was surprised who could have taught innocent souls such indecent things."[12] Thomas joined this bandwagon. Speaking through Garande's column, he assailed the likes of Kanda Bongo Man as "alien culture without decency" and said, "everything that happens at a rumba show is satanic."[13] A popular cartoon that year lampooned Thomas with the scene of a man running into a party and shouting, "Quick, quick, hide the rumba records—Mukoma [Brother] Thomas Mapfumo is here!" Not yet fifty, Thomas was acquiring a new persona—the stern elder, wagging a finger at errant youth but also, importantly, educating people about AIDS.

Thomas's next single, "Magariro," takes the debate about foreign culture to the metaphysical realm. In this mournful mbira swoon, the singer asks an old man what he is leaving his children now that he has lost his culture.

You are gone with the arrow, like a hunted animal . . .
You said appeasing the spirits was for rural folk.
What do you do now the creator is angered?[14]

Tinaye Garande wrote that "Magariro" was accusing Zimbabweans of be-coming "white people in black skins." He criticized Radio 3 DJ Kudzi Marudza for cutting the song off halfway through on his Hitsville program in order to segue to Salt N Pepa's "Let's Talk about Sex." The paradox was that the same people who danced to Kanda Bongo Man's "Sai," or Leonard Dembo's sungura megahit "Chitekete," or even "Let's Talk about Sex," also danced to "Magariro." Zimbabweans could not resist Thomas's music, even if they disregarded his counsel.

The early 1990s were a time of political paradox as well. Mugabe had ma-nipulated Cold War dynamics, tarring his most potent rival, Joshua Nkomo, with half-true charges of Soviet connections, earning praise in the West and providing cover for his massacres in Matabeleland. After the Unity Accord of 1987, Mugabe saw no need to codify his one-party state with controversial laws. Opposing him was a fool's errand.[15] There had been much to praise in Zimbabwe's first decade. Adult literacy had reached over 90 percent, unprece-dented for an African country. Primary heath care was widely available, and peasant agriculture had reportedly risen 1,400 percent in the first four years after independence.[16] But the government had paid for these achievements by borrowing, or simply printing, more and more money. Economic growth was stalled, inflation crept up steadily, and unemployment rose each year, to reach 26 percent by 1990. Historian David Blair sums it up: "Better educated, healthier Zimbabweans were becoming poorer."

Mugabe was at the height of his popularity when he surprised the world by embracing the International Monetary Fund's economic prescription, the very free-market approach he had resisted all through the 1980s. The Economic Structural Adjustment Program (ESAP) called for austerity—a floating Zim-babwe dollar, lower import tariffs, an end to state controls, and the privatiza-tion of industries. Mugabe as free-market champion amounted to a virtuoso drag performance, barely skin deep, for he implemented few actual reforms. Later, Mugabe would blame ESAP for everything, but for the moment he al-lowed others to snipe, like the reggae singer Man Soul Jah, who sang, "Born in the war, grew up in AIDS, dying under ESAP."[17] Probably the most formi-dable ESAP critic was Morgan Tsvangirai, head of the Zimbabwe Congress of Trade Unions. Tsvangirai accused Mugabe of making the country's workers his "sacrificial lamb," and he was rewarded with a five-week prison stay in

1991 on bogus charges of spying for South Africa, the first of many outrages Tsvangirai would suffer at ZANU-PF hands.[18]

In February 1992, economic worries were swept aside as Zimbabweans absorbed the shock of Sally Mugabe's death from kidney failure. "Amai Sally" had crusaded for the rights of women and children and had been universally loved for it. Mugabe cut a sympathetic figure in mourning. During the wake, he reached out to people from many walks of life, including Thomas Mapfumo. Whatever bitterness Thomas harbored, a presidential invitation could not be ignored. "Orders arrived," recalled Chris Bolton, "and he was gone in a New York minute." A photograph in the *Sunday Mail* shows Thomas dressed in suit and tie, hat in hand, kneeling before Mugabe, whose limp hand rests on his own furrowed brow. The griever in chief's gracefully barbed words to Thomas appear in the accompanying story: "We recognize the greatness of artists who perform not only for profit but for the benefit of humanity. We hope this spirit continues."[19]

"I had never met him," recalled Thomas, acknowledging a certain admiration. "He actually was a good man. He went to Mozambique to lead the liberation struggle. He promised the people freedom, and he actually brought that freedom." Thomas, unlike Mugabe, actually believed in the ESAP reforms. Finance minister Bernard Chidzero, the man charged with making ESAP work, was Thomas's "uncle" and mentor. "I remember meeting him in his office, and he said, 'If people can just abide by the rules of ESAP, this country is going to be rich,'" Thomas recalled.

To an optimist like Thomas, life in the early 1990s looked promising. His career was on the move despite the loss of the Island deal; the Chimurenga Music Company held out the prospect of independence from Zimbabwe's music monopoly; his band was marshaling its status as a national legend and forging new creative ground. The *Hondo* deal with Music Express aside, sales were good, and Thomas's concerts now commanded a door fee of Z$10, before long Z$15, the highest of any act in the country. It was a time to dream, display generosity, and look for ways to give back. That was the spirit in which Thomas began sponsoring a soccer team from Mbare, a group of unemployed boys from the neighborhood who had begged him to take them under his wing. Soccer was on par with religion for Thomas and his brothers, and during the band's 1991 travels, the subject of these boys in Mbare had dominated conversation during their bantering, tour-bus card games.

At the card table, the players had nicknames, and Thomas's was "Sporting Lion." Somewhere in Europe, as the spliffs burned and the cards went down, something clicked, and not long after the band got home, a *Sunday Mail* headline gave fans a jolt: "Mapfumo Forms Soccer Club." "Some years ago," writes Tinaye Garande, "Elton John bought Watford Football Club in a trail-blazing move. Now, Zimbabwe's Thomas Mapfumo is building his own club, Sporting Lions, on the cheap."[20] Thomas romanticized his players as "natural footballers" whom he could save from becoming "thieves like their unemployed friends." The team's showing in friendly matches soon earned it a shot at a franchise in the third of Zimbabwe's six professional divisions. Thomas purchased the team for Z$25,000, and the Sporting Lions took to the field. Money shortages were an impediment from the start. "Mugabe likes cricket," Thomas groused, noting the lack of state support for his game of choice.

Thomas devised a plan to keep the Sporting Lions franchise afloat; every Sunday afternoon the Blacks Unlimited would play an afternoon concert to benefit the team. From the start, Thomas treated his soccer players better than his musicians, something that would inevitably lead to tensions. Thomas's daughter Chiedza recalls the team visiting the house in Mabelreign, whereas the band—with the exception of Chartwell—was something "totally separate." Athletes working for a better life made more suitable company for Thomas's wife and children than hardscrabble musicians from Mbare and Chitungwiza, for the Mapfumo home was a warm, wholesome place. Chiedza remembers Thomas as a playful father. She recalled, "He had a rifle, and I had this toy gun. And he wore his hat, and I would wear my hat. There's a picture where we're both wearing our hats and aiming our guns." In the picture, which hung in the Mabelreign house as part of a framed montage of family scenes, it looks as though the two are on safari in the living room. Chiedza, with her rifle and hunting hat, can't be more than four at the time.

"He was the less strict parent," said Chiedza, "easygoing, and very generous with allowances. My mom was the strict one. Me and my brother, if we did anything wrong, we knew we wouldn't get into as much trouble if we told *him* first." Chiedza and her brother saw more of Vena's family than Thomas's. The exceptions were Uncle Lancelot and her grandfather John Mapfumo, who lived with Lancelot, his wife, Florence, and their daughters in Mbare. Chiedza was particularly fond of her grandfather, a kindly, loving presence always, and she fondly recalled those visits to Mbare.

Lancelot was also well remembered, playful like Thomas, fond of a joke, perhaps a little hapless. A favorite story for Thomas was the time the band played the Everly Hotel in Bulawayo sometime in the mid-1980s. Lancelot had had quite a bit to drink at the show. He was sharing a hotel room, and a bed, with Douglas the doorman. The bathroom was out in a hallway, and on returning from a visit there, Lancelot mistakenly returned to the wrong room and slipped into bed alongside a strange woman. "Douglas has a light complexion," Thomas explained with a twinkle. "This woman *also* has a light complexion. Lancelot thinks this is Douglas. He gets in bed!" The woman's husband soon returned, and pandemonium ensued.

Although Thomas kept his bandmates at a distance from his wife and children, it was important to him to have his brothers, and his uncle Jira, prominent in his musical life. No doubt there was a business strategy behind this; he trusted his own blood. But also, he deeply enjoyed having family around. No Blacks Unlimited concert was complete without the spectacle of Thomas, William, and Lancelot, telling stories and laughing like schoolboys during band breaks.

The Blacks Unlimited's 1992 world tour opened with summer dates in the United States—including a show at New York's Central Park Summerstage, a side trip to Maui for gigs at a posh resort, and two California festivals, at one of which the young mbira player Bezil Makombe was initiated into a new world of pleasure when he was dragged into a muddy swimming hole by a naked hippie girl.[21] With Island out of the picture, Ken Kutsch struggled to meet the budget, calling in favors and cutting corners. Ron, the Louisiana bus driver, had acquired a crack habit since the last tour. After one Illinois gig, he left the band at their hotel and headed off with a friend to look for drugs. As they approached the home of a potential dealer, the door swung open and a shot rang out, lodging a bullet in the friend's leg. Somehow the police did not get involved, and the tour continued, but easygoing Ron was now a worry.

In San Francisco, the band encountered the Kronos Quartet, then promoting its 1992 *Pieces of Africa* CD, a set of collaborations with African composers.[22] Kronos's David Harrington had proclaimed Thomas one of his favorite musicians and, after attending a show, expressed a desire to collaborate. The unlikely pairing of chimurenga and chamber music actually occurred, just once, in a London concert that fall. Ken found the performance "loose around the edges," but hopeful. He pushed for a joint recording, but it was not to be, said Ken, due to a lack of "commitment from Thomas."

From his new base in London, Ken had been negotiating a deal with WEA Sound Wave in Los Angeles to release songs from *Chimurenga Masterpiece* and *Hondo*. When the deal collapsed, Thomas blamed WEA for promising money and not sending it. "This guy had no money," said Thomas, "and he was a *liar*." Ken told a more tangled tale involving lawyers to whom Thomas owed money.[23] Thomas proposed dividing the WEA advance between himself, Ken, and the Sekurus, with nothing for the lawyers or other band members. Ken thought this "unethical" and objected, effectively falling on his sword by informing the lawyers of Thomas's plan. "The law firms put up a lien on WEA," said Ken. "They called up and said, 'If you do this deal, there are going to be problems.'"[24]

This was the end of the chimurenga road for Ken. On top of the WEA fiasco, Thomas had abandoned Ken's payment policy for the band, and three years after he first heard Thomas's voice booming moral clarity from a radio in New York City, Ken had a "bad taste" in his mouth. He left disorder and bitterness in his wake at the end of 1992. Chris Bolton called him a "New York hustler" who should have been fired long ago.[25] "Kenny was a good manager," recalled Thomas, "but at the same time, he was a *crook*." Thomas believed Ken had taken two $45,000 payments from Island and never paid him "any cent" of it.[26] "I complained to him," said Thomas. "'Where is all this money going to?' He was telling me about expenses and things like that. Well, with me, it didn't go down very well."[27] Ken insisted he had abided by his contract, taking 20 percent and nothing more.

Chartwell alone defended Ken, crediting him with brilliant tours, putting Thomas on the front page of the *Guardian* and booking the band's first gigs in Japan. "That period was the best," said Chartwell. "I was paid eight hundred pounds after a two-month tour. To get that, it took Ken Kutsch." Whether a fantasist, a crook, a champion of the little guy, a sharp-elbowed hustler, or an innocent victim, Ken had shepherded the Blacks Unlimited through a period of remarkable expansion in the early 1990s. The task of maintaining that momentum now fell to people with more modest talents and ambitions.

Bob Diener, the band's Illinois angel, offered a guerrilla-style workaround for releasing music in the United States. He would manufacture CD copies of *Hondo* to sell during tours. *Hondo*—with fiery artwork by Saki Mafundikwa—would be the first Zimbob release and would inaugurate Thomas's adventure with small, independent—even homemade—record labels. If Island had been making "coffee-table records," these releases would amount to little more than vanity pressings. When sales numbers came in, Thomas would be no happier than he had been in league with the devils of industry. Bob had begun visiting the band in Harare, staying in Thomas's house and entering a fateful love affair with the country. He helped Thomas buy a used Mitsubishi in Champaign and shipped it to Zimbabwe. He invested in materials to stock a video rental, music, and variety store Thomas and Vena were setting up in Harare—T'n'V Music Sales and Video Hire. Even before *Hondo* came out, Bob said he had already loaned Thomas US$20,000.[28]

After the 1992 tour, Thomas got to work on a new album, *Chimurenga International*.[29] The recording incorporates guitar work by Ashton "Sugar"

Chiweshe, the ebullient policeman musician who was in every way Ephraim Karimaura's opposite. Where Ephraim played taut, rhythmically precise lines deeply married to mbira rhythms, Sugar painted in bold strokes, riding over the beat with surging rock lyricism.

Musa Zimunya studied the shifting lineup. He was pleased to see Charles back on bass guitar. Charles was "passionate," though perhaps too studied, lacking "that fine integration of movement and feeling" that Washington had displayed.[30] As for the guitarists, Musa's gold standard remained Sithole, who "made you listen with your heart." Musa liked Ephraim, who had no need to move his body, because "his mind is working on the guitar." Sugar, on the other hand, was a showman. "He's turning his head like a blues guitarist," said Musa, "like B. B. King. He looks soulful for certain members of the crowd after a few drinks. But just when he thinks he's playing the most exciting stuff, suddenly he is missing his notes, and you hear this jarring *rrrrriff* in the melody."

These were the glory days for Chris Bolton as Thomas's sound man. Black smoke billowed from his Volkswagen Beetle as he made his way to and from Mapfumo gigs around Harare. "Looks like one of the Kuwaiti oilfields that got away," Chris quipped, adding, "I am actually a supporter of Greenpeace. It's just that my rings have gone." At shows, Chris handled sound, worked the crowd, maybe found a pretty African girl to seduce. He socialized with Thomas and the guys, collected his pay, and went home to his Ndebele wife. On the way, near dawn, Chris might stop at Baker's Inn downtown, a normal fast-food franchise except that if you asked the right clerk for "the special," you would receive a French fries bag filled with marijuana.

When the Blacks Unlimited played their first concert in Bulawayo in almost five years, a reviewer noted that whites, blacks, Shona, and Ndebele came together in an unusual way. It was a step toward reconciliation after Thomas's ups and downs with the Ndebele audience in Matabeleland. Now Thomas's stock was rising in all rebel camps, for he had shown he could make direct assaults on Mugabe and his corrupt ministers—the *chefs*—and survive. In January 1993, Thomas's face peered from the cover of *Southern Africa Monthly* under the headline "Thomas Mapfumo: A Cultural Ambassador?" The accompanying article by music journalist Fred Zindi puzzles over Thomas's contradictions: the singer believed that Zimbabweans were being punished by angry ancestors, but how could this be reconciled with foreign tours, the Kronos Quartet, and exposing, writes Zindi, "our musical heritage and culture to Western audiences who will probably steal ideas from it and use them to their own advantage?"[31]

Thomas confronted an ever more crowded field in Zimbabwe's music market. Sungura star Leonard Dembo, with eight albums, was the top seller—"what the music industry is all about these days," one journalist wrote.[32] Gospel music was also ascendant, in grim lockstep with the mounting hardships of drought, disease, and economic stagnation. The new crop of electric mbira bands flourished creatively but sold few records. Forever tarred with the charge of imitating Thomas, they could never gain traction and establish mbira pop as a viable genre. Pio Macheka and the Black Ites came closest to success, but Macheka too faltered after a few albums. By the mid-1990s, his career in decline, the once-dreadlocked singer turned up bald, claiming he had been abducted along the roadside and forcibly shorn, supposedly by a gang of Mapfumo doormen. Thomas never dignified this story with a rebuttal, and it later came out that Macheka had cut his own locks to please the family of a woman he hoped to marry.[33] His feint failed as a publicity stunt, but lived on as urban myth, still believed by many.

All this rough-and-tumble enhanced Thomas's graybeard grandeur. He had introduced his Chimurenga Music Company as a vehicle for promoting young artists he liked, and expressed hopes that some of these would eventually surpass him. But when no protégés emerged, some accused Thomas of undermining the new mbira bands. Thomas's public comments probably reinforced this impression. "Everyone is just following his nose," he scolded. "You don't just become a footballer if you are not a footballer, so we must be very careful of people who mislead the nation trying to turn themselves into musicians. They won't last long because this road is full of gravel. It's a hard road. We are like guerrillas. If you are not strong, we will leave you on the way." This was hardly nurturing. Nor was it the cause of any band's demise. The media and public never embraced the new mbira groups because their music ran counter to the rushing tide of Zimbabwean popular culture, ever more infatuated with foreign ideas and influences. Thomas's success was an anomaly. Its persistence now had less to do with his use of mbira, or any other Zimbabwean traditional music, than with the sustained force of his songwriting, especially his trenchant lyrics.

On the international front, the opposite held true. Words meant little; sound was everything, and for Thomas, the mbira has a huge draw. The only Zimbabwean band to rival Thomas's success in the global domain had been the Bhundu Boys. From their base in Scotland, the mighty Bhundus had swept through the United Kingdom and out to the world on the strength of two barn-burner records.[34] But they faltered when they gave in to pressure and sang in English on a third album, *True Jit*. The release fell flat with lyrical banalities about "jit jive in the bhundu" and "foolish" love. English spoiled the mystery. The Bhundu Boys might groove and croon like the Beatles, but in the heyday of reggae and punk their words lacked edge and, once understood, disappointed Western fans.

More devastating still, the Bhundu Boys' lead singer and guitarist, Biggie Tembo, had become unstable, rejecting the perks of international touring life on moral grounds, while at the same time demanding star billing. Biggie had physically attacked his Scottish benefactor, Gordon Muir, and in 1989 left the band outright, reportedly saying, "I quit. Fuck the lot of you."[35] Chris Bolton, who had done business with Biggie, recalled him "getting funny." Chris said, "Biggie went into Christianity as well, which is always a sign of madness, I think." Biggie became a gospel singer, and the Bhundu Boys went on without him. Then bass player David Mankaba became the first Zimbabwean musician to publicly acknowledge having AIDS, shortly before he died in June 1991. Shepherd Munyama, of Blacks Unlimited fame, stepped in, but when both he and keyboard player Shakespeare Kangwana also died, reportedly from AIDS, in 1993, the Bhundu Boys lay in ruins.

In May 1993, Thomas played a double bill with Manu Dibango of Cameroon at Harare's gleaming new convention center. The union of the respective "Lions" of Zimbabwe and Cameroon kept Thomas in the headlines for a month, and soon afterward, he played his first ever concerts in South Africa—a significant event for Zimbabweans. The behemoth to the south was shaking off the vestiges of apartheid, having miraculously avoided civil war and freed Nelson Mandela. Two shows at the Tandoori Theatre in Johannesburg sold out, and the band moved on to a festival in Grahamstown, a midsize university hamlet in the Eastern Cape, and site of the International Library of African Music—repository, as it happens, of some of the world's oldest mbira recordings.

Despite Grahamstown's air of enlightenment, the local police were unaccustomed to the sight of dreadlocked musicians walking their quiet streets. Acting on a tip, officers mounted a search of the band's villa. As the police were about to leave, an officer caught sight of Sugar, nervously hovering by a bedroom door. Perhaps some unspoken policeman-to-policeman code triggered suspicion, for when they searched that room, they found the band's ganja supply. They also found money in Thomas's briefcase—payment for the Tandoori gigs—and concluded he must be a drug dealer. To the embarrassment of festival organizers, the musicians were forced to remain in town and face this charge in a courtroom. "A very beautiful woman lawyer," Thomas recalled, defended them ably, and in the end the magistrate dismissed the charges and reprimanded the police for treating visitors so inhospitably. Thomas credited his guardian ancestors, perhaps with reason, for his resilience seemed to know no limit.

Thomas began his fourth U.S. tour that summer with one of his strongest lineups ever—Chartwell and Bezil on mbira; Ephraim and Sugar on guitars; Charles on bass; Lancelot on keyboard and congas; Everson on trumpet; Canaan Kamoyo on trombone; and Tendai and Kudzai reunited as backup singers and dancers.[36] When they arrived in New York, Bob Diener greeted them driving a car loaded down with mbira commissioned from Chris Mhlanga and boxes of *Hondo* CDs to sell at the shows. The band had no established record label or international management—a nerve-wracking scenario for booking agent Chris Goldsmith, who adored Thomas but had his hands full touring more commercial acts.

Thomas and Bob had business to settle. They had agreed on a $5,000 advance for the U.S. release of *Hondo*, but when the tour reached California, and Bob pressed for a signed contract, Thomas named a different figure: $20,000. Bob stood up and said, "Well, that's it then. I'm going home." Bob recalled Charles "jumping up with a face that was just: *no, no, no.* And then Thomas meekly adding, 'Uh . . . Zimbabwe dollars,'" which were valued four to one against the U.S. currency at the time, returning the debt to the expected $5,000.

Saki Mafundikwa created artwork for two of Thomas's three Zimbob releases, *Hondo* and later *Chimurenga International* (retitled *Vanhu Vatema,* or "Black People" for its U.S. release). Saki was now close to the band. He had filmed them at New York's Central Park Summerstage and at the swanky Harare Sheraton with Zimbabwean government ministers dancing in the crowd. Filming a rehearsal at Club Hideout, Saki had observed Thomas giving musicians their parts and understood for the first time his centrality to the band's evolving sound. So much of what everyone played came directly from Thomas's head. "The music was magic," recalled Saki,

> but the musicians were unhappy. I met them at a show in San Diego at this club, the Belly Up. Everybody saw the relationship between me and Thomas, and they would just come to me and say, "Please talk to him." There was something that was going on with the money, and the girls felt they were not being respected, so I brought everybody together. I actually said, "Mukanya, I want to talk to you. There are problems in the band. Let's try to solve them." And we had a powwow, but Thomas just brushed the stuff off. He wasn't really someone to deal with issues.

Ephraim was sick. He had lost weight after a painful bout with shingles. As the band approached New York for one last show at SOB's, he became too ill to perform and had to go home. Saki drove him to JFK Airport. The band had dined at Saki's Brooklyn home the night before, and Ephraim, shirtless, bone-thin, and sweating profusely, had conceded he was suffering from tuberculosis. On the way to the airport, the guitarist seemed to revive, reminiscing about the Blacks Unlimited guitarists he had known, clearly proud of the way he had come from nowhere to earn a place among them. Ephraim had no ticket or reservation, and Saki had to fight to get him on a plane. At the gate, the two embraced, and Saki knew he would never see the guitarist again. The band moved on to a gig in London, and before they got back to Harare just days later, Ephraim was dead. The official cause was "immune deficiency and tuberculosis," but when my obituary for him in *Beat* magazine suggested the true cause was AIDS, Ephraim's wife responded with a heartbreaking letter saying, first, that the clothing Ephraim had mailed to her from America had been claimed, along with everything else, by Ephraim's relatives, leaving her nothing—and also that her husband had *not* died of AIDS.

Ephraim was not the first of Thomas's guitarists to die young. In 1990, Leonard "Pickett" Chiyangwa—whose forceful guitar work had gilded some of the most important "chimurenga singles"—had quietly slipped away. Such deaths had been an early, scarcely noticed harbinger of the AIDS menace. Soon, so many Zimbabwean and Congolese musicians were turning up in obituary pages at young ages that international journalists began to take note. Neil Strauss from the *Village Voice* spoke with Ephat Mujuru for a piece headlined "Plague of Silence," a survey of deceased African musicians. Ephat was outraged by the premise. "Whenever there's a health problem," he protested, "Westerners always point to Africa. They think we don't know anything about AIDS. They want to say African people are loose people. It's very exaggerated."[37] But it was no exaggeration to say that Zimbabweans were dying of AIDS, and too many of their countrymen were in denial. Strauss cited euphemisms such as "slimmers disease" or "a bad bottle of beer"—anything but acknowledge the possibility that a loved one had died of AIDS.[38]

When Tinaye Garande published his review of *Chimurenga International*, he made no mention of Ephraim's passing. For him, the story was the fact that this release had been delayed while Thomas patched up his distribution deal with Gramma Records. Garande called the new music "worth the wait," and it was. The session's three mbira adaptations easily outclassed the era's aspiring mbira bands. Bezil Makombe's older brother Ngoni had joined the band on mbira, adding strength in this key area. In a township jazz-inspired number, "Ndinofarira Zimbabwe (I Love Zimbabwe)," Thomas reassures fans that no amount of touring will make him "sell out" Zimbabwe, "home sweet home." The album is barbed with messages of wounded patriotism, as in "Vanhu Vatema (Black People)," which says, "Self-seeking rule has ruined us / Nepotism has ruined us / Ignorance has ruined us / Oh, black people!"

Chimurenga International appealed to poet intellectuals, disenfranchised workers feeling the pinch of ESAP, and families burdened with the shame and loss of disease-stricken loved ones. Its songs fed the slow simmer of dis- enchantment building in Zimbabwe, but in his review, Garande treats the politics gingerly. Commenting on "Amai Vemwana," he writes, "Lyrics like 'Mr. Headman you have failed to rule us' could be misconstrued to mean something more sinister and yet they are well intended, however critical." Garande brushes off Thomas's rhetorical excesses by allowing that "militant" lyrics and "hard-hitting social commentary" are "as synonymous with Map- fumo as his dreadlocks."[39]

Ephraim Karimaura had come to the band as a neophyte who had to be taught everything. He departed as a player whose shoes would be hard to fill. "We had very few guys who could play this type of music," recalled Thomas. One of those was Joshua Dube. Dube was playing in the band of mbira mae- stro Ephat Mujuru, and he was loyal, but his earnings there were insufficient for a married man with a house, an ailing wife, and a son to look after. Over the years, Dube had resisted Thomas's proxies who visited from time to time to see if he might return. When Thomas's emissary arrived this time, Dube again demurred, laying low for a few days in the hope that some hungrier guitarist would surface.

One night as the band was getting ready to start up at the Nyamutamba Hotel, Sugar was nowhere to be found. Dube recalled, "Thomas sent William to my place." Broke at the time, and faced with Thomas's most persuasive recruiter, Dube agreed to play as a temporary solution. He took the stage with the Blacks Unlimited for the first time in more than ten years. At the end of the night, Thomas paid him Z$400. Dube recalled, "Thomas said to me, 'Josh, please, you must come back to the band. Look at what these people are doing to me.' So I said, 'Okay, I will come.'" For the third and final time, Dube became Thomas's lead guitarist.

Thomas also shook up his stage show by introducing the Mudeka sisters, Anna, Patience, and Mutsa. The Mudekas' unveiling at a Christmas Eve show in 1993 at Mushandira Pamwe delighted fans with a flurry of sharp new dance routines. Memories vary. Tendai recalled returning late from a trip to Zambia and getting ready to take the stage with the band only to find "three ladies" already on stage. She feared "they were going to chase me like a dog." Bob Diener, newly arrived for his third stay in Zimbabwe, recalled Tendai and another singer-dancer being asked to step aside after the first set while the Mudekas finished the show. "There was all this uproar," said Bob, "and Tendai was running to me and saying, 'Thomas is firing us. Thomas is firing us.'" The Mudekas were fine dancers, though Thomas was never fully satisfied with their vocal sound. Like their predecessors, the sisters soon found that adulation on the stage came as a package with hard work and low pay. The Mudekas' run proved exhilarating but brief. Patience left first, joining Bob in Champaign, where they were married in August 1994—a development that Thomas had keenly predicted from the moment the Illinois entrepreneur laid eyes on the singing, dancing Mudekas.

By that time, bigger dramas were rocking the Blacks Unlimited. In May, Sabastian Mbata, the band's sterling drummer had died at home in Mbare. Tinaye Garande noted the appearance of a new drummer, Sam Mukanga, at the Heroes Day gig that summer but made no mention of the veteran he was replacing. Heroes died in wars, not from sickness. Meanwhile, Chartwell, arguably the backbone of the band for seven years, was weighing his options. The deaths of so many musicians had shaken him. Chartwell had been in-vited to participate in a British Arts Council stage production in England, *Strong Winds*, along with the mbira maker Chris Mhlanga. As the date drew near, Chartwell made a plan to stay in England afterward to study sound engineering.

Chartwell no longer believed in the dreams he and Thomas had nurtured. Along with Charles and William, they had signed papers and agreed on titles and responsibilities in the Chimurenga Music Company. "Thomas had to put percentages to people," recalled Chartwell. "That was hard for him, to make a decision like that." But four years had passed, and nothing had progressed. "All these record companies have benefited," said Chartwell, "but not even one of my children is going to benefit from what I did." As Chartwell saw it, the band was Thomas's third priority, after the Sporting Lions and T'n'V retail store. Washington, Everson, and Joshua Dube also spoke of jealousies between the band and the team. The soccer players traveled in a bus, while musicians rode emergency taxis. Thomas invested in new uniforms for players but not for musicians. He threw a year-end party for his team but not for his band. And still, the musicians were asked to play gigs to support the Sporting Lions. What had begun as an act of charity now felt like exploitation. For Chartwell, it was finally too much:

> It was sad to see that the money we were working for at the weekend was to pay for the football players. I indicated that to Charles. I think he didn't

have the control to say anything because there was always William. And there was Jira. It's the relatives who come into the business that really made me want to leave the Blacks Unlimited. I'm not saying that I should have money like Thomas. He made his name. He made his history. I respect that. But someone is in Mabelreign having a house with an electric gate and two cars. Someone is in Highfield, living in a ghetto, in a house that doesn't even have a fence. I told him, "I'm going to go." He understood. But nobody took it seriously.[40]

Chartwell left for England as promised, not to return for seventeen years. His departure went unnoticed by the local press, though in November 1993 the *Sunday Mail* did run a splashy story dispelling a rumor that Thomas had been stabbed to death after a show. A telephone call to Vena put that notion to rest; Thomas once again proved himself a survivor. But he had lost a lot that year, including his U.S. booking agent, Chris Goldsmith. The Lion of Zimbabwe would spend most of the next four years at home in Zimbabwe, rebuilding once again.

> There is God the almighty, but then there are also smaller gods,
> and these are our ancestors. We must honor them and talk to
> them all.
> THOMAS MAPFUMO

One more death shook the Blacks Unlimited in 1994. On August 31, Thomas's beloved friend and favorite bass player, Charles Makokowa, succumbed to kidney injuries he had suffered years earlier from a drunken soldier's rifle butt. Many deaths had reshaped Thomas's band, but this was personal. Thomas had discovered his true power as a songwriter in Charles's group, the Acid Band. He and Charles had huddled around a shortwave radio listening to the Voice of Zimbabwe during the war and made the trip to Wedza together to meet the guerrillas. They were as close as brothers; they were soul mates and confidants, and afterward, friends of the band would say that Charles had been the only musician—maybe the only person—able to talk Thomas out of an ill-considered idea.

Allan Mwale, the bass player Thomas worked with in the Springfields, had joined the Blacks Unlimited a couple of years earlier, taking up the bass when Charles played keyboards, and spelling him during the long live shows. As Charles had grown weak, he had spent time coaching Allan on repertoire and on the fine art of creating mbira bass lines. Allan recalled his mystification when he first studied Charles's unique style: "I said, 'Where did you get this bass from?' He said, 'Listen to the mbira.' Sure enough, the notes were there." Charles had pioneered a modern tradition, one imitated and extended by subsequent generations of bass players in Zimbabwe. Now Allan became its inheritor and standard-bearer, and while he would never match Charles as an innovator, he played with an almost brute forcefulness that belied his elfin physique.

Allan assumed Charles's place in the band, but not in Thomas's inner circle. Allan never touched a spliff. Gin and Lion Lager were his vices, and he had an astonishing capacity for both. This allied him with Bezil, whose appetite for alcohol was also prodigious. Bezil and Allan were always at play—the mischievous boy and his irritable uncle. Bezil needled Allan with the nickname Saidi—their private code for "short," and a surefire provocation.[1] Ngoni, a teetotaler, completed this comic trio as straight man, with a gift for physical humor. On stage, in the midst of music, Ngoni would suddenly hoist a knee in the air and look up in shock, as if that knee had become possessed by a spirit and was acting on its own. Allan would laugh, then become similarly stricken, and the two would raise knees and trade worried glances like mimes while Bezil scowled disapprovingly. Shenanigans aside, these three connected musically. Their mbira and bass were the engine—fueled by shared blood and alcohol—that powered the Blacks Unlimited through the late 1990s.

In the spring of 1995, as the band was touring in Europe, Saki Mafundikwa telephoned with an idea. Thomas had no agent, manager, or record label in the United States, but he had fans. Saki proposed a bare-bones, "unplugged" tour—Thomas performing with *only* mbira and hosho. Saki offered to fly Thomas, Ngoni, Bezil, and Lancelot over from London for a limited set of shows. He would invest up front and be reimbursed from tour proceeds. Thomas agreed, but as Saki made arrangements, Thomas kept calling from the United Kingdom to revise the plan, insisting, first, on drums and then, a week later, on bass.

"Then it's no longer *unplugged*," said an exasperated Saki. "Are you aware of that?" Thomas said he was, but: "No bass, no tour."

Saki rebranded the tour as Thomas's fiftieth birthday celebration. SOB's signed on for the first show. Saki reached out to friends of the band and got help with visas and bookings. Mai Chi Maraire—Dumisani's ex-wife—offered to organize shows in hired halls in the Pacific Northwest. This tour would not be strictly unplugged, but it would present the sparest band Thomas had ever staged.

In a matter of weeks, Saki had become a tour promoter, and one with much to learn. Three airplane tickets had now become six, as Thomas insisted on Chris Bolton as soundman. When SOB's made the advance available on the morning of the first show, Thomas and Chris swung by the New York club to collect it, using the cash to book themselves into a hotel, rather than the private home Saki had arranged. Thomas rejected the van Saki had rented for the trip to Ithaca, insisting on a spacious car instead. Bills were mounting, and the tour had just begun.

After the show in Boston, word arrived that the Seattle promoter was reneging on his offer to fly the musicians west. The only way to continue was to rent a van and drive. But a second driver would be needed, and that honor fell to me.[2] Throughout the eight-thousand-mile, round-trip journey that followed, Thomas sat in the passenger seat, sleeping, smoking, telling stories and laughing, controlling the radio and cassette machine with an iron hand, or just turning the radio off and singing. As the van approached Rochester in early morning light, Thomas crooned Bobby Darin's "Beyond the Sea": *If I could fly like birds on high, then straight to her arms I'd go sailin' . . .*

Far from the social and professional support of home and surrounded by musicians with whom he was not close, Thomas seemed exposed, lonely, perhaps still grieving. A big moon hovered low, and the sloped backs of the Alleghenies emerged from the mist, like huge, slow creatures feeding in a steamy swamp. A heat wave was searing the nation. The death toll in Detroit and Chicago had reached eighteen and would soon top one hundred. Eight people in a van could not hope to stay cool. Crammed in among instruments and merchandise, Bezil, Allan, Ngoni, and Sam languished, shirtless and half sleeping, cheek by jowl in the backseats. "We are soldiers," sighed Thomas, drawing on war memories to steel the band for another rough passage. After nearly twenty-four hours, he at last called for a rest.

The van pulled up at a Holiday Inn outside South Bend, Indiana. In the blessed cool of the motel lobby, Thomas surrendered two soggy hundred-dollar bills as though they were the last things he owned. Chris asked the desk clerk if the sauna was open. When she gazed back in disbelief, he waved his hand. "Never mind, dear," he said politely. "I'll just go outside." Chris shared with Bezil—as he once had with Chartwell—a deep habit of humor; between them, play was everything. As the musicians unloaded, Chris instructed Bezil, "Now, you go down to that parking lot. You'll find Hugh Grant there. We told him we were sending him a nice black girl, but being Hugh Grant and a bit fuzzy, he probably won't notice. Make sure he *pays* you."

Chris worked hard to lighten the mood. But once back on the road, he and Thomas bickered more than laughed—over when to stop, what to eat, and other small matters. The musicians, tired and apprehensive, kept to themselves. There were no card games, and fewer boisterous reminiscences of the old days. When Thomas lit up, he mostly smoked alone, and music was his pleasure. He might wheeze out a rendition of "Purple Haze," break into an excoriation of dance hall and rap ("I'm of the opinion that people must *sing*") or lavish praise on some bygone rocker, like Ian Anderson of Jethro Tull ("That was the time when rock music was good"). The band detoured briefly to visit Mount Rushmore. The monument appeared smaller than they had imagined, and the instant they laid eyes on it, Thomas announced, "We have seen it. Let's go. Anyway, I don't see why we should be carving the faces of presidents into a rock."

In Alberton, Montana, Thomas called his wife in Zimbabwe and returned jubilant with news that the Sporting Lions' new "striker" had scored five goals and led the team to a key victory. The team was now within a few games of promotion to Division One, a coveted prize. The news was a welcome boost. Back home, Thomas had earned a reputation for challenging referees during matches, even taking to the field to protest calls. Despite some notorious incidents, he insisted the referees respected him: *Mukanya is a bit cheeky, but he is a nice man.* "You know why they like me?" boomed Thomas in a burst of enthusiasm. "Because my team is well dressed. They always look smart." The same could not be said for his four musicians as they marathoned through punishing heat.

The American road evoked memories of Bob Diener, Thomas's former angel, and now a disappointment—mostly over money, but also Bob's marriage to Patience Mudeka. "I have never shot a man," muttered Thomas, "but I would shoot Bob. I will get out my 9-millimeter and that will be the end of his story." Menacing words, leavened with a smile, were but the lingering bravado of Thomas's ghetto youth. When it came to someone closer, "our brother Chartwell," Thomas spoke more personally, and more gravely.

"Chartwell killed Charlie," Thomas declared, his voice heavy with sadness. "Yes, Chartwell and his wife. They poisoned Charles. Chartwell is a *witch*." This notion went back to the time when Chartwell and his first wife, Linda, had lived at the house in Mabelreign. Vena had been haunted by dreams from which she would awaken in tears. The Mapfumos had concluded that Linda was causing these dreams and had asked the couple to leave. Later, when Charles died and Chartwell did not call Thomas to offer condolences, Thomas deduced that Chartwell—not drunken soldiers—had been his friend's true killer.

In a modest apartment he rented in London in the late 1990s, Chartwell reacted to this charge. He did not share Thomas's view of Christianity as a religion that could be seamlessly blended with Shona beliefs. Chartwell had never forgotten that his birth name, Shorayi, was stripped from him by Christian missionaries and replaced with the name of Winston Churchill's summer home. Chartwell believed in ancestors but doubted that humans could wield magic, as in the outlandish stories that fill the pages of Zimbabwe's Shona-language tabloids. "Imagine if we really had magic in Zimbabwe," mused Chartwell. "We could have killed Smith and his bloody army. Why did thousands of people have to die with guns if we have got magic? If I had magic, I would use it to make things work. Why do I kill Charles? If I wanted to kill anybody, I would kill *Thomas*, because he owes me a lot." For Chartwell, Thomas was a man mired in his own misdeeds, creeping into madness like an African King Lear, his wild accusations "the last kicks of a dying horse."

In Portland, Oregon, Bezil and Ngoni stayed at the home of an American mbira player who owned a large collection of African music.[3] Bezil dubbed as many mbira recordings as he could fit on a ninety-minute cassette, and from the moment Thomas became aware of this tape, it was all he wanted to hear. He studied it, parsing songs closely—rejecting some as too modern, praising others, and singing along with those he knew. Two vintage tracks by the group Yekwa Chiboora were instantly familiar, unmistakably Thomas's models for the Blacks Unlimited's versions of "Hwa Hwa" and "Pidigori."

"Thomas has *stolen* these songs," cooed Bezil with wicked delight each time one of them played. Thomas showed no hint of self-consciousness about his appropriations. "This is our music," he declared as the mbira tape rolled yet again. "It is not just ordinary music. When we play this music, we are protected."

Chris's tolerance for mbira reached its limit. He took to wearing earplugs while driving. In Arizona, a state trooper pulled the van over in 120-degree heat. "Evening, officer. Was I speeding?" asked Chris cheerily, hopping out of the ganja-perfumed van, still in drive, then hopping back in to throw it into park. "A little tired tonight?" asked the officer, surveying Thomas and the van's too many passengers. When he let the van go with a warning, Thomas crowed, "You see what I was telling you? This music is protecting us."

At a truck stop outside Spokane, Thomas called Harare and learned that Biggie Tembo had hanged himself. The ex–Bhundu Boys star had checked into a hospital a day earlier, then escaped from his straitjacket and used it to fashion a noose. "Biggie was doing church work," said Thomas, puzzling through yet another death. "I think he was out of sorts with his ancestors and he tried to fix it by going directly to God. But you cannot disregard your ancestors." Thomas believed that Biggie's troubles went back to his discovery that the man who had raised him was not his father. Biggie had learned his father's identity and traveled to the man's village to present himself as a lost son. Unfortunately—

unlike Thomas's paternal clan in Guruve—Biggie's family had shunned him, making him a stranger to his paternal bloodline. Thomas had never been close to Biggie, nor an admirer of his music. Yet this story, with eerie parallels to his own, now preoccupied him.[4]

Thomas had been skeptical that this small band would "satisfy" fans. But as the tour neared its end, he became convinced of its minimalist power, particularly after Zimbabweans in Santa Monica told him this was the best Mapfumo lineup they had ever seen. Thomas arranged with Manny Rettinger—the guitarist and engineer who had mastered the Zimbob CDs—to record the final performance at the El Rey Theatre in Albuquerque. That recording would redeem an otherwise difficult tour, beautifully documenting the Blacks Unlimited's one-and-only stint as a full-on mbira band.

Saki met the band at JFK Airport. His heart sank when Allan greeted him as "Mukoma Saki." (Mukoma means "older brother," but Allan was Saki's elder!) "Mukoma," Allan pleaded, "I have a wife. I have kids, and I am going home with fifty dollars." Instead of being paid, Saki was besieged with musicians expecting *him* to pay them. Meanwhile, Thomas, "strutting there in his hat" and his "long leather coat," became evasive. Saki challenged Chris Bolton, who, acting as manager, should have set aside a promoter's cut—generally 10 to 15 percent—after each gig. Chris shuffled nervously. "We don't have any money left, Thomas, do we?" he asked. At last, Thomas spoke softly to Saki, promising to give him money in Zimbabwe. "I felt powerless," recalled Saki. "That tour made around $14,000, and Thomas couldn't give me my money. It was the lowest moment in our relationship. And I was very angry, for a long, long time. But—it's crazy—I had so much respect and love for Thomas that my anger wasn't really at him. My anger was at *Bolton*." Not for the first time, the bulldog Brit had proven a useful lightning rod.

Back home, Thomas reunited with his full band and produced the fourteenth Blacks Unlimited album, *Sweet Chimurenga*. This is largely an album of upbeat pop songs, many featuring prominent keyboard riffing from a new band member, Richard Matimba. The songs neither acknowledge nor explore Thomas's personal grief over the loss of so many musician friends. Instead, we get folktales, a meditation on tragedies, a condemnation of tsotsis (hooligans) set to old-school African jazz, and even a love song.[5] One of just two mbira-based songs here, "Mvura Ngainaye (May the Rains Fall Down)," is a prayer to God to end droughts that had caused so much hardship in recent years. Dube plays a single, resolute guitar line that gathers power as it interweaves the mbira, cycle after cycle, never changing. Thomas's vocal translates the wretched angst of poverty and starvation into a plaintive melody that arcs over the music with devotional urgency. "Mvura Ngainaye" would become a staple of Thomas's live shows for years to come.

Early in 1996, Jonah Sithole joined the Blacks Unlimited one last time, and for over a year, the two greatest guitarists in the band's history shared the stage.[6] "He was the old Jonah Sithole," recalled Dube, "like when we were boys. There was no jealousy between us now." Dube and Sithole mostly took turns rather than playing together. The crowd at shows favored Sithole, flashy, charismatic, and draped in the aura of the liberation war's chimurenga hits. But Sithole resisted adulation, often leaving the stage to let Dube play.

Dube was emerging from a personal tragedy. His wife had suffered a long illness, and his mother had pressed him to turn to spirits. A n'anga had ordered Dube to buy alcohol, an ax, and a knife—accoutrements for a healing ritual. When his wife had died anyway, Dube had burned these things in his yard, swearing he would never again consult a n'anga. "Poor people believe in that," he declared afterward. "So if spirits are protecting you, why are you still poor?" For Dube, things came clear now: mbira was just music; its occult trappings were, for him, nothing more than devilry.

Dube had resorted to drink. When Cathy Mteya first laid eyes on him performing in a Harare nightclub, he was slumped in a chair on stage, cradling his guitar, his narrow face withered and glum. "Someone was actually feeding him pills during the show," Cathy recalled. "I assumed he was an AIDS victim." A self-styled Christian with a good heart, Cathy married Dube and made his rehabilitation her mission, with encouraging results.

The Sithole-Dube period peaked with the 1996 release of *Roots Chimurenga*, which features Sithole with the full, three-man mbira section in a set of eight, tradition-based songs, some of them adapted from tracks on Bezil's Portland mbira cassette. The standout is "Mukadzi Wamukoma (My Brother's Wife)," an adaptation of the traditional song "Nyamaropa." The band's recording barely tops five minutes, but Thomas was soon performing twenty-minute versions on stage. Within the scant words he composed for "Mukadzi Wamukoma," fans heard a moving lament for those lost to AIDS, but also, between the lines, a more sinister tale.

At independence in 1980, Albert Mugabe—the prime minister's brother— had been the popular leader of the Zimbabwe Congress of Trade Unions (ZCTU). When Albert turned up dead in his swimming pool a few years later, police suspected foul play. Many found it suspicious that Robert—"well known for speechifying over other people's bodies"—spoke little about his brother's death, and investigators never turned up a killer or motive.[7] Ever since, the rumor has lingered that when Robert and Sally Mugabe returned childless from Mozambique, the Mugabe clan feared their powerful son was impotent and arranged for Albert to impregnate Sally. This was a customary Shona solution to the problem of childless couples, but when Robert found out about it—so the story goes—he ordered the child aborted and the brother drowned. Thomas denied that this was his subject in "Mukadzi Wamukoma," but the mere title—"My Brother's Wife"—was enough to raise suspicions he could not quell.

At all-night pungwe concerts, the band sometimes reprised "Mukadzi Wamukoma," letting it fill most of the sunrise set. "One song, one hour," complained Dube at the end of one long night. But fans craved such songs. Revelers seemed compelled to linger indefinitely in the ceremonial trance they provided. Veteran session drummer Sam Mataure lauded the Blacks Unlimited's spellbinding performances during this era, though he was chilled by the memory of so many departed musicians. "Too many ghosts," Mataure shuddered—a common sentiment in the AIDS-depleted beer halls of Harare in the late 1990s.

Thomas kept the band in the studio as much as possible, diligently recording new songs, even though he then acknowledged that studios in Zimbabwe were obsolete and poorly maintained and produced substandard product.[8] Still, inferior recordings were better than none at all. Chris Bolton had reestablished contact with WOMAD, and in the summer of 1996, the Blacks Unlimited played at the UK festival and stayed on to track a fine, live-in-the-studio album at Real World Studio in Box.[9] The session features a reduced lineup—essentially the same as the American birthday tour, but with Chaka Mhembere on third mbira and Jonah Sithole playing guitar in his final recording with the band.[10]

That summer Zimbabweans looked on uneasily as Robert Mugabe married his former secretary Grace Marufu in a Roman Catholic ceremony. Grace was forty years younger than Mugabe and had already become the president's junior wife in a tribal ceremony two years prior to Sally Mugabe's death. Sally's life of service had epitomized the idealism of the liberation struggle; Grace's ambition smacked of its demise, an embodiment of corruption and rot. Grace would be hated for her shopping binges in Europe and for the palatial home Mugabe would build her in Borrowdale. Grace would surpass Sally in only one department, demonstrating the president's fertility with three children.

A few days before the August presidential wedding, Vena Mapfumo had a minor traffic accident on the Bulawayo Road. She was not hurt, but police found a corn-husk-wrapped "cob" of ganja in her car, and she and Thomas were arrested and made to appear before a magistrate. This case, like others before it, was thrown out for "lack of evidence." Thomas's relationship with state authorities maintained an uneasy equilibrium. He could sing about rigged elections, broken promises, and the suppression of dissent within ZANU-PF. He could even seem to be hinting at delicate personal matters, yet the machinery of power was not used against him, even when opportunity presented itself. Whether protected by ancestors, feared by the state, or just plain lucky, Thomas remained untouchable.

For the Blacks Unlimited, the darkest day of 1997 came in August when Jonah Sithole died in a Harare hospital. Sithole's wife, Gladys—along with Joshua Dube and his new bride, Cathy—urged Sithole into an eleventh-hour dalliance with Christianity. Cathy introduced the idea, and at first Sithole resisted. "Ah, Catherine, forget about it," she recalled him saying. "You're telling me about this Bible, the book that was brought here by a white man, thieves. Don't be cheated by these things." But, near the end, when Cathy offered to pray for him, Sithole accepted. "He was longing for something like that," she said. "I think Jonah had jumped his rope. He was already on the other side."

Gladys Sithole arranged for a pastor to come to the hospital to bathe and baptize her dying husband. Meanwhile, Thomas and members of Sithole's family marshaled traditional forces. "They decided it was better to do it the spiritual way," Gladys recalled with a sigh. "I didn't like it, but Jonah had to decide. And in the end, his relatives, and Thomas, his friend, had to bring him to one of these n'angas. When I took Jonah back, the doctors were angry." Sithole died at forty-three, leaving behind three children and many great recordings, but also a sense of missed opportunities. An architect of chimurenga music, and a first-rate composer and guitarist, he had never made it to American stages or received due recognition overseas. A compilation of his Deep Horizon recordings on the Zimbob label remains the only international release under his name. Kudos to Bob Diener for that.

Thomas's intervention into Sithole's treatment—like his accusations against Chartwell—was rooted in dark beliefs. Thomas and certain Sithole relatives thought the guitarist had been the victim of witchcraft by a malevolent elder brother, Phineas, who had been a ZANU lieutenant in the early days of the struggle when Ndabaninge Sithole had led the nationalist movement. "They were all Sitholes," said Thomas. "This guy was into black magic. He had what they call a *chikwambo*. This thing needs a lot of blood, so you have to kill people to feed this chikwambo of yours." According to Thomas, Phineas Sithole ultimately killed his entire immediate family, including some who had tried to save the ailing guitarist. Thomas understood that Jonah Sithole had been ill for some time, but the ultimate cause of death was the failure of the guitarist's ancestors to protect him. "There is a saying in Shona," said Thomas. "If a person is sick, it's not God who actually kills you, it is your ancestors. If they turn their back on you, you are a dead person."

Thomas was reexamining his religious beliefs. Over the years, he had entertained doubts about the power of ancestors, but recent events—Chartwell's alleged betrayal and the deaths of Ephraim, Saba, Charles, Biggie Tembo, and now Jonah Sithole—had revived his ancient faith. Even mundane matters now appeared in a new light. The Blacks Unlimited had suffered a decline in attendance at shows. There were explanations for this: weak sales for Thomas's Afro-rock release *Afro Chimurenga*, Sithole's failing health, Thomas's preoccupation with the Sporting Lions, the country's worsening economic plight. But Thomas looked to the spirits for an answer. "We paid some visits to certain medium spirits or n'angas," he explained. "We were told exactly what was happening, the reasons behind the low turnouts. This medium spirit told me we had to perform certain rituals. We did exactly that, and everything was back to normal." There was no debating such logic.

Not long after Sithole's death, the WOMAD recording was released—internationally as *Chimurenga: African Spirit Music* (WOMAD Select), and in Zimbabwe as *The Lion of Zimbabwe* (Gramma). Phillip Magwaza reviewed the session in the *Sunday Mail*, briefly noting Sithole's passing but mostly complaining that there were too many songs repeated from *Roots Chimurenga*.[11] Now, with Dube once again the sole guitarist, the Blacks Unlimited returned to the studio to record a new set of "political" songs under the title *Chimurenga Movement*. This album sidelines traditional grooves almost entirely in favor of reggae, throwback rock 'n' roll, and Afro-rock—catchy pop songs with words that lacerate acts of official corruption and greed, as if Thomas were spoiling for a fight.

The cheery sing-along "Tipeiwo Mari (Give Us Money)" was the hit, with its boisterous demand that politicians share their ill-gotten wealth. In the fall of 1997, as Thomas's audiences sang this song delightedly—*We want money. Give us money!*—the powerful Zimbabwe War Veterans organization was delivering that very same message to Mugabe and was getting results. War vets leader Chenjerai "Hitler" Hunzvi had threatened to withdraw support for ZANU-PF unless the government rewarded them financially for past service to the nation. Mugabe gave in, authorizing a cash payout of Z$50,000 per veteran family, plus monthly Z$2,000 payments for the rest of their lives—an immediate expenditure of some Z$2.5 billion.

Mugabe's decision would trigger a decade-long slide into oblivion for the Zimbabwe dollar. It would embolden Morgan Tsvangirai, who had taken over the Zimbabwe Congress of Trade Unions and was leading mass demonstrations that brought soldiers to the streets of Harare. It would open the door to a chaotic wave of farm seizures carried out by Hunzvi's "war veterans," a good number of them born after the liberation struggle had ended. These events would inspire the creation of Zimbabwe's first viable opposition party and lead to some of the most brutal deeds of Mugabe's bloody reign. The stage was now set for Thomas Mapfumo's second—and most fateful—showdown with the government of the day.

12 / Breaking the Cycle

The problem with mbira music is that it's very difficult to break the cycle and the melody sequence. Sometimes I think this must have something to do with African history and the fate of African communities. You go round and round until you swoon. Robert [Mugabe] can't break that cycle. That's why we are not going anywhere.

MUSA ZIMUNYA

We will finish what we started.

THOMAS MAPFUMO

Ian Douglas Smith appeared in the open doorway of his stone house in the Belgravia neighborhood of Harare. "Can't shake your hand," he said with a quick smile and a flash of blue eyes. "Mine are full." Tall, fit, and nearing eighty, he was carrying avocados and tomatoes just picked from his garden, which flourished in view of an even larger Victorian mansion next door: ironically, for this fierce anticommunist, the Cuban embassy. Smith took a seat in the living room—spacious, cream colored, and full of light on a spring afternoon. In this house Smith had been writing and speaking a lot about the world leaders who had undermined his government in the 1970s, and about the "terrorists" and communists who had been ruining the country ever since. He would bend visitors' ears about these things, but he would also show himself to be a peaceful old man, equally content to rhapsodize about the weather. "I have always said," he remarked, "that April and May in this country are as perfect as weather can be."

I wanted to talk to him about music. "Well, I'm not a musician," Smith demurred. "I love listening to music, classical music and opera mostly. I like African music. The melodies and harmonies are beautiful, especially the singing. On my farm, the Africans used to brew beer and sing and play guitars. I could hear it. It was lovely." As a young man, guitarist Joshua Dube had been one of those musicians, and he remembered it well. "The whole country was fighting against Smith," Dube recalled, "but on his farm people were very free." Smith reprised one of his memorable phrases from the old days, describing these celebrants as having "the happiest black faces in Africa."

But what did Smith remember about his government's confrontation with the popular singer Thomas Mapfumo? The former prime minister looked puzzled. It took a few tries to get him to focus on the idea of music *recorded* during the liberation war. "This chap you keep mentioning," he said. "I'm not familiar with him."

"Thomas Mapfumo?"

"I don't know him," Smith insisted. "I know the mbira. I've heard it since I was a boy. It's a lovely instrument. But as for chimurenga *music*, we weren't aware of that. And I don't ever recall anyone being arrested for singing. But you know, while I love music, I don't give a damn what the words are. I hear Mimi singing on her deathbed. She's supposed to be dying of consumption, but she's singing her lungs out. The meaning doesn't matter to me. What I like is the sound, the emotion. So if they were singing political things, that would have gone right over my head."

Was this surprising? Not really. It would have raised eyebrows in America if Ronald Reagan had never heard of Michael Jackson, or Richard Nixon had asked, "Who's this guy Bob Dylan?" The American melting pot demands a modicum of pop culture fluency from its leaders. Not so much in Rhodesia, or Zimbabwe, where separate cultural universes persist tenaciously after a history of division. Smith had insulated himself from so much of local life, during the war and since. "I haven't read the *Herald* in fourteen years," he said with a note of pride. "It's just propaganda. And the television is worthless. Even the radio. You can't listen to that rubbish. I mostly learn by talking to people. Lately I've had a lot of the young black professionals coming to talk. Do you know what bothers them? It's the fact that the first black government has brought shame to black people. I am now more hopeful for this country than I have been in years. People are standing up and saying they won't take it anymore. They can't afford to eat. I've always said a hungry man is a dangerous man." Strangely, this was a line Thomas Mapfumo also liked to quote, echoing Bob Marley, of course.

Outsiders marveled that Smith still lived in Zimbabwe; most leaders on the losing end of an African liberation war wind up dead or in exile. But sitting in the presence of this graceful, sly, brazenly hopeful old gentleman, one realized that he was both here and not here. Ensconced within the hubbub of Harare, Smith lived in a world of garden produce, family, and the sustaining narratives of his fateful betrayal at the hands of feckless Western leaders. Like President Mugabe surrounded by supplicants and yes-men, like the rebellious war veterans crying for reward two decades after the fact, like the Christian evangelists making converts among the ranks of the miserable, or like Thomas Mapfumo himself, holding court in beer halls, surrounded by the dispossessed—poor under Rhodes, poorer under Smith, poorer still under Mugabe—Smith inhabited a private universe, unavailable to persuasion, and oddly safe.

In his year-end *Sunday Mail* recap, Phillip Magwaza wrote that 1997 had not been Thomas's year and that he was "a pale shadow of the mystical and vibrant Mukanya we know." Magwaza failed to note the loss of Jonah Sithole, or that *Roots Chimurenga* had been on Gramma's best-seller list through the entire year, even as two additional Mapfumo releases had come to market. In his bathrobe and fresh from the shower, Thomas groused, "This writer has never even attended one of my shows." He picked up the phone and rang Magwaza to "set him straight." Magwaza acknowledged Thomas's rebuttal in his next column, describing it as "educative."

At the stroke of midnight, a woman in a lime green skirt jammed her thumb into a bottle of locally brewed Bollinger's beer. Shouting, "Happy New Year!" she gave it a shake and released a plume of spray. The crowd ignited, and beery fountains rained down on the worn wooden floor of Bulawayo's Large Town Hall. Patrons cried out in gleeful surprise, their fancy clothes bathed in the libation. Their voices merged with the boom of bass and drums and the robust plinking of amplified mbira, all reverberating off the massive auditorium's dark oaken panels, pale blue walls, and high, frosted windows edged with curtains as red as the stacks of plastic beer crates mounting by the doorway. High above the christened dance floor, empty balconies, and enormous stage where the Blacks Unlimited played, a portrait of Robert Mugabe looked faded and small. It was the first day of 1998 in the heart of Matabeleland, and Thomas Mapfumo had returned after another long absence.

William and Jira were unhappy with the gate, well short of the full house they had expected. Thomas, dressed in black and white formals and prepping for the second set, had no time for bad news. He was committed to performing in Bulawayo regardless of the turnout. He showed off his sparse command of the local tongue, even though he considered it a language "imposed on Zimbabwe, like English." Thomas said, "My wife speaks Sindebele, but not our kids. I don't know why." Then, with a chuckle, he added, "They like their Shona." Some Shona viewed Ndebele culture as richer and better preserved than their own. "The Ndebele are united," said one Shona man, "more proud of their language, names, and practices than we Shona." Others saw things differently, like the young mbira player at Bezil's rural home, who alluded darkly to "those people down in Bulawayo." Everson, around long enough to recall the tensions of the past—the shebeen killing in 1979, and the victory song "Nyarai (Be Ashamed)"—was not surprised by the low turnout.

The father of all Zimbabwean music writers, Leo Hatugari, was in attendance that night, dancing at the side of the stage in a gray trench coat. Hatugari had been in Hwa Hwa prison with Mugabe but now allied himself with malcontents like Mapfumo. As the beer flew at midnight, the band played "Mvura Ngainaye," Thomas's prayer for rain, and the urbane Hatugari tucked his head low and shimmied like a villager. This song had been Thomas's anthem through a deathly dry fall. Now, too late to do the country's farmers any good, the rains were coming. Fierce, daily storms blackened the sky, carved streams through stunted maize fields and washed out roads everywhere. Even the ganja crop in Malawi had been affected, causing smokers to settle for low-grade local herb or scrounge for rare caches of hashish smuggled in from port towns on the Mozambican coast.

The band's Monday meeting at the Elizabeth Hotel opened with a lecture from Jira about foul language overheard on the tour bus. The musicians endured Jira's fuss and fury in silence, half embarrassed, half amused. Thomas had been hearing rumors that one of the musicians was helping the women in the band, Florence and Mutsa, find work with other artists. William wanted answers, but no one seemed to know anything about that. Thomas took the floor to inveigh against lies. He told the story of four friends who find a cache of money. They decide to eat first and divide the spoils later. Two of them go out for food, but upon their return, they are ambushed and killed by the others. But when the killers eat the food they too die, for their late friends have poisoned it. "So you see," Thomas concluded merrily, "we must not have lies. We must be like a family." The story generated a burst of laughter. Then William began dispensing pay envelopes.

Next door to the Elizabeth Hotel was a forlorn establishment called the Star Bar. It opened to the street, its sign and façade in sunlight, its interior all shadows. This was a favored lair for veteran musicians, some going back to the 1960s, when Thomas sang with the Springfields. Many had left music for other professions, but they gathered here, often dressed in suits, to drink beer and talk, a fraternity of the forgotten. After band meetings, the older Blacks Unlimited musicians habitually retired to the Star Bar to commiserate. Dube peered at three Z$100 bills in his envelope. "Four shows," he sighed. "Three hundred dollars." To be sure, it wasn't much. But Thomas had many mouths to feed. He was then making regular payments to the families of some of his deceased musicians, notably Charles and Saba. With the economy sinking by the day, pressures on the band's earnings were mounting—from musicians, crew, family members, and, of course, Thomas's soccer team. There was no way to satisfy everyone, but musicians like Dube and Allan Mwale, who put in such long hours and performed so consistently, seemed especially aggrieved.

The band played a rare downtown show at Job's Nitespot that week. Between sets, William—dressed smartly in pinstripe suit and fedora, setting off his stylish pencil-thin moustache—discussed the Sporting Lions with Thomas. The brothers had been stung by the team's recent demotion. Thomas said it had come down to one bad call by a referee. "I told him," he blustered, "you are lucky I don't have my gun. You'd be a dead dog." William and Thomas touched hands and laughed, their voices roaring like engines.

A group of Sporting Lions officials joined Thomas in his "backstage" room during a Friday show at the Seven Miles Hotel. In high spirits, Thomas presided grandly, holding forth on a variety of subjects. There was a story in the *Herald* about the pope's bodyguards. "Why does he need bodyguards?" Thomas boomed, switching to English. "He knows if he dies he is going to heaven. He is a *holy man*. Did you know that there are telephones at the Vatican and you can speak your prayer into that phone? Who is supposed to be on the other end? Is that God? No. This is where we part ways. The Roman Catholic Church owns the world." Thomas's commentary had the flow of stand-up comedy, and everyone enjoyed it. For the soccer men, this was a night on the town, a chance to unwind amid the glow of Thomas's celebrity and wit. Music was secondary, and Thomas knew it, so he shared beer, bravado, and hilarity backstage, then returned to the garden and his fans, whose needs ran deeper.

Amid the tense early days of this new year, 1998, local events were fueling a new level of outrage in Harare. In a single day, the price of corn meal, "mealies," the stuff of Zimbabwe's beloved sadza and the nation's staple grain, rose 21 percent. There were rumors of unrest in the city. Driving through Highfield, Thomas noted crowds walking along the roadside, a quiet exodus of citizens too poor to afford transport. "It's like the early days when we were fighting Ian

Smith," Thomas reflected. He gestured toward the township, adding, "After all these years when people were fighting for freedom, you build them a toilet instead of a house? And why blame Smith? If you go to Mbare and look at those houses, they are much better." Thomas knew it was provocative for him—of all people—to credit Ian Smith on any count. But his attitude had changed. He was bracing for confrontation. "Without violence," Thomas said grimly, "nothing changes here in Africa."

Willard Karanga—policeman by day and Blacks Unlimited trombonist by night—warned there would be a "go slow" among the city workers, and many businesses would be closed the next day. Morgan Tsvangirai's trade union had organized nationwide protest rallies. Workers were to take the day off from their jobs and march to central locations where they would hear speakers condemning the government's hastily devised 5 percent tax on workers, Mugabe's latest strategy to fund his payoff to war veterans. Tsvangirai had fought all the way to the High Court, which had allowed the demonstrations, as long as they remained peaceful. Rallies in Gweru, Mutare, and Bulawayo did stay calm, but when a massive crowd marched out of Highfield toward downtown Harare, a wall of armed police turned them back at Charter Street. The police resorted to tear gas. Enraged protesters stoned policemen and overturned vehicles, even a few ZUPCO buses.[1] Hooligans and tsotsis took advantage of the chaos, looting stores and robbing people, especially whites.

Thomas tried to drive to Seven Miles for rehearsal but was forced to return home. "There was violence, man!" he recounted the next day. "I myself had stones thrown at my car." Allan was tear-gassed in the back of an open truck while trying to make his way to rehearsal. He showed up nursing a bottle of cough medicine. Everyone had a story. "The police were at fault," Thomas declared. "But that does not excuse the looters."

Thomas had often credited the Mugabe regime for getting "one thing right," creating a police force that was "close to the people." Policemen lived in neighborhoods, not in separate barracks like their Rhodesian forebears, and people, even Thomas, had come to trust them. Back in the 1980s, the band had labored to conceal their ganja smoking at shows. Now Thomas smoked openly at rest stops during road trips. Cop cars honked hello to him as they passed. But political unrest was different. Rumors circulated that the police had built surveillance sites, hidden amid the green slopes overlooking the Charter Street entrance to Harare. "There are guns in those hills," said Thomas, "big guns."

After the "food riots," Morgan Tsvangirai was beaten nearly to death in his office during daylight hours. Despite "investigations," his attackers were never identified. Broadcast media and the *Herald* were in editorial lockdown, unable to explore or even fairly report on such events. Meanwhile, critical voices were spitting fire in the pages of Harare's independent newspapers.[2] The *Zimbabwe Independent*'s Muckraker column was particularly pungent, responding to one Mugabe speech with characteristic sarcasm: "One would have been excused for thinking that the president was speaking from Mars for very little of what he said bore any resemblance to what the masses have experienced over the past 12 months. Indeed, while he was waxing lyrical about democracy, that very democracy was in flames in the streets of Harare courtesy of those expected to maintain law and order."[3]

"Mugabe is just a bastard," said Thomas upon reading these words. "The people fought a war of liberation. They must not feel that they fought and died for nothing." Soon new violence erupted, once again turning Harare into a conflict zone with cars smashed and burned, stores stoned and looted, and the army dispatched to subdue Chitungwiza. When the band next met at the Elizabeth, Thomas vented his rage that Indian shops had been raided and people had rushed out of Mbare with shopping bags to loot anywhere they could. "It was chaos," he declared. At the same time, Thomas could sympathize, noting, "People in this country have been very patient."

Ian Smith had a joke he liked to tell that year: "President Mugabe, you should have told me that all you wanted to do was to rename the streets. I would have helped you. You didn't need to fight a war for that." Jaundiced humor was becoming instinctive for Zimbabweans, like scratching a wound, agonizing but irresistible.

"*Asingade, anenge asingade*," sang a group of young men in the crowd at a Blacks Unlimited show: "When he says no, it means no." Thomas's song was a hit that season. It defends the people's right to refuse "the king" and ridicules ZANU-PF's intolerance of dissent. But one of those singing young men conceded that, although the party had squandered the dreams of a generation, he nevertheless pulled the ZANU-PF lever when elections came around. "There is no alternative."

"We have no opposition party," echoed Thomas. "So now the people are becoming the opposition. That is very dangerous." Mugabe had managed to maintain a certain dignity prior to these disturbances. His intransigent hold on power may have boiled down to simple greed, for which many Zimbabweans blamed the new wife, Grace. "She has tasted power," said one former Mugabe supporter, "and she doesn't want him to let go. Last year, Mugabe could have left and still been a hero. Now, he is becoming a hated man."

Thomas channeled his anger into songwriting, and soon the band was rehearsing an incendiary number called "Nhamo Zvakare (Trouble Again)," a screed against national leaders for betraying the promises of the liberation struggle. The lyrics were blunt and bitter—to Dube, dangerous. Not all Thomas's musicians shared his eagerness to speak out; but, as he said, they were like a family, and he was the head of household. Interestingly, Thomas chose not to record this song amid the turmoil of 1998. He saved it for a later album—musical reasons, he said, not political ones.

Bezil had retreated to his mother's rural home during the riots. The day he returned, the mood at Seven Miles was high as the management had slaughtered a goat and was feeding the band a midday feast. Bezil stood at the doorway to the kitchen watching a woman carve meat. "Someone was looking for his dog," he murmured sourly. Bezil rarely came to rehearsals these days. He drank heavily at shows and crabbed often about low pay, poor conditions, and lack of recognition for his contributions to creating songs. Familiar stuff, but with Bezil, all of this swirled into a stew of confused thinking. Arriving drunk for a show at the Nyamutamba Hotel, he complained about his wife, pregnant for a second time. "When women are pregnant," he cried, "they become troublesome. You can't understand them." Mutsa and Florence objected, and Bezil snapped back at them, "Get out, you singing daughters!"

"Bezil is going around with bad characters," said Thomas, clearly concerned, "people who are not of his size, people who have already achieved their goals. Bezil is not even paying his rent. So, what sort of a person is he?" Thomas lamented that the best musicians were always somehow difficult. "Even in football," he said. "You find that the notorious ones are the talented ones." Had Bezil been a lesser musician, Thomas might have sacked him. But this was "a major player" in Thomas's view, and the band's mbira section sounded "not very sweet at all" when he was absent. "Bezil is a genius," sighed Thomas, "but he must not be told. I myself have never told him."

Bezil was unrooted. Fatherless from boyhood, he had grown up in awe of his elder brother, Gordon, a prodigy mbira player on his way to becoming a spirit medium when Bezil was born in 1972. Gordon owned a car, traveled to South Africa, and had girlfriends: all this was impressive to Bezil as a boy. But recently Gordon's spirit had abandoned him, and he had descended into poverty and isolation. "During the rains last year," Bezil told me in a rare moment of reflection, "he got into a fight over money. He killed a man by beating him with a shifting spanner. A big one." Bezil said the law had spared Gordon, though afterward his victim's widow had resorted to witchcraft, and Gordon had died mysteriously. This death turned Bezil away from Shona religion, once an anchor in his life. Meanwhile, as all this was going on, Bezil had traveled to Europe and America, where he had entranced young girls, tasted wine and whiskey, and seen the bright lights of London and New York. Like Zimbabwe itself, Bezil had experienced too much too fast. Now he was reeling. Beneath all the belligerent poses and the alcoholic fog was a young man of extraordinary sensitivity, and this emerged movingly whenever he played mbira.

Douglas, a veteran Blacks Unlimited doorman, lost his mother that year, and band members attended the funeral—"a poor funeral," said Dube, "not a religious one." The Mbare compound where people gathered was unswept and dirty. Charred rocks lay among cooking fire ashes near a corner where a few meager stalks of corn poked out among weeds. Wooden chairs and benches had been set up, though nearly everyone was standing. When Thomas's musicians arrived, they were surrounded by *vaoora*, wives of the deceased woman's sons. A hunchbacked woman approached in black, hair glued to her bony head, eyes bloodshot from crying. She held a white strip of cloth in one hand and gestured toward Dube, addressing him in Shona, pointedly mentioning "Thomas Mapfumo." Dube surrendered Z$15, real money for him. Had he refused, the old woman would have tied her white cloth around his wrist to advertise his negligence. Vaoora begin collecting money at the moment of death and continue up until burial a day or two later. "Even at graveside," said Dube, "they form a line around the grave. They won't move until you pay. And let me tell you something. That money is all for *them*, not for the family. Funerals used to be serious. No beer, no swearing. Now they drink and even fight, especially here in Mbare. It's *worse*."

Dube and his wife, Cathy, still walked in the shadow of Jonah Sithole's death. As with so many premature deaths in Zimbabwe, few wished to acknowledge a particular cause. "It wasn't like that before," said Cathy. "That was the first thing people could ask when you got to a funeral. 'Oh, what caused his death?' But now with this AIDS, people are scared. It's like you will be suspecting the family members. 'Ah, he was just sick.' That's what they tell you." She paused before adding, "In life, you must have room for lies. This is the attitude in Zimbabwe."

Gibson Blathewick, the saxophone player who had replaced Chartwell, looked thinner by the day. He had retired from the Zimbabwean army after twenty years' service and joined the Blacks Unlimited. He honestly couldn't say which life was harder. "Gibson is sick," warned Dube. "You can see it in his face. He won't last out the year." This was true. By the time the Blacks Unlimited arrived in America that summer, Gibson too would be dead.

The band left Harare for a weekend tour, starting at the Sebakwe Hotel in Kwekwe. A craggy-faced, forty-something white Rhodie stood out in the black crowd. He wore a T-shirt that read, "Down the Scud." Scuds were barrel-shaped plastic jugs of commercially produced Chibuku, millet beer. The product had come to market just after the Gulf War, which brought the Scud missile into common parlance—hence the Chibuku name and slogan. This old Rhodie had lost both parents and a brother in Zimbabwe's liberation war, yet somehow the experience had brought him to sympathize with blacks. More than sympathize—bars like the Sebakwe were now his milieu. His white peers shunned him as a "nanny fucker," but he didn't care. Downing scuds all night, he danced amid the mostly male crowd, rolling his large belly in time with the music, fitting in nicely.

At Hwange Stadium, not far from Victoria Falls, the band played under klieg lights for a big crowd that sang and danced in the bleachers, overjoyed at the chance to see "this old man of ours." The band was exhausted from travel. They had been forced to sleep under trees in a public square in Kwekwe, after being abandoned by a negligent bus driver. Sam Mukanga labored at the drum kit in bare feet, struggling to sustain power and speed. Thomas was frustrated, turning back often to urge the poor drummer on through three long sets. The band played five shows that week, for which Dube and Allan each received Z$700 in their envelopes at the Elizabeth Hotel on Monday. "Ah, but that guy is poor when it comes to money," said Allan, his voice still wheezy from tear gas. Dube offered a mild defense of Thomas, saying he was at heart "a good guy," only beset with needy relatives and the steady financial drain of his soccer team.

Musa Zimunya had heard all this before. Like Hilton Mambo, the poet was unsympathetic to the complaints of musicians in bands like Thomas's and Oliver Mtukudzi's. Musa considered these musicians lucky to be in such bands, and he rejected the notion that they lived lives of exploitation and economic brutality. "What do you say about a man who has worked as hard as Thomas?" asked Musa. "After all that he has given, he still has to play four nights a week just to support his family. Is there not brutality in that?" Musa noted that Thomas's best musicians had always craved the freedom to express themselves, but when they split off on their own, they invariably failed to distinguish themselves as individual artists. "You would have thought they would say, '*This* is what we meant.' Instead, no statement whatsoever. And then they go back to Thomas."

Musa had been waging a lonely fight on Thomas's behalf at the University of Zimbabwe. In his role as chairperson of the Department of African Languages and Literature, he had drafted a proposal arguing that Thomas should receive an honorary degree for his contributions to the nation. The proposal cited Thomas's "prophetic vision" and stressed that "together with a generation of lesser known musicians," Thomas had "rescued Shona music."[4] The idea had met resistance from another professor at the university, Dr. Dumisani Maraire, who had returned from his post in the United States some years earlier.[5] Dumi argued in a memorandum that Thomas should be seen as a businessman, not an educator. "He lifts, rearranges, gives the material a new identity and gives credit to himself," wrote Dumi. "This is called clever in music industry, while other specialists call it stealing from the culture."[6]

Musa dismissed Dumi's critique of Thomas as "small-minded," the result of "corruption, jealousy, or downright dumbness." Nevertheless, Dumi did influence the process. Musa's initial proposal was to make Thomas a doctor of literature, but the University Council had approved only the recognition of an honorary degree. Now the matter lay in government hands. President Mugabe customarily awarded such honors, but his office kept citing scheduling conflicts to delay the ceremony. Musa was baffled. Why didn't Mugabe just "get rid of it" and put the issue behind him? "Robert does not understand irony," the poet fretted. "Perpetually, the man is caught in ironies!"

Reading Harare's private print newspapers in 1998, one might easily have concluded that Mugabe's regime was in its final days. Editorials tirelessly cataloged evidence of corruption, frequently accusing the president of "postponing the inevitable."[7] But in the countryside, ZANU's electoral base, people had access only to state media, which blamed their suffering on meddling outsiders, never on failed politicians. Meanwhile, big names from the liberation struggle were becoming embroiled in scandals no newspaper could ignore. Ndabaninge Sithole, whose writings had sparked the nationalist movement, and who had challenged Mugabe all the way up to the 1996 elections, had been convicted of conspiring to assassinate the president.[8] More stinging still for the famously homophobic Mugabe, former president Canaan Banana, Mugabe's right-hand man at independence, was enduring a sensational public trial for sodomizing boys on his soccer team.[9]

Few subjects inspired such scorching rhetoric from Mugabe as homosexuality. Most commentators dismissed these antigay rants as a tactical diversion from more pressing issues—the slumping economy and stalled progress on land reform. But Mugabe's bigotry was heartfelt, rooted both in his Catholic faith and in his firm conviction that homosexuality was fundamentally un-African—a belief contradicted by anthropologists but widely held nonetheless.[10] Vilifying homosexuals also distinguished Mugabe from a rival of sorts,

Nelson Mandela. Just a few years after Mandela's brave fight to enshrine gay rights in the South African constitution, Mugabe had drawn the battle lines in Zimbabwe when he banned the Gays and Lesbians of Zimbabwe (GALZ) from the 1995 International Book Fair. That year, Mugabe had barnstormed the country denouncing homosexuals as "lower than pigs and dogs" and vowing they would never enjoy any rights in Zimbabwe.

Alarmed by Mugabe's tirades, international human rights organizations had rushed to GALZ's rescue with generous donations. Coffers had swelled, and black membership in the organization had grown dramatically. "Homosexuality was supposed to be a white thing," recalled Keith Goddard, the composer and music professor who had done so much for musicians at the Zimbabwe College of Music. Quietly, Goddard had also led GALZ since its founding in 1990. Goddard—white, bearded, long-haired, and hunchbacked—had now emerged as an unlikely international spokesperson for African gays. Meanwhile, GALZ's membership had become three-quarters black by 1998—a big change from its white, ex-Rhodie beginnings eight years earlier. Homosexuality was becoming an obsession in Zimbabwe's national media.

Goddard always remained on good terms with Thomas, though he never dared ask the arch-defender of traditional culture for his views on homosexuality. Thomas's social politics could be stern. He believed in strict schools, segregated by sex and with a uniform dress code, and agreed with Malawian president Hastings Banda that women should be barred from wearing short skirts. Yet Thomas also defended freedom. Presented with a direct question about homosexuality in Zimbabwe, Thomas gave a conflicted answer. "It is a taboo in African culture," he began, echoing conventional wisdom that homosexual identity was a "white" notion. Then he pivoted, saying, "Actually, in African culture, they *think* it's taboo, but to put it straight, it's the way one feels. We are all equal in the eyes of God. We are the same people, but we differ in character. That's how we were created." Thomas had tolerated problem drinkers, philanderers, wife beaters, thieves, and at least one homosexual among his musicians. He had no quarrel with Africans who led a gay lifestyle. Nor could he bless them. That "mandate" belonged to God.

On major holidays, many Harare residents make their amends with God and the ancestors by going *kumusha*, home to their "rural areas" where the bones of their forbearers lie buried. It's a ritual of remembrance oddly separate from their city lives. Cosmopolitans who typically dress Western and display an almost studied ignorance of traditional culture suddenly find themselves clapping to greet one another, recalling Shona proverbs, and dancing to mbira music with their village relatives. People who would never attend a Mapfumo show in Highfield might well turn up at the Rainbow Inn in rural Murombedzi for Thomas's Christmas and Easter pungwes, packing the vast space before the stage, singeing their fingers as they flipped meat on the sizzling braai pits, and drinking cold beer and warm Chibuku, sometimes straight from its missile-like jugs. Near dawn at Thomas's Easter show that year, during a roiling performance of "Mukadzi Wamukoma (My Brother's Wife)," the Rainbow Inn staff handed out roses. As the sun poked above the horizon, people held their flowers aloft, and a flock of white mourning doves flew from the branches of tall *musasa* trees. As if on cue, they circled and swooped over a huge crowd high on beer, braai, and chimurenga music. In that fleeting moment, country and city lives came together.

Back in Chitungwiza, Thomas sat before a television in his break room at the Nyamutamba Hotel, watching Mugabe talk tough to the ZCTU. The trade union leader Morgan Tsvangirai had been floated as a possible challenger to Mugabe, and the president was keen to nip this candidacy in the bud by saying over and over that Tsvangirai was "unqualified" to lead. "Was *he* qualified?" parried Thomas, referring to Mugabe. "He's just a fool." When the ZTV newscaster resumed her bland commentary, Thomas said, "Let's leave this woman to her lies." He reached for his cough syrup and fedora and headed for the stage. The band was playing "Wenhamo (The Sufferer)," and Thomas began to sing.

The next Monday at the Elizabeth, Thomas rebuked his band over their behavior at shows. "You are destroying the music," he told them. "This band is now very unruly." Bezil was "busy drinking" all night and "sleeping on the stage." Gibson and Everson were "two sick guys who should not be drinking at all." Thomas cited Everson's diabetes, his need to control his sugar intake, and the special danger that drinking posed for him. Turning to Dube, he said, "You too are a culprit, always turning up that guitar." Then to Allan, "Washington played that bass. Charlie played that bass. They did not drink the way you are doing. This is very disappointing. You can't have a Christmas party every night." The musicians slumped in their seats and endured the scolding. Afterward, at the Star Bar, they reacted. "Allan is an old man," said Dube. "Mukanya must not tell him what to do." But, Dube allowed, when it came to the subject of drinking and the health of his musicians, Thomas had in fact been "talking a lot of sense in that room."

"Sekuru Mukanya," said Tendai Ruzvidzo, with grudging admiration. "I love his music. I hate his attitude. Ah, but I want to sing with Mukanya." After the Mudeka sisters had supplanted her in the Blacks Unlimited, Tendai had sung with Oliver Mtukudzi for a while but found his music "too light." Now, she said, the dancers working with Thomas were lazy. "Thomas finds his girls in pubs," she grumbled. "They don't dance, just swinging their arms and stepping side to side, the same thing every time. It's sad." Tendai had been one of the original Singing Daughters, and Thomas announced her return to the band "to teach these girls dancing" with unusual fanfare. Tendai appreciated the recognition. "I am going to work nice with Mukanya this time," she said. "It doesn't matter there is money, there is no money. When you are on stage, you have to do what you are supposed to be doing there. Look at Tina Turner. She is an old woman, but she can dance, that one."

Under Tendai's tutelage, Mutsa and Florence improved sharply. The band had revived the song "Ndave Kuenda (I'm Now Going)," a brooding Korekore number first recorded for the album *Zimbabwe Mozambique* eleven years earlier. Thomas said bringing this song back had nothing to do with Mugabe's ever-diminishing status. One had to wonder, though, hearing him sing, "I am leaving, boys. I am leaving, girls," prompting the backing singers to answer, "Go. Leave. What is so special about you?" Tendai choreographed the song in short order, and when the dancers hit the stage, a big Mushandira Pamwe audience cheered them loudly as they leapt and turned to the song's ferocious groove. Thomas was elated and made a point of complimenting the girls for "bringing the stage alive."

Thomas announced that the band would return to Shed Studio within days to record the songs they had been rehearsing. The musicians were sitting in the garden at Seven Miles, the summer sun pouring over them and over the white metal chairs, cracked concrete, burned-out oil-drum trash bins, and spiky, untended greenery. Set up in the middle of the dance floor, amps turned low, no PA for the vocals, the brass players far off to one side and the women practicing their dance moves on the other, the Blacks Unlimited prepared for the studio in their traditional way: playing long, unhurried versions of song after song while Thomas moved around the circle, listening closely, changing and adjusting everyone's parts in search of an elusive satisfaction. Dube, on guitar, had a sense of what would please Thomas's ear and could sometimes come up with parts that Thomas would approve readily; other times Thomas would stop him cold and sing a completely different line. Veteran players learned not to become attached to their contributions. "He knows what he wants," said a later guitarist, Gilbert Zvamaida. "That's the bottom line. If you hear him complaining, you will have to change that line. He is a straightforward man." So it was that a man who played only a little guitar and did not read music or study its theory could nevertheless qualify as one of the most distinctive and accomplished African composers. In a very real sense, Thomas's band was his instrument.

Shed Studio at that time was a sixteen-track, reel-to-reel outfit located in the basement of a Harare office building. It was barely adequate for the band. Compromises had to be made, like recording two or even three mbira on a single track. Work proceeded quickly, with most songs recorded in just one or two takes. Thomas was inscrutable in the recording studio. He might request key changes, new parts or arrangements on the fly, even as the engineer's finger hovered above the "Record" button. There is a mysterious Zen to his music making, leisurely and fluid during rehearsals, sudden and decisive in the studio. The band had been working up another piece from Bezil's Portland, Oregon, mbira cassette—still a fascination for Thomas three years later. Then Thomas abruptly abandoned the idea, replacing it with the Shona song "Chig-waya," part of the karimba (small mbira) repertoire, arranged by the musicians on the spot. Sweet and simple, "Chigwaya" refers to the fish known as bream, which has "complete control over its territory." Some mbira players interpret "Chigwaya" as a metaphor for *njuzu* (mermaid spirits). But the metaphor works equally well for a bandleader, feeling at the top of his game.

While the players recorded, the women, Mutsa, Florence, and Tendai, drank beer in an adjacent storage room and engaged in girl talk. Mutsa complained about her "jealous" husband. "He doesn't want to see me with a white man," she said. "He thinks, 'Ah, you are going to be like Anna, like Patience.' Even drinking. If he hears I was drinking beer, he will shout. He is very, very African, like our ancestors." When at last they were called to sing, the women were too drunk to hit the notes, and Thomas called it a day.

The band tracked ten songs in two days, but, strangely, none gave full voice to Thomas's boiling anger toward the ZANU regime. Even the starkly beautiful "Ndiyani Waparadza Musha (Who Has Destroyed My Home?)" plays more as requiem than protest. Thomas wore his gray suit and tie the night he went to Shed to record vocals for this album, entitled *Chimurenga '98*. Shona singer and bandleader Robson Banda—once called the "prince of chimurenga"—had died that morning, but that was not the occasion for Thomas's formality. He simply liked to dress well when singing for history.

In those days, you entered the offices of Gramma/ZMC—Zimbabwe's merged record company monolith—to confront a life-size black-and-white photograph of Thomas Mapfumo circa 1988. Company headman Julian Howard was proud of his businesslike relationship with Thomas. "All he wants is his check," said Howard, revealingly. "He doesn't even check the figures." Checking the figures was Howard's job, and he confirmed that Thomas had been the biggest-selling artist over the long haul of Zimbabwe's popular music history. He hastened to add that, at that particular moment, rumba singers Simon Chimbetu and Leonard Zhakata were outselling both Thomas Mapfumo and Oliver Mtukudzi, and that most of those rumba sales were in rural areas.

That big rural market had once been Thomas's honeypot. Musa Zimunya had handled Thomas's distribution during the late 1980s, and recalled being "shocked" to discover that rural people had purchased the majority of Thomas's records. Not any more. Like independent newspapers, Thomas's music was now city fare. He could travel to the hinterlands on holidays and entertain urbanites gone kumusha, but the locals now preferred good-timing *sungura* and rumba, devoid of social warnings and political critiques. "There is something horribly askew in this society," said Musa.

Julian Howard seemed almost embarrassed by his company's success amid the worst economic crisis Zimbabwe had seen. He noted that catalog sales had been particularly strong that year and speculated that the war veterans' payoff might be a factor. For these newly moneyed customers, a cassette of chimurenga singles had the power to evoke a time when heroes were black, enemies white, and suffering had a tangible purpose.

"*Mari, mari! Money, money. We want money!*" Thomas's song was everywhere—in restaurants, bars, emergency taxis—everywhere but on state-run radio. Kudzi Marudza, one of the Radio 3 DJs blamed for suppressing local music, made no apology. "Chimurenga music will be remembered as the music of the struggle," he declared, "nothing more. After Mapfumo, there will be no more chimurenga music." Independent music producer Tendai Mupfuridza agreed. "Mapfumo has personalized the music," he said, "just as our president has personalized a political party. That is a typical Zimbabwean problem. We want to be the only one. 'Without me, there is nothing.'"

Marudza and Mupfuridza were not alone in the opinion that Thomas's glory days had passed. Harare's unofficial sound track told a different story. The very "personalization" these music pros assailed—the same quality that made Thomas a sometimes authoritarian bandleader—was also a key to his success. Zimbabwe's economics and politics, as well as its social and stylistic trends, all worked against him, and yet the beer halls where Thomas appeared remained packed night after night after night.

Business-minded observers told Thomas he was killing himself, and his musicians, by doing so many and such long shows. If he played once a month in a stadium, they argued, he'd make more money and live longer. Thomas believed his fans would never accept that. He needed to go to their neighborhoods and give them the catharsis they craved—every weekend. The catharsis was his as well. For by now, all artifice and showmanship had vanished from Thomas's stage act. He led no sing-alongs, delivered no practiced patter, participated in none of the organized dance routines. He did not even use a set list, calling the tunes on the spot according to his mood. Half the time Thomas kept his one good ear buried in a speaker so that the audience could barely see him. The musicians too found sanctuary in the sound. They might be hungry, frustrated, bitter, or drunk, but on the stage they knew a kind of grace, the truest reward for all they had sacrificed.

At the end of a Sunday afternoon ceremony at the Mapfumo home, a heavy urn of seven-days beer sat in a band of bright sunlight slashing across the living room carpet. For once, the television was dark and silent. Vena served a meal of sadza and chicken. The children, Tapfumaneyi and Chiedza, rallied to help out, and baby Mati was the object of doting affection. Thomas's brothers and sisters were present, along with his mother, Janet, quiet but cheerful, and John Mapfumo, sprightly and merry with drink. Thomas and his family were at ease that day, together in harmony and undistracted by musicians, fans, or soccer players. Despite its air of ordinariness, this would be among the last such gatherings. Thomas would soon depart for a long summer in America. John Mapfumo would die suddenly the next September. Janet would mostly live out her remaining days on a remote homestead, for she had always felt most at home on the land. At century's end, Thomas would face a changed world and would have to reevaluate everything, breaking the cycle at last.

Thomas Mapfumo's legendary crouch, here at
New York's Central Park Summerstage

Thomas Mapfumo before his first gig at New York's SOB's, 1989

Thomas Mapfumo, SOB's in New York City, 1991

Thomas Mapfumo and Chartwell Dutiro, SOB's, 1991

Sabastian Mbata on drums, SOB's, 1991

Chartwell Dutiro and Bezil Makombe, New York, 1993

Tendai and Kudzai at Central Park Summerstage

Thomas Mapfumo in Philadelphia, 1992

The three-mbira juggernaut: Bezil Makombe, Ngoni Makombe, and Chaka Mhembere, 1998

Bezil Makombe, along the road to Mutare, 1997

Thomas Mapfumo and Chartwell Dutiro in a Harare studio recording the album *Vanu Vatema*, 1993

Thomas and Vena outside their new establishment in Harare, 1993

Sam Mataure (drummer) and Washington Kavhai (bass), San Francisco, 2000

Tom Terrell and Thomas Mapfumo at Celebrate Brooklyn, 1999

Allan Mwale, Bezil Makombe, Thomas, Ngoni Makombe, Chris Bolton,
and Samson Mukanga, Lake Powell, 1995

Al Green and Richard Crandall at Thomas's house in Eugene, Oregon, 2009

Billy Gibbons, Cuthbert Chiromo, and Thomas, Houston, 2001

Thomas outside the Middle East Café in Boston, 1993

Thomas, freshly shorn, and the band at the Kola Note in Montreal, 2004

Thomas and the crowd at Johnny D's in Sommerville, Massachusetts, 2004

Thomas with Beninois vocal star Angelique Kidjo, after sharing the stage at a benefit at Jazz at Lincoln Center, New York, 2005

The only known photograph of Tapfumaneyi Mupariwa, Thomas's father

Vena receives her green card in Eugene, Oregon, 2009

Thomas with William Mapfumo, on a return trip to Harare from Eugene, Oregon, 2003 (PHOTO: BROOKS BARNETT)

Thomas, Gilbert, and Chaka rehearsing for their performance with dancer
Nora Chipaumire, 2010

Nora Chipaumire performing with Gilbert, Thomas, and Chaka, 2010

Tapfumaneyi, Vena, Chiedza, and Thomas at Thomas's house in Eugene, Oregon, 2013

Thomas and Vena's children, Mati, Chiedza, and Tapfumaneyi, at Thomas's house in Eugene, Oregon, 2013

Thomas Mapfumo performing at the World Financial Center
in New York, July 2012

Thomas Mapfumo and Banning Eyre on stage at Carnegie Hall's Zankel Hall, 2012
(PHOTO © 2012 JACK VARTOOGIAN / FRONTROWPHOTOS)

III AMERICA

13 / Striking at Empires

Ours shall soon become a nation of liars. We lie to our wives.
We lie to our husbands. We lie at work. We lie in parliament. We
lie in cabinet. We lie to each other. And what is worse is that we
have begun to believe our lies. What I fear most is that we will not
leave anything to our children except lies and silence.

HERBERT CHITEPO FROM A DREAM SEQUENCE IN ALEXANDER
KANENGONI'S NOVEL ECHOING SILENCES

Al Green was born in New York City in 1952. He was the son of a physics
professor who spirited his family through a succession of university towns
before settling at Sandia Labs outside Albuquerque. Al's grandfather on his
mother's side was Stuart Hedden, the first inspector general of the CIA and, in
Al's view, an "American war criminal." Hedden's mid-1950s doings on behalf
of United Fruit had triggered a coup in Guatemala, and some 200,000 deaths,
a defining achievement in a long career of international meddling. Upon his
own death in 1976, Hedden left Al a trust fund worth just under $2 million—a
boon to the young man's finances but a blight on his conscience. At high
school in Albuquerque, Al had played drums in a rock band whose guitarist,
Manny Rettinger, became a musical mentor and lifelong friend. When Manny
was recruited to work on Thomas Mapfumo's CD releases for Zimbob, he
telephoned Al to say he had found "the real musicians in this world," and they
lived in Zimbabwe. His children grown and his bank account flush, Al was
ready to listen, and to help.

Al first saw Thomas on stage at the OK Hotel in Seattle during the 1995
mbira-band tour. There was a moment during the song "Chemutengure" when

Allan Mwale's bass line swooped up to fill the role of the absent lead guitar. The sound levitated Al's heart into his throat, and once he heard it, he never looked back. Al offered to drive Thomas to the band's next show in Eugene, Oregon, where he owned a house. So began a professional relationship that would outlast all Thomas's other international record deals. Serengeti, Earthworks, Shanachie, Island, WEA, Virgin, EMI, Zimbob, Real World, Nascente, Sheer Sound in South Africa—only Gramma Records in Zimbabwe would produce more Thomas Mapfumo albums than the company Al Green created for that purpose in 1998, aNOnym reCOrds.

Al's inexperience led to some missteps, like keeping Thomas's title for aNOnym's debut release, *Chimurenga '98*, which did not reach the U.S. market until 1999. But Thomas saw right away that Al was all about the fair deal. Al offered Thomas 55 percent of revenues, "with no deductions," by far the best percentage the singer had seen. Beyond releasing new recordings, Al would also labor to secure rights for Thomas's back catalog. He would examine every recording deal and distribution contract he could find, demanding back payment or, if the deal seemed invalid, cessation of sales. Al approached his task free of emotional attachments to those who had "helped" Thomas in the past. Al suspected everyone, from the pious "gatekeepers" of the "world music mafia," to the most minor players in an industry he considered designed and built to exploit artists like Thomas.

For Al, Bob Diener was "a snake." Jumbo Van Renen and his Brit cronies at Island had signed Thomas only as a way to get back at Mugabe, who had spoiled their imperial Rhodesian picnic, and EMI had falsified a licensing contract to get an extra five years of selling rights. Faced with Al, Shanachie Records claimed to own no more copies of Mapfumo titles. Yet using the Internet, Al kept ferreting out caches of Shanachie product. Al's crusade was a dizzying mix of dead-on bravado and bilious paranoia. It yielded money for Thomas, even as it soured potentially useful relationships. Al did not compromise to avoid ruffling feathers. He had his eye on a bigger picture, one in which the global crimes of his grandfather and the abuses musicians had suffered at the hands of producers, distributors, and record labels were all the deeds of an overarching foe. Al called it "The Empire," and you were either with it or against it. Chris Bolton had displayed the demeanor of a junkyard dog on Thomas's behalf, but it was the slender, soft-spoken Al Green, with his vision of the just fight, who planted teeth and drew blood where it counted.

Al's tenure as the man behind the Blacks Unlimited curtain officially began in July 1998, when Chris Bolton pulled into Eugene driving a rental van that was "smoking . . . on its last legs." Chris's musician passengers weren't faring much better, and Thomas was worryingly ill. His T-cell count was low, he had boils on his legs, he was anemic, and his urine swam with bacteria. A doctor in Seattle asked him, "Do you want to live?" and when Thomas said he did, the doctor emphasized a need for rest and for protein, ideally red meat, two big steaks a day. Tendai Rudzivo, the only woman on the tour, assumed a motherly role, fretting over Thomas's health but also Allan's. "Allan has fungus on his tongue," she said. "My mother had that. It goes from your tongue down your throat and you *die*." As the band camped in Al's Eugene home, Tendai pleaded with Allan not to drink or smoke. In private, she sized things up coldly: "Allan is a bass man. You can replace him. But what about Thomas? Who can replace him?"

A shiatsu massage helped Thomas rally for two performances at WOMAD-USA in Seattle. But he was not himself. At a forum on politics and music, he sidestepped a chance to air his dissatisfaction with Mugabe. "Certain elements in the government are corrupt," Thomas said mildly, "but we can't blame everyone. We still think the president is okay." Chris Bolton recalled "audible gasps" when Thomas added that Mugabe was actually doing a "good job." Perhaps a tent full of American music fans and rolling cameras seemed the wrong place for Thomas to vent against Zimbabwe's revolutionary president, but for Chris, this evasion smacked of ethical failure and marked a turning point in his assessment of Thomas. Under a blazing northern sun, before a hillside of blissful fans, the band delivered a sublime show at the Edmonton Folk Festival in Alberta. Tendai's explosive vocals, free-flying arms, and solar smiles delighted the crowd. Thomas, who had welcomed Tendai to the band with acclaim and encouragement, told her to tone it down for the evening show. Tendai was crushed. "Thomas can be such a *rotter*," fumed Chris. "I told Tendai, 'You'll be dancing when he's gone.'"

Chris had always backed Thomas, however stern his regime. Now he was using words like "jealous," "stubborn," and "childish" to describe his boss. When the band returned to Zimbabwe, this simmering conflict reached a boil. Thomas accused Chris of profiting deceitfully from the 1996 WOMAD CD. Thomas brandished the contract, which Chris had signed in his place, and accused Chris of pocketing a 7,000-pound advance.[1] Chris went into hiding, "sleeping rough" in his car and eventually throwing himself on the mercy of the British embassy, which refused to shelter him, even though, he claimed, Thomas's friends in the police force were out to "fix" him. Joshua Dube and Tendai protected Chris, housing him with relatives until he could slip out of the country on a sunrise bus to Johannesburg. When Chris spotted his name on the border agent's list, he placed his passport over it, and the agent's stamp fell. "He wasn't looking at the list," said Chris. "Just name, face, passport, stamp. But it was shitting-bricks time."

Chris now joined the list of so-called crooks who had worked for and betrayed Thomas. Tendai left the band to create her own folkloric group. But a year or so later, defying Chris's prediction, she died in Zimbabwe following an illicit abortion. As for Thomas, fears about his health proved unfounded. A little downtime in America and a few months of hearty eating, and he was good to go.

Thomas now turned his Zimbabwean affairs over to Cuthbert Chiromo, an entrepreneurial young music fan. "At first I thought he was just a guy that Thomas would send to pick girls," recalled Vena, "but he's a smart guy. He wanted to help." Cuthbert helped Vena first, getting her out of debt from the failed T'n'V enterprise and helping to launch her, along with her sister, with a more successful downtown dress shop called Strawberry's Boutique. Some in Thomas's band and family suspected a romantic liaison, but Cuthbert and Vena were just a good business team. Convinced that Gramma/zMC was still cheating Thomas—and always would—they set up an in-house distribution operation using the Chimurenga Music Company name and planned to make *Chimurenga '98* their maiden release. The timing was good. Thomas had at last won control of his Gramma masters, including nearly everything he had recorded since independence.[2] Al Green met Cuthbert in Nashville, Tennessee, and they spent a night in a hotel room making copies of Mapfumo master tapes, some of which went straight to a cut-rate cD duplication house.

In Harare, Thomas's onetime nemesis at the *Sunday Mail*, Phillip Magwaza, was reassessing the "Chimurenga Guru." Magwaza published a glowing account of the 1998 tour, heralding Thomas's ability to drive crowds "crazy with musical ecstasy."[3] He reported that Thomas had signed a "million-dollar contract" (presumably Zimbabwean dollars) to rerecord catalog music for the international market—an imaginative take on the Al Green deal. Magwaza hailed *Chimurenga '98* as a "masterpiece" that "oozed with originality."[4] When Thomas staged a joint concert with Oliver Mtukudzi at Club Hideout, Magwaza called it "a show that, when I have grey hairs, I will recount to my grandchildren around the fireside." By April 1999, the band was preparing to embark on another foreign tour, starting with a gig at the Reggae Sunsplash Festival in Jamaica. Magwaza summed things up with prescience, warning "Mapfumo fans" that "your weekends will never be the same."

Thomas was the subject of more salacious press in the *Herald*. His paternal uncle Jeremiah had died a few months earlier. Suspecting foul play, Thomas had gone to the family compound in Guruve, with a n'anga on hand to "cleanse the village." The n'anga had determined that Thomas's cousin, Noah Makore, had killed Jeremiah and other family members using what the *Herald* called "non-natural means." Thomas described "dirty things" associated with witch-craft, all found on Noah's property by the n'anga. The key evidence was the horn of an animal, uncovered in a granary. "Noah was the culprit," Thomas concluded. "Labeling" Noah "a witch" appeared to violate the colonial-era Witchcraft Suppression Act, which bars such accusations. Noah pressed charges on this basis. By the time the case went to court, however, Thomas had left for Jamaica.[5] In the end, witnesses refused to testify, and the case was dismissed, leaving Thomas certain he had done "the right thing" by following African custom. Despite this, Noah continued to care for Thomas's cattle in Guruve. "He is like a brother to me," said Thomas without rancor, "but he is a jealous man."

While the band traveled and performed, Al prepared a second aNOnym CD release, *Live at El Rey*, the concert Manny Rettinger had recorded in Al-buquerque at the end of the 1995 mbira-band tour. *El Rey* came out first in Zimbabwe and sold massively with its unique sound—mbira untrammeled by guitars, brass, or keyboards. Phillip Magwaza called it "pure murder . . . Mukanya at his best." This success put Cuthbert and Vena's new distribution arrangement on solid ground and cemented Thomas's confidence in his new team. Meanwhile, Al faced a sluggish music market in the United States and the looming decline of the CD format. Al's distributor, Stern's Music in New York, urged him to invest in advertising. "This is *Mapfumo!*" railed Al. Paying for display slots in record stores struck him as legalized payola. "It was pay to play, pay to sell, pay to *pray*," he said scornfully. Stern's had revealed themselves as servants of "The Empire" and "whores of Babylon." Al refused to advertise, and each successive aNOnym release sold fewer CDs than the previous one.

Al's lawyer secured P1 performance visas for Thomas and the band, tech-nically allowing all of them to bring their families to the United States. Most of the musicians had more pressing agendas, which they unfailingly brought to Al. Dube wanted Al to release music he was recording in Zimbabwe with his own band, Shangara Jive. Ngoni and Sam required medical attention. "Everyone needed a lot," recalled Al. "Everson needed insulin, which he was pulling a hundred units of and shooting himself up every day. I told him, 'That's gonna kill you, man.' And he said, 'No. My doctor told me this is what to do.' Then he's drinking Cokes and alcohol all day, and then another hundred units." Al focused on business. If the money flowed, other problems would take care of themselves.

In the summer of 1999, the Blacks Unlimited moved through America in a Bounder recreational vehicle Al had purchased on the used market. Al was a hands-off manager. When driver Richard Crandall clipped a turn too tightly and scratched up the side of the RV, Al had only one question: "Was anyone killed?" Thomas received an award at the Houston International Festival in Texas, where he rubbed shoulders with Angelique Kidjo of Benin and Billy Gibbons of ZZ Top. Cuthbert kept Thomas in the news in Zimbabwe by feeding glowing reports on the band's triumphs abroad to Magwaza at the *Sunday Mail.* Vena—who accompanied Thomas on tour for the first time in years—shopped tirelessly, purchasing a computer to keep track of business, and, to Thomas's exasperation, mountains of new and used clothing to sell in her boutique back home.

In Amherst, Massachusetts, Lancelot Mapfumo learned that his own wife, Florence, was dying of liver cancer. Thomas rushed his brother to Bradley Airport, but before the flight reached Harare, Florence had died. Thomas was shattered. His reaction was striking in light of all the deaths he had so gracefully absorbed in recent years. He was low for days, his performances noticeably subdued. Before the band returned home that fall, Allan Mwale, Thomas's sideman since the Springfields, and the backbone of the Blacks Unlimited rhythm section for seven years, would also be dead, along with Ashton "Sugar" Chiweshe, the bombastic policeman guitarist. Allan had been too sick to travel, and after some quick training, Chris Muchabaiwa had replaced him on this tour.[6]

In September, the band landed at Al's house in Eugene to record a new album. Singers Memory Makuri and Rosa Sande worked in the kitchen each night, preparing sadza for everyone.[7] Bezil liked to slip out on a bicycle and party with local friends after dinner, returning in the morning with outlandish tales. Bezil's behavior both angered and amused Thomas, pitting his persona as disciplinarian elder against fond memories of his own rapscallion past.

The Blacks Unlimited's 1999 recording session was the first of five to take place at Gung-Ho Studio, a cozy Eugene facility renowned for its vintage gear. Engineer and owner Bill Barnett took pains to accommodate Thomas's idiosyncrasies—his penchant for changing keys and arrangements in the midst of a session, his need to hear heavy bass in the mix at all times, and his reluctance to announce plans in advance. The key changes came when Thomas wished to sing in a more comfortable or effective pitch register. With mbiras tuned in three different keys, the mbira players could generally adjust to changes readily; for guitarists things could be more problematic, forcing the player into awkward fingerings and preventing desired use of open strings. Barnett knew little of Thomas's history but quickly recognized his artistic prowess. The weeklong session yielded sixteen tracks, including definitive remakes of mbira classics "Mukadzi Wamukoma," "Mvura Ngainaye," and "Pidigori."[8] Barnett achieved an impressive result, capturing the three-mbira sound with noteworthy crispness and presence. Ten new songs from this session would make up the bulk of Thomas's incendiary upcoming release, *Chimurenga Explosion*.[9]

The band returned to Zimbabwe that fall just as trade union leader Morgan Tsvangirai held a massive rally in Rufaro Stadium to proclaim the formation of a fledgling political party, the Movement for Democratic Change (MDC). This party would contest Mugabe's ZANU-PF for the presidency and seats in Parliament. Mugabe and his minions branded the MDC as a front for British and Rhodesian interests, out to reclaim what they had lost in war twenty years earlier. The MDC slogan was *chinja maitiro* (change your ways). As far as ZANU was concerned, it might as well have been "recolonize Zimbabwe." The ruling party viewed the MDC as nothing short of treason and insurrection, to be countered by any means possible.[10]

In November 1999, Thomas at last received his honorary master of arts degree from the University of Zimbabwe. He was recognized along with five others, including the sitting vice president, Simon Muzenda, and the late Ndebele leader Joshua Nkomo. Thomas wore a black cap and gown for the occasion, and a photograph of him bowing his head before President Mugabe appeared in the *Sunday Mail*. Disc jockey James Maridadi was struck by the "good-natured" tone of Mugabe's remarks as he praised Thomas's chimurenga music. "In his face," noted Maridadi, "I didn't see any hard feelings."

"It was very good watching that," agreed Dube, surprised by the ceremony's power. "I felt proud." Thomas was also touched, though he held a dagger up his sleeve that day. On returning to Harare, he had taken the band into Shed Studio to record two additional songs for *Chimurenga Explosion*. "Mamvemve (Tatters)" and the reggae-tinged "Disaster" matched neither the musical verve nor the production quality of the Eugene recordings. Yet these were the songs that would upend Thomas's life in Zimbabwe.

The political climate could not have been more charged when *Chimurenga Explosion* was unveiled in early December. Zimbabwe's government was preparing for two separate elections, beginning with a referendum on a new constitution that would give the government explicit power to seize white-owned land without compensation.[11] Gangs under the direction of Liberation War Veterans Association chairman Chenjerai "Hitler" Hunzvi were already doing this; Mugabe's constitution would simply make it legal. When *Chimurenga*

Explosion hit the market, the *Sunday Mail* warned it was "not for the faint hearted." Thomas was "a lone hungry lion," brazenly condemning conditions in Zimbabwe and "leaving the public to look for answers."[12] The reviewer, Stanley Gama, identified "Nhamo Zvakare (Trouble Again)," with its accusations of liberation war promises never fulfilled, as the "most controversial" song. But it was "Mamvemve" and "Disaster" that hit a raw nerve with the public, not with high poetry or philosophy but with blunt, simple words.

"Mamvemve" says: "The country you used to cry for is now in tatters . . . run by crooks. Let's get out of here." And "Disaster":

Mother of my child, there is disaster here
Disaster within our family
Disaster within our house . . .
Our country is full of corruption
The crooks are going to finish us[13]

Chimurenga Explosion is provocative in every way. Its cover presents a black-and-white photograph of "the capture of Nehanda" in 1897, and on its inner sleeve, ZAPU leader Joshua Nkomo kneels with a traditional fur hat on his head as he receives a ceremonial ax from an Ndebele spirit medium at Salisbury Airport in 1962. First Chimurenga, Second Chimurenga. . . . Lest anyone miss the point, Al Green's own sleeve notes exclaim, "The explosion is imminent. I fear for the lives of my friends."

As the new millennium dawned, Zimbabweans were learning to cope with unprecedented shortages—food, medicine, and gasoline, for which one had to wait hours, even days. But Mugabe wagered that taking land from whites and giving it to blacks would play well in the eyes of history, so while others cried over gas lines and broken bones, he looked ahead, planning the final undoing of Rhodesia's primal sin. Zimbabwe's constitutional referendum in February 2000 was a genuine national showdown. State media blared hyperventilating support for the "Yes" campaign, even as the MDC moved through the land recruiting candidates and voters to oppose it. Geoffrey Nyarota, the journalist who had broken the Willowgate scandal in 1988, had recently launched a sensationally popular newspaper, the *Daily News*, which kept a rapt urban readership well fed with frank reportage and excoriating commentary on the ZANU government.[14] And everywhere was the familiar voice of Thomas Mapfumo singing "Mamvemve" and "Disaster," implicitly urging Zimbabweans to reject a new ZANU power grab. In the end, the referendum dealt Mugabe his first taste of electoral defeat: 54 percent of a small but committed turnout voted "no" on his constitution.

The following month, while in London for a concert with Oliver Mtukudzi at the Barbican Center, Thomas spoke to the *Telegraph* and rubbed salt in ZANU's wounds. "After all our struggle," he said, "I never expected our own black government was going to destroy our country. People are saying enough is enough." Thomas's remarks were reprinted in the *Daily News* and widely assailed by Zimbabwean officials and state journalists. The *Sunday Mail* had recently celebrated Thomas's selection as "Arts, Culture, and Literature Person of the Century." Now a headline jeered, "Tuku Outclasses Mukanya in London." Then, as June's parliamentary elections approached, reports surfaced that "Mamvemve" and "Disaster" were being restricted from radio play on ZBC. No ban was announced. The songs everyone had been talking about just quietly went away, another sign that Thomas's days in the sunlight of Zimbabwean state media were ending.

Mugabe's wounded regime now set about fixing courts, infiltrating churches, intimidating voters, and suppressing the ideas of formerly right-minded artists. Mugabe fielded a powerful new henchman on the cultural front, Jonathan Moyo. An American-schooled writer and professor, Moyo had first made a name for himself as a Mugabe critic, writing columns for Geoffrey Nyarota's *Financial Gazette* in the early 1990s. Moyo's Ndebele father had been killed by Mugabe's Fifth Brigade, so his attacks had carried a sharp personal edge.[15] But Moyo had gone on to be tainted by accusations of financial wrongdoing, first at the Ford Foundation in Nairobi and then at Witwatersrand University in South Africa. He had returned to Zimbabwe in 1999, emerging unexpectedly as Mugabe's point person for selling the new constitution. "He was a man on the run," said Geoffrey Nyarota. "He sought refuge and security behind the ZANU-PF fortress, knowing he would become untouchable there. His calculations were correct, but you don't get anything for nothing in this world, least of all from ZANU."

Moyo had failed to sell the constitution, yet Mugabe did not blame him. "Moyo was creative," explained Nyarota. "He must have taken Mugabe by surprise on more than a few occasions by his zeal and creativity, and by the extent of his venom. Because he *was* venomous, especially against the independent press." ZANU came within a few seats of losing control of Parliament in the June elections. Immediately afterward, Mugabe appointed Moyo as minister of information, a post from which he would torment both Geoffrey Nyarota and Thomas Mapfumo for the next four years.

Venom became the vogue. Members of the Blacks Unlimited had their houses searched. "This came from the top," an officer told Dube by way of apology as his men rummaged through the guitarist's house in Chitungwiza.

As Thomas prepared for a summer tour, police arrived at his Mabelreign home and impounded five BMWs.[16] A special fraud team including high police officials claimed the vehicles had been linked to a carjacking ring in South Africa, and Thomas and Vena were accused of knowingly purchasing stolen property. Cuthbert was also questioned. Thomas immediately branded the investigation a charade, "organized" to discredit him. But it hurt to lose those cars. Worth some Z$2 million each, they were both an important way to preserve wealth amid rising inflation and—for a car enthusiast like Thomas—dearly loved. Thomas later wrote the song "Ndaparera (I Have Been Destroyed)," condemning the government for harassing him, simply because he spoke up for "the welfare of the people."[17]

The car charges worried Musa Zimunya, who also found himself put off by the specter of Thomas as a potential MDC partisan. "Thomas Mapfumo of all people shouldn't find himself on the same side as Ian Smith," said Musa. The poet was relieved when Thomas disallowed the MDC from playing "Disaster" and "Mamvemve" at rallies. But when Thomas arrived in New York in July 2000, there was no mistaking his exultation over the election results. "The government has been cut down to size," he gloated:

> I've been with this thing for too long now. I remember when they [ZANU] were in the bush. I was supporting them through my music. They liked me. They talked about me as a hero. Today I am a villain, an enemy of the state. He [Mugabe] was angered by my statement in England. Back home, everyone read about it and said, "He's done it. He's going to jail." I went to the newspaper myself and I said, "I am not afraid. If the president is doing the wrong thing, I have to point it out." I wasn't insulting him. I was only talking about the problems that my fellow countrymen are facing. The president has to change his ways. . . . For me to go into hiding? Run away from ZANU-PF people? I am not going to do that. This is my country. My family is here. We are citizens.

Thomas boasted that *Chimurenga Explosion* was "the biggest-selling record in the country," and said Blacks Unlimited shows around Harare had drawn overflow crowds all through the spring, effectively serving as unofficial MDC rallies in the run-up to the June elections. But even as he basked in the aura of principled protest and victory, Thomas had made arrangements for his closest family members to escape Zimbabwe. He had rented a house in Eugene, Oregon, and during the spring of 2000, his wife and children quietly moved there, unnoticed by the Zimbabwean press for months.

At school in Zimbabwe, Chiedza had used the neutral family name

Chikawa. "I would never say anything about who my family is," Chiedza recalled. "At school, people would just know me as Chiedza Chikawa." The truth emerged one day when Thomas dropped her off at school. Afterward, classmates would sing his songs in class and rib Chiedza for having been so secretive. "That was near the end," she recalled. "When we left, my friends didn't know I was leaving. *I* didn't even know until the night before. My mom came home and she was like, 'You guys are going to go into America tomorrow. Pack your bags.'" Chiedza was thirteen at the time.

The three children flew to San Francisco with their uncle William, whom they had scarcely known prior to this moment. Al Green met them all at the airport and drove them to Eugene. "The first place we ever ate food in America was Denny's," said Chiedza. "We were so wowed by the freeways, and all these different cars and big trucks." That first summer in Eugene was lonely, and Chiedza had to take on new responsibilities caring for her younger sister before Vena arrived. Then came fall, and the relentless gray skies and rain of the Oregon winter—"depressing" for this Harare girl—and soon, the arrival of Thomas and the band to share the house with them. Things could scarcely have been more different from the secure and carefree life the family had known in Zimbabwe. It was not easy for them to understand that the security, comfort, and opportunity they had enjoyed there were rapidly dissolving. Tough years lay ahead, but Thomas had done what he felt was necessary to protect what he cared about most: his own family.

"The thing was to get the *family* here," recalled Al Green, insisting that Thomas and the band had intended to keep their own base in Zimbabwe. Al understood that the musicians would now spend more time in the United States. "We hoped we would be accepted by the left wing," he said, "or the underground, or somebody. But by the time we got everybody here, there was nobody left on the left." Andrew Frankel, an old hand in promoting African music in America, warned Al it was a career mistake for Thomas to leave Zimbabwe. He argued that it would undermine his credibility at home and that the band would never find enough U.S. gigs to work year-round. "It's not about touring the fucking country," Al steamed. "We're here to *escape*. And, yeah, we want gigs." Al heard Frankel's warning as just another voice of "The Empire," out to prevent Thomas from "poaching in the king's forest."[18] But the 2000 tour that Al organized suffered from hasty planning and too little support. "I lost $75,000 that year alone," recalled Al.

Cuthbert served as the band's road manager that summer. He traveled with a laptop and introduced Thomas and Vena to the Internet, which they used to buy and import a Nissan Civilian minibus for the band and the soccer team to travel in back home. As the tour progressed, Thomas remained preoccupied with developments in Zimbabwe. He groused about Mugabe's legacy of failing hospitals, closing schools, farm seizures, voter intimidation, and, most galling of all, worthless local currency. "Now you have Z$1,000!" Thomas exclaimed. "You have *nothing*. And if you don't have money in that country, you are a dead man." In the smoke-filled back compartment of the rolling Bounder, Thomas riffed away, sometimes with frightening bluntness. "I hate my country," he said once. "I don't hate my country. I love my country. But right now I hate it because of Mugabe." Thomas called Mugabe "a worried man" and predicted that when he fell, people would "hang him high."

No day on tour with the Blacks Unlimited ever felt like Christmas to Joshua Hlomayi Dube. Least of all these. "Joshua is a sick man," Thomas announced in Chicopee, Massachusetts. Dube had battled tuberculosis for much of the past year and had nearly beaten it, but complications kept arising. Thomas made plans to bring in another guitarist from Zimbabwe. His brother William had recruited Zivai Guveya, not yet twenty years old at the time. Al had planned two recording sessions for the band at Gung-Ho in Eugene, first a collaboration with avant-garde Rastafarian trumpeter Wadada Leo Smith and his band N'Da Culture—which became the album *Dreams and Secrets*—and then a session to record new Blacks Unlimited songs. But before the recording was over, Al was forced to fly Dube home.

Dube asked that Al be present when the guitarist negotiated his final payment from Thomas. Al understood that Dube needed to leave with honor, "because when you left the band, you always left in dishonor," he observed. "It was the only way, like the Hell's Angels." Dube brought a lifetime of demons to that meeting: the night his first wife had died and Thomas and Jira had pressed him to perform anyway, all the times he had been lured away from his own musical pursuits, or felt unrecognized or taken for granted. Thomas was as generous as he could be, but there was no way to set right all the wrongs in Dube's head. "When Joshua was packing his stuff," recalled Al, "he said, 'Let me tell you one thing, Mr. Green. You work hard and you die poor.' And that's the last I heard from Joshua Dube."

News reports in Zimbabwe suggested that Thomas had moved the band permanently to the United States. "My home is Zimbabwe," he protested to the *Sunday Mail* in a telephone interview. "I can't abandon my fans for anything." A new album Thomas and Cuthbert had pulled together from the three Gung-Ho sessions hit the market that fall. *Manhungetunge* refers to a nagging pain in the stomach, and the title song uses Shona proverbs to describe the decline of Zimbabwe in poetic terms.[19] But the album leads off with a song from the Wadada session, a playful romp called "Big in America," which proclaims in English, "Everything is big in America. . . . Everyone wants to be in America." From his new posting at the University of Virginia, Musa Zimunya wrote in a private e-mail that Thomas's stay in the United States "seems to have blinded him to the wickedness of this society to the point where he could compose such fawning praise and actually record it." Musa was not alone in finding Thomas's America-boosting unseemly. "It's not a joke," Thomas protested. He said "Big in America" was a prod to Africans, and Zimbabweans in particular, to strive harder and improve their lots, as Americans do. But combined with the news that Thomas's son and daughter had enrolled in schools in Eugene that fall, "Big in America" played for many as a love song to the singer's new home.

None of this seemed to matter when a sellout crowd of more than four thousand fans mobbed the Aquatic Complex in Chitungwiza on November 24, 2000. Crowds had greeted Thomas at the airport days earlier, perhaps half expecting to watch him be arrested. When instead he went about his business as ever, Thomas took on an air of invincibility. Laying bitterness aside, he criticized "mudslinging in the newspapers" and spoke of a "common purpose" and "uniting the nation for one goal."[20]

Thomas was entering a combative cultural landscape in Zimbabwe. Letters to the *Herald* now called him a self-serving hypocrite who hid behind the delusion that Zimbabwe was somehow unsafe for him or his family. Thomas's criticisms of ongoing farm seizures set him up for especially pointed attacks. One *Herald* letter charged, "If Mukanya's songs do not reflect characteristics of military resistance against political and economic injustices that we are suffering from at the hands of our former colonizers . . . then his songs do not deserve the title Chimurenga."[21]

In March 2001, the Danish human rights organization Freemuse, which monitors artistic censorship around the world, sent me to Harare to investigate the alleged banning of "Disaster" and "Mamvemve."[22] Thomas had by then rejoined his family in Eugene, but many of his musicians were still in Harare, working out visa and transport issues. There was no way to prove that Thomas's songs had officially been banned. "You don't have to issue an edict," said Iden Wetherell, editor of the *Independent*. "You just pick up the phone and that's the end of that." My Freemuse report painted a picture of "fear and self-censorship," nothing to grab headlines. As it turned out, Mugabe's still confident regime was just beginning to flex its muscles in the cultural sphere.

Thomas was the only prominent singer who dared criticize the ZANU government openly. "You have to be big to lock horns with Mugabe," said Geoffrey Nyarota. "There could be dire consequences. Your sungura boys are too small. They don't have the teeth." Two veteran black DJS, James Maridadi and Comfort Mbofana, had come within hours of joining an independent, white-run radio station badly in need of the credibility their African voices would have provided. These DJS agonized before declining to participate. "When ZANU hits back," explained Mbofana, "they hit dirty." The station, Capital Radio, gamely went on air anyway, only to be closed down within days. The government had no intention of honoring its decades-old promise to open the airwaves.[23] This left dissent in the hands of independent journalists and a few brave writers, like novelist Chejerai Hove and playwright Cont Mhlanga of Bulawayo. Thomas aside, musicians and broadcasters, whose voices could have reached many more ears, were cowed in a deepening milieu of intimidation.

Fear had many faces. In the rural areas elderly people might be shown binoculars and told these miraculous eyes would be used to observe their votes on election day. A young boy in a rural compound demonstrated the open hand—the signature gesture of the MDC—noting that it was "very dangerous" if the soldiers saw you do it. Urban dwellers faced random acts of violence. "They go in crocodile trucks," said Debbie Metcalfe, Oliver Mtukudzi's manager during these years. "They go in fully clad and looking as intimidating as possible, into restaurants where you have a pretty random group of people, often with their kids, made to lie down, all their drinks poured on top of them, food thrown on top of them, squashed on the floor by soldiers' boots—and then beaten. Purely as intimidation." Beyond uniformed tormenters, there were the ZANU youth and the so-called war veterans, many of them too young to have participated in the struggle, "Hitler" Hunzvi's shadow army. In one two-week period in 2001, Harare's independent press served up a litany of dire reports, including the following:

"War Vets Shoot Two Epworth Residents" (*Daily News*, March 8)
"Woman Loses Houses to War Vets" (*Daily News*, March 10)
"MDC MP Gets Death Threats" (*Financial Gazette*, March 8–14)
"War Vets Storm Club" (*Standard*, March 11–17)
"War Veterans Gloat as Farm Goes to Ruin" (*Zimbabwe Independent*, March 16)
"Even the Police Are Horrified at the Happenings" (*Daily News*, letter from Sgt Leave Me Alone, Harare, March 22)
"War Vets Close Two Schools" (*Daily News*, March 22)

"It's got all the hallmarks of fascism," observed Comfort Mbofana. "I don't know what it is about this country that people accept that sort of thing. If this were happening in South Africa, do you think that president would last two weeks?" The *Independent*'s Iden Wetherell blamed a "culture of deference." He said the under-thirty population, the so-called born frees, felt abandoned and preferred to further personal interests rather than lay their lives on the line as their parents had. "People don't like to be involved in politics," concurred Radio 3 DJ Kudzi Marudza, who catered to the born frees. "All they want is entertainment. That is why Oliver is doing so well, because he doesn't say anything about the government." But while Marudza, a government employee, lauded artistic disengagement, James Maridadi, who had nearly joined Capital Radio, noted that it was "becoming fashionable to identify with the music of Thomas Mapfumo." A new generation now referred to Thomas as "Gandanga," sometimes translated as "guerrilla" or even "terrorist," but in essence a reference to fearsome dark powers.

Thomas was now Sly Stone, or maybe Gil Scott-Heron, to Harare's hip-hop youth—old school but authentic, and on point. Comfort Mbofana, part of Harare's intellectual establishment, praised Thomas's political courage but described him as "a character out of a gangster movie with bodyguards and all." Mbofana believed that Thomas had "lost the plot" of his freedom-fighting past and become "a hero with criminals in this town." The BMW charges, later discredited, seemed believable to Mbofana at the time. The broadcaster said he had seen carjackers at Mapfumo shows. "I know these guys," he said. "They've all got the same kind of look—the leather jacket and the hat. And they're in there spending money from having robbed some poor old lady. I think that is a stigma, something that is going to haunt Mapfumo for the rest of his life." Mbofana bought into this urban mythology but failed to see the other side of it—Thomas as musical minister to the disenfranchised, something like Johnny Cash at Folsom Prison.

It was no surprise that DJs like Marudza and Mbofana took their shots at Thomas. For years he had condemned them as corrupters who pedaled decadent foreign music and lured young Zimbabweans away from their African culture. Ironically, the government media overlords who now sought to vilify Thomas were at the same time saddling these DJs with the burden of having to broadcast 75 percent local Zimbabwe music. This was a rule Thomas actually applauded, while the DJs found it hopelessly unworkable. Yet even DJs now confessed to missing Thomas. "The saddest thing," said Maridadi, "is that Thomas Mapfumo is not in Zimbabwe at this moment. That is the *saddest* thing."

"Everyone loves him actually," said ZANU official and author Alexander Kanengoni. "He's the one guy they would protect. . . . Oh, God, now he goes to America? It's so disappointing. We miss him. We *miss* him." Kanengoni wondered, perhaps naively, why other singers did not criticize the government as Thomas had. The only explanation he could muster was the land issue. "It's so close to everyone's heart," he said, "that there is a real possibility of forgiving people for the manner in which they are handling it. You end up agreeing with them."

So it was that reasonable, cultured men could reconcile themselves to the spectacle of unruly mobs armed with axes and guns, forcing farmers to sign away their land, beating and driving off farmworkers, then seizing everything of value and letting fields go fallow as they charged on to the next conquest. For a ZANU idealist like Kanengoni, praising Mapfumo provided cover. If Mugabe's overriding goal—reclaiming the land—was just, and an artist like Thomas was there to critique any flaws in the process, somehow the society seemed in balance.

Chenjerai Hove, a writer long past excusing ZANU abuses, sized things up differently as he sipped gin and tonics under the watchful eye of CIO minders at his favorite bar, the Queensdale Sports Club in Braeside. In a bemused, silk-smooth voice, Hove elucidated the "art of intimidation" in Zimbabwe. "They go to the soft spot," he observed. "If you are stubborn, they intimidate your wife, reminding her every day that 'your husband is going to die very soon.' And if your wife is stubborn, they trail the children, follow them to school, giving the impression that they could kidnap them or throw them in the swimming pool to drown." Hove wondered what tactic had finally persuaded Thomas to move his family to the United States. "That soft spot was touched," he concluded, "and he made his decision, which might ruin his career."

Thomas's career was certainly compromised, if not ruined, by his move to America. Life in Oregon would be expensive and challenging. "When we first came," Thomas would later observe, "we didn't know nothing about America. And we made a lot of mistakes." In the early years, Vena could not yet work. There were school expenses for the children. Money was tight, and credit, while available, had hidden costs and consequences. Meanwhile, Thomas's recordings and U.S. gigs were being handled by Al Green, generous and well-meaning but also volatile and inexperienced in the music business. Still, even in their darkest moments in Oregon, neither Thomas nor Vena ever doubted that they had done the right thing in leaving Zimbabwe.

Everson Chibamu died in Harare in March 2001. It was sudden. His wife was out all day, and he didn't eat properly. That was all it took to end the life of a diabetic, and the longest-standing Blacks Unlimited member other than Thomas himself. Joshua Dube was among just three band members to attend

Everson's funeral. An angry Thomas called the band to a Monday meeting at Strawberry's Boutique, Vena's dress shop in Harare. Speaking by telephone from Eugene, he berated his musicians for their negligence and for daring to request money at this solemn moment. "You must stick together," he insisted, "like one family." But as brave and bold as Thomas's voice might ring out on the political front, he was distant now and was losing his power to make demands back home, even of his own musicians.

Gifted musician, your songs of liberation and emancipation
helped bring freedom to the people of Zimbabwe. . . . Known
as the "Lion of Zimbabwe," you have been the eyes, ears and
mouth of your people for the past 30 years. You have clearly
demonstrated that an artist can have a major impact on social
transformation. A hero to the politically oppressed of Africa
and to legions of fans of contemporary African music, you are a
leading figure in the "world music" phenomenon and have helped
popularize mbira music around the globe. Stalwart leader and
talented artist, you are an icon for liberty and justice.

THOMAS MAPFUMO'S CITATION FROM OHIO UNIVERSITY

In June 2001, Thomas once again donned cap and gown as Ohio University
presented him with an honorary doctorate in music. He flew to Athens on
the university president's plane and received red-carpet treatment, returning as Dr. Mapfumo.[1] The band left Harare that spring, arriving in Eugene
shortly after Thomas, Vena, and the children moved into a modest ranch house
on West Twenty-Seventh Place. In Zimbabwe, Thomas had kept the lives of
his family and band separate. Now, when the Bounder RV rolled into town,
everyone lodged together in this quiet neighborhood, the family upstairs and
the band downstairs.

Thomas was doing his best to keep the Blacks Unlimited intact in the face
of newly daunting obstacles and expenses. Close quarters led to tension among
the musicians, even an onstage skirmish between drummer Gordon Mapika
and Chris, the young bass player. Gordon, along with singers Rosa and Mem-

ory, pressed Al Green to rent them rooms at the Downtown Motel, a prelude to their departure from Eugene. Thomas telephoned Sam Mukanga in Harare and asked him to rejoin the band. Sam had recently emerged from three months in prison after being implicated in a land sales scandal. Overly trusting, and barely literate, the drummer had fallen under the spell of a manipulative war vet bandleader who used musicians as unwitting pawns in a scheme to profit from seized white farms. At first, presented with this offer from Thomas, Sam hesitated, having been dismissed from the band two years earlier. Now, laid low and frightened, he agreed to come to Eugene, accompanied by singer Felistas Bisiwasi.

The September 11 terrorist attacks occurred days after their arrival. As the world convulsed, Thomas and his musicians hunkered down at Gung-Ho to record *Chimurenga Rebel*, an album he would later assess as one of his best. This is a gloves-off set of songs: sneering at Mugabe's yes-men in one, decrying political violence in another, and predicting divine retribution for human misdeeds in a third. Thomas comes close to naming names on "Huni," a thinly veiled diatribe against marauding war veterans' leader Chejerai Hunzvi. Hunzvi had been elected to the Zimbabwean Parliament in 2000, but after just a year in office, he had died, possibly from malaria, possibly AIDS, possibly the divine retribution Thomas had so often warned about. A vile and opportunistic man, Hunzvi was also a fraud who himself never fired a shot in Zimbabwe's liberation war. Despite Hunzvi's death, Thomas went ahead with the song, for its message—"Don't play with the people"—survived the man.

Chimurenga Rebel's most consequential song is a mournful lament called "Marima Nzara (You Have Harvested Hunger)." It is an unsparing meditation on the land troubles plaguing Zimbabwe. Thomas now ventured beyond the relatively safe position that land redistribution was a good idea handled badly. In press interviews, he paraphrased his new song, questioning the very impulse to oust white farmers. "These are not the same white people who stole your land," he insisted. "They are just like you and me. They are Zimbabweans. If they can utilize the land for us to feed the rest of Zimbabwe, give them the land. We are not just there to grab land when some of our people don't even know what agriculture is all about. That means we are inviting hunger into Zimbabwe."[2]

Thomas had grown up on the land, in the midst of peasant farmers. He had standing to address this subject. But to defend white farmers from the vantage point of his American roost riled his critics. Zimbabwean literary scholar Maurice Vambe led the charge, excoriating "Marima Nzara" in the *Sunday Mail*. "Mapfumo's version of Chimurenga," writes Vambe, "has clearly come under support from Western-oriented media and corporate demands to leave the status quo of inequality as it is. . . . He thinks Africans cannot farm [and] whites are God's chosen farmers."[3]

In fact, Thomas's position was more nuanced. A decade earlier, in the song "Maita Kurima Hambuvire (You Thought Farming Was Easy)," he had expressed the idea that commercial farming requires knowledge. During the previous thirteen years in power, the government should have been educating Africans in agricultural sciences and techniques, preparing them to assume control of the land and "feed the whole nation." The thorny saga of British support for Zimbabwean land reform—promised by Thatcher, reneged on by Blair—is well covered elsewhere. For Thomas, the central issue had always been simple: *the ZANU government never had a plan for land redistribution.* And now, by turning farms over to people who lacked the experience to make them fruitful, the government had "harvested hunger" and sown despair.

During the recording of *Chimurenga Rebel,* Thomas got word that his uncle Marshall Munhumumwe of the Four Brothers had died in Harare, some years after suffering a crippling stroke. Then mbira player Ngoni Makombe learned that his wife had passed away, brutal news as their son had also died recently. Ngoni flew home as soon as the recording was finished.[4] On October 5, 2001, riding high after strong reviews for a comeback recording, and on his way to a prestigious teaching fellowship in the United States, Ephat Mujuru suffered a heart attack in London's Gatwick Airport. The legendary mbira player died en route to the hospital, leaving behind a widow and ten children. Then it was Joshua Dube's time. His wife Cathy took him to the hospital on a Wednesday, and he died two days later. Thomas sent Z$20,000 to the family, but William Mapfumo delivered it to Dube's brother, Jonah Moyo, not to Cathy. Moyo collected his brother's body and took it to Gokwe for a swift burial. Cathy did not even attend her husband's funeral. "It's just terrible with the relatives here," Cathy said by telephone with astonishing good humor. She remarked that Dube's relatives would have happily "put me out of this house" had Dube not taken legal steps to prevent that. The Zimbabwean music community was shaken by another season of death. "People are just falling down like leaves," said one musician. "It's like death has become fashionable."

As Christmas approached, Thomas questioned the wisdom of going home. A magistrate's ruling had temporarily revived the issue of the supposedly stolen BMWs, once again an uncertain threat. More consequentially, minister of information Jonathan Moyo was flexing his muscles in creative ways, even releasing his own propaganda album on which he sang popular songs retrofitted with "patriotic" lyrics. Minister Moyo had begun pressuring musicians to sing in support of the land invasions. His converts included the liberation war–era singer Comrade Chinx, Zimbabwean rumba king Simon Chimbetu, and even Andy Brown, who had once been respected as a rare musical critic of government shortcomings. Thomas knew the songs on *Chimurenga Rebel* would be banned, and he was determined to perform them in Harare, despite "frightening" reports from friends there. The band was booked for a New Year's Eve show in the massive Boka Tobacco Auction Floors. Press reports were erratic: Thomas was coming, then not coming, then he was. In early December, Al Green urged Amnesty International to send observers to Zimbabwe because there were "plans to eliminate" Thomas during his visit.

Chimurenga Rebel hit the street in Zimbabwe just before Christmas 2001 and sold thirty thousand copies within days. The *Herald* dubbed it Mukanya's "Xmas present" in an article that carefully avoids any discussion of lyrics. Meanwhile, a letter to the *Herald* called Thomas a "scared man" and advised him to "enjoy the small club circuit in the USA and let some of us at home try to improve our lot without giving interviews to colonizers."[5]

Thomas offered cautious comments to the ZBC at the airport in Harare. He acknowledged that the land issue had been the primary motivation for the liberation war and that Mugabe was "a hero in this country." He added cryptically, "Let us advise him properly." Thomas's principal message was a call for unity and an end to violence, but the *Herald* spun this to say he had "fully backed the land reform programmes and praised President Mugabe for leading the country from oppression to independence."[6] However skewed in its public presentation, this interview served its purpose, defusing a potentially dangerous arrival and allowing Thomas to be heard in the venue that mattered most—the concert hall.

At Boka, Thomas wore his Sporting Lions colors in honor of the team's recent achievement of a nine-year dream, winning a place in the Premier League. He took only short breaks during a long night of music that showcased hard-hitting songs from *Chimurenga Rebel*. Under heavy police guard, an officially estimated eight thousand fans reveled all night and marched away at sunrise chanting, "Mukanya woye!" (Up with Mapfumo!).[7] Thomas said there were ten thousand people at this show, and Cuthbert, who actually supervised ticket sales, insisted the correct count was fourteen thousand. In any case, Boka was the scene of the biggest concert Thomas had ever staged.

Print attacks on *Chimurenga Rebel* continued in the state media. A letter in the *Sunday Mail* branded Thomas a "fair weather patriot" and no longer an "authority on Zimbabwe" now that he spent so much time abroad.[8] Two days later, the *Herald* published a lengthy broadside under the headline "Fame

Creeps into Mukanya's Head—Again." Accredited only to Entertainment Reporter—could this have been Minister Moyo himself?—the article needles Thomas on sensitive issues: his "surrender" to play music for the "puppet government of Bishop Muzorewa," his unfair treatment of band members, court cases involving unpaid child support, and the alleged purchase of stolen cars. The article assails the song "Big in America" as a cultural sellout featuring "heavy rock guitars," and dismisses "Disaster" and "Mamvemve" as little more than pleas for attention from a paranoid man who has lost touch with his audience.[9]

When Thomas telephoned the *Herald* demanding to know who had written such an outrageous story, Entertainment Reporter responded with "Factual Story Riles Mukanya," a sanctimonious editorial that sneered, "Papers are not printed to shower praises where they are not due."[10] After years of fawning coverage full of comical exaggerations, this freewheeling attack exemplified Jonathan Moyo's new brand of cultural journalism. Entertainment Reporter mocked Thomas's claim that the ZBC would ban the songs on *Chimurenga Rebel*. But Thomas said that a ZBC DJ had described a meeting of radio staff at which Moyo himself branded Thomas "a terrorist"—this Smith-era slur was back in fashion—and made it perfectly clear that the new songs must not receive airplay. And they did not.

Before leaving Zimbabwe, Thomas paid a visit to his biological father's village near Guruve. His car was followed by a group of "youngsters . . . looking for trouble." They approached Thomas outside a butcher shop and greeted him, saying, "Mr. Mukanya, can you show us your ZANU-PF party card?" Thomas instead produced a pistol from his glove compartment and scared the children away. But during ceremonies at the village, police arrived to question him about the incident. They confiscated his gun, forcing him to return to Harare the next day and fetch documents. Thomas laughed off this harassment, minor compared with what others were experiencing in the run-up to the March 2002 presidential elections. Food aid was reportedly being distributed only to those with ZANU-PF cards—an effective tactic when parts of the country were verging on famine. In the weeks to come, voters would be beaten and election observers stoned, and Morgan Tsvangirai himself would be charged with treason for presumably plotting Mugabe's assassination. Yet Thomas remained convinced that Mugabe would lose the election. "Everyone is saying," he reported gleefully, "'We will meet at the polling station!'"

Thomas returned to Eugene with a bare-bones lineup: Chaka alone on mbira, no brass section, and no singer-dancers. Drummer Sam Mukanga was too ill to travel with the band, but he flew in just in time to play the House of

Blues in Cambridge, Massachusetts. This would be the first Blacks Unlimited performance for trumpeter Brooks Barnett, a University of Oregon graduate, blond, blue-eyed, and one day shy of his twenty-third birthday. Of all the American musicians who moved in and out of the band during the years of Thomas's exile, none would leave a greater mark than Brooks. He would rapidly learn and transcribe brass parts for much of the Mapfumo repertoire and find and train a number of other horn players who would accompany him on the stage and in the studio. Brooks's musical education had begun with "Baptist hymns and pop-Christian hits in church on Sunday." His grandfather—a doctor and pastor who was born in Kenya and lived there and in Congo most of his life—had played valve trombone, and Brooks's father had learned trumpet at missionary school in Kenya. But by the time Brooks reached college, he had moved on from "Trumpet and the Swan" to a fascination with Miles Davis, "the prince of darkness." Brooks distilled Miles's wisdom into a personal credo: "Rule number one: trumpet stars make their own rules."[11]

This was the confident, precociously talented young man who took the stage in Boston, having practiced Thomas's music only in hotel parking lots and gas stations as he and nineteen-year-old Tapfumaneyi Mapfumo, Thomas's son, piloted the band in a rented minivan across the country from Oregon. That House of Blues gig marked the debut of the Blacks Unlimited redux, its pared-down, punchy sound carried by musicians young enough to be Thomas's sons. On bass, Chris Muchabaiwa literally looked the part, his lanky body, long dreadlocks, and smooth stage moves recalling video of Thomas's first gig in Germany twenty years earlier. Zivai on guitar was the opposite: short, stocky, and sullen, rarely breaking a smile but fully in command of Thomas's repertoire and style. Brooks was entranced, writing later, "On TM's command, the band can play triple pianissimo or triple forte, and everywhere in between. The music seems like it already exists on another dimension. Starting a set is like turning on a faucet."

As the band headed for Montreal, it became clear that Sam, the drummer, was suffering from more than exhaustion and a bad diet. He was so sick that, despite a trip to the hospital and various unspecified medications, he could not play the Montreal show. Brooks telephoned his physician father for advice, but there was no simple remedy for what ailed Sam. In London, Ontario, the barely conscious drummer was hospitalized and cared for by a doctor who treated him for meningitis and salmonella without charge, and arranged for him to be flown home to Zimbabwe. Sam died soon afterward. "God is our judge," said Lancelot with a detachment Brooks found chilling. "Each man must face death alone."

Thomas had told the *Boston Globe* that performing on the same stage with Bob Marley in 1980 had been the "greatest joy" in his life. His "greatest hope" was that Zimbabweans would "vote ZANU-PF out of power."[12] This was not to be. The March presidential election was a sham. The opposition had been muzzled in state media while ZANU-PF blanketed the country with propaganda, including a relentless barrage of radio jingles under the banner *Chave Chimurenga*—roughly, "it's now war"—in which popular singers touted the ruling party and its aggressive land policy. The vote itself was riddled with irregularities, yet the government declared a record turnout and a Mugabe victory. There was the usual international outcry, but when Nigeria and South Africa, the country that mattered most in Harare—accepted the result, Mugabe's hold on power was secure for another six years.

Jonathan Moyo was now a ZANU hero, and his minions in Zimbabwean state media indulged in an orgy of gloating. A letter to the *Herald* branded "Dr. Mapfumo" a sellout and lauded musicians who had sung in favor of the farm seizures as "true sons of the soil."[13] Disgusted urbanites, sustained by acid commentary in the independent press—to which they alone were privy—voted with their feet. Attendance at Simon Chimbetu's Harare shows plummeted, and once-popular singer Andy Brown could scarcely book a gig. "People are in no mood to forgive musicians who took the wrong side," noted one musician.[14] Brown made no apologies for his actions, saying that the *Daily News* had "killed my career." Brown freely admitted being paid by Moyo, whom he called a "good musician" and a "social scientist." And Brown criticized his old friend Thomas as overheated and paranoid. "They're not going to worry whether Thomas sang this or that," scoffed Brown. "Thomas still comes home and enjoys his houses. Nobody cares. They forgive him. Because they are much more clever than he. Do you think they would give him a degree because they don't *know* him? This is where education comes in. Thomas is working on a natural vibe, which is cool. But there is an element of study that one has to have for you to be able to make those statements." There is also an element of corruption, perhaps envy, in Brown's remarks, for the singer had clearly been bought off by the regime and paid a heavy price for it with his former fans.

Some musicians sided with ZANU for reasons of their own. In London, Chartwell Dutiro was troubled by his onetime mentor's turn against the Mugabe regime. If in fact Thomas had harbored doubts about Mugabe all the way back to independence, why had he praised the new leader then? "If he could sing a praise song for somebody who he knew was wicked then," asked Chartwell, "are we not dancing with devils?" Like Andy Brown, Chartwell found Western reporting on Zimbabwe hypocritical. Both men reflexively cited the

2000 Bush victory in Florida, suggesting that any nation that could validate such a result had little standing to cast aspersions on other people's elections. Chartwell dismissed MDC partisans as "Rhodesians," plain and simple.

"We are all former Rhodesians," Thomas rebutted, aligning himself with Nelson Mandela's "rainbow nation" rhetoric. But to Chartwell and others, the MDC, with backing from "Anglo-American companies" and trade unions, was part of a conspiracy aimed at nothing less than reclaiming what had been lost in the battles of the 1970s. Supporters of ZANU argued tenaciously that the current fight was ultimately a continuation of the liberation struggle—the African village versus the colonial city. And the village supported Mugabe.

Chartwell had not been to Zimbabwe for ten years, and from his English refuge, he was unwilling to distinguish the violence of the independence fight from the brutal theft of a democratic election. In his 1978 book, Bishop Abel Muzorewa writes about "'exiles' disease'—a condition of disorientation, division and general confusion which results when politically-minded persons are separated for too long from their people."[15] Chartwell would surely reject this comparison, but his remove from on-the-ground realities in Zimbabwe inevitably weakened his authority. Exile would now pose a similar risk for Thomas, one reason his annual returns to Zimbabwe remained so vital to his art.

"Beautiful countryside, isn't it?" mused Thomas, driving his black Mercedes-Benz SUV past Eugene's golden fields, tall stands of pine and fir, and hills and buttes rendered nappy by logging. The multi-CD player moved from Culture's trenchant reggae to Louis Armstrong singing "Body and Soul," as Thomas piloted down the steep driveway of his new home. Lancelot got out to fold in the side-view mirrors and direct the Mercedes slowly into its tight fit in the garage. Inside, the house had a familiar feel—black vinyl furniture, a huge central TV and stereo, a clean and tidy look, a framed photo of Thomas in cap and gown, and Vena in the kitchen, cooking. She felt unsettled, missing home, worried about people there, still unable to work legally and a little lost in Oregon. "But it's all right," she allowed with a stiff upper lip.

The house was crowded. Thomas, Vena, Chiedza, and five-year-old Mati shared the main floor. Lancelot and Chaka took the laundry room. Chris, now replacing Sam on drums, and Tsepo Makhaza, the new twenty-something bass player, slept on a foldout bed in the basement rehearsal room, while Zivai and Tapfumaneyi shared an upstairs bedroom, festooned with sports jerseys and caps and photos of family and musical stars. The only telephone was in the kitchen within earshot of the TV, and, although Vena had set up her computer there, Thomas would grow antsy if anyone used the phone line to get on the Internet. "We are expecting calls from home," he would say. Thomas kept his watch set to Harare time. The Sporting Lions' place in the Premier League was on the line, and team reps called often with updates and game results. At mealtimes, Mati would produce small folding tables and plates, equally portioned for all, and Thomas would lead a brief silent prayer before everyone ate—just as he had in Harare.

Beer drinking was banned, which meant it had to be done in secret, easily accomplished since the young musicians adored it and had friends to bring it to them. In setting house rules, Thomas contrasted alcohol with ganja, which he said was "created by the Lord." He considered its illegality an injustice, "oppressing a section of the population." Thomas acknowledged that marijuana was not for everyone, and he never offered his spliff to someone he considered too young to make a mature choice. His countless songs contain not a single reference to smoking. He was never an advocate, only a person "born to smoke ganja." Smoking was not an act of "partying" for Thomas. "I have no time for celebration," he said often. "I don't even celebrate my birthday." Instead, ganja helped Thomas do his creative work. It was his way of turning off the noise of the world.

No less an achiever than Carl Sagan once extolled "the devastating insights achieved while high" on marijuana. Sagan's sole complaint about the drug was that it interferes with short-term memory. Thomas's tape recorder was his defense against losing the momentary insights that mattered most to him: song ideas. The larger forgetting of the world was precisely his objective in smoking. Forgetting, writes Michael Pollan, is "vastly underrated as a mental operation." For Pollan, "memory is the enemy of wonder, which abides nowhere else but in the present."[16] "If I smoke ganja," said Thomas, "I feel motivated to get into action and start working. I joke with my children and my wife. I say a lot of stories to them, always thinking of my family as the first priority of my life." So it was that the ganja bag sat on the table in the family room in Eugene, while the boys hid their beers in the basement.

Thomas's musicians found him a sometimes arbitrary head of household. They had become honorary children in a newly extended family. Vena wielded considerable influence, as befits a "woman of the house" in Thomas's view. Children, on the other hand, were "always under the rule of their parents." Thomas rejected the notion that a child becomes an independent agent at age eighteen. "In African custom," he explained, "you can grow up to be sixty years, and you will be still under your mother's rule and father's rule." *Parents are the gods you can see.* And when they die, they must be honored through prayers and ceremonies.

Yet children could wield power in the Mapfumo household. One night after dinner, the television was tuned to a featherweight boxing match (Sena vs. Gaitlin). Little Mati turned up at Thomas's side to say that only five minutes remained until "the contest." Thomas spoke to her firmly in Shona, but the child would hear none of it. "Daddy," she protested, "every day, boxing. Every day, soccer. Every day, news. Every day, boxing. Every day, soccer . . ." When the gladiators on the screen collided in an accidental head butt, the challenger was injured and the fight called early. Mati saw her opening. Chiedza and Vena abandoned duties in the kitchen and took seats before the TV. "The contest" turned out to be the semifinal round of the first season of *American Idol*, with only Justin, Nikki, and Kelly remaining. The women of the house were riveted, each rooting for her favorite. As the singing proceeded, Thomas perused an American tabloid, the *Globe*, where he found a splashy two-page spread under the headline "American Idol Is Fixed!" The girls paid no heed as their patriarch—who had established his own career in a Rhodesian singing contest thirty years earlier—read aloud about the corruption behind America's favorite reality show.

Thomas was counting his dollars that fall. He would need them to get the band back to Harare for Christmas to launch his new album, *Toi Toi*. A "toi toi" is a defiant display of dance and song seen in both South Africa and Zimbabwe as blacks stood for freedom from colonial rule. The idea of toi toiing against Zimbabwe's black government was sure to enrage the likes of Jonathan Moyo, himself targeted in a song from the album called "Mukoma J (Brother J)." But the lyrics on *Toi Toi* confront the crisis in Zimbabwe more reflectively than those on *Chimurenga Rebel*. Thomas mostly pleads with God, rather than with people or politicians, to rescue the country. On the album's most penetrating song, "Pasi Inhaka (This World Is Our Inheritance)," Thomas muses over the temporary nature of all things, as an mbira-driven groove—one not based on any traditional song—gallops ahead beneath volleys of sad, silvery guitar and stoic blasts of brass.

Again, Thomas had qualms about returning home in 2002. There were new rumors that he and Vena would be arrested upon arrival. Thomas contacted Musa Zimunya in Virginia and asked what he was hearing. Musa had a line to a former student who now worked closely with Mugabe and Moyo. "I got hold of him," recalled Musa, "and I said, 'What's going on out there? You guys want to arrest Thomas Mapfumo? Don't we have enough trouble as it is?'" Musa's contact looked into these reports and called back to declare them baseless. He said that President Mugabe had been "very upset" to learn that this rumor was circulating and had personally challenged the CIO and the police during his morning briefing, demanding to know if such a plan existed and receiving assurances it did not. If this discussion in fact occurred, it might explain why the docket for the case concerning Thomas's BMWs mysteriously vanished around this time. "No docket, no case," said Saki Mafundikwa, who believed that a Mapfumo admirer on the police force had likely destroyed the paperwork.[17]

Thomas flew back to Harare in December 2002, with a band that included Brooks Barnett. No one had coached the American trumpeter about what to say at Zimbabwe customs, so when asked the reason for his visit, Brooks said he had come to perform with Thomas Mapfumo and the Blacks Unlimited. The agent wrote "holiday." But Zimbabwe was no holiday for Brooks. Thomas convened seventeen musicians for lengthy rehearsals at Mushandira Pamwe, and they soon began performing the marathon concerts Harare fans had been craving. "They were just *into* it," recalled Brooks. The crowd at Thomas's Christmas Eve show at the Harare International Conference Center was smaller than the one that had greeted him at Boka a year before. The *Sunday Mail* put the turnout at three thousand and speculated that Z$5,000 tickets and Z$800 beers had surely dissuaded many. But even this state newspaper conceded that Thomas and the band performed exceptionally, and that when they left the stage at 4:30 on Christmas morning, "no-one complained, no-one."

Riding shotgun around town in Thomas's Japanese-bought BMW, Brooks sensed that the whole city was "on Thomas's side . . . the best side." He said, "Every person we met had nothing but the highest respect when they were dealing with him." Meanwhile, state radio and television filled airtime with talk about the "Third Chimurenga," a new ZANU-PF crusade driven home by constant replays of Moyo's *Chave Chimurenga* jingles. These jingles would blanket the airwaves until March 2003, when they were at last withdrawn in response to public complaint—not about the politics but the ceaseless repetitions. Thomas had sold his house in Mabelreign, and his relatives now lived in a five-bedroom home in Mount Pleasant with a yard and swimming pool. Brooks said they kept Radio 2 playing loud in the kitchen all the time, but rarely did he hear a song by Thomas Mapfumo.

Reviewing a mid-January Mapfumo concert in Gweru, the *Herald* reported that fans had to choose between buying mealy-meal for their families that week or paying the Z$2,500 admission fee to hear Thomas. Plenty chose to feed their souls rather than their bellies. The *Herald* refrained from attacking Thomas during this visit, opting instead to write about him as a mere celebrity rather than as a political force. The *Daily News*, on the other hand, used Thomas's presence to tweak the government. One story surveyed musicians' attitudes toward the "crisis" in Zimbabwe. Fred Zindi—musician, chronicler of Zimbabwean music, and now professor at the University of Zimbabwe—said only, "There is no freedom of expression in Zimbabwe and I can't comment on that issue. I have children to look after." Dr. Mapfumo showed no such caution. He called on the seventy-nine-year-old Mugabe to "act like a mature citizen and gracefully leave the presidency so that someone else can take over."[18]

In the wake of its defeat, the MDC was splintering, and while Thomas was now willing to call openly for Mugabe to step aside, he had also cooled on Morgan Tsvangirai. In one interview, Thomas bade Zimbabweans to "forget about Mugabe and Tsvangirai" and seek grassroots solutions to the nation's ills.[19] He also slammed fellow musicians like Chinx, Chimbetu, and Andy Brown, who, he told the *Daily News*, had "fallen for money." Such stories were deeply irksome to Minister Moyo. Moyo had been harassing and detaining *Daily News* editors and reporters for two years, with little effect. By the end of 2003, he would force the paper to stop publishing altogether, relegating opposition voices to the Internet, where still fewer Zimbabweans would hear them.

Toi Toi hit the market shortly before Thomas and the band returned to the United States in February 2003. The *Herald* once again bypassed the politics, dubbing it a "jazz album" and noting that "the once undisputed Chimurenga music king has now set his sights on the American market and lost the mbira beat."[20] Just the same, Gramma Records' music charts were already listing *Toi Toi* as the top-selling album in the country, even though it was receiving no radio play.[21] The *Daily News* queried ZBC's chief executive as to why such a popular release was being ignored. "Which one is Mapfumo's 'latest album'?" he replied. "Get me a copy of it so that I can listen to it."[22] This from the head of the only legal radio broadcaster in the country in reference to the best-selling album of the day. The Blacks Unlimited played one last show in Mutare. Under heavy police guard, fans sang and shouted along with Thomas "things they wouldn't dare say."[23] For that alone, Thomas's return had been worth the risk.

Al Green, now living in San Francisco, was running low on cash and reining in expenses where he could. "The horn players wanted money too," Al wrote in a private e-mail referring to the *Toi Toi* recording sessions. "Fortunately they were young and easily intimidated, so they're still in the band." Al could be equally blunt and far more prosaic in public e-mail missives to Thomas's fan base. After a short U.S. tour, he thanked those who had attended the shows, noting that they could now consider themselves "terrorists like us." He wrapped up, "So goes Zimbabwe, so goes America. All the money spent on War, the rest lost to corruption in High Places. Both leaders mockeries of innocence as they wash the blood from their hands."

Al fired up the newly repaired Bounder and personally drove the band from Eugene to Michigan, where they were refused entry to Canada because the American authorities would not guarantee reentry for the Zimbabwean musicians. Oregon congressman Peter DeFazio's office got involved but could not provide the needed assurances, and lucrative Canadian shows had to be scrapped. Al's e-mail account of this ill-fated tour, "Two Weeks in the Pirate Ship," chalked the Canadian fiasco up to "a simple mistake on the part of USCIS (Homerland Security)."[24] Al wrote, "The Canadian Official was resolute in first determining if we were indeed musicians. He asked us to sing a little tune, right there, for free. We sang a bit of 'Hey Jude,' feeling it appropriate for the moment. We sang with little joy, and I'm afraid our pirate version didn't impress him."

The year 2003 would be the first in Thomas's career when he would record no new music. He had the songs, but not the means to produce them. The band would make its annual pilgrimage to Harare and record the new music there, where costs were lower. On the eve of departure, Thomas was uncharacteristically glum, blaming Al for the Canadian fiasco. "How can you do that?" he asked. "How can you cross an international border when you have not arranged all your visas? All the people that were working in that office—this guy has laid them off. He is now running things from his house with his girlfriend. *Toi Toi* is a good album. But this guy is not promoting it. I cannot record any more music for Al. I am looking for a label. I have told him."

Al Green too had reached a decision point. "I had sold two houses," he recalled. "And I had to mortgage another house. My credit was shut down. All the money had been pissed away on America. Every gas station. Every hotel. Every phone call. I paid for everything. And I'm glad I did it." Al could be cantankerous, but he was also self-aware. In a personal e-mail around this time, he wrote, "I know they say I fucked Andy Frankel out of thousands of dollars, forced his booking agent to put a voodoo curse on me, was mean to Ken [Braun, of Stern's], and scared Thomas Brooman [WOMAD], that I insulted Randall Grass [Shanachie Records], attacked Bob Diener [Zimbob], and generally brought an unpleasant feeling to an industry that was just doing business as usual." Al had no regrets, though he was beginning to doubt that either he or Thomas would live to profit from his crusade to close down "pirates" and redirect Thomas's royalties. Perhaps, Al mused, their children would benefit.

Brooks Barnett spent much of 2003 living with the band, in and out of Thomas's house and the Downtown Motel. He had become one of them, learning Shona, going on weekend fishing trips and cooking up the catch, and rehearsing and transcribing new music even though there was no money to record it. Brooks disliked the atmosphere of noncommunication within the band, the tension between Thomas's family and his musicians, the unpredictability of payments. But, like so many Blacks Unlimited musicians before him, Brooks found spiritual succor in Thomas's music, and each time he would resolve to leave, he found himself unable to do so. "As a musician," he reflected, "you have dreamed your whole life to be on that stage playing music that is relevant to people, singing to their soul and their heart with what you are playing. I've seen people, certain types of people, old women, who would cry when we play these horn lines. I would actually see them weeping—just an incredible feeling. And that's addictive. You want it more and more. And yes, he uses that."

On stage in Revolution Hall in Troy, New York, the band showed little sign of all this wear and tear. They ripped into the new repertoire with energy and gusto. Zivai was sporting a Telecaster guitar and plugging into a powerful Marshall amplifier. Tsepo too played through new gear, a six-string bass and a Genz-Benz cabinet rig. Thomas sang with passion and focus, but something was off in his appearance. His hairline had receded dramatically. The long, clumpy ropes of his asymmetrical dreadlocks now hung from scant roots at the back of his head. Curly wisps of black hair still grew up top, but the clean line between hair and scalp had moved back past the crown of his head, a little more on the right than the left. Those pendulous dreads mirrored Thomas's financial condition, and his ability to operate in America or Zimbabwe—for all hung by threads. As he left Revolution Hall that night, Thomas acknowledged as much, saying, "We're in a mess."

Thomas arrived in Harare in mid-December 2003, once again faced with rebuilding his band after three of his young musicians chose to remain in London rather than return to Zimbabwe or America. He would look for more experienced players this time, and his top priority was to put Bezil Makombe back in the lead mbira chair. Bezil's brother Ngoni lay in a coma at the time, dying—"another great loss to a world that couldn't give a rat's ass," sniped Al. When Ngoni died in January 2004, Thomas attended the funeral and made a gift to the family. Afterward, Bezil rejoined the band.

Thomas's best new recruit was lead guitarist Gilbert Zvamaida, who would endure in this crucial seat for more than a decade. Gilbert grew up playing music in the Eastern Highlands. Though he displayed early ability, he never took music seriously until, ironically, he mangled a finger in a fan belt during reaping time at the mill. Eighteen years old and unable to work, Gilbert fashioned himself a three-string "banjo" and began learning songs off the radio. He mastered Thomas's Acid Band hits, current at the time. Nearly thirty years later, the prospect of joining Thomas on stage was "like a dream come true." Gilbert had spent all that time as a professional guitarist, most notably in a successful outfit called Zig Zag Band. But by the time Thomas approached him, most of his bandmates, and his wife, had all died of sicknesses. Gilbert's only personal ties to Zimbabwe were his ailing father and teenage son, already living on his own. Slipping off to America as Thomas Mapfumo's guitarist offered more than musical fulfillment; it was an escape from a life of tragedy.

For the first Christmas in memory, Thomas released no new music in Zimbabwe.[25] The downward dive of the local economy was evident in petrol and food shortages, declines in all public services, and also skyrocketing admission prices at Thomas's shows, now Z$15,000 or even Z$20,000. Two years earlier, this amount had been enough to finance Joshua Dube's funeral. Now, it barely covered admission to a Mapfumo show. Still, with "Mukanya fever" gripping the city, plenty of fans were willing to pay. But there were problems. Thomas suspected foul play when the power was cut shortly after the start of his show at Club Hide Out. When he tried to book time at Shed Studio to record, he got a runaround. "They were not fully booked," Cuthbert complained to the press, suggesting that someone at Shed was clearly "not happy with the message in the music." Then, with eleven songs fully recorded and ready to be mixed, one of the studio engineers accidentally erased the hard drive of the session, forcing the band to change travel plans and rerecord the album.[26]

Outside Harare, it was even worse. Onetime guerrillas and CIO agents crowded into a show in Chinhoyi, scene of the first firefight of the liberation struggle back in 1966. Veterans of that battle danced with joy as Thomas launched into his classic repertoire, but when he moved to newer songs critical of the regime, an officer approached a doorman to say that if Thomas did not stop singing such songs, "people will be beaten." As Thomas sang a new song criticizing Zimbabwean soldiers and police, an Ndebele CIO agent approached the band's Ndebele drummer—a friend from the old days in Bulawayo—and whispered into his ear: "Today we are going to take Mudhara [the old man]." William Mapfumo recalled, "It was very tense. They were after the band. Thomas was supposed to play until 6:00 AM, but he said, 'I will just play one more song and then stop the show. I don't want to be threatened.'" Thomas denied ending the show early and insisted that although the band left town that night, he himself slept in a local hotel. But the atmosphere was unnerving. Said Thomas, "The country was becoming lawless."

Thomas labored to persuade the press that he would soon be coming home, that he had never intended to abandon Zimbabwe, that things were now "looking promising," and that he was "not in exile."[27] But incidents like these fed the growing impression that he was the target of unseen enemies determined to trip him up at every opportunity and make the option of coming home seem as unappealing as possible.

Vena and the three children, along with Lancelot's daughter Cleopatra, had all returned to Harare early in 2004 to update their U.S. visas. Despite daunting obstacles, Vena succeeded in securing the visas and getting everyone back to Eugene safely. She and the children were now legal U.S. residents, but she still could not work and earn money to support them. Thomas, meanwhile, remained in Zimbabwe tending to his own raft of problems, including a contentious shake-up of Sporting Lions management after a disappointing season. Before leaving Zimbabwe, Thomas gave a lengthy press interview in which he sought to put to rest rumors that he was in ill health, losing his hearing, dependent on a "songbook" on stage to remember his lyrics, that he was shying away from politics, that his family was losing contact with Zimbabwean culture, and that his soccer team was at death's door. Thomas defended himself gamely on all fronts, ending this four-month visit with a vow to reverse his ill fortune and come back to stay the following year. He flew out of Harare on April 4, 2004. As of this writing, in February 2015, he has never returned.

15 / The Land of the Horses

I am a marked man.

THOMAS MAPFUMO

Leaves continued to fall during Thomas's years in exile. Ian Smith succumbed in Cape Town at eighty-eight, ending in a state of "gloomy delight" at Zimbabwe's myriad failures. Smith's successor as prime minister, Bishop Abel Muzorewa, saw out his years in Harare, nursing his own bitter tonic of self-vindication until the Lord called him home at eighty-five. Hakurotwi Mude, whose mbira singing voice had captivated Thomas, passed away in Highfield, Harare, at seventy-two, his skill and renown having failed to deliver him from poverty, and Thomas's beloved uncle, John "Jira" Munhumumwe, also died in his early seventies. These were natural deaths for men who had lived long lives. Crueler fates felled others. Guitarist Emmanuel Jera was still in his fifties when he had the misfortune of collapsing on the street during a week when Harare's doctors and nurses were striking to protest pay cuts. Manu died unattended at Harare Hospital. Benny Miller, Thomas's favorite recording engineer, fell to a heart attack at fifty-eight. Prostate cancer, diagnosed late, took the life of Tom Terrell, the writer and DJ who had so memorably road-managed Thomas's first U.S. tour. Terrell was fifty-seven. Composer, educator, and gay rights activist Keith Goddard was just forty-nine when he died in a hospital, and singer Andy Brown was fifty when he, like Goddard, succumbed to the proverbial "undisclosed ailment." Brown's onetime wife, Chiwoniso, daughter of Dumisani Maraire, also died, of pneumonia, at just thirty-seven in a Chiungwiza hospital, ending what had become a promising international career as a singer-songwriter. Simon Chimbetu, scion of Zimbabwean rumba, was fifty when he perished in a fiery road accident not long after receiving a farm from the government—a gesture of thanks for his support of Mugabe's land campaign.

"ZANU-PF declared him a hero," said Thomas of Chimbetu. "Well, I think that is a good thing." Thomas had dismissed Chimbetu's music as derivative and shallow, and excoriated his participation in ZANU propaganda, but in the end, gut-level affection for a flashy dresser and a man of his word counted more.[1]

Thomas had given up his house in Eugene, so when he and his musicians returned from Zimbabwe in the spring of 2004, they landed at the Downtown Motel. By then, a friend from Ghana had helped Vena apply for state aid and find a small house, big enough for her and the children. For four years, Vena had looked after Thomas's musicians without complaint. Now she yearned for family life. She had hoped Thomas would join them in the new house and let the musicians find places of their own, but Thomas opted to rent a separate house for himself, his brothers, and the band.

This was a difficult period for Vena and Thomas. She had confronted him over "girlfriends" in the past. There had been blowups and frank discussions, but no lasting resolution. Thomas viewed his occasional dalliances as a fact of his professional life. "I am a musician," he explained. "I have a lot of pressure on me. I have friends out there who can call me in the middle of the night on my phone. Some of them are female friends. When such incidents happen, I expect my wife to understand. A woman who is married to an artist has to realize that."

"You can be a musician," allowed Vena. "But do it with respect. Your family has to come first."

Thomas had, of course, put his family first by bringing them to America. "The kids could have stayed in Zimbabwe," noted Al Green. "Instead, they grew up in Eugene and played soccer, and went to the ice cream store, and had a pretty nice life without all the suffering." Thomas's overriding objective had been to give his children opportunities in life, something he felt Zimbabwe could no longer offer them. In the process, he had surrendered the economic engine that had driven his career. Between 2004 and 2014, Thomas and his musicians recorded enough new material for at least six studio albums and composed many more songs that were never recorded. From all that creative output, only three physical albums have made it to release, and only one on an international label. None of this music was promoted or performed in Zimbabwe, where it would have meant the most, and none of it generated much income. During these years, Thomas worked with at least eight different

American agents and "managers," none of them able to organize his business sufficiently to support all who depended on him.

Thomas's critics in Zimbabwean state media would delight in the hardships exile posed to his musical career. Thomas's family, on the other hand, would feel deep gratitude for his decision to bring them to America. After all, how many legendary musicians have made the opposite choice—career over family—with disastrous consequences for their loved ones? Prioritizing the interests of his wife and children over his professional goals showed character and integrity for an artist of Thomas's stature. He gave up a lot by leaving Zimbabwe. But, in the end, the work that makes Thomas Mapfumo an African music legend was already there; no one could take that away. For his family, on the other hand, especially his young children, the future was at stake. Thomas knew what he had to do, and he never looked back.

Even without the complications of a tricontinental music career, family had never been a simple proposition for Thomas. From the age of ten, he had made his way with the Mapfumos and Munhumumwes, although his own father belonged to another clan, a difference that could be neither erased nor forgotten. Thomas's wife and children sometimes felt distant from their in-laws on Thomas's side. Even when Thomas became the breadwinner for the clan, Janet, his mother, would visit Harare and more often than not stay with William and Lancelot rather than with Thomas. During the family's last visit to Zimbabwe, Thomas urged Tapfumaneyi and Chiedza to visit Janet: "Go and see Gogo." For whatever reason, Janet chose not to receive them. "As we entered the gate," Tapfumaneyi recalled, "she opened the curtain and I could see her. And then she just shut the curtain." Thomas's children left Zimbabwe without seeing their grandmother one last time.

In July 2004, the Blacks Unlimited flew to Boston for a set of East Coast shows. Thomas was the first to emerge from the gate at Logan Airport. Something was different. His fedora sat low on his head, no hint of dreadlocks showing. With a sly tip of his hat he revealed a head shaven cue-ball clean, a look that would convince some Zimbabweans he must be dying of cancer. In fact, he had been liberated from a twenty-year burden that had grown unwieldy and painful. "We are feeling some breezes," quipped Thomas. William had recently arrived from Zimbabwe, and he and Lancelot were also close-cropped. The three Mapfumo brothers cut a striking image as virtual skinheads.

Bezil, who had always maintained a clean-cut look, now sported short, nappy dreads, matching those of Chris and Chaka.[2] Bezil was subdued this time, less the jovial rascal of past tours. In South Africa, he had been supporting his wife and children by playing with a band called Movement. Movement had a sponsor with ties to the African National Council, so the band enjoyed a degree of stability and security, though no major success. Still, Bezil already questioned his decision to come to America. "Here, I am poor," he muttered. "But I just keep quiet. I don't say anything."

In the Gateway Inn in Somerville, Massachusetts, Thomas and Lancelot bantered about the situation back home. "The MDC is planning to go to war," Thomas boomed feistily. "They are preparing their fighters in South Africa and Mozambique. They are going to attack Zimbabwe." Mugabe had "closed all the openings," just like Smith before him, leaving people no choice but to fight. "People don't want to hear about ZANU," echoed Lancelot, tossing out aphorisms about the chicken being "out of the pot . . . it won't go back in." William sat in the corner, smoking, listening, as quiet as Bezil.

The band had played England and Austria—the site of Thomas's shearing—and two big shows in Barcelona, Spain. But due to accrued expenses, there was little cash to show for it. Money, and its continual scarcity, seemed to weigh on William especially. He needled Thomas, pointing out that sungura bandleader Alick Macheso was outselling every other artist in Zimbabwe. "Your CDs are not selling because they are not played on the radio," William declared in a humorless baritone. "Macheso is making more money there than we are in America." Thomas parried gamely that Zimbabwean money was worthless anyway, but William pressed him, certain that Mugabe's people would forgive everything, if only Thomas would soften his line. "They like him," said William privately. "But they don't like the messages in his songs. If he just sings in praise of the ruling party, I know he can get a farm. Just like that. I *know*."

Bezil agreed, showing rare compassion for Thomas. "Sometimes I feel sorry for him," he said. "One day he will have nothing. He will have destroyed his band, and he will have no money at all. Like Safirio Madzikatire."[3]

Thomas had been forced to sell the Sporting Lions that week.[4] "I loved that team," he said softly as sweet smoke filled the crowded motel room, "but I had to realize my own children were going to starve." Thomas said all he had wanted was to help young men from Mbare find a better life in sport. Sponsors had shunned "Mukanya's team," undermining him at every turn. Politics, celebrity, and the shoddy state of soccer in Zimbabwe had all conspired against Thomas's dream, and losing it left him raw.

"Thomas is very brave," said Gilbert, the new guitarist, just a few months into his American sojourn. "Now in Zimbabwe, his life is in danger. Those guns can come out at any time. He shouldn't move alone there. But he shouldn't sing politics." More tactful than William, more polite than Bezil, Gilbert too seemed to be nudging Thomas to ease up on criticizing the regime in Zimbabwe. Thomas, for his part, had lost the company of his wife, his soccer team, his dreadlocks, his ability to perform for the audiences that loved him most, and far too many friends, relatives, and colleagues. He was not about to lose his message and artistic mission, no matter what family members and musicians might tell him.

Vena had been urging the family and the band to apply for political asylum, which, among other advantages, would allow them to work legally. "At first Thomas didn't want to do it," Vena recalled. The reason was clear: asylum status would rule out any near-term visits to Zimbabwe. But after William overstayed his tourist visa, he began to see things Vena's way. Asylum would return him to legal status and allow him to bring his own family to America. With his brothers and wife in agreement, Thomas came around, and the family, along with some band members, prepared asylum applications.

Help came from an unlikely source. A live Mapfumo CD called *Chaputika* (Explosion), recorded during the band's spring 2004 visit to the United Kingdom, had been swiftly packaged and released in Zimbabwe by local producers.[5] The CD included an otherwise unreleased track called "Masoja ne Mapurisa (The Soldiers and the Police)." With its frontal attack on ZANU's use of men in uniform to brutalize critics, this was the song that had nearly triggered violence at Thomas's last show in Chinhoyi. No sooner did *Chaputika* hit the market than ZANU youth raided Harare flea markets where it was being sold. They attacked the father of one of the producers and torched his car. Resulting reports in the international press provided fresh documentation to support the Mapfumos' asylum claims, and by the end of 2006, Thomas, his family, and a few key musicians would all become political exiles. After that, only U.S. citizenship—the fruit of two more lengthy and uncertain bureaucratic processes—would allow them to visit Zimbabwe with full confidence that they could return to the United States.

Thomas's contact with fans back home would now be mediated by the Zimbabwean press. *Sunday Mail* reporters telephoned him in Eugene, fishing for incendiary comments, seemingly out to portray him as a politician rather than a people's poet. "I don't want to be the president of a country," said an exasperated Thomas. "I am a musician, an entertainer, and what I'm saying is that people's rights should be recognized. Our people are facing poverty today because of mismanagement. It's our own fault. We have to put our house in order." For Thomas, putting one's house in order had always involved a spiritual dimension, from his liberation war pleas to the ancestors, to the prayerful lyrics on *Toi Toi*. Literary critic Maurice Vambe sought to portray this as weakness. In academic writings, Vambe tries to dismantle Thomas's revolutionary credentials.[6] Vambe portrays Thomas's resort to prayer as a cop-out, a dead-end substitute for positive action. Thomas never read Vambe's essays, but the title of his next CD offered a pithy reply: *Rise Up*.

Recorded at Sprout City Studio in Eugene—after original tracks from Zimbabwe were mysteriously lost, twice!—*Rise Up* is well summarized by its opening song, an anthem of quiet resolve called "Kuvarira Mukati (To Suffer in Silence)." A shimmering organ vamp lends a hymnlike quality to the sound, but the lyrics are a call to action.

> It is up to you slumberers
> You don't talk, guys, huh?
> You just keep quiet, guys
> When things get tougher
> You will be losers, guys
> You just hurt inside
>
> Twenty years, but nothing have we developed
> The great war we fought has proved nothing
> The bondage we suffered then is never ending . . .
> If you don't speak, gentlemen, this will not end

The "eight years" mentioned in the song "Corruption" has become twenty, and now the call is more urgent, an entreaty to "slumberers" to wake up and resist. Geoffrey Nyarota had broken the Willowgate scandal in 1988, launched the *Daily News* a decade later, and in 2003, fled Zimbabwe after a series of arrests and detentions. While lecturing at the Kennedy School of Government in Boston, Nyarota attended a Mapfumo show at the Somerville nightclub Johnny D's. During a break, he made his way to the club's snug, downstairs green room to greet the man. "When I saw Thomas Mapfumo that night," he recalled, "I saw myself, because we are now sinking in the same boat. I thought about the punishment that Mugabe unknowingly inflicts on the children of Zimbabwe. If he knew that this great man stood in front of two dozen people and called it a night of entertainment, maybe Mugabe would be persuaded to change. But for Thomas, this is a dangerous game. There is no gold mine here for him. His gold mine—and he *does* have a gold mine—is six thousand miles away."

Elias Mudzuri, Harare's former MDC mayor, attended another Boston Mapfumo show and danced gleefully until the last note played. Mudzuri had been elected mayor in 2003, only to be driven from office by ZANU-PF a year later. During his tenure in office, police had threatened his business associates, attacked his bar in Budiriro—forcing him to close it to protect patrons—and repeatedly arrested him during town meetings at which he was trying to help citizens address their problems. "I never saw the inside of a jail cell in my life," Mudzuri told Thomas in the dressing room at Johnny D's, "until I was elected mayor."

Mudzuri had been a reluctant politician, well aware that Mugabe would "stop at nothing, other than reduce you to rubble." Mudzuri was particularly offended by Mugabe's unvarnished racism. "[Mugabe] still thinks in the sixties," said the mayor, "and unfortunately, the West, the whites, because of some guilty conscience, they think he has a point. But you can never reverse history by attacking the children of those people. In 1980, it was Mugabe himself as president who declared that we shall never again fight on racial grounds. And we *believed* him." Thomas's political evolution, on the other hand, made perfect sense to Mudzuri, whether the subject was Bishop Muzorewa or President Mugabe. Both these leaders had earned the people's trust and then betrayed it. "But if a man marries a spirited bride," said Mudzuri, "and then is hurt when she cheats on him, it does not mean he was wrong to marry her. I don't think Mapfumo owes anyone an apology for singing at that [Muzorewa] rally. Just like today, when Mugabe has failed, there is no apology needed to explain why he once praised him. We are not gods. We cannot foresee what will happen."

Mudzuri was going back to Zimbabwe, and he urged Thomas to do the same, saying, "Your people need you." Later he said, "Mapfumo is not young. He should be able to stand his ground and say, 'If you want to kill me, kill me.' He has to make his choice. Is he really going to be an American, with all his roots? What part can he play?"

Al Green's April 2004 press release opened: "Please note the following Revolutionary Events with David Hilliard and the Black Panther F.U.G.I.T.I.V.E.S." Al had been confident that three Bay Area concerts pairing chimurenga music with old-school rap would put well-needed cash in Blacks Unlimited pockets. Thomas embraced the Panthers as fellow "freedom fighters" and savored Hilliard's war stories about J. Edgar Hoover and the epic clashes of the 1970s. But he was not surprised when these concerts failed to attract large audiences. Afterward, Al circulated an e-mail titled "Goodbye Forever!" It opened, "Hello! aNOnym reCOrds (NOCO) is evolving finally into what it was meant to be. Nothing."

Al's crisis of faith coincided with yet another management breakdown. The contract for Thomas's Spanish concerts had directed most of the proceeds to cover past car payments, air tickets, visa fees, and restaurant and gas station bills. Trumpeter Brooks Barnett described an ugly scene in Barcelona when

Thomas learned he would not be paid in cash and treated the festival director to a titanic rage.

But, mere months after Al's "Goodbye, Forever" declaration, rays of hope appeared on the royalty front. Money was trickling in from Gramma and EMI, and customers around the world were finding their way to legitimate sources of Mapfumo music like CD Baby and iTunes. Al celebrated by renewing his impolitic e-mails. He urged a boycott of the "world music" industry: "a disgusting sham of racist exploitation." He reported on his ongoing hunt for any and all who had abused Thomas financially. Mike Wells of Serengeti was "a big game hunter" who reminisced about his lifelong pursuit of African master tapes "like he was Pearl S. Buck." A tribute to Thomas in the EMI compilation liner notes was "just like the patriotic reach-arounds on Fox News." While the Blacks Unlimited were left to "die in poverty" in Oregon and Zimbabwe, "these rich fucks take the credit and release their 'compilations,' as 'experts' in their field."

At the Kola Note in Montreal, a young Zimbabwean rapper called Stepper opened the show. Backstage after sound check, Thomas lectured Stepper about hip-hop: "I don't want to hear people talking shit about America and then imitating American music." His point made, Thomas handed the rapper a small bill and sent him off to hunt for ganja. Despite improving fortunes for the band, the musicians were not earning enough to send much money home, and they let their dissatisfaction be known. "People always complain," said Vena, citing Chaka as the one musician who seemed to understand the big picture, and actually felt grateful to be in America. Chaka had left a job in a factory to join the Blacks Unlimited and had no regrets about the decision. "It's not Zimbabwe," said Vena. "Where do they expect a lot of money to come from? It's a struggle."

In January 2005, singers Mavis and Naomi, along with Bezil and Nyoni (the Ndebele drummer), decided to return to Zimbabwe. They might suffer more there, but at least they would be with their families. Thomas accepted the musicians' choice gracefully and even helped arrange their travel. Once back in Harare, however, Bezil went to the *Sunday Mail* and charged that the band had been forced to live "hand-to-mouth . . . like beggars." Bezil revealed that Thomas no longer lived with his wife. When a reporter telephoned from Harare, Thomas confirmed the separation but denied that anyone went hungry in his household. "[Bezil] is angry with me because I tried to build him into a responsible man," said Thomas. "He is very talented when it comes to making music, but he has serious problems with alcohol. At one time my brother William gave him a thumping for his wayward behavior and that made him want to leave." Thomas expressed undiminished affection and concern for his favorite mbira player. "I see that confused young man as my own son," he said. "He is free to return to the band. I am not vindictive."[7] Despite this rift, the two musicians would remain in close contact, and Bezil would join the band for future concerts in South Africa.

Chris Muchabaiwa stayed in Eugene, but on his own terms. Unwilling to live under the watchful eyes of Thomas and his brothers, Chris had moved in with an American woman and fathered a child with her. Musically, Chris was now a vital asset to the Blacks Unlimited. He could play either bass or drums, even guitar, and was essential to the process of training American musicians to play with the band. Given the difficulties of recruiting musicians from Zimbabwe, especially without going there, finding American players became unavoidable at this point.

Meanwhile, people living in Thomas's house were getting sick, in Chaka's case, sick enough to be hospitalized. The culprit turned out to be mold growing in the walls. In March 2005, Thomas, William, Lancelot, and Gilbert found a new house on Capitol Drive, near the top of a high hill overlooking Eugene. It was a sunny two-story home with wooden porches and pleasing views. Just weeks after they moved in, William accidentally walked through a sliding glass door leading from the living room to one of the porches. The sun was in his eyes, and he thought the door was open. His head hit the heavy glass—not shatterproof—breaking it into large, bladed projectiles, one of which nearly severed the index finger of his right hand as it fell. An emergency room doctor sewed up the wound but did little to repair tendons, muscles, and nerves. William would experience restricted movement and pain that would make manual work difficult for years to come.

Bob Coen, the filmmaker who had helped guide Thomas to his first American tour, visited Eugene and found Thomas "in a dark place." Bob was among those who had been urging Thomas to go home to refresh himself emotionally and creatively. Now he saw that this was both impossible and pointless. "I am a marked man," said Thomas. "Me and William and Lancelot. And my family. We cannot go there. We will not be safe."

After March gigs in the United Kingdom, Gilbert flew to Zimbabwe to renew his passport, not realizing that he would be stranded there for nearly a year.[8] Thomas continued to accept gigs, though he now lacked both a drummer and a lead guitarist, minimal requirements for a show. The year 2005 was the low ebb of Thomas's exile, a time when he had neither the Zimbabwean musicians he needed to present his music effectively nor a solid core of American substitutes.[9] Al was finding that American promoters and agents now saw Thomas Mapfumo and the Blacks Unlimited as "more of a bar band," meaning, to Al, "not the type you'd have at a performing arts center where the rich throw money at themselves and revel in their domination." It was actually easier to pull together a show in England, as during a brief visit that Cuthbert had arranged for Thomas to perform at the Live 8: Africa Calling concert in July. With Brooks the sole horn player, just Chaka on mbira, no backup singers, and Londoners Zivai and Tsepo on guitar and bass, respectively, the band looked sparse spread across a vast outdoor stage, but the chimurenga sound was there, and the band was treated well and paid properly.[10]

As the Oregon contingent made their way home from the United Kingdom, Immigration and Naturalization agents at Newark Airport tried to deport Chaka, citing an irregularity on his passport. Chaka was still recovering from his mold-related sickness. He relied on medications that would have been prohibitively expensive, if available at all, in Zimbabwe. Desperate to save Thomas's last remaining mbira player, Al Green forced his way into a secure area of the airport. "My friend is upstairs and he's going to *die* if you send him home," Al told an official. The official gave Al a cell phone number, which he called so persistently that the authorities agreed to release Chaka. "I'm finished with everybody," Al said afterward. "I'm Gulliver, back from the land of the horses, and I never want to hear the words 'world music' again."[11]

But if 2005 was a rocky year for Thomas in America, it was worse in Zimbabwe. The MDC had vacillated over whether to compete in parliamentary elections, first boycotting, then joining the race, then losing in a rigged April vote. International outrage and street protests were met with swift violence, dragnet arrests, and Mugabe's smug pronouncement that the opposition should be "sporting enough to accept defeat and not look for excuses." In the process, the MDC now split into factions. "These guys are not thinking big," Thomas complained. *Rise Up* was released in Zimbabwe during the heat of that spring campaign. The *Daily Mirror* called it "a real gem . . . a blockbuster," but this and all other news was soon buried beneath the rubble of President Mugabe's most outlandish stratagem to date. Murambatsvina, officially Operation Restore Order—also Operation Drive Out Trash—was presented as a crackdown on illegal structures and black market street vendors. In practical terms, it involved bulldozing whole neighborhoods of Harare, generally MDC strongholds, including Mabvuku, where Thomas had spent his teenage years. The UN estimated that some 1.5 million people were directly displaced, and 2.4 million affected, as the homeless filtered into the countryside.

Even Mugabe's defenders were mystified by such wanton destruction. Some blamed the Chinese, supposedly after the street vendors' business. Others feared the president had succumbed to madness. Thomas had no trouble discerning the logic behind Murambatsvina. With municipal elections on the horizon, Mugabe wanted to expel opposition voters from the city, "into the rural areas where they will have to buy ZANU-PF cards." Thomas said, "They need those cards to eat. If you can't get food, what else can you do? You end up saying, 'I am one of you.'" Thomas had told an interviewer at the Live 8 concert that Zimbabweans would have to resort to armed struggle to end the Mugabe regime. Now, in comments on CNN, he again said the unthinkable: the country had been better off under Ian Smith.

As he waited for his visa in Harare, Gilbert spent ten months laying low at Thomas's family home, mostly hiding in fear. The guitarist ventured out only once to visit his dying father in Chimanimani and a few times, when absolutely necessary, to the passport office downtown. "I didn't play music," wrote Gilbert in his political asylum plea. "I didn't meet my friends. I didn't work. I didn't want to be noticed because of my ties to Thomas." Gilbert was overjoyed to rejoin the band in time for a benefit concert in Boston in January 2006. He emanated cherubic radiance on stage, his upbeat demeanor at odds with that of the other musicians, who had weathered a slow, thin year in Eugene.

In April, Thomas took the stage at SOB's in New York, sprouting short dreadlocks and fronting a band with as many Americans as Zimbabweans.[12] He sang a newly composed song called "Ruregerero (Forgiveness)," including the refrain "I forgive you, if you forgive me"—a song that would actually receive radio play in Zimbabwe. Thomas began this song seated and strumming an acoustic guitar. His execution was a little tentative, but as the band took charge, the sound lifted and a trademark Blacks Unlimited song structure unfolded—sweetly urgent vocals with call-and-response, melodious brass passages, and an exuberant guitar-driven jam to finish. Other new songs were also unexpectedly sunny. Thomas talked about singing "for joy" and showing his fans "the other side of my life." Cuthbert had recently pulled together a reissue compilation for the Zimbabwe market called *Love Unlimited*—all romance, no politics. Thomas said he wanted to reveal a softer, happier face of his artistic persona. This did not mean he was abandoning politics or protest—far from it. But distance from the problems at home, and exposure to so much contemporary music in America—notably from his children—was awakening new curiosities and musical avenues to explore.

On a Sunday morning in September 2006, William appeared at the Capitol Drive house in suit and tie. Gilbert came upstairs in a jacket and dress shirt, and William joked that he looked like "the minister of mines." Laughing and happy, Thomas, William, Lancelot, and Gilbert headed for the United Methodist Church in Eugene for their weekly ritual of public worship. William, his wife, and two of his daughters now lived in their own house in Springfield. Thomas's and Lancelot's children shifted between the Capitol Drive house and Vena's small place in town. Lancelot worked nights in a cafeteria at the University of Oregon. Gilbert ran the household, cooking and cleaning. Music went on mostly late at night once Lancelot got off work and made the grueling climb up the steep bends of Capitol Drive on his three-speed bicycle. After sadza and smoke, Lancelot would bring out his keyboard and a portable cassette machine, and Gilbert would break out his nylon-string guitar. Gilbert had now become Thomas's principal cocreator, taking on the role once held by Jonah Sithole, Joshua Dube, Chartwell Dutiro, and Bezil Makombe.

With some twenty new compositions at the ready, Thomas booked time at Sprout City Studio and swiftly recorded ten of them. The songs included some with English lyrics, and mixed political messages—"Ruvengo (Hatred)" and "Somebody Got to Pay"—with gentler fare, like his song about forgiveness and "Universal Love," a kind of rebuttal to so-called bedroom love songs.[13] The session's most poignant entry was a new composition called "Ndangariro (Remembering)," expressing the pain of separation from fans in Zimbabwe. Its warm harmony and straight-from-the-heart vocal would have broken hearts in Harare. As it was, these tracks would languish, recorded but unmixed, at Sprout City, while Thomas scrounged for money and continually revised his concept of the project. Some of these songs would find their way onto an eventual album, *Exile*, which finally reached the Zimbabwean market four years later.

In May 2006, Zimbabwe's inflation rate stood at 900 percent. A roll of toilet paper cost Z$400,000. By August, prices were so unwieldy that the government knocked three zeros off the currency, reducing Z$20,000 to just Z$20—about 10 American cents—overnight. Inflation soared unabated to 1,700 percent early in 2007, and unemployment reached 80 percent nationwide. As disease, hunger, and death spread, Harare's six official cemeteries neared capacity. The government recommended cremation, a violation of Shona custom but, officials argued, a necessity. Thwarted by a shortage of coal, grieving relatives shipped bodies to be burned in wood fires in Mutare, and even across the border in Mozambique.

In March 2007, the world saw images of MDC leader Morgan Tsvangirai's face so swollen from prison beatings that he could not open one eye. Mugabe responded succinctly to the resulting condemnations: "Go hang."[14] By May, electricity in Harare had to be rationed to four hours a day, and inflation reached 3,714 percent. The government forced shops to lower prices beyond the break-even point. Police, militias, and desperate citizens moved through

Zimbabwe's cities in a parade of commercial destruction. The police would demand price reductions; if merchants refused, militias would beat them; when prices dropped, citizens would rush in to empty the shelves. Many businesses closed, and by November, inflation reached 15,000 percent after doubling in a single month. Despite all this, Mugabe's system of patronage—a toxic blend of threats, bribes, and orchestrated scandals directed at critics—held firm. The quintessentially audacious despot announced his candidacy for another presidential run in 2008, and Michael Wines of the *New York Times* opined that, given his methods, "Mugabe may yet win."[15]

Thomas observed these events with surprising optimism. Seeing the bruised faces of Tsvangirai and his comrades broadcast on CNN, he said, "The whole world is watching. They know who Tsvangirai is now. Things are moving in the right direction."

In September 2007, the Blacks Unlimited performed at Philadelphia's Constitution Hall for the Liberty Award ceremony. The honoree was Bono and his organization DATA (Debt, AIDS, Trade, Africa). Former president George H. W. Bush attended the ceremony, along with various leaders the Irish rocker had improbably engaged as allies in his campaign to uplift Africa. In his acceptance speech, Bono lauded "the poetics of Allen Ginsberg, Edward R. Murrow, Miles Davis, Quincy Jones, Mary K. Blige, Frank Gehry." Surrounded by members of the aid-to-Africa elite, as well as by a children's choir from Uganda, Bono rhapsodized about America. "Of thee I sing," he intoned. "All of thee. These are the reasons I am a fan of America." At the dinner afterward, where Thomas would perform, Al Green paced the hall in silence, passing within striking range of former senator Rick Santorum and other stalwarts of "The Empire," but never showing his true colors. The patrons were well into dessert by the time Thomas performed, and some did not stay. Bono danced at stage-side during the mbira prayer "Mvura Ngainaye," plainly enraptured, but he too slipped away before the set ended.

Thomas was pleased to have participated. But singing about Zimbabwe was "becoming boring" he said afterward. It was time to "focus on the whole world." In the past, Thomas's inspiration had come from events unfolding around him in Zimbabwe: political doings, challenges people faced, and stories and scenes he encountered as he made his way around the country. Now, Thomas faced the world as an exile, watching CNN, dealing with airports and highways, American officialdom, and the pain of separation from his homeland and people. In his songwriting, he was trying to speak to a broader public and was becoming increasingly interested in doing so in English rather than in Shona.

Over Christmas, the Mapfumo family gathered in number in Oregon—Lancelot and his daughter Cleopatra; William with his wife, Sylvia, and two of his daughters, Marcia and Michelle; then Thomas with Vena, Tapfumaneyi, Chiedza, and Mati, as well as Thomas's older daughter, Janet, who had come from London with her half sister Charmaine and young daughter Lelani. This was an unprecedented reunion, and though potentially awkward, it presented an opportunity for healing within the extended family. Then, on Christmas Day, the Mapfumo brothers received word that their mother had died in Zimbabwe, and mourning rather than celebration became the order of the day.

Thomas guessed that Janet Chinhamo was around eighty when she died. Her passing had been preventable, the result of high blood pressure, which could easily have been treated had Zimbabwe's health system been functioning properly. Just as when his blood father had died in 1973, when the Hallelujah Chicken Run band was off at the remote Mhangura mine, Thomas was unable to perform the normal duties of a grieving Shona son, and he was devastated. He later said he was not even certain where his mother had been buried, yet another reason for him to crave a return to Zimbabwe.

"She was a strong woman," he reflected. "Very, very strong. And strict." Janet had passed on her steely constitution, as well as an ironclad sense of rules and order, to her three sons. "She was somebody powerful to Thomas," recalled Vena. "She was a believer." Even during Thomas's childhood years, when they had mostly lived apart, Janet had been "in the forefront," organizing bira ceremonies at her parents' home in Marondera. Vena believed that these events in the Communal Lands were "where Thomas got most of his influence in the culture." This was Janet's great contribution to her son's artistic life.

Thomas soldiered on in 2008. Two years earlier, planned WOMAD shows in the United Kingdom had been scuttled when British immigration had denied the musicians entry visas; with asylum applications pending at the time, officials had determined that their return to Oregon could not be guaranteed. Now the musicians had asylum status, though foreign gigs still remained problematic. A "Legends of Zimbabwe UK Tour" in 2008 promised the first joint appearances by Thomas Mapfumo and Oliver Mtukudzi—Mukanya and Tuku—since their ballyhooed Barbican show in 2000. Opening night in Dublin delivered, with the two icons on stage at the end to sing "God Bless Africa" together. But the next day's show was canceled after the venue failed a safety inspection. A near riot ensued when some two thousand fans learned they would not see the legends after all. The cancellation left the promoter unable to pay Thomas the rest of his advance—about 10,000 pounds. No money, Thomas told them, no show.

At Stratford Rex in London on Saturday night, Tuku took the stage with his band. But when the audience learned that Thomas would not appear, patrons rioted again, trashing the PA speakers and fighting with police. The tour was a financial and public relations fiasco. The promoters argued they had done their best to respond to circumstances beyond their control. Thomas's representative, Cuthbert, agreed with them, saying that Thomas's decision not to perform had undermined efforts to correct the situation.[16] "Sometimes even if you are my friend," he told newzimbabwe.com, "I have to tell you when you are wrong, and I have told Mukanya."

"Cuthbert is a thief," declared Chris Muchabaiwa, for once taking Thomas's side. "He was working with the promoters behind Thomas. I could smell it at the shows. Cuthbert knew they were playing Thomas rough." Chris was not the first Blacks Unlimited member to doubt Cuthbert. From the first U.S. tours Cuthbert participated in, musicians had watched him buying computers and "expensive gadgets," while they earned scarcely enough to feed their families. Now, in his role as "replications manager," Cuthbert was arranging high-profile gigs like the Legends shows and pulling together new Mapfumo CDs for the Zimbabwe market, sometimes using unreleased and reissued tracks. One of Thomas's colleagues, who observed Cuthbert at work in Zimbabwe during Thomas's exile, wondered whether even Thomas understood all that his young agent was doing: "Sometimes I think Cuthbert is more in control of the music than Thomas."[17]

"Thomas has been abused," said Cuthbert, looking back on his tenure. Cuthbert had indeed known the British promoter for the Legends shows and had felt a special responsibility, having played a key role in brokering joint appearances between Thomas and Oliver going back to the Barbican show in 2000. Cuthbert genuinely believed it had been a mistake for Thomas and the band not to perform. As to any criticism that he had profited unfairly from Thomas, Cuthbert was equally unapologetic. Unlike some of Thomas's agents over the years, Cuthbert *had* made sure he got paid for his efforts, at least in the beginning. And he had always left decisions about compensating musicians strictly to Thomas. But Cuthbert insisted that he had never sought to take advantage of Thomas, only to help him.

"I have been very protective of him," said Cuthbert, speaking in 2014, and he noted, "When Thomas left Zimbabwe, he had eighteen CDs on the market. Today, he has got a catalog of fifty-five. Nobody appreciates me for that."[18]

After the UK Legends debacle, Al Green withdrew from the world. He lived for months in a tent near Harbin Hot Springs, in Middletown, California, in the company of a "Cherokee mystic woman." Everyone in the Blacks

Unlimited, and in Thomas's family, was concerned. They felt an overwhelming gratitude toward Al—with good reason. Thomas called him "one hell of a good guy" who was "not into material things or the riches of this world." Vena too attested to Al's "good heart." She knew he had shouldered many expenses for the band and the family. Despite his circumstances, Al had no regrets. "I could have just gone broke in subprime housing starts," he noted wryly from his California retreat. "But the Mapfumo stories will be better at the rest home."

At the start of 2008, the Zimbabwe government issued new bank notes valued in the millions of dollars. On the day the new currency hit the street, $5,000,000 was enough to buy three loaves of bread. But not for long. Inflation reached 66,000 percent in early February, and 100,580 percent by the end of the month. On March 30, 2008, Zimbabweans went to the polls and elected an MDC-majority Parliament. Most observers believed that MDC leader Morgan Tsvangirai also won the presidency that day. But Mugabe's police commissioner, August Chihuri, had promised before the election that he would "not allow puppets to take charge," and he proved as good as his word. After a month of dithering, the government called for a runoff election, and Chihuri's police went to work, arresting and harassing MDC operatives, killing more than one hundred. Tsvangirai withdrew, citing intimidation, and lost the June rematch. South African president Thabo Mbeki then convened slow and arduous negotiations aimed at forming a government of national unity. It took until September to reach an agreement, which Mugabe promptly ignored by appointing his own handpicked cabinet. In February 2009, almost a year after the election, Morgan Tsvangirai was sworn in as prime minister of Zimbabwe, and an uneasy stasis prevailed.

"Right now the military is running the country," said Thomas. "There is no government." Thomas and others believed that Mugabe had been ready to accept defeat, but that generals, and his wife, Grace, had forced him into the runoff, fearing retaliation under an MDC government. In Australia that spring, Thomas told an interviewer that Zimbabwe was "a lost country." He noted that even now he had supporters in the government, but that neither they nor Mugabe any longer called the shots. Were Thomas to return, his life would be in danger not from politicians or police but from "people who have nothing, who don't care whether they are paid fifty dollars to kill someone."[19]

Thomas disapproved of the unity government, saying that Tsvangirai had "jumped in the river with crocodiles" and was now "sharing the same table with the devil himself." He poured these sentiments into a song called "Vagere Kunaka (They Are Sitting Pretty)," a jab at MDC officials who now partook of the tarnished spoils of power. This song became part of an unusual collaboration between the Blacks Unlimited and Nora Chipaumire, a Zimbabwean modern dancer living in New York City. A striking, statuesque figure with long limbs, powerful musculature, and a shaved head, Chipaumire had visited the Capitol Drive house in Eugene and danced in the living room as Thomas and his musicians played. She had adored Thomas's music as a girl in Zimbabwe and had always approved of his politics. The ensuing collaboration would culminate in a full-length theater show called *lions will roar, swans will fly, angels will wrestle heaven, rains will break: gukurahundi.*

Nora, Thomas, and the Zimbabwean members of his band toured this show successfully at universities and prestigious performing arts venues in 2009 and 2010. But even this success could not deliver Thomas from his financial woes. As his options narrowed, he reached out to old allies, even Chris Bolton, who offered to help book the band in Europe. Thomas continued to believe Chris had "stolen" 7,000 pounds from him. On the other hand, the Brit was "family," a person who had also done good for the band. "To us," said Thomas, "that 7,000 pounds is a small issue." Hot-tempered at times, but indeed not vindictive, Thomas knew the difference between "jumping in the river with crocodiles" and genuine forgiveness.

Meanwhile, Zimbabwe approached its grim nadir. Cholera ravaged the nation, overwhelming the country's battered health care infrastructure and killing as many as six in ten victims. More than four thousand people would die in southern Africa before the epidemic ended. After inflation reached an estimated 8 quintillion percent—the number 8 followed by eighteen zeros—the treasury issued a Z$10 trillion bank note—worth about US$8.00 the day it hit the street—and soon, a Z$100 trillion note.[20] Finally, in April 2009, the currency was suspended altogether, and for the foreseeable future, Zimbabwe would run on Euros, rands, and U.S. dollars.

Then something unexpected happened. Diamonds—the greatest prize Cecil Rhodes had dreamed of but had never found on the Zimbabwean plateau—were discovered in abundance in the Marange fields outside Mutare. The 2010 find was spectacular, enough to remake a ruined nation into one of the world's top diamond producers.[21] Now, guarded by the Zimbabwean army and overseen by zanu loyalists, these diamond fields would afford Mugabe's regime a lifeline, allowing it to ignore pressures for democratic reform and ensuring that Thomas Mapfumo and the Blacks Unlimited would remain distant, corralled, and all but silent, still six thousand miles from their own waiting gold mine.

You can take the baboon out of the mountain, but you can't take
the mountain out of the baboon.
SHONA PROVERB

Musa Zimunya's earliest recollection of Thomas Mapfumo was his shyness.
Over the years many associates have noted Thomas's sporadic manner of
communicating, the way he can withhold information and change his mind
without warning. Those who have worked with him know that to be successful
they must suspend personal agendas and enter Thomas's psychic world. That
world is first and foremost rooted in land and open spaces, the sun, the cattle,
the herd boy's switch—Thomas's boyhood seduction into a realm of songs
and the spirits of benevolent ancestors. This sacred space had already formed
within him when he came to Mabvuku in his tenth year and began his life as
a cultural chameleon, adhering to his parents' churchly ways at home while
learning to maneuver the mean streets of Mbare, Harare's oldest township.
Gilbert Zvamaida described Mbare as a domain where only the wise and wily
survive. "You have to champion every situation," he said, "tough, soft, whatever. You face it the way it comes." It is no accident that many of Zimbabwe's
best footballers and boxers, as well as musicians, have emerged from Mbare.

In 1980, Thomas boasted to Fred Zindi that he had been "mischievous"
from his earliest days. "I was always fighting with other boys," he recalled,
proudly proclaiming himself "a really good fighter." In the shadow of the liberation war, Thomas was eager to portray himself as a pugilist. Later, reflecting
on the godly life lessons of Janet Chinhamo and John Mapfumo, he called
himself a peacemaker. "I've never fought anybody in my life," he said in 1998.

"I've always lived peacefully, and I've got lots and lots of friends who are very close to me." Somewhere between the personas of the curious child of nature, the obedient, reverential son, and the devil-may-care Mbare street kid lies the essence of Thomas Mapfumo. So it is that this man of many names can be honest, "straightforward," "not vindictive," and "a good guy," while at the same time being tough to pin down, let alone predict, guide, or manage. One moment Thomas will brandish harsh words, or even the pistol in the glove box of his car. The next he will be pliable, forgiving, serene, and bemused.

"I am coming from Dande," said Thomas, and the pride in this statement goes beyond that region's centrality in the liberation struggle. Dande is Thomas's true home, the shrouded bedrock of his identity. Janet and her parents may have directed him to the path of Shona tradition, but that path eventually led him back to Dande, away from the Mapfumos and Munhumumwes, to his paternal ancestors, the Mupariwas of the Makore. Thomas's belief in this path fills his songs, which persistently call on Zimbabweans to revive and embrace their African culture. This, more than any political message, is the core of his oeuvre.

Not all of Thomas's admirers find the notion of a cultural return wholesome, especially as a prescription for a troubled African nation. Geoffrey Nyarota said: "The influence of ancestors cannot be nationalized. My ancestors do not protect Thomas. Neither do his protect me. Ancestors protect their own. The people of a certain clan would go to their ancestral tree and kneel there, and pray for food. But Harare has no clan, no elders in the traditional sense. So we are living in a totally different world now, where our culture has been uprooted. You can't go to the polls and vote for a dictator and then go back home and wait for your ancestors to deliver food to your table."

"Unfortunately for us, we were colonized," said the broadcaster Comfort Mbofana. "We have to live with it. We have to incorporate it. This is how societies move forward. A lot of people will go and see a medical doctor and pray for the sick. If that doesn't work, they will go and see a n'anga. We still do traditional things, but we've also assimilated a lot. Now if I understand Mapfumo to be saying, 'Let's go back to the old ways and forget everything else,' well, you can't do that."

"There is nobody, no culture in the whole world, that has remained intact," declared Bishop Abel Muzorewa. "Cultures change. There are some elements of the culture that people continue to develop, and there are some they drop." This idea of winnowing tradition is a strong thread in postcolonial African thinking, but the tally of what should be kept and what discarded will vary widely in the minds of Thomas Mapfumo, Abel Muzorewa, or Robert Mugabe—let alone among the members of the Gays and Lesbians of Zimbabwe. Thomas would "throw away" practices that spread virus and disease. He has rejected polygamy and despises corruption. But when it comes to appeasing ancestor spirits and honoring parents—"the gods you can see"—there can be no compromise. This tradition must endure for Shona people, whether they live in Harare, Dande, London, or Eugene, Oregon.

In America, Thomas can never reproduce the rich ties to Shona religious practice that were once so readily available to him. In this regard, he is a private man. He prays before meals and often attends church on Sunday, but the African side of his religious life is harder to see. Surely it is a privation for him to be so far from extended family members and the traditional religious figures and places that long nurtured his spiritual life back home. Thomas expresses no particular concern about this, presenting it as just another consequence of his exile. His wife and daughter, however, both acknowledge a more pressing need for Thomas to return to Zimbabwe and to renew himself in ways that can only happen there, including through Shona spiritual practice.

Some have called Thomas's diverse cultural appetites—mbira, traditional healers, Jesus, ganja, soccer, professional wrestling, golf, BMWs, vampire movies, and reality crime shows—contradictory. Another word might be "human." Thomas believes in freedom, and while he is often eager to offer an opinion, he has mostly tolerated the cultural paths others follow, leaving judgment to God. Thomas's overriding concern is that African people not lose their *identity*, something Zimbabweans of his generation have witnessed personally. Musa Zimunya used to taunt his students at the University of Zimbabwe. "I see you are wearing a baseball cap," he would say. "I see you are wearing the LA Lakers, the Chicago Bulls. I respect your excitement. But where are you going? *Where are you going?*" Musa did not want to stop his students from strutting down Robert Mugabe Avenue as though they were in Bedford-Stuyvesant, Brooklyn. He simply wanted them to reflect on their cultural choices. "I think that the biggest tragedy of colonialism," said Musa, "is to have so brainwashed generation after generation, and to continue to lure those who know no better into a world where they will remain eternal aliens. This is one of Thomas Mapfumo's great battles, because as a creative person, he knows what is available to all." In other words, Thomas is a cultural omnivore, free and willing to embrace whatever artistic expressions and social practices he likes, beginning, first and foremost, with his identity as a Shona Zimbabwean, and then as a citizen of the world.

Thomas's loyalty to his origins also shapes his politics. For as much as he has soured on Mugabe and his self-serving regime, Thomas remains a patriot, and a man who believes in a better future for Zimbabwe.

Thomas Mapfumo and Robert Mugabe—two strong Shona men with dominant mothers and complexity in their paternal lines. Both are shy in public and persuasive in private. Both are gifted with rare talent even as they emanate authority and resist counsel. These lions of Zimbabwe embody the paradoxes of their young nation, which grew up too fast for comfort and now careens into an awkward adolescence in the early twenty-first century. Aggrieved Blacks Unlimited musicians have at times taken bitter comfort in comparing Thomas with the leader he first boosted and later excoriated. Said one musician in a moment of anger, "They are not the same, but they are the same." This is tempting rhetoric for a frustrated musician, but it is far from accurate or fair. Among the things that separate the two men: a generation, years of education, the wounding personal ordeals of Mugabe's broken youth and decade-long imprisonment. Mugabe gave his country independence, then robbed it of its wealth and productivity and tarnished its long-standing culture of civility with an atmosphere of hostility and divisiveness. Thomas, on the other hand, created music and poetry that inspired a people to win freedom, reaffirm their African identity, and reject the very tyranny that Robert Mugabe has imposed on them. For that last deed alone, Thomas must be remembered as one of the bravest figures in twentieth-century popular African culture. It is unlikely that history will be so kind to Robert Mugabe.

"It's we people who create dictatorship," Thomas often said, lamenting the "hero worship" that turned Mugabe into a kind of god in the nation's psyche. Outsiders find it easy to vilify Mugabe as an icon of evil. For those who fought the liberation struggle, it can never be so pat, one reason Zimbabwe's political divide remains difficult to chart. Thomas even crossed swords with his longtime friend and ally, Musa Zimunya, as the poet returned to Zimbabwe in 2004. "Musa is such a good writer," recalled Thomas with some regret, "but at the same time, he said there is nothing wrong with grabbing land." Many clear-eyed Zimbabweans were won over by Mugabe's crusade to right the wrongs of history—Chartwell Dutiro, Tute Chigamba, Andy Brown, Simon Chimbetu, even the gifted novelist Alexander Kanengoni, who, despite reservations about Mugabe's methods, wrung his hands and allowed that the quest to reclaim land was so ultimately just that "you end up agreeing with them." For all Thomas may lack in formal education, and all the complications in his life, the Chimurenga Guru has never been willing to travel *that* twisted moral road.

"When the real cultural studies begin to be seen in our universities," Stephen Chifunyise once predicted, "like the African studies departments of the 1970s in America, then Thomas Mapfumo will have a place in our education system." The playwright and ZANU minister of sports, recreation and culture added, "We will then be asking: What does 'Bhutsu Mutandarika' mean? What is the meaning of 'Magobo'?"

Future students and scholars will no doubt examine Thomas Mapfumo's songs, finding within them meanings to suit their times. They will assess Thomas as a cultural messenger and a force of history in his nation's birth, and, of course, as a composer and bandleader. They will address the question of "originality," a favorite word for Thomas. Some Mapfumo critics find it ironic that an artist who made his career, in significant part, by adapting indigenous traditional music might be called an original. But this is no paradox. Stravinsky said famously, "A good composer does not imitate; he steals." The late Malian guitarist Lobi Traore—an African maestro who, like Thomas, crafted a hybrid of tradition and modernity—held a similarly liberating view: "You cannot play anything without touching someone, or someone touching you. Once you play it, it's not yours anymore. It's for the whole world." Thomas has borrowed and refreshed many ideas from Zimbabwean tradition, and not just from the mbira repertoire, which underlies no more than 30 percent of his canon. Thomas also drew inspiration from *shangara, mande, jerusarema,* and *muchongoyo* rhythms from Manyikaland. He has borrowed from his own musicians and from recordings he admires, be they rock 'n' roll, reggae, Afro-jazz, Zulu vocal music, or West African folklore. His claim to originality stands because, for all this borrowing, Thomas has never merely imitated. His collected creations, with all their associations, amount to a sprawling and consequential personal genre in which every song—good or bad—bears his unique stamp. Because of him, cultural expressions that might well have been ignored or forgotten are now woven into Zimbabwe's popular culture.

Thomas's "chimurenga" canon could not have been built without help from brilliant collaborators, many of whom have vanished into obscurity, or died poor. Thomas may not have recognized or rewarded them as they would have liked, but their sad fates are also rooted in a young society that denigrates and devalues all but a few musicians, and raises its leaders to reign large, not to share glory. Thomas has struggled mightily and risked much for what glory he has attained. His own reward has in no way been commensurate with his achievements.

Chimurenga music has never riveted the larger world the way Bob Marley's reggae or Fela Kuti's Afrobeat have. Many of those closest to Thomas and his story are left with a nagging sense that he could have, *should have*, counted more. Perhaps had he vanished in custody in 1979, or been slain in the violence of 2000 or stricken by illness in his prime like Marley and Fela, the radiance of martyrdom would have uplifted his life's work in the eyes of a distracted world. Yet this is unlikely. To begin with, Thomas's greatest artistic power lies in his rarefied sound and in his inspired adaptations of Shona language and musical idioms. While Thomas sings with one of the most distinctive and memorable voices in all of contemporary music, his English lyrics lack the universal appeal of Fela's or Marley's magnificently idiosyncratic ones—the song "Corruption" being a clear exception. For non-Shona speakers, the deeper allure of Thomas's music lies in the sound, not in the words, and here it matters that the Shona people were spared involvement in the Atlantic slave trade, which lurks darkly beneath the most successful strains of black music, from jazz to hip-hop to Afrobeat. Ironically, a safe remove from Western slavery excluded the Shona from perhaps the most formative cultural exchange undergirding the world's popular music. The Afro-Atlantic trail of tears has watered many gardens, including those that produced Marley, Miles, Fela, James Brown—the list is endless. Shona swing and soul are undeniable, but for most Western ears, they remain "other," an exotic realm disconnected from our own hidden musical DNA and, so, beyond the fringes of our cultural mainstream.

Writing in the mid-1990s, ethnomusicologist Thomas Turino dwells on Thomas's commercial motivations, suggesting that the Blacks Unlimited's emphasis on mbira in the 1980s was an accommodation to the "worldbeat" phenomenon that grew up in the wake of Paul Simon's *Graceland*. Turino detects a calculated effort by Thomas to adopt "cosmopolitan aesthetics and style in order to succeed in the transnational market."[1] To the extent this is true, it masks both Thomas's lifelong adoration of mbira music and also his larger unwillingness to cater to popular trends. Had his driving concern been commercial success, why would Thomas have ditched the two-guitar sound to favor keyboards in the late 1980s, when so many world music insiders were telling him this would alienate foreign listeners? Why would he play grueling all-night concerts in the poor townships of Harare, when he could have made more money performing in a stadium once a month? Why would he brush aside potentially advantageous collaborations with Ry Cooder, or the Kronos Quartet, or, later on, the opportunity to record for an album of African covers of U2 songs?[2] Most crucially, why would he separate himself from his core market and his most powerful source of inspiration and income in order to ensure a better future for his children?

Thomas could likely have gone further had there been an impresario—a

Chris Blackwell—guiding him over the years. When Blackwell took on Bob Marley and the Wailers, he imposed his will. Peter Tosh and Bunny Wailer jumped ship, but Marley saw opportunity and yielded, bearing the consequences and reaping the rewards. Thomas, on the other hand, has always looked to managers and agents to project *his* ideas, not to guide him with their own. Many African musicians have raged at the injustices of a profit-driven music industry, but few with Thomas's stature have responded by putting their careers in the hands of maverick enthusiasts like Bob Diener or Al Green. These are the acts of a romantic, an idealist, a supremely confident creator— hardly a commercial strategist.

One common reason Thomas's musicians and managers have cited for his failure to prosper as he might have is "relatives," including extended family members and in-laws, the Mapfumos and Munhumumwes. Joshua Dube called them "hungry lions." Chris Bolton and others used stronger words still. One person close to the family noted, "Thomas is a very nice person, but he is overly controlled by his brothers" (William and Lancelot). Thomas is the eldest and most successful of the three brothers, but because he has a different father, he has always maintained a distinct identity and has shouldered a special responsibility in their company. Whether backstage at a Seven Miles show in the old days, or on a visit to the house Lancelot shared with William and his family in Springfield, Oregon, in 2013, Thomas instinctively played the confident jester, lifting the mood with feisty banter and "funny stories." No matter how dark William's mood might be at the outset, he could never resist Thomas's well-honed antics for long. The two always seemed to wind up touching hands amid a duet of baritone laughter. For Thomas, this was more than good form; it was duty. And it has always been hard for him to separate familial loyalties from the nuts and bolts of managing his career as an entertainer.

In Zimbabwe and America, Thomas has at times had to conduct sensitive diplomacy in order to keep harmony within his extended family. The issues go back to his divided parentage, and they extend not only to the realm of business and family matters but even into spirituality. Thomas's brothers became deeply involved with their Christian church in Springfield, much as Janet and John Mapfumo had been with the Christian Marching Church in Mabvuku and Mbare. Meanwhile, Thomas's own wife and daughter continue to yearn openly for him to reconnect with his paternal family in Guruve and with the African spiritual practices of his past.

Thomas vaguely acknowledged these intrafamily dynamics, though he did not wish to discuss them in any detail. He portrayed the clan as having come together in their Oregon exile. Despite disagreements with William, it was

Vena, along with Tapfumaneyi and William's daughter Edith, who spared William the ordeal of returning to Zimbabwe when his American visa neared expiration in 2005. "We made Thomas change his mind and bring William here," said Vena. Later, in 2011, it was William, Lancelot, and sisters Edith and Tabeth in Zimbabwe who came together to urge Thomas to reconcile with Vena. "They actually talked sense into me," declared Thomas. "That's my family." As to the idea that his brothers control him, Thomas reflected, "Someone is saying, 'You love your brothers too much.' I say, 'No, no, no. I just love everybody in my family.' I am the eldest brother. There is no father now, no mother. I shouldn't be seen dividing the family."

Many successful bandleaders have been criticized for giving family members too much power in their business affairs. Such conflicts are a trope of popular music history. In Thomas's case, the family plainly comes first, so it is not surprising that he has given relatives—along with maverick enthusiasts—important roles in his operation. "My family members are good people," said Thomas. "They are always by my side, and I don't think they deserve blame." If things have gone wrong, and achievements fallen short of expectations, said Thomas, "I have to blame myself."

Not that there aren't other culprits behind Thomas's misfortunes—exploitative record companies, inexperienced managers, political adversaries, jealous peers. Years into his exile, back in Zimbabwe, the saga of Thomas's confiscated BMWs reached a sordid conclusion. When no one ever emerged to claim the cars as their own, the police concluded they had not been stolen after all. Cuthbert was called in to collect them, but when he arrived, the four vehicles were nowhere to be found. "They were sold by somebody," said Thomas. "I'm sure it was some top official in the police force." Thomas sought to right this wrong by seeking financial compensation through a lawyer, but given his remoteness in exile and the state of corruption in Zimbabwe, his prospects for success looked dim indeed, and the taint of this elaborately conceived smear lingers.

Meanwhile, in 2011, Thomas and Vena sold the house in Mount Pleasant and, soon afterward, what land in Zimbabwe had remained in the family.[3] This marked another painful separation from their heritage, another sacrifice for the good of the family. After all, what was the liberation struggle fought for, if not for land?

In 2013, Thomas, Vena, and the children all longed to return to Zimbabwe. Thomas, who had once called himself a "marked man," no longer felt afraid. "For what?" he asked. "I was born there. And my father, my spirits, my forefathers are there. They will always look after me." The problem was no longer the threat of intimidation and violence, but rather the difficulties of financing and logistics. Thomas had a vision of his return. He dreamed of assembling a large band with Blacks Unlimited musicians from America, the United Kingdom, and Zimbabwe, the biggest ensemble he had ever staged. He imagined an epic "welcome home" concert, in a stadium, joined by Oliver Mtukudzi and one of the popular young acts in Zimbabwe, maybe a band from South Africa as well. Thomas also spoke of a second large-scale concert—to raise money for the economic victims of Mugabe's misrule. Only such a scenario, and nothing short of it, would befit the return of the Lion of Zimbabwe. The problem is, no such concert seems possible without the cooperation and assistance of the government, and so far, it has been impossible to arrive at terms acceptable to both parties.

Thomas dearly hoped that Mugabe and ZANU would be defeated in the 2013 elections, creating a natural opening for his return. But the eighty-nine-year-old despot carried 61 percent of the vote in the official tally, and ZANU took commanding control of the Parliament in what the New York Times called "a stunning comeback."[4] As Thomas had predicted, the MDC's involvement in a coalition government had damaged the party's credibility and that of its leader, Morgan Tsvangirai. This, combined with Mugabe's road-tested stratagems for predetermining the results of elections, carried the day once again.

As of this writing, Thomas, his family, and the band's Zimbabwean musicians all have green cards. They can work in the United States—and even visit Zimbabwe with reasonable assurance of being allowed to return to Oregon afterward. Chaka the mbira player and Gilbert the guitarist moved into places of their own in Eugene,[5] as did Chris the bass player and drummer, who is an avid fisherman and is looking into agriculture while raising his American son and two Rhodesian ridgebacks. Thomas and his son Tapfumaneyi have moved into a small house in town, very near Vena's larger place. Vena is a caretaker for the elderly, a calling that brought her comfort during the time when her own father died in Zimbabwe, and she was unable to return and mourn him.

A self-described "workaholic," Vena generally spends her days off from work with Thomas, the two of them eating, laughing, and enjoying movies together. The family—sometimes joined by musicians—gathers often at his house, and the warmth and goodwill among them is instantly evident. To visit with Thomas is to revel in an endless supply of stories from the old days—the time guitarist Ephraim Karimaura went out to a liquor store in London and got lost, wandering the streets for two days in a city where "all the buildings look the same," or the time William performed a mock "citizen's arrest" on a Zimbabwean police officer who had joined the band backstage to smoke ganja.

Living with the past—but not *in* it—Thomas, his wife, and their children savor a new ease of living, hard won for an African family in exile in America.

Exile has given Thomas time to reflect. He has become particularly close to his daughter Chiedza. After graduating from the University of Oregon, Chiedza took a job as an accountant at the nonprofit HIV Alliance in Eugene. At age twenty-six in 2013, she had spent half her life in Zimbabwe and half in America. Only in Eugene had she truly come to know her father, and the experience inevitably made her curious about his past in Zimbabwe. "When I look at his old band," said Chiedza, "a lot of them have passed away. Almost everybody. I look at it and say: he's still here. Coming from where we're from, I feel like there was a purpose, a *reason* for that." Chiedza described one unusually candid conversation within the family. Thomas's children together confronted him about how they had shared in Vena's suffering during the years of exile, suffering they now understood as young adults—children no more. Thomas listened, reflected, and later came back with an unprecedented apology. "To me," said Chiedza with evident satisfaction, "it seemed very sincere." Full reconciliation between Thomas and Vena may yet come. For her part, Vena said she still loves him and remains his "number one fan."

Back in Zimbabwe, Thomas used to complain that the stories of Shona ancestors were too often absent from school curricula. "This is our history," he would inveigh, "and if children are not taught it, they won't know. If you ask Tapfumaneyi today, 'Who is Chaminuka?' *he doesn't know.*" Yet in his exile, Thomas did not worry that life in America would weaken his children's connection to Africa. "That won't change them," he insisted. "They will still remain my kids, and they will remember always to preserve their culture. There are things that you won't take away from them—the African in them, and the Shona in them. You won't take that out of them."

Tapfumaneyi was sixteen when he left Zimbabwe, and at twenty-eight he agreed, "I know what my culture is. It's like riding a bike. You don't forget about it." This confidence is impressive, but one wonders whether the family is underestimating the steady and persistent process of cultural erosion that America has always exerted on generations of immigrants. Tapfumaneyi has delved into rapping, and Thomas has even invited him to rap with the Blacks Unlimited on stage and in the studio on a few occasions. Thomas listens to the music his son admires, approving of a few artists, like T-Pain, "because there is music in his songs." But Thomas harbors stubborn reservations about hip-hop as a cultural force, particularly what he sees as its tendency to promote violence. He has often challenged his son on these grounds, saying, "This is gangster music. A lot of youngsters have perished through this music." This hot debate will not be settled between them; nor will it destroy their bond.

The Mapfumo brothers' conservative social values have sometimes put them at odds with young Americans, with their own children, even with school authorities in Oregon. Once, on a visit to his daughter's high school, William witnessed a boy and a girl kissing in a corridor. "He went mad," said Thomas. "He said to the person in charge, 'If this was in Africa, these two would have been expelled from school. We don't allow this nonsense. You give too much freedom to youngsters.'"

Thomas was sympathetic to William's stand. But, as an artist, Thomas thinks in larger terms. Regardless of the misdeeds committed in life, the power or riches gathered, we all face death naked and penniless: "The earth is our inheritance. We are just passersby."

In June 2009, Thomas was working in a recording studio in Albuquerque, New Mexico, when word that Michael Jackson had died flashed on the television screen. The news transfixed him. Thomas seemed to lose interest in his own work and sat mesmerized as a cascade of images recalled the life and death of the fallen superstar. All the talk about Jackson's personal morality, his powerful family, his morphing image, anything other than the art itself and its impact on fans, meant little to Thomas. "This man was *loved*, everywhere in the world," he said indignantly. "If you tell my daughter he was not a good person, she will cry." For a man who had endured many losses and sacrificed so much for his family and for his art, this preoccupation with the drama of another artist's death was striking. We are all passersby, but in the end, some pass more brightly than others.

In 2012, at work on a fresh set of songs, Thomas took up an offer from a young DJ named Charlie (Charlie B. Wilder) in Los Angeles to provide "modern beats" for some of his songs. Together, they created a new, stripped-down version of Thomas's song "Shebeen (Speakeasy)" (1989). Thomas spoke excitedly about finding new blends of style and sound, something to "surprise the people, not something you have heard before." Life in America and the passage of time have heightened Thomas's sense that he must reach future generations, and for the first time, he contemplated the idea of remixing old songs from his catalog to make them sound more contemporary. Remixing had once seemed a violation of his art, and Thomas was not pleased when others sampled his work without his permission. Now, suddenly, this modern practice appeared to him as a challenge, an opportunity, even a mission as he sought to find a new voice and a new way forward as an artist in exile.

Despite the financial and management obstacles to releasing new music, Thomas continued to compose, rehearse, and record with his musicians in Oregon. Among the songs he tracked between 2012 and 2014 were a number sung in English, clearly aimed at a broad audience. "Danger Zone" is a tour of conflicts and hot spots around the globe; "Music," created with DJ Charlie, and "Are You Ready" are both hymns to the dance floor, light and celebratory; "Nhamo Urombo (Problems of the Poor)," a Shona-language song, continues Thomas's career-long focus on the hardships of the impoverished, though without pointing fingers this time; "Hatidi Politics (We Don't Want Politics)" seems to preempt questions about why he's not pointing fingers, proclaiming instead, "Stop politicking, and give us what we want": good schools, health care, and a better life; and "Zimbabwe" echoes that message in a more expansive and sentimental way. The resulting album, *Danger Zone*, is no olive branch to the Mugabe regime, but it does mark a de-escalation of a long-running war of words. These are the benevolent musings of a man who has come through this and other wars, and emerged wizened and mellowed. More than three decades after the exuberance and electricity of that Rufaro Stadium dawn in 1980, Thomas has long since tired of celebrating Zimbabwe's leaders and, by this time, of hurling barbs at them as well. To the extent he has anything more to say to them, it comes down to a pragmatic plea that they should simply do their jobs: "Leave politics aside and work together to rebuild the economy of that country."

These new songs were mostly produced by a Eugene-based keyboard player named Fernando Bispo. Bispo had little background in African music. There are few mbira adaptations or traditional songs amid this work, in all a set of lushly produced dance grooves—reggae, straightforward club beats, and a few classic chimurenga romps spiced with layers of electric and acoustic guitars and backing vocals from Gilbert Zvamaida. "We are from the old school," Thomas said proudly. "But these are modern times and things are changing. We have to be with the time." Thomas even experimented with using Auto-Tune on some of his vocals—now a commonplace technique in contemporary African pop—and Gilbert worked jazz and rock guitar riffs in among phrases reminiscent of chimurenga oldies. The ingredients are new, but Thomas's creative process is essentially unchanged. His band is his instrument, and the sound they produce is shaped more than anything by the music in his head.

The potential impact of Thomas's late exile music is hard to assess. Without an international label and effective management behind them, the songs will be hard-pressed to win attention in today's fractured and diffuse global music market. The arrival of a U.S.-based Zimbabwean manager, Austin Sibanda, an old friend of Thomas's, in 2013 has been a promising development. Meanwhile, in Zimbabwe, music piracy has become so rampant that Thomas rightly fears releasing new music there until he can return to perform it live. Given who he is, all he has accomplished, and the desire—distilled over a decade—of so many Zimbabweans to see him on the stage again, Thomas is well positioned to make a comeback in his homeland. In fact, his return to Zimbabwe is inevitable. Whether it happens before or after the curtain falls on the slow-motion final act of the Mugabe era is anyone's guess. But whenever and however it comes, Thomas's next performance in Zimbabwe will be one for the history books.

In 2012, Thomas made a number of visits to New York City, one to perform at the World Financial Center and another to play Carnegie Hall's second auditorium, Zankel Hall, which has presented some of the city's most prestigious concerts of African music since it opened in 2003. Thomas also accepted an invitation to speak on a panel following a screening of Zimbabwean filmmaker Simon Bright's *Robert Mugabe . . . What Happened?* (2011). Dressed in a tweed jacket and tie, the only black person on the panel, Thomas challenged the overflow crowd by calling out Afrocentric Americans who sometimes turn a blind eye to Mugabe's excesses. "Most of you support him for grabbing the land, and you think he is giving it to the rest of the black Zimbabweans," needled Thomas from the stage. He corrected this misimpression, and as the conversation veered toward racial issues, he again asserted that Zimbabwe's fight, like so many around the world, was not about black versus white, but rather about improving the lives of poor people. Thomas raised eyebrows when he called on America and Britain to intervene with force in Zimbabwe, to overthrow Mugabe and his "torturers." Here was the resident African revolutionary and poet-maestro mischievously espousing what sounded like neoconservative foreign policy. No surprise that his fellow panelists—two white Zimbabwean liberal activists and an American human rights lawyer—politely took issue with Dr. Mapfumo's prescription.

Thomas enjoyed the exchange, pleased to provoke debate. What impressed him most, though, were the organizers of this event—thirty-something Zimbabweans, "born-frees," too young to remember the liberation war but keen to understand its legacy and take up its unfinished business. Politicians and singers at home had disappointed him, but here were countrymen to whom Thomas felt he could pass the torch.[6] "I'm still fighting," he told these young men, "but I'm getting older. It's your fight now." He urged them not to be intimidated, adding, "You must have the heart of a lion." With that, Thomas Mapfumo returned to his family and musicians in Eugene, neither vanquished nor victorious, for the chimurenga—the struggle—continues.

ACKNOWLEDGMENTS

First and foremost, I would like to thank Thomas Mapfumo, his wife Vena, brothers William and Lancelot, children Tapfumaneyi, Chiedza, and Mati, and all other extended family members who have shown me such hospitality, insight, and friendship over the past twenty-seven years.

Deep thanks also to all the musicians of the Blacks Unlimited I have been privileged to know, especially Jonah Sithole, Ephraim Karimaura, Chartwell Dutiro, Joshua Dube, Gilbert Zvamaida, Chris Muchabaiwa, and Bezil and Ngoni Makombe, all of whom taught me things about Zimbabwean music I could never have learned simply by listening.

Thanks also to the many Zimbabwean musicians beyond the Blacks Unlimited fold I have come to know through this endeavor, starting with the mbira players: Ephat Mujuru and his wife Emely Chimanga, Chris Mhlanga, Tute Chigamba, Hakurotwi Mude, Richard Selman, Beaular Dyoko, Stella Chiweshe, Garikayi Tirikoti, Forward Kwenda, Erica Azim, Wiri Chigonga, Musekiwa Chingodza, Chaka Chawasawira, and Cosmas Magaya. And to these great musical creators beyond the world of mbira: Oliver Mtukudzi, Simon Chimbetu, John Ngwandangwanda, Andy Brown, Chiwoniso Maraire, and Leonard Zvakata.

Thanks to Lyda Kuth and the Lef Foundation for early support of this project, to filmmaker John Riber for supplying me with an invaluable collection of Zimbabwean news clippings about popular musicians, and to Musa Zimunya for some of the most enjoyable and illuminating dinner conversations I've ever had. Thanks to Marie Korpe, Ole Reitov, and Freemuse for making it possible for me to return to Zimbabwe in 2001. Thanks to my loyal, wise, and patient agent, Sarah Lazin, and to my chief editor, Jeff Hush, who read this manuscript with an unsparing eye more times than either of us would like to recall. And to CC Smith for meticulous copyediting and an epic effort on this book's indexes. And thanks to Ken Wissoker, Elizabeth Ault, Liz Smith, and everyone at Duke University Press for believing in this book and bringing it to the world.

Thanks to Dirck Westervelt for sharing this journey with me both in Zimbabwe and beyond, to Nora Balaban for never letting me forget to actually *play* Zimbabwean music all these years, and, especially, to Sean Barlow, Georges Collinet, Michael Jones, and all the dedicated members of the *Afropop World-wide* team who have stood by me through everything.

Researching and writing this book has been such a significant part of my life for so long now that it is impossible to recognize all the people who have helped in the process, and to cite the innumerable ways they have contributed. So I resort to a list, in no particular order, with gratitude to all I can name, and apologies to those I have inevitably overlooked:

Saki Mafundikwa, Thomas Terrell, Bob Coen, Al Green, Jennifer Kyker, Paul Berliner, Thomas Turino, Tony Perman, T. M. Scruggs, Cuthbert Chiromo, Richard Crandall, Crystal Sloan, Jon Kertzer, Andy Warshaw, Milo Miles, Ian Anderson, Christoph Borkowsky, Jumbo Van Renen, Gerald Seligman, Marg Tobias, Rob Allingham, Samy Ben Redjeb, Andrew Seidenfeld, Cathy Mteya, Debbie Metcalf, Fred Zindi, Jack Vartoogian, Robert Smith, Ken Braun, Bonnie Raitt, Angelique Kidjo, Brooks Barnett, Paul Prince, Peter Vaughan Shaver, Manny Rettinger, Bob Diener, Chris Bolton, Stuart Carduner, Louisa Bradshaw, Ed Klinger, Armando Ortega, Alyson Steinman, Brad Powell, Erich Ludwig, Lazarus Williams, Parker Smathers, Soloman Murungu, Tendai Mupurutsa, Alexander Kanengoni, Geoffrey Nyarota, James Maridadi, Comfort Mbofana, Elias Mudzuri, Sam Mataure, Peter Godwin, Jon Garelick, Peter Manuel, Lucy Duran, Robert and Helene Browning, Maure Aronson, Susan Weiler, Isabel Soffer, Nyasha Gutsa, Lisa Walters, Andy Frankel, Benny Miller, Bill Barnett, Thaddeus Moore, Fernando Bispo, Ted Mason, Richard Woodin, Dawn Elder, Henry Kaiser, Mhoze Chikowero, Chris Berry, Rujeko Dumbutshena, Don Gillard, Virginia, Leigh, and Henry Rhett, Pam Friedman, Kate and Tom Kush, Chester King, Jody Cormack, Marika Partridge, Anne Peters, Ellen and Mark Barlow, and Phyllis Rose.

Finally, thanks to my family, my late parents, Jack and Cornelia, my brother Stephen and Jonathan Ochoco, my sister Alison and her family, Stephen, Sarah, Olivia, and Joshua Kester. As Thomas has often said, everything begins with family, and I have been blessed with an especially supportive, loyal, and inspiring one.

NOTES

PREAMBLE

1. An mbira is a handheld instrument consisting of tuned metal tongues clamped to a base of hard wood. This general type of instrument is popularly referred to as a "hand piano" or "thumb piano," although ethnomusicologists and mbira players prefer the more technical term, "lamellophone." The plural is also "mbira."

2. In this case, *sekuru* means uncle; it can also mean grandfather.

3. A. S. Chigwedere, *From Mutapa to Rhodes: 1000 to 1890 A.D.* (London: Macmillan, 1980). Early Shona history is complex, disputed, and far beyond the scope of this book, but Chigwedere is not alone in citing Murenga as a godlike figure, the father of Chaminuka and Nehanda, two of the most revered *mhondoro* spirits.

4. Joshua Dube and Jonah Sithole are the key guitarists in the early history of the Blacks Unlimited. Because their first names are similar, I mostly refer to them by their last names to avoid confusion.

5. Throughout this book, I use the same format as in this sentence for providing English translations for songs with Shona titles. The English translations are my addition, not part of the original song title.

6. The term *pungwe* came into common use during the liberation struggle to describe all-night political gatherings featuring group singing of "chimurenga songs."

7. I had known Thomas for ten years when I made this return to Zimbabwe. I had written my first piece of music journalism about him, just months after Sean Barlow and I traveled to Harare to do early research for the public radio program *Afropop Worldwide*. When Thomas began to tour in the United States, we came together in places like Boston, New York, Philadelphia, and Atlanta. In 1995, I was the band's driver during one tour, moving from Boston to Seattle, into western Canada, and down to California and New Mexico. I first played guitar with the Blacks Unlimited during a sound check in Georgia in 1989 and debuted on stage with them in Harare about three years later.

As a musician, I knew what it felt like to be inside this band's deeply chiseled grooves, though I still had much to learn. Mbira songs, important in the Blacks Unlimited reper-toire, are elusive. They can trick me to this day. On stage, Bezil Makombe might start out playing a simple part he had coached me on, but he never stayed there long. After a while, displaced fragments of melody exchanged among the three mbira players could suddenly shatter, leaving me adrift in a disorienting echo chamber. If I held to my part, it was as close as I would ever come to playing guitar amid the off-kilter genius of Thelonious Monk in midsolo. But if I strayed even slightly from the beat, the bass and drums would sound suddenly unfamiliar, and I'd be treading broken glass, lost in a sonic wilderness before a roomful of sharp-eared fans. Forgiving patrons in those hotels and beer halls would clap my hand and say, "I like your beat," or "Man, you know how to tune your wires." But there were others, including my musician friends, whose critique could be unsparing.

"Pidigori," a song celebrating the demise of a bad man, was the first number I was trusted to play while Thomas was on the stage. I never knew when it would come, as Thomas rarely relied on set lists. At any point during the night, that signature sequence of mbira notes might sound, summoning me to the stage, where Dube would hand off his guitar. "Pidigori" could be the best or the worst fifteen minutes of my week. When it soared, I felt the music was connecting me with the spirits of the guitarists who had taught me. Thomas once told me, "I almost felt like I was listening to Mr. Sithole." Praise didn't get better than that in the Blacks Unlimited.

I was proud to play with Joshua Dube on a recording of "Pidigori" in 1999, one high point of my studio experiences with Thomas. Another high point—the song "Ndiyani Waparadza Musha" from *Chimurenga '98*—grew out of a West African guitar piece I had learned in Mali and introduced to the band. The song became part of the band's warm-up set, and Thomas became intrigued by the groove and conjured a beautiful falsetto vocal that transformed it with the question, "*Who has destroyed my home?*" This song—with its underlying Malian harmony—became popular in Zimbabwe, for it captured the sense of loss and recrimination there at the close of the twentieth century.

1. ENGLAND IS THE CHAMELEON, AND I THE FLY

1. Adding a final *s* to *sekuru*, to make the plural term *sekurus*, is Anglicized Shona, which I use at times in this book for the benefit of English speakers. In standard Shona, the plural of *sekuru* would be *vasekuru*.

2. Marshall Munhumumwe led one of Zimbabwe's best-loved guitar bands, the Four Brothers. But because he was born after Thomas, Marshall became that unusual uncle who is younger than his own nephew.

3. David Beach, *The Shona and Their Neighbors* (Oxford: Blackwell, 1994), 25.

4. Said Hamdun and Noël King, *Ibn Battuta in Black Africa*, rev. ed. (Princeton, NJ: Markus Wiener, 1994), 22.

5. Beach, *Shona and Their Neighbors*, 85.

6. Scarcity of water, climate change, shifting trade routes—these theories have their proponents, but they somehow fall short of explaining such a radical retreat from the grandest city in all southern Africa.

7. Beach, *Shona and Their Neighbors*, 104. The first was Mutota, an elephant hunter. Munhumutapa kings levied a 50 percent tax on new gold mines, and for every elephant

felled, the king took the tusk nearest the ground. Ivory, gold, and copper also brought them fortunes in trade goods from the coast.

8. Beach, *Shona and Their Neighbors*, 100.

9. Statistics on gold yields from the plateau tell the story: 1,500 kilograms in 1667; 425 kilograms in 1758; 267 kilograms in 1790. Beach, *Shona and Their Neighbors*, 114.

10. Beach, *Shona and Their Neighbors*, 109–14.

11. Beach, *Shona and Their Neighbors*, 115.

12. Beach, *Shona and Their Neighbors*, 132–33.

13. Beach, *Shona and Their Neighbors*, 49.

14. Anthony Thomas, *Rhodes: The Race for Africa* (Harare: African Publishing House, 1996), 240.

15. Thomas Parkenham, *The Scramble for Africa: The White Man's Conquest of the Dark Continent from 1876–1912* (New York: Random House, 1991), 375–76.

16. J. G. Lockhart and C. M. Wodehouse, *Rhodes* (1963), 69–70, cited in Parkenham, *Scramble for Africa*, 377. In 1877, before he became prime minister of the Cape Colony and launched his bold land grab on the Zimbabwe plateau, Rhodes prepared a grandiose "Confession of Faith" bidding his benefactors to form a secret society whose goal would be "the extension of the British rule throughout the world . . . the occupation of the whole continent of Africa, the Holy Land, the valley of the Euphrates . . . the whole of South America . . . the ultimate recovery of the United States as an integral part of the British Empire . . . then finally the foundation of so great a power to hereafter render wars impossible and promote the best interests of humanity." Wow.

17. Thomas, *Rhodes*, 63.

18. Thomas, *Rhodes*, 14.

19. Parkenham, *Scramble for Africa*, 385.

20. Parkenham, *Scramble for Africa*, 380, 386.

21. Parkenham, *Scramble for Africa*, 384.

22. Thomas, *Rhodes*, 194.

23. Parkenham, *Scramble for Africa*, 386–88.

24. Thomas, *Rhodes*, 216. The phrase comes from Frank Johnson, *Great Days* (London: G. Bell and Sons, 1940).

25. Thomas, *Rhodes*, 220. The quote is attributed to Selous.

26. All quotes from Chenjerai Hove from author's 2001 interview with the writer in Harare. See note on the song "Chemutengure" in chapter 2.

27. Parkenham, *Scramble for Africa*, 494.

28. Parkenham, *Scramble for Africa*, 500–501.

29. Many believe that Nehanda's hanging tree still stands in downtown Harare, preserved, though unmarked along a stretch of Josiah Tongogara Avenue. The tree is a powerful symbol for many, including feminists who have come to embrace Nehanda. However, there is considerable evidence that this is not in fact the tree from which the medium, or anyone else, was hung.

30. Terence Ranger, *Are We Not Also Men? The Samkange Family and African Politics in Zimbabwe 1920–64* (Portsmouth, NH: Heinemann, 1995), 24.

31. Ranger, *Are We Not Also Men?*, 44.

32. One reviewer of this manuscript has noted that in recent times, Shona girls have been known to become pregnant deliberately before the payment of lobola, in order to demonstrate their fertility. Beach's statistics would seem to indicate that such a practice was not widespread—if it existed at all—in precolonial times.

33. Beach, *Shona and Their Neighbors*, 56–57.

34. Ethnomusicologist Thomas Turino deconstructs the "essentialist" dichotomy between rural and urban culture in Zimbabwe, a distinction commonly referenced in writing and speech, including by Zimbabweans themselves. Turino makes a good case that this division is often exaggerated, masking the steady flow between people's city and rural homes. I would add only that, for all the movement and exchange between urban and rural areas, these remain distinct environments. The same person may feel and act quite differently in each, a phenomenon touched on later in this book. The interaction between these worlds is complex, but a certain separation is quite real.

35. This quote comes almost entirely from one of my 1997 interviews with Thomas, but it incorporates elements from Zindi's 1984 interview: Fred Zindi, *Roots Rocking in Zimbabwe* (Harare: Mambo Press, 1985), 25.

36. *Mapira* is the plural of *bira*.

37. Zindi, *Roots Rocking in Zimbabwe*, 24.

2. SINGING SHONA

1. Thomas Turino, *Nationalists, Cosmopolitans, and Popular Music in Zimbabwe* (Chicago: University of Chicago Press, 2000), 96.

2. Julie Frederikse, *None But Ourselves: Masses vs. Media in the Making of Zimbabwe* (Harare: Anvil Press, 1982), 8.

3. Frederikse, *None But Ourselves*, 16. This quote comes from a Rhodesia Ministry of Information pamphlet called *The Man and His Ways*.

4. The year 1948 was also when George Nyandoro helped organize a brief general strike by black workers, one of the earliest acts of protest in the liberation struggle.

5. Turino, *Nationalists, Cosmopolitans, and Popular Music in Zimbabwe*, 98, quoting Peter Fraenkel, *Wayaleshi* (London: Weidenfeld and Nicholson, 1959), 17.

6. Zimunya interview with author, Harare, 1998. He went on to say, "There were many, many songs that looked down on black people. I don't know who composed these songs but everybody sang them. [*Sings*] 'This is our land, this land of Rhodesia. It attracted many nations. So what do we do, Africans? They came to take our things away, and they brought in their place machines and cloth.' It's a very beautiful song. If it hadn't been so ambiguous, I think it would have been the national anthem. It was sung countrywide during my generation."

7. The term "jazz" is used loosely in a number of southern and East African contexts, especially in band names. The "township jazz" or "African jazz" that Thomas and others refer to emerged out of South Africa in the early and mid-twentieth century, and it has continued to evolve ever since. Today, South African jazz is highly developed and still influential beyond the country's borders. Broadly speaking, it hews closer to dance music and cool jazz than to the explosive expressions of bebop and post-bop. African jazz represents yet another African reprocessing of an American genre that already had Africa deeply woven into its fabric.

8. The high-water mark of originality in the Rhodesian jazz scene was August Musa-ruwa's composition "Skokiaan," which became a worldwide hit in the 1950s after it was recorded by Louis Armstrong as "Happy Africa."

9. Musa's example here, sadza, is itself interesting. In fact, the cornmeal sadza Zimba-bweans eat today is a colonial construct. The original sadza was made from millet or sor-ghum. Corn (maize), which was introduced to Africa in the sixteenth century, only reached the Zimbabwean plateau in the nineteenth and became the staple food of Zimbabweans relatively recently. To this day, spirit mediums do not eat cornmeal sadza.

10. *Shatini* is not a Shona word but rather from Chilapalapa, a simplified pidgin language mixing Zulu, Shona, Afrikaans, English, and other tongues. Chilapalapa was developed in mining communities to allow basic communication among all parties present.

11. The Zutu Brothers were older guys, neither popular nor good enough to compete with top bands like De Black Evening Follies or the Melodians, whose stage show featured a comedian gorging himself on two loaves of bread.

12. Alice Dadirai Kwaramba, *Popular Music and Society: The Language of Protest in Chimurenga Music: The Case of Thomas Mapfumo in Zimbabwe*, IMK Report No. 24 (Oslo: University of Oslo, Department of Media Communication, 1997), 3. She is citing statistics from C. Stoneman, ed., *Zimbabwe's Inheritance* (London: Macmillan, 1981), 69.

13. Fred Zindi, *Roots Rocking in Zimbabwe* (Harare: Mambo Press, 1985), 24. Thomas apparently told Zindi this was in 1962, but in our 1998 interview he insisted that he finished school in 1961.

14. Turino, *Nationalists, Cosmopolitans, and Popular Music in Zimbabwe*, 126–27.

15. Coon carnivals, so called, are still presented annually in the Cape Town area. A com-petition among costumed troops of musicians, dancers, and acrobats, the tradition seems to trace its roots to an American influence. During the nineteenth century, ships with black American crews—mostly from New Orleans—spent time in the port of Cape Town, and elements of minstrelsy, vaudeville, and the coming jazz age made their way into the black South African cultural mix. On a visit to Cape Town in 1988, I was surprised to hear the term "coon carnival" used without a trace of irony, as Thomas uses it here.

16. *Africana: The Encyclopedia of the African American Experience*, ed. Kwame Anthony Appiah and Henry Louis Gates Jr. (New York: Basic Books), "Zambia," 2042.

17. *Africana*, "Malawi," 1230.

18. This is the same black institution that key South African leaders, including Mango-suthu Buthelezi and Nelson Mandela, attended.

19. David Blair, *Degrees in Violence: Robert Mugabe and the Struggle for Power in Zim-babwe* (London: Continuum, 2002), 17–19. Most of the key facts in this short biography of Mugabe come from Blair.

20. The jailed singer was William Kashiri.

21. H. Ellert, *The Rhodesian Front War: Counter-insurgency and Guerrilla Warfare, 1962–1980*, rev. ed. (Harare: Mambo Press, 1993), 3–5.

22. Ellert, *The Rhodesian Front War*, 7. Ellert also notes that Smith himself was nearly killed by an assassin with a grenade disguised in a can of beans, but when the man boasted about his mission over beers, the Special Branch was listening and leaked word back to ZANU. The loose-lipped assassin wound up in a shallow grave.

23. "Chemutengure" is a fascinating song, later recorded and performed by Thomas, as

well as many other artists. Many mbira musicians play it, though with its simple two-phrase structure, it is not part of the sacred repertoire. It appears to have been written around the time Rhodes's Pioneers arrived on the Zimbabwean plateau. Jennifer Kyker (pers. comm.) says the name refers to a wheel going round and round. The singer is poking fun at the cart driver, using playful language, but also delivering a veiled criticism of the Africans who worked for Zimbabwe's earliest white settlers.

24. Turino, *Nationalists, Cosmopolitans, and Popular Music in Zimbabwe*, 258–61. I have Professor Turino to thank for letting me hear these archived recordings of the Springfields. He was able to copy them when he had research access to the Zimbabwe National Archives in 1992–93.

25. Most of Thomas's account of this Rambanai incident, including this intriguing remark, come from Zindi, *Roots Rocking in Zimbabwe*, 28.

26. Entrepreneur Paul Ndoro put up money for the liquor license, and Mutanga himself managed the club. The venue was later known as Machipisa, named for the Highfield neighborhood it made famous.

27. Zindi, *Roots Rocking in Zimbabwe*, 29.

28. Joshua was born in 1953 to a musical family in Gokwe. This was the Midlands region where Ndebele, Tonga, and Shona-speaking Shangwe people intermingled. Joshua picked up finger-style guitar from his gifted brother Jonah Moyo, who would go on to lead the Devera Ngwena Jazz Band. "My father saw me playing my brother's guitar one day," Joshua recalled. "I thought I was alone, just busy practicing. I guess he loved what I was doing, because when he bought me one—a Carlton—it was a good guitar, a box guitar, very strong."

29. Kwaramba, *Popular Music and Society*, 32.

30. Turino, *Nationalists, Cosmopolitans, and Popular Music in Zimbabwe*, 99–101.

31. Turino, *Nationalists, Cosmopolitans, and Popular Music in Zimbabwe*, 100. Few broadcasters knew where to look for mbira players, so they aired invitations and waited to hear from them. Turino says, if more Zezuru players showed up at the radio station, that was likely a matter of geography rather than bias. Players from other regions were recorded, though not in any systematic way. "Simon Mashoko lived in Masvingo," mbira player Ephat Mujuru recalled, "but he also got recognized. He played *njari* [another type of mbira]. If people were good, it didn't matter where they were. Someone would say, 'If you go to Mutoko, there is somebody who plays mbira very well.'"

32. Turino (*Nationalists, Cosmopolitans, and Popular Music in Zimbabwe*, 75–78) deconstructs the notion of an mbira—specifically *mbira dzavadzimu*—"revival" in the 1960s. Citing Hugh Tracey's work in the 1930s, Turino characterizes mbira dzavadzimu as a "rather specialized, small-scale tradition, at least by the early 20th century." Even if this specific instrument's exalted status in Zimbabwe today is a relatively new development, it seems clear that there was a more general African cultural "revival," involving mbira and occurring alongside the growing nationalist movement in urban centers like Mbare during the 1960s.

33. The International Library of African Music (ILAM) was moved to Grahamstown, South Africa, where it remains, by Hugh's son Andrew Tracey.

34. *Wait a Minim* was decades ahead of its time. The Tracey family was on its way to establishing a global legacy as preservers and defenders of African traditional musical culture, but the fact that this play ran Off-Broadway, at the John Golden Theater, for 456

performances in 1966 and 1967 is remarkable. A year later, Dumisani Maraire would arrive to teach at the University of Washington in Seattle, sparking the growth of a grassroots movement to promote Shona music in the United States, but that would take years to reach fruition.

35. Turino, *Nationalists, Cosmopolitans, and Popular Music in Zimbabwe*, 100, 101.

36. Turino, *Nationalists, Cosmopolitans, and Popular Music in Zimbabwe*, 101. Turino argues that the notion of indigenous culture "dying out" in Rhodesia was and is overstated. Many city dwellers, and rural people raised in areas of heavy missionary activity, notably by the Seventh-Day Adventists, had effectively lost their culture. But this did not characterize the whole country. Nationalists like Robert Mugabe saw traditional culture as a way to tap into mass emotions. The African pageantry he had witnessed in Ghana had moved him as spectacle, and he wanted to harness similar feelings back home. But for the power brokers of the liberation struggle—white and black—African traditions were often an abstraction, often just tools used to manipulate hearts and minds.

37. Turino, *Nationalists, Cosmopolitans, and Popular Music in Zimbabwe*, 149. The quotes come from M. E. Kumalo, "City Tribal Dancing Display," *Parade*, February 1959.

38. Turino, *Nationalists, Cosmopolitans, and Popular Music in Zimbabwe*, 101–5.

39. Musa Zimunya, "Proposal to Honour Thomas Mapfumo with Honorary Degree," 1997. This quote comes from Zimunya's draft of this proposal, which he shared with me privately.

40. Thomas Turino told me that Jacob Mhungu, an mbira and bow player, was doing guitar versions of village songs as early as 1951 for musical, not nationalist, reasons. John Nkomo's recording "Haruna" (1966), played with bottleneck guitar, is a version of the Shona war song "Bayawabaya," originally a drum and vocal piece, though it is often performed on mbira. Nkomo's may be the oldest recording of traditional Shona music played on guitar, but the practice surely predates it.

41. There are various ways to conceptualize this progression. Some mbira players might begin the progression on the G at the end of the third line, rendering it G C Em, Am C F, Am Dm F, Am C Em. Others might start on Dube's second line, the one beginning with Dm. The symmetry remains in all cases, but the sense of the cycle's beginning and ending changes, altering the listener's perception of the piece considerably.

42. This is the only Thomas Mapfumo single that credits a cocomposer. The credit reads, "Thomas and Joshua." Asked how this happened, Thomas said years later, "We never had a conversation about it," suggesting that if there had been a conversation, Afro Soul might have credited the song differently.

43. Thomas Turino, through his extensive research in the Zimbabwe National Archives, finds one, roughly simultaneous, example of an electric guitar being played damped to imitate mbira. "Kumutongo," a 1973 single by M.D. Rhythm Success (Gallo GB-3815) is an adaptation of the mbira song "Kuzanga," although the composition is credited to Dominique Mandivha. The guitarist is not identified. Turino stresses that the innovations of the Hallelujah Chicken Run Band should be seen in the context of a succession of popular bands that were beginning to experiment with adapting Shona folklore, including Jerusarema dance percussion, and the 12/8 sound that would later be called "jit." These bands, active in the late 1960s, would include the Harare Mambos, the All Saints Band, the Beatsters, the Zebrons, the Saint Pauls Band-Musami, M.D. Rhythm Success, and, importantly, the band

Joshua had played with prior to joining Thomas, the Lipopo Jazz Band, under the direction of Malawian bandleader Jackson Phiri. These bands' recordings in no way undercut the Chicken Run Band's originality but simply put it in a context. What would ultimately distinguish Thomas would have less to do with his being the first to adapt traditional folklore, and more to do with his being the most committed to it, and the most effective.

3. WHEN THE SPIRIT COMES

1. This is also Anglicized Shona for the standard Shona plural form, *dzin'anga*.

2. The first known notation of an mbira piece comes in an 1872 entry in the diary of German traveler and geologist Carl Mauch. A century later, Paul Berliner and others would develop a system of notation for mbira pieces, although to this day, most players, whether in Zimbabwe or elsewhere, learn the music aurally, not from notation.

3. Some Western recordings of mbira do not use the deze and mute the bottle caps on the instrument to eliminate the buzzing. The result may be appealing in its own way, but this approach fundamentally distorts the musical tradition. To buzz or not to buzz remains a hot topic of debate among Westerners who play and record mbira.

4. I have found no evidence that the Rhodesian government specifically tried to "ban" mbira. But Paul Berliner writes, "As early as 1973, I received unconfirmed reports of performers in northern Zimbabwe who were fined or arrested for their performances of mbira music." Paul F. Berliner, *The Soul of Mbira: Music and Traditions of the Shona People of Zimbabwe* (Berkeley: University of California Press, 1978), 245.

5. Mude was not Ephat's "uncle" in the strict sense. Ephat's use of this term is an expression of respect, affection, and closeness, not a literal description of family structure.

6. Playing hosho is difficult, and different players have their own styles and techniques. This description reflects my best effort to characterize it as I hear it, but it should not be taken as definitive.

7. Again, the term *pungwe* derives from the liberation war era—describing all-night political gatherings featuring singing and dancing—not from older Shona religious tradition. But pungwe has now entered general Shona vernacular, hence this boy's usage in this context.

8. Ephat never liked the term *mbira dzavadzimu*, saying that all mbira were "of the ancestors." He considered it a confusing term created by anthropologists. It is, however, still widely used.

9. David Lan, *Guns and Rain: Guerrillas and Spirit Mediums in Zimbabwe* (Berkeley: University of California Press, 1985), 32.

10. M. Gelfand, S. Mavi, R. B. Drummond, and B. Ndemera, *The Traditional Medical Practitioner in Zimbabwe* (Harare: Mambo Press, 1993), 3.

11. Lan, *Guns and Rain*, 34.

12. Terence Ranger, "The Death of Chaminuka: Spirit Mediums, Nationalism, and the Guerrilla War in Zimbabwe," *African Affairs* 81, no. 324 (1982): 349–69. This account of Chaminuka and Muchatera is mostly drawn from Ranger's provocative essay. These are complex matters, and much has been added since. My intent is not to resolve knotty historical debates but to dramatize the complex psycho-spiritual underpinnings of this unique African conflict.

13. Ranger, "Death of Chaminuka," 349.

14. For the record, writing in 1994, D. N. Beach cites "contemporary sources" showing that in fact, the Ndebele had long been on good terms with Pasipamire. They clashed over the issue of ivory hunters arming Pasipamire in exchange for permission to hunt, and "in April 1883, the ruler summoned the medium to his country and had him executed." For Beach, the rest is mythology, however widely held. D. N. Beach, *A Zimbabwean Past: Shona Dynastic Histories and Oral Tradition* (Gweru, Zimbabwe: Mambo Press, 1994), 60.

15. Ranger, "Death of Chaminuka," 352.

16. Ranger, "Death of Chaminuka," 352.

17. Ranger, "Death of Chaminuka," 353. Muchatera's version of Pasipamire's death goes further than any before. Ndebele aggression here stems from King Lobengula's anger that God has abandoned his people in favor of Chaminuka and the Shona. When at last the old medium falls silent at the hands of the young boy, Muchatera reports, "The voice of Chaminuka was heard by all gathered, telling them that Lobengula would be defeated by another race who would come from the east."

18. Berliner, *Soul of Mbira*, 45. Berliner, in turn, cites Gelfand as the source for the connection between Muchatera and Chaminuka. Berliner's book fits generally into Ranger's argument about Muchatera's influence on scholars, but it is clear in Berliner's writing that he is skeptical of Muchatera as an informant on matters beyond mbira playing.

19. Ranger, "Death of Chaminuka," 355.

20. Ranger, "Death of Chaminuka," 363.

21. Ranger, "Death of Chaminuka," 354.

22. Ranger, "Death of Chaminuka," 355.

23. Tute Chigamba, interview, 1998.

24. Lan, *Guns and Rain*, 9.

25. Lan, *Guns and Rain*, 4.

26. Lan, *Guns and Rain*, 157–58. There were no schools, shops, or beer halls in Dande as the war began, but there were three types of Christian churches. The Evangelicals were openly hostile to Shona religion and insisted that their followers reject spirit mediums as Satanic forces playing on "heathen fears." The Catholics were more lenient and so attracted by far the most followers, many of whom continued to attend biras and visit n'anga. Then there was the small but growing Apostolic Church, founded by an African prophet named John Marange in the 1930s, whose followers can still be seen dressed in white and gathered under trees in open fields. Apostolics accept the truth of spirit possession but brand ancestor spirits as dangerous and evil. Their own ceremonies can also result in possession, but by the Holy Spirit, not by African spirits.

27. Lan, *Guns and Rain*, 92–93. Lan also argues that the realization that mediums, not only chiefs, were now "a vital weapon in counter-insurgency" came about "virtually overnight." He writes, "Every single medium at every level of seniority was to be interviewed. Standardized questionnaires were prepared. The tone of the instruction circulated in February 1973 among the district assistants who were charged with assembling information on the mediums in the north-east suggests how the attitude to mediums had hardened." Unresponsive mediums were to be arrested. Lan, *Guns and Rain*, 192–93.

28. Lan, *Guns and Rain*, 148.

29. Thomas Turino, *Nationalists, Cosmopolitans, and Popular Music in Zimbabwe* (Chicago: University of Chicago Press, 2000), 208.

30. Julie Frederikse, *None But Ourselves: Masses vs. Media in the Making of Zimbabwe* (Harare: Anvil Press, 1982), 105. The most potent venue for these songs was the all-night, musical teach-in known as the pungwe. When guerrillas came to a village and announced a pungwe, security demanded that everyone attend. For some, it was a burden, and for many a source of fear, but the singing provided distraction and pleasure to while away a long night. The messages focused not on the Maoist theory that animated the guerrilla leaders but on spiritual matters and, above all, on the idea of reclaiming land, the most persuasive rationale for the war.

31. Lan, *Guns and Rain*, 157.

32. Lan, *Guns and Rain*, 57.

33. Ranger, "Death of Chaminuka," 362.

34. Ranger, "Death of Chaminuka," 365.

4. SONGS FOR THE BOOK OF HISTORY

1. Peter Godwin and Ian Hancock, *"Rhodesians Never Die": The Impact of War and Change on White Rhodesia, c. 1970–1980* (Harare: Baobab Books, 1993), 8–9.

2. Godwin and Hancock, *"Rhodesians Never Die,"* 84.

3. Godwin and Hancock, *"Rhodesians Never Die,"* 102.

4. Thomas Turino, *Nationalists, Cosmopolitans, and Popular Music in Zimbabwe* (Chicago: University of Chicago Press, 2000), 268, citing a *Parade* article from 1971.

5. Turino, *Nationalists, Cosmopolitans, and Popular Music in Zimbabwe*, 271. Dube said this directly to Turino, who uses the statement to support his thesis that political consciousness was an afterthought for Thomas. I see this differently. Turino was writing in the late 1990s, before Thomas showed his true mettle by standing up to Mugabe. But even in this earlier phase, the trajectory of Thomas's political awakening is clear from many sources. The divergence of views on "Ngoma Yarira" highlights the two musicians' opposite natures: Thomas was quiet, complex, and guarded, and Dube was straightforward and practical to a fault. If the two had different understandings of their own song, it was hardly the only time they would stand side by side and still be worlds apart.

6. Turino, *Nationalists, Cosmopolitans, and Popular Music in Zimbabwe*, 285. Turino describes this translation as "literal" and notes that his interpreter had difficulty expressing some of the lines in this song in English.

7. Musa finds veiled suggestions of protest in other Hallelujah Chicken Run songs as well, like "Zai Ona Zai Ona," set to the rhythm of a work gang with Thomas singing, "Work, work," and the chorus responding, "There's no money. There's no money." Or "Mutoridodo," adapted from a children's song about a man who goes to Dande—the guerrilla stronghold—looking for salt only to have his fish stolen from his frying rack in his absence. For Musa, such scenarios posed "a challenge to the imagination" and "touched a raw nerve in the wounded dignity of the African people."

8. This and other quotes attributed to "a Teal manager" come from a reliable Teal source, interviewed in 2005 from South Africa. He did not wish to be identified.

9. Turino, *Nationalists, Cosmopolitans, and Popular Music in Zimbabwe*.

10. In Dube's account, Thomas sold a microphone from the band's kit, but the result was the same.

11. Godwin and Hancock, *"Rhodesians Never Die,"* 29.

12. Zexie's career had started back in 1957, by coincidence, at Mhangura mine, where he and his brother used to play South African styles, *kwela* and *marabi*.

13. Marshall, who would later lead a superb band, the Four Brothers, was Janet's youngest brother, so technically Thomas's "uncle," though Thomas was actually a few years older than Marshall.

14. The master tapes for these songs did not survive, though collectors do have singles. As yet, these great songs have appeared on no compilation releases.

15. The single, AS 1031, is actually titled "Yarira," although everyone seems to recall it as "Yarira ne Hosho." It is undated and does not appear in Emmanuel Vori's list, or Musa Zimunya's, or Alice Kwaramba's. But based on its catalog number, it comes before the Acid Band singles. It is one of four sequential singles, and, interestingly, it is the last one that Thomas credits to "tradition." Henceforth, even clearly traditional songs are always credited to him. Guitarist Gilbert Zvamaida says the song uses what is known as the *pfumo jena*, or "white spear," rhythm.

16. The station's only nod to any form of African music had been Hugh Masekela's "Grazin' in the Grass," recorded in 1969 in New York.

17. Godwin and Hancock, *"Rhodesians Never Die,"* 117.

18. Thomas recalled in an interview, "When [Oliver] was paid for the record, he actually came to me and paid me eight dollars. Eight dollars! I used that money buying beer and Cokes for my friends."

19. When Thomas left Wagon Wheels "for greener pastures," his goal, as ever, was to find a band he could lead. Solomon Tawengwa invited Thomas to come and sing with the Pied Pipers, who had a contract at Mushandira Pamwe. The Pied Pipers took Thomas into the studio to record a new single, but when it came to delivering the sound he was after, they fell short. The single they recorded reprised the first Shona song Thomas had performed with the Springfields, "Shungu Dzinondibaya," and the flip side was a traditional song for the mhondoro spirit, "Chaminuka." The record was "no good at all," as Thomas recalled. "People didn't buy it."

20. Thomas was still a guest with the Acid Band, and his balancing act grew still more conflicted when he took a daytime gig with the house band at the Skyline Motel. He began inviting the Acid Band to come out to the Skyline and back him on the songs they were developing, and one day, the jam was so hot the guys played long and arrived late for their night jobs. Thomas was fired on the spot. At last forced to choose, he severed ties with the Pied Pipers and the Skyline, and officially joined the Acid Band.

21. Fred Zindi, *Roots Rocking in Zimbabwe* (Harare: Mambo Press, 1985), 35. The Acid Band then was Thomas, Charles, Pickett, James Chimombe, a guitarist named Lucky, though not Lucky Mupawaenda, Albert Gweshe on drums, and Enoch Manda on saxophone—a "very strong" lineup, by all accounts.

22. Asked to name his four most important songs in 2012, Thomas put "Pfumvu Pa Ruzevha" at the top of the list. The others were "Tozvireva Kupiko" (another Acid Band single from 1977), "Marima Nzara," and "Havasevenzi Vapfana" (both from *Chimurenga Rebel* in 2002).

23. The Selous Scouts' feats of psychological manipulation are legendary. H. Ellert's chap-

ter on the Scouts (*The Rhodesian Front War: Counter-insurgency and Guerrilla Warfare, 1962–1980*, rev. ed. [Harare: Mambo Press, 1993], 124–60) is a fascinating and seemingly balanced account of counterterrorist operations during the war.

24. Ellert, *Rhodesian War Front*, 127–28, 135.

25. *Rhodesia Herald*, December 8, 1975.

26. Turino, *Nationalists, Cosmopolitans, and Popular Music in Zimbabwe*, 289.

27. Terence Ranger, "The Death of Chaminuka: Spirit Mediums, Nationalism, and the Guerrilla War in Zimbabwe," *African Affairs* 81, no. 324 (1982): 368. Ranger cites a 1975 gathering of mediums where one reportedly claimed to be possessed by Chaminuka, a challenge to Muchatera Mujuru. As for Thomas's venture, he recalled four in the party: himself, Pickett, Charles, and producer Crispen Matema.

28. *Mitemo* also means taboos in the traditional context, suggesting a deeper message about keeping right with the ancestors.

29. Julie Frederikse, *None But Ourselves: Masses vs. Media in the Making of Zimbabwe* (Harare: Anvil Press, 1982), 108.

30. This quote combines comments far apart in time. The first part comes from 2004; the second from 1981.

31. *Dangarembwa* in Shona means "a pack of dogs."

32. In an interview with me in 1988, Sithole recalled that "nobody was chucked away" when the Storm and the Acid Band merged. "Pickett was playing the sound of the Acid Band, while I was playing the sound of the Blacks Unlimited. As time went by, Thomas said Pickett was not practicing, so he ended up playing only sublead. There was nothing you could do about it. Anyway, he was good. But then the bass man, Finos, was getting too drunk, so I had to replace him with Charles." Sithole's recollection that it was he who had sacked Finos and brought in Charles on bass also supports the case for his leadership role in the band, as do statements by some other musicians. Only longtime fans would remember these first Blacks Unlimited support musicians, guitarist Pickett, the drunken bass man Finos Magaramombe or his replacement Charles Makokowa, the drummer Jonasy Sarutawa, or saxophonists Enoch Manda and John Sibanda, whose surname even Thomas could not recall.

5. BISHOP AND PAWN

Tom Hama epigraph quoted in Julie Frederikse, *None But Ourselves: Masses vs. Media in the Making of Zimbabwe* (Harare: Anvil Press, 1982), 264, 216.

1. Abel Tendekai Muzorewa, *Rise Up and Walk: The Autobiography of Bishop Abel Tendekai Muzorewa*, ed. Norman E. Thomas (Nashville, TN: Abingdon, 1978), 10.

2. Muzorewa, *Rise Up and Walk*, 45.

3. Muzorewa, *Rise Up and Walk*, 50–53.

4. Muzorewa, *Rise Up and Walk*, 80–85.

5. Robert Cary and Diana Mitchell, *African Nationalist Leaders in Rhodesia: Who's Who* (Johannesburg: Africana Book Society, 1977), 229. The African National Council was distinct from the earlier African National Congress, formed in 1934 and banned in 1959, and the South African ANC.

6. Cary and Mitchell, *African Nationalist Leaders in Rhodesia*, 233.

7. Cary and Mitchell, *African Nationalist Leaders in Rhodesia*, 170. Mugabe was semi-officially elected to lead ZANU upon his release in 1974. Kaunda backed Ndabaninge Sithole.

8. Tekere would serve in Mugabe's government but would turn against him, and even run against him in the 1990 election. His recent comments, cited here, should be weighed in that light.

9. Heidi Holland, *Dinner with Mugabe: The Untold Story of a Freedom Fighter Who Became a Tyrant* (Johannesburg: Penguin, 2008), 176. Filmmaker Simon Bright explores the question of whether Mugabe changed or simply hid his violent nature in the excellent film *Robert Mugabe . . . What Happened?* (2011).

10. Muzorewa, *Rise Up and Walk*, 176.

11. Muzorewa butted heads with Mugabe and Nkomo and came away feeling that their Patriotic Front was "an exercise in negativeness" (Muzorewa, *Rise Up and Walk*, 220). The bishop's own bottom line, an election on the basis of one man, one vote, was more than Smith could stomach, but Muzorewa stood for it to the bitter end and returned with his reputation intact. Again, large crowds welcomed him.

12. Peter Godwin and Ian Hancock, *"Rhodesians Never Die": The Impact of War and Change on White Rhodesia, c. 1970–1980* (Harare: Baobab Books, 1993), 211.

13. Among the three Africans—all Shona—only Sithole had real political experience, and he had been shunned by ZANU and the guerrillas. Smith's own party thought the internal settlement was radical, even though it guaranteed twenty-eight white seats in a hundred-seat assembly.

14. Frederikse, *None But Ourselves*, 266. A Rhodesia Broadcasting Corporation letter from August 28, 1978, instructed all employees to "ban any mention" of eight major political organizations.

15. This attack occurred on September 3, 1978. The Soviet-made Strela 2 missile hit the plane's starboard wing, forcing it to crash-land. Of the fifty-six people on board, thirty-eight died.

16. These attacks were so unacceptable to Muzorewa that he threatened to withdraw from the transitional government. It was an empty gesture, for the bishop had nowhere to turn. His only real success was to liberate the disease-ridden protected villages, providing a small boost to his credibility but also a tactical advantage to the guerrillas.

17. Thomas Turino points out that histories of the war tend to gloss over the bishop's popularity in the late 1970s. "Back then we were *all* for Muzorewa!" a middle-class black friend told him (Thomas Turino, *Nationalists, Cosmopolitans, and Popular Music in Zimbabwe* [Chicago: University of Chicago Press, 2000], 195).

18. Alec J. C. Pongweni, *Songs That Won the Liberation War* (Harare: College Press, 1982), 148–50.

19. Alice Dadira Kwaramba, *Popular Music and Society: The Language of Protest in Chimurenga Music: The Case of Thomas Mapfumo in Zimbabwe*, IMK Report No. 24 (Oslo: University of Oslo, Department of Media Communication, 1997), 36–38. Kwaramba says this song came out in 1974, but this appears to be wrong. Its catalog number, AS 1090, indicates that the song came later, and its question, "Where is Mr. Chitepo to lead us?," would make no sense prior to Chitepo's 1975 assassination.

20. Thomas also sang, "Where is Mr. Parirenyatwa to lead us?" Dr. Stephen Parirenyatwa,

Rhodesia's first black doctor, had served as the original deputy president of ZAPU prior to his death in a car crash in 1962.

21. Frederikse, *None But Ourselves*, 105.

22. *Rhodesia Herald*, January 22, 1979.

23. The B-side of this record, "Tamba Wachenjera (Play the Game Carefully)," also evokes the war, warning that you never know who may be listening to you, so watch what you say.

24. Most of this comes from a lecture Thomas gave in New Orleans in 1991 and from my own interview with him in Harare in 1998. The part where he is accused of being the "Chimurenga singer" and the detail about "bad translations" come from Frederikse, *None But Ourselves*, 109–10.

25. Frederikse, *None But Ourselves*, 264. In a footnote, Frederikse writes, "The Emergency Powers (Maintenance of Law and Order) Regulations allowed the police to detain people without trial for 30 days. Thereafter, ministerial approval was needed." Ashton "Sugar" Chiweshe, who says he worked with the band during this time, recalls Thomas's stay in Chikururbi as "twenty-eight days."

26. This paragraph (from Frederikse, *None But Ourselves*, 264) is more detailed and comes from an interview conducted closer to the actual event than most other accounts here. This version somewhat contradicts Everson's recollection of being taken straight from a show to the rally, but the idea is consistent.

27. *Herald*, April 2, 1979.

28. In fact, the photo is so little like Thomas's memory that when I showed it to him, he claimed it was the wrong one. However, he also insisted that the picture he remembered appeared in the *Herald* on the morning after the Bulawayo rally, and this is the only edition of the paper I could find that covered this rally.

29. I interviewed Muzorewa in May 2005, in Washington, DC, at a conference of Methodist bishops. He seemed mildly defensive in recalling this rally and insisted he had "nothing to hide." In essence, I believed him. If he was hiding anything, it was probably from himself. As to his limited awareness of Thomas, it seemed genuine. During the year we spoke, there had been many stories in the Zimbabwean press about Thomas's life in exile in the United States. Despite this, as we parted, the bishop asked me, "Is he still living?"

30. Fred Zindi, *Roots Rocking in Zimbabwe* (Harare: Mambo Press, 1985), 34. The Frederikse reference comes from Thomas Turino's handwritten transcript of her complete interview in the Zimbabwe national archives.

31. In theory, it is possible that the April 2 *Herald* article covered one Muzorewa rally at which Thomas performed, but not the *first* one, the one that directly followed his release. This would contradict Muzorewa's assertion that they appeared together only once, but it would support the musicians' recollections of multiple rallies and perhaps also Thomas's memory of a more damning photograph. However, I carefully examined every *Herald* edition from January through April and found only this one report of the Blacks Unlimited playing a Muzorewa rally. If official documentation on Thomas's detention exists to clarify the sequence of events, that remains for future researchers to uncover.

32. Muzorewa crushed his only serious opponent, Sithole, who had claimed the ZANU name for the purposes of his campaign.

33. Godwin and Hancock, *"Rhodesians Never Die,"* 244.

34. *Herald*, May 9, 1979.

35. Frederikse, *None But Ourselves*, 110.

36. Thomas recalled attending but not playing at this event. However, his name definitely appeared on the posters, and Zexie's son, Aaron Manatsa, recalled growing up with the family photo album, including photographs of Thomas singing in Rufaro that day. Incidentally, Zexie's wedding ended in near mayhem as fans outside stormed the fences, sending two people to hospital.

37. The Green Arrows, *The Green Arrows* (Analog Africa No 1. AACD 061, 2004). From sleeve notes by Samy Ben Redjeb. The notes go on to say that Zexie's band, the Green Arrows, later grounded on their own political shoals when two members publicly accused Zexie of pocketing money given to him by a political party. The party in question was not amused by the publicity, and after receiving a death threat, Zexie was forced to fire two of his best players. The band was never the same. On the subject of going to the movies, once again, Thomas's and Zexie's memories don't match. Possibly bitterness over later events clouded Thomas's memory. Possibly guilt over those same events, or his serious car accident in 1987, clouded Zexie's. In any case, Thomas insisted that Jonah Sithole and Allan Mwale were the guys he went to the movies with, "not Zexie."

38. A number of people close to the guerrilla movement have noted the ruthless violence reserved for dissenters within the ranks. One example is the recollection of a Catholic woman who "supported Mugabe despite inklings of his cruelty." See Holland, *Dinner with Mugabe*, 148–49.

39. Godwin and Hancock, "*Rhodesians Never Die*," 261.

40. Holland, *Dinner with Mugabe*, 133.

41. All the dramas of the prior year, so consequential for Thomas, were swept aside by electrifying new headlines. On December 27, ZANLA's top commander, Josiah Tongogara, a strong candidate in the coming election, was killed in Mozambique when his car crashed into an oncoming vehicle. Investigations would conclude it was an ordinary traffic accident, but as with the death of Herbert Chitepo, some would always suspect the powerful hand of Mugabe behind yet another potential competitor's convenient demise.

6. AGONY OF VICTORY

Epigraph: Mudereri Kadhani and Musamura Zimunya, eds., *And Now the Poets Speak* (Harare: Mambo Press, 1997), 158–59. *Tichatonga* means "we shall rule."

1. White Rhodesia also scrambled to influence events. Military bands were instructed to play "numbers with an African flavor," as if this would discourage voters from supporting ZANU and ZAPU! There were plots to assassinate Mugabe, attack his assembly points, and rig or annul the election. A phony edition of the Catholic newspaper *Moto* hit the streets with a front-page article defaming Mugabe. When a *Moto* printing press in Gweru was subsequently bombed, people were supposed to conclude it was a ZANU reprisal. Evidence pointed instead to the Special Branch of the Rhodesian government. Peter Godwin and Ian Hancock, "*Rhodesians Never Die*": *The Impact of War and Change on White Rhodesia, c. 1970–1980* (Harare: Baobab Books, 1993), 268–69.

2. Shed Studio had opened in late 1979 with superior eight-track recording equipment that engineer Steve Roskilly had managed to import. Teal now did most of its recording at Shed, but the 1980 election had created so much uncertainty that the company had slowed its release of new records, curtailing Thomas's most reliable source of income. Among the

handful of Blacks Unlimited singles from this period are four songs Jonah Sithole recorded and sang, none of them apparently political or particularly successful. Thomas mostly sings about social topics like infidelity and divorce in traditional society, and the struggle of a poor man to win respect among the wealthy. One song, "Muchandiuraya (You Will Have to Kill Me)," refers to the land issue with defiant words: "This is my land. I'm not getting out. This is where I belong. So you will have to kill me."

3. This characterization of the judge comes from my interview with Willard Masantula.

4. Kadhani and Zimunya, *And Now the Poets Speak*, xiii.

5. *Haarari* means "one who never sleeps"; the name was given to the chief of the referenced Zezuru clan, Chief Neharawa, because he was never surprised by his enemies.

6. Even Nkomo's appearance at the independence ceremony telegraphed unease. As Geoffrey Nyarota noted, "He was with the people, not with *them* [Mugabe and his power circle]. And he was extremely bitter." Meanwhile, Bishop Muzorewa was so devastated by his resounding defeat that he boycotted the ceremony in Rufaro Stadium. "I chose not to go," he recalled in our interview. "It was very difficult, very disappointing for me. I knew what Mugabe believed in. I thought that our hope for freedom and liberty was dashed down, that democracy was defeated." The bishop did not even remember where he was that day.

7. Musa Zimunya believed Thomas sang "Nyarai" against Muzorewa and his supporters, and that some Ndebele people had simply "misinterpreted" it. Everyone knew the history of Ndebele dominance over the Shona in precolonial times. Still, Musa insisted, any hint of a new conflict—African against African—was too awful for Zimbabweans to contemplate. This is why Thomas could reprimand dissenters in "Nyarai" and be, in Musa's words, "unashamed to perform it."

8. Julie Frederikse, *None But Ourselves: Masses vs. Media in the Making of Zimbabwe* (Harare: Anvil Press, 1982), 328.

9. Roger Steffens, "Zimbabwe Victorious: Bob Marley's African Triumph, I-Witness Dera Tomkins," *Beat* 17, no. 3 (1998): 48–55.

10. Timothy White, *Catch a Fire: The Life of Bob Marley*, rev. ed. (New York: Henry Holt, 1989), 3.

11. John Masouri, *Wailing Blues: The Story of Bob Marley's Wailers* (London: Omnibus Press, 2010), 485. In Masouri's account, Marley approached Chris Blackwell for funding to travel to Zimbabwe, but Blackwell did not see enough promotional value in the trip, and balked. But Marley was adamant and declared he was going to bankroll the whole thing himself. Eventually, Blackwell advanced $90,000, which wasn't enough; Marley wound up spending $250,000 of his own money on the trip.

12. Some details from Ras T. Henry, "When Bob Marley Caused Riot inna Africa," *Rasta Times*, September 30, 2001.

13. Godwin and Hancock, *"Rhodesians Never Die,"* 313.

14. Memories of the performances vary. Oliver recalled groups playing all day and then stopping after Marley's set. Thomas remembered Marley as the first to play, and music lasting until sunrise. Dera Tomkins describes traditional groups and choirs performing at the far end of the stadium starting at 6:00 PM.

15. *Exodus* was named "best album of the 20th century" by *Time* magazine.

16. Marley played a second concert at Rufaro the following night, and things went more

smoothly. For Zimbabweans who attended both concerts, events merge, all part of one long, expansive celebration. I interviewed a number of people who had a hard time distinguishing the two performances.

17. Ras T. Henry claims that Marley did not take the stage until twenty minutes *after* the exchange of flags, but this time line does not appear to be correct.

18. Thomas Parkenham, *The Scramble for Africa: The White Man's Conquest of the Dark Continent from 1876 to 1912* (New York: Random House, 1991), 670.

19. Fred Zindi, *Roots Rocking in Zimbabwe* (Harare: Mambo Press, 1985), vii. This is one of many places where Robert Mugabe's famous remarks of April 18, 1980, are cited.

20. Heidi Holland, *Dinner with Mugabe: The Untold Story of a Freedom Fighter Who Became a Tyrant* (Johannesburg: Penguin, 2008), 72.

21. Parkenham, *Scramble for Africa*, 671.

7. SNAKES IN THE FOREST

1. Andrew Whaley, "We Are for the People, Says Blacks Unlimited," *Herald*, December 10, 1980.

2. The record reprieved war-era Acid Band songs "Tozvireva Kupiko" and "Pfumvu Pa Ruzevha" and mixed in victory salutes from the Blacks Unlimited's recent repertoire, "Africa," "Nyarai," and "Kwaedza mu Zimbabwe."

3. This was the first Thomas Mapfumo song I ever heard, on a mix tape Sean Barlow sent me from London in 1984. I was hooked instantly.

4. Maurice Vambe and Alice Kwaramba both try to make a connection between the song "Shumba" and Mugabe's brutal suppression of Matabeleland. Thomas has repeatedly rejected this, arguing that the song was performed during the war, although it was not recorded until 1981. The lyrics are allegorical and offer little clarification on the point. I take Thomas at his word that an anti-Ndebele message was not his intent here. But given the ferocity of Mugabe's Matabeleland campaign, it is not surprising that some listeners would have interpreted the song in that context.

5. Everson Chibamu, joined now by Temba Moncube on trumpet and a saxophonist remembered only as Bobby.

6. The imprint of Cuban clave—strong in Congo music—fades in East Africa and is fainter still in sungura, which emphasizes a straight 4/4 beat, superlively bass playing, and dueling electric guitars.

7. Maurice Taonezvi Vambe, "Versions and Sub-versions: Trends in *Chimurenga* Musical Discourses of Post-Independence Zimbabwe," *African Study Monographs* 25, no. 4 (2004): 167–93. Vambe writes, "After Zimbabwean Independence, the *Sungura* beat helped provide hard-hitting commentary on the slowness of leaders in delivering on promises of independence to the African masses." This is interesting, but according to my research, the politically engaged impulse in this music did not survive long beyond that. In any case, sungura caught fire in Zimbabwe's towns and villages, and it has remained the lifeblood of the local record industry ever since. After Jonah Moyo would come John Chibadura, Leonard Dembo, Khiama Boys, System Tazvida, Alick Macheso, and many others, all remaining quite faithful to the 1980s sound, the rise of Africa's hip-hop generation notwithstanding.

8. The Hallelujah Chicken Run Band had left Mhangura in 1976 to become the house act at a beer hall in Chitungwiza.

9. In honor of the third anniversary of independence, the Blacks Unlimited released an upbeat commemorative number called "Pamberai (Rejoice)." The single went gold. The flip side, "Haruna," is an adaptation of a traditional song about a woman who gossips too much. Dube's lead guitar sears with rock edge, and Thomas's crying vocal gives this village song a brooding air, leavened only by a bright brass section refrain.

10. David Blair, *Degrees in Violence: Robert Mugabe and the Struggle for Power in Zimbabwe* (London: Continuum, 2002), 29.

11. Catholic Commission for Justice and Peace in Zimbabwe, *Breaking the Silence, Building True Peace: A Report on the Disturbances in Matabeleland and the Midlands 1980 to 1988. Summary Report* (Harare: Catholic Commission for Justice and Peace in Zimbabwe, Legal Resources Foundation, 1999). This report is my principal source for facts concerning the activities of the Fifth Brigade. Many Fifth Brigade recruits had been guilty of war crimes but had avoided culpability under the general amnesty of 1979. The Catholic Commission for Justice and Peace in Zimbabwe wrote that "the very men who had tortured people in the 1970s used the same methods to torture people again in the 1980s" (*Breaking the Silence, Building True Peace*, 5).

12. Catholic Commission for Justice and Peace in Zimbabwe, *Breaking the Silence, Building True Peace*, 9.

13. Blair, *Degrees in Violence*, 32.

14. Catholic Commission for Justice and Peace in Zimbabwe, *Breaking the Silence, Building True Peace*, 12.

15. Blair, *Degrees in Violence*, 29.

16. I have not found independent confirmation of this account. There is much yet to be written about this history. But even if this encounter did not happen as Thomas reports, it captures the dark reality of Nkomo's acquiescence.

17. The record is an Afropop classic, although it cannot quite live up to Van Renen's title. A *true* collection of Thomas's chimurenga singles would have to include the Hallelujah Chicken Run Band's "Ngoma Yarira" and "Murembo," the first Blacks Unlimited's "Yarira ne Hosho," and Acid Band numbers like "Pamuromo Chete," "Tumirai Vana Kuhondo," and "Hokoyo."

18. Willard had adopted the surname of a Congolese fire-eater who had agreed to "demonstrate," but not teach, his trade. "It took me almost a year," the fire-eater recalled. "I used to get burned because he didn't tell me which chemical he was using." After painful experiments with alcohol, Masantula at last discovered that the key was to use paraffin, and he incorporated the stunt into Thomas's stage show.

19. *Fodya* literally means "tobacco," though in musicians' circles it is often understood to mean marijuana.

20. Emmanuel Jera (Manu) recalled that some of the *Mabasa* tracks were originally recorded during the *Ndangariro* session. But after Manu quit the band, frustrated with low pay and his inability to move the sound in a more "international" direction, tracks were either scrubbed or reworked. "I had a row with Thomas," said Manu. "I had no future in his band." Manu believed that his parts were retracked, probably by Dube, and new songs were added. "Ndanzwa Ngoma Kurira (I Hear the Sound of Drumming)" is the standout, a masterful workout of mbira-esque vocal and guitar. The song "Mari (Money)," a mournful, brassy, rumba variant, makes the point that money is not bad per se; blame goes rather

to the people who use it to oppress and manipulate others. "Usatambe Nenyoka (Don't Play with a Snake)," a reworking of a war-era single, might be read as further commentary on the dissidents, but its mood is light and its lyrics vague: "Don't play with the enemy."

21. Paradzai Gore plays the mbira on this track. Turino says that the first popular recording to blend mbira and guitars came three years earlier from Pamidze Benhura—also playing bottleneck at this time. "Zvamunozhema" (1980, TEAL ZIM-4) is an mbira song. The flip side is "Chemutengure," played on slide guitar, with mbira on the recording.

22. This period of change in the band lineup generated confusion. Columnist Leo Hatugari actually reported that Thomas was maintaining two complete bands and could put on separate shows simultaneously, shuttling himself back and forth between clubs. Thomas admired Hatugari but laughed this report off as the fantasy of a man who "sometimes drinks too much beer and forgets what to write about."

23. Lacking the musicianship of Dube, Manu, and Washington, *Mr Music*'s five tracks can't match the creative force and punch of *Ndangariro* and *Mabasa*. Nevertheless, the Blacks Unlimited sound remains essentially intact and even shows evolution. Two traditional adaptations, "Kufa Kwangu (The Day I Die)" and the war song "Tondobayana (We Are Going to Kill Each Other)," incorporate prominent mbira performances—although the mbira players are not credited on the album jacket. "Kufa Kwangu" is especially good with its minor-key tonality and testosterone-pumped chanting. Overall, though, the album feels a little flat, its tracks overly long and guitar work perfunctory.

24. James Chimombe was the rhythm guitarist in the Acid Band when Thomas joined. As a singer, he went on to record very popular songs with O.K. Success and, especially after 1980, with the Huchi Band and Ocean City Band. Chimombe died in 1990, reportedly from AIDS.

25. The mbira players, who had become part of the band's local gigs, did not join this tour; neither did Masantula the fire-eater, who recalled the bitterness of those left behind: "Thomas promised us heaven, but it turned out to be hell."

26. The Kenyans who had licensed Thomas's early albums to Van Renen's Earthworks label had now formed a distribution company called Serengeti headed by Mike Wells, whom Van Renen remembered as "dreadful . . . a real, old colonial system guy." Wells first tried to cut Earthworks out of the Mapfumo deal and work directly with Rough Trade, the UK distributor. When that failed, *Mabasa* and *Mr Music* were released in the United Kingdom as Gramma Productions for Serengeti Records on Earthworks / Rough Trade. A small pie was being divided into many thin slices, and Thomas—not to mention his musicians—fell low on the food chain.

27. Back in Harare at the end of 1984, Thomas denied a London news report that he was planning to leave Gramma. "We have been with Gramma for such a long time that we can't part now," he told the *Sunday Mail*, but added that he and Gramma would need to "redefine" their deal to give him "more control."

28. While other young nations, especially in West Africa, uplifted local art forms and traditions, teaching them in schools and underwriting performance ensembles, Zimbabwe sidelined its artists. Rather than underwrite popular musicians, the new government slapped a prohibitive luxury tax on imported instruments and musical equipment. This blindness to culture offended Thomas's values and helped to further alienate him from the national leadership.

29. Joshua Dube recalls a different incident in which Charles was badly beaten, again by soldiers. It was in Zambia, probably around 1983, after the band had played a show in the Keystick neighborhood of Lusaka. When the other musicians returned to the hotel, Dube and Charles remained in a bar drinking, and on the way home they were harassed by soldiers at a roadblock. "I was the trouble," recalled Dube. "I was drunk. I started shouting at those soldiers. 'Hey, *pfutseki* [fuck off]! Why are you doing this? Did you know we are from Zimbabwe?' What, what. They were speaking this Chichewa, and I know a bit of that language, so I was shouting in their own language. But instead of attacking me, they went straight for Charles. Yah. With the butt of a gun. And I was still shouting at them, but they didn't do anything to me."

30. Not long after releasing *Chimurenga for Justice*, Rough Trade collapsed as a label and went back to its niche as an offbeat London record store.

31. Ian Anderson, "Zimbabwe Gold: Ian Anderson on the Folk Roots of Thomas Mapfumo," *Folk Roots*, no. 28 (October 1985): 28–31. Anderson had interviewed Thomas during the *Chimurenga for Justice* studio sessions, and the story he wrote holds up well despite some oversimplified mythology, such as the idea that no one in Rhodesia had sung in Shona before Thomas did.

32. *Sing Out* 32, no. 3 (1987).

8. CORRUPTION

1. Brian Cader of Gramma reported Thomas's sales for 1987 at 20,000 copies; Jonah Moyo and Devera Ngwena at 40,000; Michael Jackson at 5,000.

2. *Zimbabwe Mozambique* was tracked at the independent Frontline Studio—with Benny Miller at the controls—and released in August 1987. It was the first LP from Thomas's Chimurenga Music Company.

3. *Zimbabwe Mozambique* also includes the triumphant, anthem-like "Serevende," built around an mbira part created by the band and voicing the nostalgic lament of a man who has lost everything. "Joyce" is an ebullient reprise of the war years and a warning to a young girl not to venture out into danger: "Beer is sweet, so stay at home." And "Ndave Kuenda (He Has Gone)" concludes the album with more dark, stirring Korekore music, this time with Jonah's prickly guitar lines seeming to pierce the lassitude descending over the country.

4. Thomas's preoccupation with automobiles had blossomed considerably since the days of his first car, the Morris Minor Charles drove to the police station when Thomas was jailed in 1979—Thomas said he himself "never drove that car." Later on, he owned an Alpha Romeo Alfasud and then a sports car with a Studebaker engine—"very fast." The leopard skin Granada was quite déclassé for Thomas and did not last long. Soon would come the American-bought Mitsubishi and the first in a series of BMWs.

5. David Blair, *Degrees in Violence: Robert Mugabe and the Struggle for Power in Zimbabwe* (London: Continuum, 2002), 30.

6. Thomas recalled that Jonah's drawing away from the band had already begun when this recording was made. This was why he called on a "friend," respected jazz/pop guitarist Louis Mhlanga, who had emerged from the progressive, mixed-race band Ilanga, alongside Andy Brown. Mhlanga would go on to become a session musician in the South African scene and to build a unique solo career as a cross-genre guitarist.

7. Thomas made this remark in a 1998 interview with me.

8. By an odd coincidence, Rappaport had known Bob Coen in the late 1970s. He had been in charge of the new Barnes and Noble chain's security when Bob had landed in the city and taken his first job unloading books from trucks at the warehouse. The two had been friendly, and no doubt this helped smooth their subsequent dealings, but more important, Jerry already loved Thomas's music and was keen to sign him.

9. Amy expressed her alarm in a March 29, 1989, personal fax to Crystal Sloan in Boston.

10. I wrote such a letter at Amy's behest. Thomas acknowledged it when we met during the U.S. tour. He was polite about it but let me know that he had his reasons for replacing Jonah and was not about to second-guess them.

11. Leo Hatugari, "Thomas Mapfumo Puts the Record Straight," *Sunday Mail*, April 30, 1989.

12. Alice Dadirai Kwaramba, *Popular Music and Society: The Language of Protest in Chimurenga Music: The Case of Thomas Mapfumo in Zimbabwe*, IMK Report No. 24 (Oslo: University of Oslo, Department of Media Communication, 1997), 88. Part of the reason Kwaramba sees "Chigwindiri" as Thomas "taking sides with the ZANU(PF) government" is that she places this song in 1983, not 1988. I have found no evidence of an earlier release of the song. Thomas says there was none and that Kwaramba has the chronology wrong.

13. I tried to interview Ephraim multiple times, once even pulling out a tape recorder while we were relaxing with a beer after a Harare concert in 1993. He would not speak on record. This may have had to do with nervousness about his limited English, or perhaps his Mozambican roots, which he was sensitive about because they had caused visa complications on that 1989 tour. He may have simply been terribly shy. He was always very warm with me and generous with his knowledge of Zimbabwean guitar. It is a pity I could never learn more of his story.

14. Thomas said that there "wasn't any kind of story" concerning Florence's eventual departure from the Blacks Unlimited lineup.

15. Although—bizarrely—Island decided to replace the Zimbabwean banknote on the cover with one from the Philippines, an oblique reference to Fernando Marcos, who was also making headlines that year.

9. BIG DADDY AND THE ZIMBABWE PLAYBOYS

1. Chris's partner in the early days was a savvy local white woman, Debbie Metcalfe, future manager of Oliver Mtukudzi.

2. Dance Theater Workshop's Andrew Warshaw was a key player in making this tour happen. He had accompanied *Afropop*'s Sean Barlow to West Africa on the then-NPR program's maiden field trip. So when Barlow called from Harare to say he'd found the perfect band for DTW, Warshaw took up the cause.

3. Thomas does not recall this event, although Bob swears by the memory. Possibly Thomas was not present when it happened.

4. *Corruption* was not Thomas's first U.S. release. Carthage Records in New York had distributed a vinyl edition of *Ndangariro* in 1984, and Meadowlark, a division of Shanachie Records, had done the same for *The Chimurenga Singles* a year later. During the years that Ken managed Thomas, Shanachie would reissue both of these titles in the new CD format,

starting with *The Chimurenga Singles*, which Ken made certain hit the street in time for the 1989 tour—no doubt further compromising his reputation with Island.

5. Though I was on a first-name basis with Tom Terrell, I refer to him by his last name to avoid any possible confusion with Thomas.

6. Carthage had licensed a compilation called *Viva Zimbabwe!*, as well as Thomas's *Ndangariro*, praised by the *Village Voice*'s Robert Christgau for its "ferocious . . . rhythm guitar attack." A vinyl release of *Chimurenga Singles* had also garnered a brief review in the *Voice*, as well as the *Philadelphia Enquirer*, and even in *Cosmopolitan*. A longer *Voice* piece by R. J. Smith had appeared in April 1986, covering *Mabasa* and *Mr Music*, which Smith likely bought as imports at the African Music Gallery in the Adams Morgan neighborhood of Washington, DC. My first article about Thomas ran in the *Boston Phoenix* in March 1988; late that year, my profile of Jonah Sithole was published in *Guitar Player*.

7. *Mbaqanga* is South African; *soukous* is Congolese. Both are music styles Thomas would have been familiar with, but these genre names do not describe his sound with much precision. Christgau would go on to write excellent articles and reviews on African music; these were early days.

8. The legendary Bembeya Jazz was more or less disbanded at this point. "Diamond Fingers" pulled this band together to showcase himself. Among the Bembeya Jazz musicians he recruited was the singer Sekouba "Bambino" Diabaté, who would soon become the most popular vocalist in Guinea and a West African superstar. For the moment, Bambino took second billing to the guitarist.

9. Ken had pled poverty and offered Saki ten free T-shirts in exchange for the use of his artwork. Saki agreed, but when Ken printed a copyright credit for Thomas on the shirts, Saki protested. He ultimately won a small-claims settlement, and although Ken never paid up, Saki was satisfied at having proven a point. Saki recalled—not for the first time—warning Thomas that he may not have found the most honest or ethical manager. Saki's actions did not play well with Island. The cover art for the second Island release, *Chamunorwa*, was assigned to a staff artist, Aldo Sampieri.

10. *Afropop* engaged a twenty-four-track mobile studio operated by Kooster McAllister to record the band's second night at sob's for *Afropop*. Despite some imperfections, that first sob's recording remains a treasure in the *Afropop* archive.

11. This smaller instrument is also called *ndimba*. Students of Dumisani Maraire sometimes call it *nyunga nyunga* (roughly "tinkle tinkle" or "sparkle sparkle"), though this is an informal term that Dumi invented, pretty much used and perpetuated only by his former students. In writings, Dumi called this instrument "the Kwanangoma mbira" or "the Jeke Tapera mbira," a reference to Dumi's mbira teacher at the Kwanangoma College.

12. Dumi inspired a fascinating documentary film about the American Shona music community: *Soul Resonance: A Cross-Cultural Celebration of Zimbabwean Music* (2012), by Douglas and Laurel Epps.

13. This was the film by Gei Zantzinger and Andrew Tracey, *Mbira dza Vadzimu: Dambatsoko—An Old Cult Center with Muchatera and Ephat Mujuru* (1978). Looking back on this film, Tracey wrote to me in an e-mail,

> Ephat was young and had to be persuaded to ask his grandfather direct questions in the film, as this was not normally polite for a child. Muchatera trod a fine line between being friendly with everyone, with the freedom fighters and the whites, and he paid with

his life. I felt he was a devoutly spiritual person. Their wonderful mbira dza vadzimu sound was the hum made by the dozen or so players together inside his banya spirit house, all of them blending in with simple or even bare versions of the songs, not outdoing each other but relying on one another to make part of the full sound. That could have been the sound described by early writers of the large mbira bands kept by rulers. Unfortunately, it did not make its way onto the film, which is mostly focused on Ephat's mbira, and I have not heard it anywhere since. Modern recordings seem to focus mostly on the two-mbira mix or the expertise of one player in imitating it.

14. Back in Harare, Ephat was putting together his own electric pop band at the time, very much in the Blacks Unlimited mold, so he and Thomas shared a great deal, including a certain enmity for Dumisani Maraire, whom Ephat had felt slighted by during his own visits to Seattle. Ephat and Dumi later reconciled, publicly proclaiming their accord with a duo CD recording, *Shona Spirit* (Music of the World, 1996).

15. Vivian Maravanyika, "Frontline Sounds Tumble Out of Sky," *Sunday Mail*, December 17, 1989.

16. Translation by Musa Zimunya. These lines are taken from various points throughout the song. The order is correct, but many lines are left out.

17. R. J. Smith, "Thomas Mapfumo, Listener-Sponsored Liberation," *Village Voice*, April 22, 1986.

18. Translation by Musa Zimunya. Jennifer Kyker, an ethnomusicologist and Shona music scholar, notes that these lyrics are very similar to those for the traditional song "Mahoro" as recorded by Mondrek Muchena's mbira group Mhuri yekwaMuchena.

19. Vivian Maravanyika, "Mapfumo's Latest Leaves Much to Be Desired," *Sunday Mail*, July 22, 1990.

20. As with *Chamunorwa*, the songs on *Chimurenga Masterpiece* are lengthy, giving the band time to build intensity. This time, the set includes only one mbira adaptation, "Dangu Rangu." The remaining four tracks are up-tempo numbers that Thomas himself described as "jit." They feature the brass section and are clearly aimed at the dance floor. The change in sound from *Chamunorwa* continues Thomas's idea that each album should have a coherent character. *Chimurenga Masterpiece* marries an exuberant sound with scolding lyrics. "Ndozvauri" taunts a "thick headed young man" for his "jungle ways." "Jairosi" is a wife-beater and a "devil."

21. This quote comes from the second publication of the *Chimurenga Fan Club Newsletter*. As far as I know, only two were ever published.

22. Chenjerai Hove, "When the Audience Becomes Part of the Song," *Sunday Mail*, January 13, 1991.

10. SPORTING LIONS

1. When I say an mbira is in a "key," I mean that its notes correspond to that key's major scale. All the Blacks Unlimited mbira uses what is known as the Nyamaropa tuning system, which defines the arrangement of pitches relative to each other. An mbira tuned this way can in fact play in two, or even three, different keys, even though the player may not have all the notes in that key available to him or her.

2. Ken asked Island to credit the album as "mixed by Thomas, Chris, and Ken, with a little help from their friends." When Island changed the credit to "Chris Bolton and Thomas

Mapfumo, with a little help from Ken Kutsch," Ken felt "an elbow in my side," presumably from Rappaport. The "brothers" overreached just once, with a misguided reworking of "Murambadoro." The original bass and drum tracks were impossible to separate, so replacing the kick drum with the pounding, "house" beat that Ken wanted meant wiping out the song's snaking bass line.

3. Kaya and Washington both left the band prior to the 1991 tour, replaced by returning drummer and bass player Sebastian Mbata and Shepherd Munyama, respectively. When Ephraim's Mozambican birth complicated the renewal of his Zimbabwean passport, Thomas lined up Jonah Sithole as a replacement. In the end, Ephraim's papers came through, and once again, Jonah stayed home. Meanwhile, Bezil lacked a passport, so Sekuru Jira recruited an old man in the communal lands, Katche Vandoro, to play mbira for the tour.

4. After seeing the band perform at the Belly Up in Solana Beach, Goldsmith was elated, and he rode the bus with them to Oregon. He gave Thomas a stack of blues and rock cassettes, but each time one of these tapes ended, the music reverted to Blacks Unlimited. "You could call that ego," said Goldsmith, "but, to me, it really didn't feel like ego. Thomas was so deep into his thing, just like John Lee Hooker, that nothing else really made sense to him."

5. The band's May 8, 1991, show, recorded by *Afropop Worldwide*, was eventually released as a cassette in Zimbabwe, and as a download internationally under the title *Live from SOB's*.

6. Thomas's departure from Island was probably unavoidable, part of a general paring down that would dissolve Mango and leave just a handful of African artists with Blackwell. Those who remained—Salif Keita, Baaba Maal, and Angelique Kidjo among them—would go on to work with producers the label suggested, something Thomas would not likely have allowed.

7. These figures may hold for Music Express stores, but it would be a stretch to take them as representative of music sales for the nation as a whole during this period.

8. "Hondo" is the name of a traditional mbira song, although Thomas's "Hondo" is different, an original composition.

9. Lyric translation by Musa Zimunya.

10. "Maiti Kurima Hamubvire" is an adaptation of the traditional mbira song "Taireva." This is the only song on the original *Hondo* that draws directly on mbira tradition. However, the extended American release included two others, both sides of the single "Magariro"/"Bukatiende."

11. Jennifer W. Kyker, "'What Shall We Do'? Oliver Mtukudzi's Songs about HIV/AIDS," in *The Culture of AIDS: Hope and Healing through the Arts in Africa*, ed. Gregory Barz and Judah Cohen (New York: Oxford University Press, 2011), 241–55. Kyker (Eastman School of Music, University of Rochester) identifies a Mtukudzi song called "Stay With One Woman" (1986) as the first popular song in Zimbabwe to address the growing threat of AIDS. This is the first in a series of songs Mtukudzi would record and release on the subject.

12. On the Beat with Tinaye Garande, "Is Local Music Repulsive?," *Sunday Mail Magazine*, January 24, 1993.

13. On the Beat with Tinaye Garande, "Splinter Group in Bid to Wipe Out Exploitation," *Sunday Mail Magazine*, December 6, 1992.

14. The author Chenjerai Hove saw this song as a dig at Mugabe. "Mugabe was beginning to make bizarre decisions, doing horrible things, which made people say, 'This guy. What's

wrong with him? We didn't expect him to do that." And then he [Mapfumo] came out with this song about an old man who had no culture, 'Your head is white. You don't have any culture. What do you do with your children? What do you teach them?'"

15. Edgar Tekere, a ZANU stalwart, mounted a brave challenge in 1990 and won just 17 percent of the vote. As for the Parliament, Mugabe put an end to the fixed quota of twenty white seats that had been guaranteed at Lancaster House, and ZANU managed to win all but three seats that year, the party's best and least violent performance in any Zimbabwean election. Blair writes of this time, "The electorate divided into three portions—Mugabe supporters, Mugabe opponents, and the completely apathetic. For as long as the first and last groups overwhelmed the second, the leader was safe." This summary of Zimbabwean politics in the early 1990s draws largely on David Blair, *Degrees in Violence: Robert Mugabe and the Struggle for Power in Zimbabwe* (London: Continuum, 2002), 36–39.

16. Heidi Holland, *Dinner with Mugabe: The Untold Story of a Freedom Fighter Who Became a Tyrant* (Johannesburg: Penguin, 2008), 112. The 1,400 percent figure is cited by Dennis Norman, a white farmer who served as Mugabe's first minister of agriculture. It's not clear exactly how Norman measures that, but he's a first-hand witness and clearly proud of the regime's early achievement in this area, even three decades later.

17. From the song "War, AIDS, and ESAP," written by Bigs Fox and performed by Man-Soul-Jah and P.A.C.E. for release on the CD *Vibrant Zimbabwe: 70+ Minutes of Music from Zimbabwe's New Bands* (Vibrant Records, 1993; Zimbob, 1994).

18. Blair, *Degrees in Violence*, 38.

19. "More Pay Condolences to the President," *Sunday Mail*, February 23, 1992.

20. Tinaye Garande, "Mapfumo Forms Football Club," *Sunday Mail*, September 22, 1991.

21. This event was offensive to Thomas and William, though Bezil himself later recalled, "And then Everson was waiting there. He wanted to be dragged in also."

22. *Pieces of Africa* included a work created with Dumisani Maraire, the progenitor of the American mbira and marimba community, so Shona music was known to the Kronos Quartet.

23. Joseph Grier in New York, and another attorney in England who—fresh off working on Sid Vicious's suit against Malcolm McLaren in a lucrative Sex Pistols meltdown—had been researching rights issues on Thomas's past recordings. Both lawyers were apparently owed money.

24. Joseph Grier did not specifically recall having any involvement with the WEA deal and said he was eventually paid. The lawyer in London apparently tried to get his money by suing Ken. Thomas recalls none of this and blames the demise of this deal entirely on WEA.

25. Chris's rap sheet on Ken is long and includes his ability to "piss off whole nations in a single gig." At a festival date in Sweden, Ken had given Thomas a James Brown–style introduction from the stage. The festival organizers had accused Ken, and Chris, of "commercializing" Thomas like "slave-driving whites." The following day, the local newspapers had written about *them* rather than about Thomas and the band.

26. This figure changed at times. In one interview, Thomas said $40,000. In a later one, the figure was $45,000, and there were two payments each for that amount, not one. Jerry Rappaport and Chris Bolton both named smaller numbers, while supporting Thomas's contention that Ken had kept more than his share.

27. Joseph Grier speculated that there probably was money floating around out there that

should have gone to Thomas and did not. "But typically," added Grier, "when they think they know who got the money, that's really not the person. Even the Beatles don't know who ended up with all their money." For his part, Ken insisted his only sin was to demand fair pay for himself and the musicians. He had made sure he received a 20 percent cut of Thomas's earnings, and nothing more. "I did a good job for those guys," said Ken without apology. "And I lived very well off of that 20 percent."

28. While in Zimbabwe, Bob made a deal with ZMC CEO Tony Hagelthorn, "a bull of a man" who first sat Bob down across an imposing desk and accused him of being a CIA spy, then made a deal with him to release Zimbob compilations of singers James Chimombe and Robson Banda. In January 1994, ZMC and Gramma merged to form a recording industry monolith in Zimbabwe. When ZMC subsequently released Bob's compilations—for which I wrote liner notes—on the Zimbabwe market, Bob called it "piracy."

29. *Chimurenga International* was released in the United States on Zimbob in 1994 under the title *Vanhu Vatema*. Chartwell and Everson oversaw the session with Thomas, determining who would play and when, and then scrutinizing overdubs, phrase by phrase. During long night sessions at Gramma, Thomas sat by sage-like, listening, nodding, his eyes sometimes slipping shut for a spell. This recording marks the return of Charles as the band's bass guitarist. Sugar's and Ephraim's contrasting guitar styles also work well, Sugar sashaying through the mbira thicket on "Hanzvadzi (Sister)" and "Amai Vemwana (Mother of My Children)," and Ephraim driving home staccato intensity as he interweaves elaborate brass arrangements on dance numbers like "Ndinofarira Zimbabwe (I Love Zimbabwe)."

30. Musa described bassist Shepherd as "raw and rural," a man who played bass as though it were a drum.

31. Fred Zindi, "Thomas Mapfumo: A Cultural Ambassador?," *Southern Africa Monthly* 6, nos. 3 and 4 (1992–93): 11.

32. Maxwell Sibanda, "Leonard Dembo, the Music Man of Today," *Sunday Gazette*, February 21, 1993.

33. Joshua Dube told me he knew this with absolute certainty, from personal sources, and I believe him. For one thing, Josh had good relations with musicians throughout the community, and he knew Pio Macheka well enough to get to the truth. Also, Josh had no overriding loyalty to Thomas and was quite willing to cast him in a bad light when he felt it was justified.

34. *Shabini* (1986) and *Tsvimbodzemoto* (1987).

35. This quote comes from a superb, heartbreaking retrospective article on the Bhundu Boys by Robert Chalmers, "The Bhundu Boys: Lost Boys," *Independent*, March 20, 2005.

36. Tendai had spent a year working with Oliver Mtukudzi and been replaced in the Blacks Unlimited by the lanky Christine Sarayi, a spectacular dancer, but no match for Tendai at the microphone. Not for the last time, Tendai's love of Thomas's music lured her back to the Blacks Unlimited.

37. Neil Strauss, "Rockbeat, Plague of Silence," *Village Voice*, January 18, 1994.

38. Thomas remains sensitive about attributing AIDS as the source of anyone's death without proof. Short of direct acknowledgment by the victim, or his or her family, which occurs rarely in Zimbabwe, Thomas believes that the survivors' sensibilities trump any value that might come from surmising or inferring a person's cause of death as AIDS.

39. On the Beat with Tinaye Garande, "Long Wait for Mapfumo's Latest Album Worth It," *Sunday Mail Magazine*, October 31, 1993.

40. Interview with Chartwell Dutiro in London, May 1998.

11. TOO MANY GHOSTS

1. Saidi is a common surname in Malawi, so this may also have been a reference to Allan's Malawian ancestry.

2. The Seattle promoter was Jean Baptiste, notoriously slippery. Knowing he could not do all that driving alone, Chris recruited me as copilot. I had come to the Sommerville show to enjoy the performance and sit in on guitar for a few songs. I had recently quit my job and was preparing to spend seven months in Mali. I made a snap decision, and within hours we were at Logan Airport renting a van for the monthlong journey. In Seattle, we would meet Manny Rettinger, also signed on by Thomas to play guitar. Chris Bolton memorably dubbed us the "Pink Spirits," but neither of us did very much playing in the shows.

3. David Bullock was the source for the music on this prized cassette.

4. There are other theories as to why Biggie Tembo took his life—alcoholism, regret at having split with the Bhundus, witchcraft, mental illness—but for Thomas, the family rift seemed the persuasive explanation.

5. "Mvura Ngainaye" is quite similar in musical structure to the traditional mbira song "Mahororo."

6. Nearly finished with the research for his book, Thomas Turino returned to Zimbabwe at this serendipitous moment when Jonah Sithole and Joshua Dube shared the stage. Finding the band sounding "better than I had ever heard it," Turino concludes his assessment of Thomas with forgiving words. Having sternly assessed the artist's commercial motivations, he now sees "a great composer/arranger and bandleader who produces great Zimbabwean music" and even allows that "this is perhaps all he ever really wanted or promised." Thomas Turino, *Nationalists, Cosmopolitans, and Popular Music in Zimbabwe* (Chicago: University of Chicago Press, 2000), 350–51.

7. This quote comes from an April 26, 2007, article posted on Zimdaily.com. Under the headline "Robert Mugabe Killed His Own Blood Brother," Theresa Nkala claims to have at last confirmed a long-standing rumor. An unidentified surviving relative of Bona Mugabe—Robert and Albert's mother—recalls that the family quietly executed a plan to have Albert impregnate Sally, providing the crucial motive for Albert's murder. For the record, Sally did in fact bear Robert one child, a son, in Ghana in 1963, but he died of cerebral malaria three years later while Mugabe was in prison in Rhodesia. For the next seventeen years, the couple produced no more children, hence the family's concern.

8. Whether Thomas used Benny Miller's Shed Studio or Gramma's Mosi-Oa-Tunya Studio, he was never satisfied with the sound of his local Zimbabwean recordings in the mid-1990s. The bass, in particular, seemed frail and mushy, and guitars, mbira, and vocals never matched the clarity of the electronic keyboards.

9. With state-of-the-art gear and veteran producer Tchad Blake at the controls, there would be no deficiencies in the sound quality at this Real World session, which was part of the studio's annual Recording Week.

10. Most of the songs in this WOMAD Select session are remakes of numbers from *Roots*

Chimurenga. Intriguingly, "Mukadzi Wamukoma" is retitled here as "Nyamaropa," perhaps reflecting Thomas's sensitivity about the Albert Mugabe rumor.

11. When Thomas recruited Sugar to fill in at a few shows, Magwaza reported excitedly—and wrongly—that the policeman guitarist was returning to the Blacks Unlimited. Whether or not Thomas seriously tried to woo Sugar back, Sugar had his own group by then, Batonga Crew, and he would not abandon it.

12. BREAKING THE CYCLE

1. ZUPCO = Zimbabwe United Passenger Company.

2. The *Financial Gazette*, the *Independent*, the *Standard*, and the newest entry, the *Mirror*. In 1998, all of these could be bought on Harare street corners on a weekly basis for a few dollars a copy.

3. Muckraker long maintained ambiguous authorship, though it eventually became clear that the column was penned by the *Independent*'s editor, veteran newsman Iden Wetherell. The column was dependably witty. One entry coined the phrase "highland laird Robbie MacGabe" after the president and his wife, Grace, were caught "castle shopping" in Scotland.

4. Musa Zimunya, "Proposal to Honour Thomas Mapfumo with Honorary Degree," 1997. Jenuguru Music Productions, organizers of the popular Zimbabwe Music Day festival, also backed the proposal. The organization had created a plaque in Thomas's honor and persuaded the city council to install it in downtown Harare.

5. While in Harare, I telephoned Dumisani Maraire to request an interview. I told him it was impossible to tell Thomas's story without recognizing his role in founding the American Shona music community. "If you want my story," said Maraire, "I must know in certain terms what will be my benefit. I would rather go to my grave with my story a secret than see someone else make money out of it." Perhaps the lingering question of Thomas's honorary degree was a special sensitivity to the man who had opposed it. In any case, we never spoke again. Maraire died of a stroke at the age of fifty-six on November 25, 1999, just weeks after Thomas at last received his degree from President Robert Mugabe.

6. Memorandum from Dr. D. A. Maraire, RE: Proposal to Honour Thomas Mapfumo with Honorary Degree, May 2, 1997. This memo was shared with me privately.

7. Kudawashe Marazanye, editorial, "Cutting Edge," *Independent*, March 27–April 2, 1998.

8. Sithole later appealed this conviction, but he died in 2000, before the case was definitively resolved.

9. Banana was convicted and sentenced to ten years in prison in 1999. He served two years and died of cancer in 2003 in London. He was denied state honors at his funeral in Zimbabwe.

10. Stephen O. Murray and Will Roscoe, eds., *Boy-Wives and Female Husbands: Studies of African Homosexualities* (New York: St. Martin's Press, 1998). The authors' preface concludes, "The colonialists did not introduce homosexuality to Africa, but rather intolerance of it—and systems of surveillance and regulation for suppressing it."

13. STRIKING AT EMPIRES

1. Chris denied the charge, and WOMAD's Thomas Brooman also doubted it. Chris did sign the WOMAD contract for Thomas. Brooman suspects that a combination of casual bookkeeping and ganja-fueled paranoia led Thomas to grow suspicious, and once he started

asking questions that Chris could not answer, the trust between them dissolved. The release came out under the WOMAD Select imprint, and Brooman says these releases never involved large advances. Remuneration came mostly in the form of product the artist could sell on tour. Whatever happened to that 7,000 pounds, I personally saw WOMAD CDs being sold at Thomas's Zimbabwe shows in 1997–98.

2. Cuthbert says it was his steady persuasion that brought Julian Howard at Gramma/ZMC to a change of heart. In the past, musicians had received an 18 to 20 percent royalty on releases. After considerable back-and-forth, Cuthbert says, Howard agreed to a much more favorable split, with Thomas receiving 85 to 90 percent, on back-catalog sales, depending on the format of the release. Cuthbert says that he and Howard wound up being "good friends," and that other major artists also soon benefited from the company's newfound fairness, negotiating similar deals for themselves.

3. Phillip Magwaza, "Mukanya Back from Successful Overseas Trip," *Sunday Mail Magazine*, September 6, 1998.

4. *Chimurenga '98* was conceived and mostly recorded during my long stay in Harare, and as promised, it offered "something different." There are requisite nods to the past, remakes of chimurenga singles "Chikonzero (The Reason)" and "Usatambe Nenyoka (Don't Play with Snakes)," and also the darkly hypnotic "Ndave Kuenda (I'm Now Going)" with mbira taking the place of the keyboard on the 1987 original. Most of the other nine tracks break new ground, from the buoyant folklore of "Chigwaya (Bream)" in which Thomas compares himself to the fish "with full control of his territory"; to the mournfully dreamy "Munongotukana (You Just Scold Each Other)" in which Dirck Westervelt's banjo is distinctly audible; to the soccer song "Shumba Dzenhabvu" with its breathless play-by-play overdub; a rocking political screed called "Set the People Free" featuring a young ragga-rapper named Yapi Banton; and prominently featured as the second track, what we had called "the Mali song" became "Ndiyani Waparadza Musha (Who Has Destroyed My Home)." Two tracks were recorded and added after the 1998 tour, including "Titambire (Dance for Us)," which borrows its bass line from Baaba Maal's "Mariama," a song heard over and over as the Blacks Unlimited tour bus drove through the Pacific Northwest and the fires of western Canada in the summer of 1998.

5. *Herald*, articles from March 15, April 10, April 16, and April 27, 1999.

6. Chris Muchabaiwa had lingered at the edges of the band for more than two years, playing guitar, bass, and drums at different times. Now he became a bona fide member. The band that would record at Bill Barnett's Gung-Ho Studio in Eugene in the fall of 1999 reflected other changes as well. In five years, keyboardist Richard Matimba had never been invited to tour the United States with the Blacks Unlimited. While Thomas considered him an excellent musician, he did not opt to bring him out for international shows. Frustrated by this, Richard eventually quit the band to join Oliver Mtukudzi, with whom he would remain until his own death from meningitis in 2004. In Tendai's place, Memory Makuri and Rosa Sande now sang and danced.

7. Making sadza is a demanding art. Corn meal, preferably white, is added to boiling water and stirred constantly with a long, heavy wooden stick or spoon. As the porridge stiffens, the stirring becomes more and more difficult, and also more vigorous. For a pot large enough to feed the Blacks Unlimited, the final strokes require enormous strength in the arms. You have to be, as I was often told, "used to it."

8. That version of "Pidigori" was released on a 2001 compilation from Nascente in the United Kingdom, *Collected*. The band also rerecorded the travelogue love song "Kariba," as well as the Acid Band's landmark hit "Pamuromo Chete (It's Only Talk)," which many Mapfumo fans had never heard because Gramma had lost or erased the original master tape.

9. *Chimurenga Explosion* included Gung-Ho recordings of the Nyabinghi-like "Musanyepere," a slow, melodious nod to South African mbaqanga called "Moto Uyo (Fire Is Coming)," three new mbira adaptations ("Chisi," "Zvichapera," and "Wachiona Chirombo"), and "Nhamo Zvakare (Trouble Again)," the brooding complaint Thomas had composed during the 1998 food riots in Harare but dropped from the *Chimurenga '98* sessions. Beyond these Oregon recordings, Thomas added two Shed Studio recordings, "Mamvemve" and "Disaster," the songs that would dominate public reaction to this album.

10. David Blair, *Degrees in Violence: Robert Mugabe and the Struggle for Power in Zimbabwe* (London: Continuum, 2002), 44–46.

11. Blair, *Degrees in Violence*, 52. The land debate of 2000 is crucial and complex, and ultimately beyond the scope of this book. At its heart lies Mugabe's deeply held belief that the British government had reneged on its 1979 promise at Lancaster House to pay compensation to white landowners for resettled land. For a variety of reasons, the validity of which has been widely debated, Margaret Thatcher and Tony Blair both declined to honor this pledge. Hence a central clause in the revised Zimbabwean constitution of 2000 used that fact as cover for Zimbabwe's own refusal to compensate white farmers. The clause read, "If the former colonial power fails to pay compensation through such a fund, the Government of Zimbabwe have no obligation to pay compensation for agricultural land compulsorily acquired for resettlement." This would have opened the door for the government to *legally* seize white farms and pay nothing to the former owners.

12. Stanley Gama, "Mukanya Releases Red-Hot Album," *Daily News*, December 13, 1999.

13. These translations were supplied by Thomas himself.

14. Nyarota edited the *Daily News* until his mysterious firing in 2002. The paper was closed down by the government the following year. Having survived six arrests and an assassination attempt, Nyarota left the country and went on to publish a memoir (*Against the Grain*) and start an online newspaper, thezimbabwetimes.com.

15. Heidi Holland, *Mugabe: The Untold Story of a Freedom Fighter Who Became a Tyrant* (Johannesburg: Penguin, 2008), 187.

16. About two years later, Cuthbert did recover one of the BMWs from the police. It had been left with the windows opened, and the interior was badly damaged. Cuthbert himself wound up buying this car from Thomas and Vena for $7,000. But they did not see the money; it went straight into expenses for the Sporting Lions football team and was gone in a matter of days. "And it pained me," Cuthbert recalled.

17. "Ndaparera" was released on the album *Manhungetunge*.

18. Andy Frankel, who had successfully managed Nigerian juju bandleader King Sunny Adé's American career, advised Al to keep Thomas and the band in Zimbabwe. He suggested that Thomas should finish the 2000 tour and go home for two years, giving the market a rest and allowing time to plan a more profitable tour. Al sized Frankel up as another world music "gatekeeper," more interested in protecting the U.S. market than helping Thomas, whose problems went well beyond finding gigs. Frankel's intentions were good, and his advice was likely sound, but it didn't help his case that he had set Al up with an

incompetent tour manager, Michel Baptiste in New York, who effectively abandoned his duties on the 2000 tour the moment the Bounder hit the highway, forcing Al to assume massive expenses. That was the end of Frankel's efforts on behalf of Thomas Mapfumo.

19. *Manhungetunge* opens with "Big in America" and closes with "Marimuka," both from the Wadada Leo Smith sessions. The album also includes "Chemutengure," "Pamuromo Chete," and "Mangoma (Big Drum)," on which I added some Mali-style electric guitar during the 1999 recording sessions in Eugene. Also from that session is the standout track "Regai Vakanganise (Let Them Do Wrong)," driving, southern African boogie, graced by inspired and nimble guitar work from Joshua Dube and powerfully precise drumming from Sam Mukanga. The remaining tracks were recorded in 2000, around the time of the Wadada sessions. "Ndini Ndega (I'm the Only One)," an indictment of selfishness, tilts toward minor-key reggae. "Magobo (Hard Work)" is a celebratory salute to workers referencing the arduous clearing of trees that was a unique and brutal feature of the Rhodesian colonial experience. The title track is three-chord boogie that winds up to a bluesy saxophone solo from newly recruited Eugene musician David Rhodes, and includes the first recorded riffs by then new Blacks Unlimited guitarist Zivai Guveya. Although this album did not prove particularly controversial on the political front, Thomas identifies social and political undercurrents in most of its songs. Internationally, the album was released as a double CD on aNOnym reCOrds under the title *Chimurenga Rebel* in 2001.

20. Shepherd Mutamba, "Mapfumo Back from Overseas," *Herald*, November 22, 2000.

21. S. Mukwenje, "Mapfumo Isn't Chimurenga Pioneer," *Herald*, January 27, 2001.

22. I wrote the Freemuse report, *Playing with Fire: Fear and Self-Censorship in Zimbabwean Music* (Copenhagen: Freemuse, 2001). Freemuse was also concerned about events surrounding an Oliver Mtukudzi song called "Wasakara," literally, "You Are Worn Out." Tuku claimed it was about an old man who preys on young girls, but many heard it as a veiled call for Mugabe to step down. Complicating matters, a lighting and sound man was jailed for pointing a spotlight at Mugabe's portrait during one performance of the song at the Harare Convention Center. This is a classic case of the public deciding what a song means, regardless of the songwriter's intent.

23. The story of Capital Radio is more fully told in *Playing with Fire*. Comfort Mbofana said that, since 1993, seven successive ministers of information had declared that the opening of the airwaves was imminent. All these years later, they were backpedaling with amusingly daft rhetoric about how the airwaves were "a finite resource." Eventually legislation was passed, although its practical effect was to restrict private broadcasting, not to enable it.

14. DANCING WITH DEVILS

1. Cuthbert accompanied Thomas to Ohio. He recalled that Thomas was not particularly interested in being honored, that he had wanted to simply keep touring. "It took a lot of effort to convince him," said Cuthbert, noting that Thomas had been similarly disinterested in receiving his honorary degree in Harare in 1999.

2. Thomas made this particular statement in an interview with me, but it is very much of a piece with what he was saying in many interviews at the time.

3. Maurice Taonezvi Vambe, "Mapfumo Becomes Reactionary," *Sunday Mail*, March 2, 2003. Ironically, Vambe's argument dovetails with Al Green's contention that even though

Chris Blackwell and Island Records promoted Thomas as a freedom singer, the real reason they gave him a contract was to tweak Mugabe. "People appreciated Thomas in '89," said Al, "because he said something against Mugabe, and the World Bank and MI5 had a big issue in Zimbabwe, didn't they? Mugabe was gonna take that land back, because the ten-year moratorium was over. So suddenly Thomas has got a big recording contract?" Jumbo Van Renen, who was involved in the Island deal, found this a bizarre stretch. Also, Mugabe's full-on land grab did not come until a decade later. Nevertheless, for Al, Chris Blackwell was not so much a savvy tastemaker as a tool of British intelligence, hanging out at "Ian Fleming's old place" and defending what was left of a prior "Empire." In Al's view, Thomas himself was not so much corrupted as used by this old boys' club. "They gave him a six-album deal," he said. "Then they cut his legs off after two."

4. The *Zimbabwe Standard* would report in February 2002 that both Ngoni and Edson Mbaisa were "fired" by Thomas, effectively not invited to return to the United States. In the article Thomas did not deny this, although the reasons and the degree of mutual agreement were left vague.

5. Manyepo Mapfumo, letter, "Mapfumo Is a Scared Man," *Herald*, December 18, 2001.

6. Rex Mphisa, "Mapfumo Backs Land Reform Programme," *Herald*, December 28, 2001.

7. Entertainment Reporter, "Up with Mapfumo," *Herald*, January 4, 2002.

8. "Mukanya Is a Fair Weather Patriot," letter from Kurai Mukanya, *Sunday Mail*, January 20, 2002.

9. Entertainment Reporter, "Fame Creeps into Mukanya's Head—Again," *Herald*, January 22, 2002.

10. Entertainment Reporter, "Factual Story Riles Mukanya," *Herald*, January 23, 2002.

11. Some of these details come from Brooks Barnett's own journal of his early years with the Blacks Unlimited, which he kindly shared with me.

12. "Questions for Thomas Mapfumo," *Boston Globe*, February 15, 2002.

13. Editor, "Shocked by Mapfumo's Hypocritical Utterances," *Herald*, March 13, 2002.

14. These observations come from Sam Mataure, one of Zimbabwe's best trap drummers, and Oliver Mtukudzi's manager following Debbie Metcalf.

15. Abel Tendekai Muzorewa, *Rise Up and Walk: The Autobiography of Bishop Abel Tendekai Muzorewa*, ed. Norman E. Thomas (Nashville, TN: Abingdon, 1978), 109.

16. Pollan and Sagan quotes from Michael Pollan, *The Botany of Desire: A Plant's-Eye View of the World* (New York: Random House, 2001). The Sagan quote is from Lester Grinspoon's essay collection *Marihuana Reconsidered*, 2nd ed. (Oakland, CA: Quick American Archives, 1996). Sagan did not allow this essay's publication during his lifetime. Pollan also cites Friedrich Nietzsche's essay "The Uses and Disadvantages of History for Life" (1876), in which the philosopher calls forgetting "a prerequisite for human happiness, mental health, and action." Finally, Pollan notes that Aldous Huxley lauded the "reducing valve" of consciousness, slowing down time, sharpening the sensations of the moment and rendering matters at hand clear and vivid.

17. Thomas says that the case fell apart early on when the man who had sold the cars and implicated Thomas after his arrest, George Sibanda, was released on bail and fled to South Africa. Without this witness, there was no way to pursue the case.

18. Maxwell Sibanda, "Artists Bemoan Zimbabwe Crisis," *Daily News*, January 27, 2003.

19. Artwell Manyemba and Phillip Chadavaenzi, "Mapfumo Slams Mugabe, Tsvangirai," *Daily Mirror*, January 30, 2003.

20. Diana Nherera, "Mapfumo's Jazz Album Tops Gramma Music Charts," *Herald*, February 27, 2003. It is interesting that Maurice Taonezvi Vambe's *Sunday Mail* piece of March 3, 2003 ("Mapfumo Becomes Reactionary") makes the opposite argument. Citing Turino, Vambe writes, "The mbira beat on Mapfumo songs has become influenced more by the taste of his North American audience." For one writer, North Americans made Thomas turn to mbira; for another, they made him turn away from it.

21. Nherera, "Mapfumo's Jazz Album Tops Gramma Music Charts."

22. Guthrie Munyuki, "Mapfumo's Protest Music Denied Airplay," *Daily News*, February 25, 2003.

23. Lifestyle and Leisure, "Mukanya, Tuku Singing the Walls Down," *Herald*, February 27, 2003.

24. This playful reference to Homer Simpson would also become the title of a 2012 collection of Al Green's own songs, *Homerland*.

25. The South African label Sheer Sound released a compilation called *Choice Chimurenga* in 2003, but nothing there was new to Thomas's Harare fans.

26. Debbie Metcalf believes that this accident happened when a young man who worked in the studio tried to bootleg the CD and wound up corrupting the master hard drive.

27. Fanuel Viriri, "I Am Coming Back Home: Mapfumo," *Daily News*, February 28, 2004.

15. THE LAND OF THE HORSES

1. Ian Smith, November 20, 2007; Abel Muzorewa, April 8, 2010; Hakurotwi Mude, January 20, 2008; Sekuru Jira, 2005; Emmanuel Jera, September 2007; Tom Terrell, November 29, 2007; Keith Goddard, October 12, 2009; Benny Miller, July 2005; Simon Chimbetu, August 15, 2005; Andy Brown, March 16, 2012; Chiwoniso, July 24, 2013. "Gloomy delight" comes from Smith's obituary in the *Times*. Regarding Thomas's softened tone on Chimbetu, he was similarly forgiving when Andy Brown died in 2012, recalling Brown as a "good friend" who had been "used" and ultimately "destroyed" by the regime.

2. The band was now Thomas, Lancelot, Chaka, Chris (on bass again), Bezil (back in the United States for the first time in four years), Gilbert on guitar, Njwaki "Gibson" Nyoni on drums, Stephan Martin and Brooks on brass, with Mavis Mapfumo (no relation) and Naomi Mkwavira singing and dancing.

3. Madzikatire had been a cultural icon in Zimbabwe, nurturing countless musicians—including Joshua Dube and Jonah Sithole—through a succession of bands, only to end jaded, poor, and inactive in Harare.

4. Cuthbert says he had been urging this move for a long time, and he finally refused to do any more work for the team. "It's me who put my foot on the ground," recalled Cuthbert.

5. Roderick Chipezeze and Jonah Sena had contracted with Thomas to film and record the band's May 2004 show at Milton Keynes for a live DVD release. The CD's sleeve copy included incorrect and misspelled titles and this over-the-top description: "The single most astonishing demonstration of the art and craft of music that can be found anywhere." Bob Coen, then serving as Thomas's interim manager, considered *Chaputika* a travesty and advised him to sue and stop it from being sold. Thomas said that he had only agreed to

a DVD release of *Chaputika*, which never actually materialized. But although the CD was flawed and, for him, unexpected, Thomas had no serious complaint, since it had provided cash flow at a critical moment. He noted pointedly that *Chaputika*'s producers were "selling more CDs than Al." No surprise there. Unlike Al, the *Chaputika* producers had access to the Mapfumo-hungry Zimbabwe market.

6. Maurice Taonezvi Vambe, "Versions and Sub-versions: Trends in Chimurenga Musical Discourses of Post-Independence Zimbabwe," *African Study Monographs* 25, no. 4 (2004): 167–93. Also Vambe, "Popular Songs and Social Realities in Post-Independence Zimbabwe," *African Studies Review* 43, no. 2 (2000): 73–86; and Vambe, "Thomas Mapfumo's 'Toi Toi' in Context: Popular Music as Narrative Discourse," *African Identities* 2, no. 1 (2001): 89–112. These articles are fascinating, if intellectually dubious. Vambe's knowledge of Shona language and culture is deep, and he provides provocative readings of popular song lyrics. But in the end, he strikes me as a polemicist couching a pro-ZANU-PF political agenda behind the rarefied language of literary criticism.

7. Robert Mukondiwa, "Mukanya, Wife Part Ways? Things Fall Apart?," *Sunday Mail*, February 13, 2005.

8. As Gilbert languished in Zimbabwe, the trombone player Willard Kalanga—once a policeman and insider—was chased by a Harare mob because of his association with Thomas. "He had to run for his life," reported Chris. "We are in danger back home." Chris said that the band had warned Gilbert and others not to return to Zimbabwe. "They thought it would not be so bad," he said in 2005. "Now they are crying."

9. Al Green himself was recruited to play drums on a few shows.

10. At the "Africa Calling" show, Thomas, Al, and Cuthbert reconnected with the Real World record label and its illustrious proprietor, Peter Gabriel. That meeting led to the international release of *Rise Up* the following year.

11. In the fourth book of *Gulliver's Travels*, the hero visits a land of horses (houyhnhnms), superior beings in wisdom and temperament. All other humans thenceforth are, for him, "yahoos."

12. Most notably the bass man, Matt Gordon, who had grown up with Shona music in Eugene and Portland and understood its rhythms and phrasing instinctively. Matt started playing guitar at eight and marimba at twelve, and by the time he was a teenager, he was picking out Mapfumo lines on bass and guitar and looking to join a Shona music band. Thomas was amazed by the speed with which he learned the music, saying, "This guy is actually better than all these bass players I have been working with."

13. On this session, Eric Miller became the first American mbira player to record with Thomas. Matt Gordon played bass, and Ian Campbell drums. I played rhythm guitar. Some of these tracks were later rerecorded with Chris Muchabaiwa on drums, and others were never used. The ultimate release, *Exile*, also includes songs from later recording sessions.

14. Michael Wines, "World Briefing, Africa," *New York Times*, March 16, 2007.

15. Michael Wines, "Memo from Harare: An Endgame in Zimbabwe That Mugabe May Yet Win," *New York Times*, March 30, 2007.

16. Cuthbert had tried to convince Thomas to perform the show, and he believed that if the band had cooperated with the promoter, they would have gotten all their money in the end. "Promoters are not enemies," said Cuthbert.

17. Thomas said he had "nearly fired Cuthbert" for siding with the Legends tour pro-

moters but decided to stick with him. "Simba," as Thomas called Cuthbert, was loyal, competent, and above all a person on the lookout for opportunities. "That's the kind of guy I want to work with me," said Thomas at the time.

18. Cuthbert told me he personally receives no royalties on these titles at present. Given the state of physical music sales in Zimbabwe, those royalties probably don't amount to much. But Cuthbert noted that having so many titles in print keeps Thomas in the public eye and has many indirect advantages, despite rampant music piracy.

19. George Negus, "Interview with Thomas Mapfumo," SBS ONE, April 16, 2008, http://www.sbs.com.au/news/dateline/story/interview-thomas-mapfumo.

20. Celia W. Dugger, "Cholera Races through a Crumbling Zimbabwe," New York Times, December 12, 2008. The 18 quintillion estimate comes from independent economist John Robertson. Clearly true precision is hard to come by in such a chaotic, fast-changing scenario.

21. Celia W. Dugger, "Diamond Discovery Could Aid Zimbabwe (and Mugabe, Too)," New York Times, June 22, 2010.

16. LIONS IN WINTER

1. Thomas Turino, Nationalists, Cosmopolitans, and Popular Music in Zimbabwe (Chicago: University of Chicago Press, 2000), 334.

2. Thomas does not specifically recall shunning Ry Cooder or declining to take part in the U2 project, only that he was waiting to hear more in both instances. In the case of Cooder, Ken Kutsch reported Thomas's reluctance. Though it is hard to say what might have happened had Thomas shown real enthusiasm, it is fairly clear that he did not, and perhaps not surprising because he had no real familiarity with Cooder's work. Thomas's American musicians recall Thomas quashing the U2 project, and Gilbert Zvamaida confirmed that Thomas was cool to the idea of covering music outside his personal tastes, regardless of the commercial upside. Thomas himself said U2 was "not my type of band." The point is that in both situations—and others—artistic considerations trumped the attraction of the opportunity, no matter how useful it might have been to Thomas's career.

3. The Mount Pleasant house was a problem. The roof leaked. The man who sold it to Thomas and Vena was "a crook." They were not there to deal with repairs, so they sold it, leaving the dress shop in town as their only remaining property in Zimbabwe.

4. Lydia Polgreen, "Mugabe Wins Again in Zimbabwe, Leaving Rival Greatly Weakened," New York Times, August 4, 2013.

5. Chaka Mhembere fell seriously ill in early 2014. All his teeth were removed, and this radical operation resulted in complications. Chaka has been unable to play with the band ever since. Thomas had hoped to return from summer gigs in South Africa with Bezil Makombe once more at his side on mbira, but Bezil remained in South Africa. In the United States in 2014, the band has sometimes performed without any mbira. On other occasions, a talented American mbira player, Eric Orem of Eugene, has joined the band on stage.

6. The organizers of this film screening were Nyasha Gusta, Fungai Maboreke, and Tapiwa Chisakaitwa.

GLOSSARY

ambuya: grandmother

assegai: (Ndebele) short spear

banya: ceremonial dwelling

bhundu: bush

bira: Shona spirit possession ritual

bute: powdered tobacco

chave chimurenga: it's now war

chikwambo: black magic fetish

chimurenga: struggle

chiremba: doctor or traditional healer

chisi: day of rest with spiritual prohibitions against working in the fields

dagga: marijuana

dandanda: ritual drumming/dance genre from Murehwa; more informally, a drumming/dance party

dandaro: social gathering with mbira

deze: gourd resonator for mbira

fodya: tobacco or marijuana

gukurahundi: rain that washes away chaff; also a term for military purge of the Ndebele

gwariva: wooden soundboard of the mbira

hacha: wild cork fruit

hanga: Guinea fowl

hondo: war

hosho: gourd rattle

hungwe: fish eagle

huro: yodeling vocal style heard in mbira music; literally, "throat"

impi: (Zulu, Ndebele) warrior

induna: (Zulu, Ndebele) chief

jit: evolution of *jiti* popularized by the Bhundu Boys as a genre of electric, Zimbabwean dance pop

jiti: rural, acoustic drumming style that developed in the mid-twentieth century out of an amalgamation of preexisting drumming styles such as *pfonda* and other influences

karimba: small mbira

kumusha: at the village

kushaura: first mbira part

kutsinhira: second mbira part

lobola: (Ndebele) dowry; in Shona, *roora*

magobo: clearing farm land

mahon'era: vocal style heard in mbira music, with an emphasis on vocable singing

mapfura: marula

mapira: Shona spirit possession ceremonies (plural of *bira*)

marabi: South African–style township jazz

masawu: dried, sour, plum-like fruit

mashave: spirits that come from outside the family lineage, often credited with bestowing talents for hunting, healing, playing mbira, and other activities

matamba: monkey orange (fruit)

mbanje: marijuana

mbira: thumb piano

mfecane: (Ndebele, Zulu) tribal war; literally, "crushing"

mhondoro: territorial spirits believed to manifest themselves as lions

mhotsi: dreadlocks

mubvamaropa: blood wood, used for mbira soundboard

mudzimu: ancestral spirit

mujiba: young boy who assisted freedom fighters during the liberation war; female form, *chimbwido*

murungu: white person or boss

Mvengemvenge/Ezomgido: a mixture of different things; name of 1990s ZBC music video show

Mwari: God

n'anga: traditional healer

ngoma: drums

ngozi: evil spirits

njuzu: mermaid spirits

painera: open-tuning guitar style

povo: (Portuguese) people

pungwe: all-night event featuring music; also consciousness-raising political rallies held during the liberation struggle

rabi: *see* marabi

rambanai: divorce; literally, in command form, "Break up!"

rombe: ne'er do well, vagabond

roora: (Shona) dowry

sabhuku: village headman; literally, "the holder of the book"

sabiedhu: submachine gun

sadza: cornmeal porridge

sekuru: uncle

shangara: musical style from Masvingo region

shatini: bushes

shave: non-lineage spirit; *see* mashave

shebeen: speakeasy

sungura: genre of Zimbabwean popular music with roots in East African rumba; (Swahili) rabbit

svikiro: spirit medium

tsotsi: hooligan, thug, thief

vadzimu: ancestral spirits

vaoora: daughters-in-law

varoyi: witches

Zimbabwe: house of stone; ancient structures

SELECTED DISCOGRAPHY

Thomas Mapfumo released many singles during the 1970s. Some of these later became available on compilations. You can find a more complete list of those singles at banningeyre.com/lionsongs. There is also a companion CD to this book, *Lion Songs: Essential Tracks in the Making of Zimbabwe*, available on this site. Here is a discography of Thomas's albums and compilations released from 1978 up to the publication of this book.

ALBUMS

Hokoyo. Afro Soul, 1978: ASLP 5000. Reissued on CD by Water in 2009: water236.

The Best of Thomas Mapfumo (Chimurenga Singles). Afro Soul, 1980. Reissued in the United Kingdom as *The Chimurenga Singles* on Earthworks International in 1982, and in the United States on Meadowlark Records, a division of Shanachie (Meadowlark 403), in 1985.

Gwindingwi Rine Shumba. Afro Soul, 1981: ASLP 5002. Reissued on Earthworks International in 1982: EMW 5506. Reissued again on CD by Water in 2009: water237.

Mabasa. Afro Soul, 1983: ASLP 5004. Released as "A Serengeti Licensed Product" for Earthworks / Rough Trade in 1984: ERT 1007.

Ndangariro. Afro Soul, 1983: ASLP 5003. Reissued on Earthworks International in 1983, and Carthage (USA) in 1984: GGLP 4414. Also reissued under the title *The Long Walk*, MI5 Recordings, in 2007.

Mr Music. Afro Soul, 1984: ASLP 5005 (the last Afro Soul LP for Thomas). Released as "A Gramma Production for Serengeti Records" and Earthworks / Rough Trade in 1985: ERT 1008.

Chimurenga for Justice. Rough Trade, 1985: Rough Trade 91. Released in Zimbabwe by Gramma in 1986.

Thomas Mapfumo & The Blacks Unlimited 12". Rough Trade, 1985: RTT 190. (Three songs recorded for Capital Radio's City Beats.)

Zimbabwe Mozambique. Gramma, 1988: TML 100.

Chamunorwa. Gramma, 1989: TML 102. Released by Mango in 1991: 162 539 900-2.

Varombo Kuvarombo. Gramma, 1989: TML 101. Released under the title *Corruption* with the addition of the song "Corruption" on Mango, 1989: Mango CCD9849.

Chimurenga Masterpiece. Gramma, 1990: TML 103.

Hondo. Gramma, 1991: TML 104. Released with two additional songs on Zimbob, 1993: TMBU 13.

Live at SOB's. Live recording by Afropop Worldwide, 1991. Later released on cassette in Zimbabwe by Chimurenga Music.

Chimurenga International. Gramma, 1993: TML 105. Released in the United States as *Vanhu Vatema,* Zimbob, 1994: TMBU 14.

Chimurenga Varieties. Gramma, 1994: TML 106.

Sweet Chimurenga. Gramma, 1995: TML 107.

Afro Chimurenga. Gramma, 1996: TML 108.

Roots Chimurenga. Gramma, 1996: TML 109.

Chimurenga: African Spirit Music. WOMAD Select / Real World, 1997: WSCD104. Released as *The Lion of Zimbabwe* in Zimbabwe on Gramma, 1997.

Chimurenga Movement. Gramma, 1997: TML 111.

Chimurenga '98. Gramma, 1998: TML 1112. aNOnym reCOrds, 1998. Also released in South Africa by Sheer Sound.

Chimurenga Explosion. Chimurenga Music Co., 1999. aNOnym reCOrds, 2000: ANON0743. Also released in South Africa by Sheer Sound.

Dreams and Secrets (with Wadada Leo Smith). Chimurenga Music Co., 1999. aNOnym reCOrds, 2000: ANON0101

Live at El Rey. aNOnym reCOrds, 1999.

Manhungetunge. Chimurenga Music Co., 2000.

Chimurenga Rebel. Chimurenga Music Co., 2002. Also released in South Africa by Sheer Sound.

Chimurenga Rebel / Manhungetunge. aNOnym reCOrds, 2002: ANON0250.

Toi Toi. aNOnym reCOrds, 2003: ANON0303.

Chaputika, Live at Milton Keynes, May 2004. Quality Video and Film Production, 2004.

Rise Up. Chimurenga Music Co., 2005. Real World, 2006.

Thomas Mapfumo "Unplugged." Chimurenga Music Co., 2006: TLM 126.

Tribute to Benny Miller. Chimurenga Music Co., 2006: TML 125.

Exile. Chimurenga Music Co., 2010: CD-TP/TM5/48.

Live at Afrofest. Chimurenga Music Co., 2010: TML 138.

Music. Chimurenga Music Co., 2014 (digital single).

Danger Zone. Chimurenga Music Co., 2015.

COMPILATIONS

Shumba: Vital Hits of Zimbabwe. Earthworks / Virgin, 1990: CDEWV 22.

The Singles Collection. Gramma, 1992: ZC 111. Released as *Legends of Zimbabwean Music—Volume 4,* Zimbob, 1996: zim 7. Released as *Spirits to Bite Our Ears—The Singles Collection 1977–1986,* DBK Works, 2005: dbk522.

Chimurenga Forever: The Best of Thomas Mapfumo. Hemisphere, EMI, 1995.

12 from 5, Collection, Volume 1. Gramma, 2000: ZCD 186. (Songs taken from *Hokoyo, Gwindingwi Rine Shumba, Ndangariro, Mabasa,* and *Mr Music Africa.*)

12 from 5, Collection, Volume 2. Gramma, 2000: ZCD 187. (More songs taken from *Hokoyo, Gwindingwi Rine Shumba, Ndangariro, Mabasa,* and *Mr Music Africa.*)
Collected, Classic Cuts & Rare Tracks from the Lion of Zimbabwe (1978–2002). Nascente. (Licensed for United Kingdom and European Union only from aNOnym reCOrds, 2001: NSCD 087.)
Chimurenga Unlimited Hits Vol. 1. Gramma, 2002: TML 116.
Chimurenga Unlimited Hits Vol. 2. Gramma, 2002: TML 118.
Zvichapera. Chimurenga Music Co., 2002: CD-TP/TM5/12.
Choice Chimurenga. Sheer Sound, 2003: slcd-059.
Hallelujah Chicken Run Band: Take One. Analog Africa No. 2, 2004: AACD 062.
Plus "Ndamutswa Nengoma" appears on *Viva Zimbabwe,* Earthworks, 1984: CTCD 4411, and "Nyamaropa" appears on *What Summer Is Made For: Live at Rivermead, Reading,* Real World, 1997: WEVEN 3.
Love Unlimited. Chimurenga Music Co., 2007: TML 127
Chimurenga Unlimited Hits Vol. 3. Chimurenga Music Co., 2007: TML 128.
African Classics: Thomas Mapfumo, the Lion of Zimbabwe. Chimurenga Music Co. / Sheer Sound, 2009: TML 131 and slcd-168.
Greatest Hits. Chimurenga Music Co., 2010: TML 136.
Zimbabwe—Our Heritage. Chimurenga Music Co., 2010: TML 141.
Golden Classics. Chimurenga Music Co., 2013: CD-TP/TM5/49.

BIBLIOGRAPHY

My principal sources in writing this book are personal interviews and conversations with Thomas Mapfumo, members of the Blacks Unlimited, musicians, journalists, DJs, managers, agents, writers, and others associated with this story. I consulted many periodicals, mostly from Rhodesia and Zimbabwe. I found the *Rhodesia Herald* on microfilm in the media archive at Harvard. And I am particularly grateful to filmmaker John Riber for providing me with a large collection of Zimbabwean news clippings from 1980 to 2004. I also consulted the following books and articles.

Anderson, Ian. "Zimbabwe Gold: Ian Anderson on the Folk Roots of Thomas Mapfumo." *Folk Roots*, no. 28 (October 1985): 28–31.

Beach, D. N. *A Zimbabwean Past: Shona Dynastic Histories and Oral Tradition.* Gweru, Zimbabwe: Mambo Press, 1994.

Beach, David. *The Shona and Their Neighbors.* Oxford: Blackwell, 1994.

Berliner, Paul F. *The Soul of Mbira: Music and Traditions of the Shona People of Zimbabwe.* Berkeley: University of California Press, 1978.

Blair, David. *Degrees in Violence: Robert Mugabe and the Struggle for Power in Zimbabwe.* London: Continuum, 2002.

Cary, Robert, and Diana Mitchell. *African Nationalist Leaders in Rhodesia: Who's Who.* Johannesburg: Africana Book Society, 1977.

Catholic Commission for Justice and Peace in Zimbabwe. *Breaking the Silence, Building True Peace: A Report on the Disturbances in Matabeleland and the Midlands 1980 to 1988. Summary Report.* Harare: Catholic Commission for Justice and Peace in Zimbabwe, Legal Resources Foundation, 1999.

Chan, Stephen. *Robert Mugabe: A Life of Power and Violence.* Ann Arbor: University of Michigan Press, 2003.

Chigwedere, A. S. *From Mutapa to Rhodes: 1000 to 1890 A.D.* London: Macmillan, 1980.

Ellert, H. *The Rhodesian Front War: Counter-insurgency and Guerrilla Warfare, 1962–1980.* Rev. ed. Harare: Mambo Press, 1993.

Eyre, Banning. *Playing with Fire: Fear and Self-Censorship in Zimbabwean Music.* Copenhagen: Freemuse, 2001.

Frederikse, Julie. *None But Ourselves: Masses vs. Media in the Making of Zimbabwe.* Harare: Anvil Press, 1982.

Gelfand, Michael. *Growing Up in Shona Society: From Birth to Marriage.* Harare: Mambo Press, 1992.

Gelfand, M., S. Mavi, R. B. Drummond, and B. Ndemera. *The Traditional Medical Practitioner in Zimbabwe.* Harare: Mambo Press, 1993.

General History of Africa. Vol. 2, *Ancient Civilizations of Africa.* Edited by G. Mokhtar. London: Heinemann; Berkeley: University of California Press; Paris: UNESCO, 1981.

General History of Africa. Vol. 3, *Africa from the Seventh to the Eleventh Century.* Edited by M. Elfasi and I. Hrbek. London: Heinemann; Berkeley: University of California Press; Paris: UNESCO, 1988.

Godwin, Peter, and Ian Hancock. *"Rhodesians Never Die": The Impact of War and Change on White Rhodesia, c. 1970–1980.* Harare: Baobab Books, 1993.

Grinspoon, Lester, *Marihuana Reconsidered.* 2nd ed. Oakland, CA: Quick American Archives, 1996.

Hamdun, Said, and Noël King. *Ibn Battuta in Black Africa.* Princeton, NJ: Markus Wiener, 1994.

Holland, Heidi. *Dinner with Mugabe: The Untold Story of a Freedom Fighter Who Became a Tyrant.* Johannesburg: Penguin, 2008.

Kadhani, Mudereri, and Musamura Zimunya, eds. *And Now the Poets Speak.* Harare: Mambo Press, 1997.

Kanengoni, Alexander. *Echoing Silences.* Oxford: Heinemann, 1997.

Kwaramba, Alice Dadirai. *Popular Music and Society: The Language of Protest in Chimurenga Music: The Case of Thomas Mapfumo in Zimbabwe.* IMK Report No. 24. Oslo: University of Oslo, Department of Media Communication, 1997.

Kyker, Jennifer W. "'What Shall We Do?': Oliver Mtukudzi's Songs about HIV/AIDS." In *The Culture of AIDS: Hope and Healing through the Arts in Africa,* edited by Gregory Barz and Judah Cohen, 241–55. New York: Oxford University Press, 2011.

Lan, David. *Guns and Rain: Guerrillas and Spirit Mediums in Zimbabwe.* Berkeley: University of California Press, 1985.

Murray, Stephen O., and Will Roscoe, eds. *Boy-Wives and Female Husbands: Studies of African Homosexualities.* New York: St. Martin's Press, 1998.

Muzorewa, Abel Tendekai. *Rise Up and Walk: The Autobiography of Bishop Abel Tendekai Muzorewa.* Edited by Norman E. Thomas. Nashville, TN: Abingdon, 1978.

Parkenham, Thomas. *The Scramble for Africa: The White Man's Conquest of the Dark Continent from 1876 to 1912.* New York: Random House, 1991.

Pollan, Michael. *The Botany of Desire: A Plant's-Eye View of the World.* New York: Random House, 2002.

Pongweni, Alec J. C. *Songs That Won the Liberation War.* Harare: College Press, 1982.

Ranger, Terence. *Are We Not Also Men? The Samkange Family and African Politics in Zimbabwe 1920–64.* Portsmouth, NH: Heinemann, 1995.

Ranger, Terence. "The Death of Chaminuka: Spirit Mediums, Nationalism, and the Guerrilla War in Zimbabwe." *African Affairs* 81, no. 324 (1982): 349–69.

Steffens, Roger. "Zimbabwe Victorious: Bob Marley's African Triumph, I-Witness Dera Tomkins." *Beat* 17, no. 3 (1998): 48–55.

Thomas, Anthony. *Rhodes: The Race for Africa*. Harare: African Publishing House, 1996.

Turino, Thomas. *Nationalists, Cosmopolitans, and Popular Music in Zimbabwe*. Chicago: University of Chicago Press, 2000.

Vambe, Maurice Taonezvi. "Popular Songs and Social Realities in Post-Independence Zimbabwe." *African Studies Review* 43, no. 2 (2000): 73–86.

Vambe, Maurice Taonezvi. "Thomas Mapfumo's 'Toi Toi' in Context: Popular Music as Narrative Discourse." *African Identities* 2, no. 1 (2001): 89–112.

Vambe, Maurice Taonezvi. "Versions and Sub-versions: Trends in *Chimurenga* Musical Discourses of Post-Independence Zimbabwe." *African Study Monographs* 25, no. 4 (2004): 167–93.

White, Timothy. *Catch a Fire: The Life of Bob Marley*. Rev. ed. New York: Henry Holt, 1989.

Zimmer, Lynn, and John P. Morgan. *Marijuana Myths Marijuana Facts: A Review of the Scientific Evidence*. New York: Lindesmith Center, 1997.

Zindi, Fred. *Roots Rocking in Zimbabwe*. Harare: Mambo Press, 1985.

Zindi, Fred. "Thomas Mapfumo: A Cultural Ambassador?" *Southern Africa Monthly* 6, nos. 3 and 4 (1992–93): 11–12.

INDEX OF SONGS AND ALBUMS

GENERAL INDEX

3, 141–42, 149, 162, 176–78, 190, 195, 197, 205–6, 209, 213, 225, 232, 234, 237–38, 243, 249–52, 257; names (noms de guerre), 77, 95, 125; as popular musical genre, 3–5, 10, 73–74, 84–85, 99, 137, 142, 144, 157, 175, 190, 208, 209, 223, 226, 243, 249–50, 259, 270, 273, 285–86, 292–93; singles, 70, 84, 133, 176, 196, 226, 314n17; songs/choirs, 65, 81, 117–18, 127

Chimurenga Fan Club Newsletter, 147, 177, 319n21

Chimurenga Guru, as name for Mapfumo, 4, 152, 234, 284

Chimurenga Music Company, 146, 165, 185, 188, 193, 198, 234, 316n2

"Chimurenga Requests" (radio program), 95, 151. See also radio

Chinhamo, Janet (mother), 13–15, 23–29, 36, 129, 157, 287, 307n13; death of, 277; estrangement from Thomas's own family, 266; illness of, 32–33; influence on Thomas, 163–64, 227, 277, 281–82

Chinhoyi, 262, 268; Battle of, 41, 54, 137

Chinx, Comrade (Dickson Chingaira), 118, 251, 259; and chimurenga songs, 65

Chipaumire, Nora, 280

Chiramuseni, Kudzai (vocalist/dancer), 159, 167, 173, 195

Chiromo, Cuthbert (manager), 234–36, 240–42, 251, 273–74, 325n2, 327n1, 329n4, 330n10, 330–31nn16–18; and BMW seizures, 240, 288, 326n16; responds to criticism, 262, 278

chisi, 15, 326n9

Chitepo, Herbert, 91–92, 95, 231, 309n19, 311n41

Chitungwiza, 60, 80, 141, 164, 189, 217, 223, 239, 243

Chiweshe, Ashton "Sugar" (guitarist), 157, 194–95, 310n25, 324n1; death of, 236; guitar style, 191–92, 197, 322n29

Chiweshe, Stella, 50–51, 79, 137, 313n8

Chiwoniso. See Maraire, Chiwoniso

Chiyangwa, Leonard "Pickett" (guitarist), 74–75, 101, 129, 136, 138–39, 141, 307n21, 308n27; death of, 196; guitar style, 77, 79, 88, 94, 127, 308n32

Christianity, 24; black churches, 28–29, 61, 90–91, 127, 194, 206, 213, 253, 305n26; church suppression of music, 45, 53–54; and Shona beliefs/practices, 36, 47, 64–65, 166, 203–4, 208, 256, 287

Christian Marching Church, 26, 28, 34, 91, 287

CIO (Central Intelligence Organization), 90, 107, 246, 258, 262

Clegg, Johnny, 145

Coen, Bob, 7, 151–52, 159, 272; Jerry Rappaport, acquaintance with, 317n8; as manager, 163–64, 167–68, 329n5

Congo, Democratic Republic of (ex-Zaire), 3, 20, 31, 40, 84, 253, 314n18; 1960s war, 31. See also Congolese music

Congolese music (rumba/soukous/Zairean), 31, 40–41, 43–44, 47, 69, 73, 75–77, 82, 118, 126, 130, 140, 147, 186–87, 196, 251, 264, 313n6, 314n20, 318n7; perception of as immoral/shallow, 186, 226

constitutional referendum, 237–38

Cooder, Ry, 182, 286, 331n2

coon carnival, 35, 301n15

corruption, 42, 117, 149, 152, 221, 245, 254, 257, 259, 283, 328n3; Corruption album, 165–66, 175, 317–18n4; of history, 17; of Mugabe family/regime, 92, 153–54, 192, 207, 221, 233, 288; in Rhodesian music scene, 42; song lyrics, theme in, 154–60, 176–78, 182, 209, 238, 269, 286

Cosmic Four Dots, 35–36, 38. See also Mapfumo, Thomas

cosmopolitans, 46, 71, 222–23, 286, 318n6

Cripps, Arthur Shearly, 60

Daily News (newspaper), 238–39, 244, 254, 258–59, 269, 326n14. See also Nyarota, Geoffrey

Dance Theater Workshop, 156, 162, 165–66, 317n2

Dande, 13–14, 50–51, 63–66, 305n26, 306n7; and Thomas's origins, 14, 36, 282–83. See also Guruve

Deep Horizon. See Sithole, Jonah

Dembo, Leonard (sungura star), 187, 193, 313n7

Devera Ngwena (band), 148, 162, 302n28, 316n1

Diabate, Sekou "Bembeya" (guitarist/band-leader), 166, 318n8
Diener, Bob, 171–72, 191, 195, 197–98, 203, 208, 232, 260, 287. *See also* Zimbob Records
dreadlocks, 3, 5, 7, 127, 130, 148, 158–59, 167, 197, 253, 268; shaving of Pio Macheka's, 193–94, 322n33; Thomas's loss of, 261, 266, 274
drums/drumming, 77, 140, 151, 157, 231, 314n20, 328n14; Mapfumo plays, 26, 32, 39, 49; modern Zimbabwe style, 1, 9, 42, 69, 114–15, 167, 171, 213, 298n7; ngoma (traditional), 15, 24, 45, 47, 57–58, 63, 65, 70, 164, 303n40, 322n30; players in Mapfumo bands, 3, 74, 112, 129, 135, 141, 169, 172, 182, 198, 201, 207, 220, 248–49, 252–53, 254, 262, 271–72, 289, 307n21, 308n32, 319–20nn2–3, 325n6, 327n19, 329n2, 330n9
Dube, Joshua Hlomayi (guitarist), 8, 36, 101, 135, 207, 212, 215, 233, 239, 246, 315n23, 316n29, 322n33; on creating "Ngoma Yarira," 48–49, 68–71, 303n41, 306n5; death of, 242, 250, 262; guitar style, 9, 205–6, 224, 298n7, 314n9, 327n19; in Hallelujah Chicken Run Band, 48–49; joins/rejoins the Blacks Unlimited, 6, 104, 129, 197–98, 209; and Jonah Sithole, 53, 73, 206–8, 297n4, 323n6, 329n3; learning guitar, 44, 302n28; leaves Blacks Unlimited, 136, 246; and Mapfumo, 136, 215, 218–20, 223–24, 237, 275, 287, 306n5; police search of home, 239; rejects animist religion, 206; Shangara Jive (band), 235. *See also* Blacks Unlimited; Hallelujah Chicken Run Band
Dutiro, Chartwell, 182, 184–85, 189, 191, 202, 275, 284, 322n29; brings mbira to Blacks Unlimited, 150, 168, 179, 195; early life and joining Blacks Unlimited, 145–51, 162, 166–171, 174, 176; leaves Blacks Unlimited, 198–99; opposes MDC, 254–55; witchcraft accusation, 203–4, 208–9, 219
Dyoko, Beauler, 50–52, 63, 180

Earthworks Records, 133, 140, 142, 232, 315n26. *See also* Van Renen, Jumbo

elections (Zimbabwe), 208, 217; of 1979, 93, 103–5; of 1980, 107, 109–12, 115, 311n41; of 1985, 155; of 1990, 177, 309n8, 321n15; of 1996, 221; of 2000, 237, 239–40, 244; of 2002, 252, 254–55; of 2005, 273–74; of 2008, 279; of 2013, 289
Elizabeth Hotel, 113; band meetings at, 214, 217, 220, 223
ESAP (Economic Structural Adjustment Program), 187–88, 197, 321n17

FBC (Federation Broadcasting Corporation), 30, 35
Federation of Rhodesia and Nyasaland, 29–30; and broadcasting, 30–31, 34, 45
Field, Sir Winston, 38, 40, 90
Fifth Brigade, 132–33, 158, 239, 314n11
Florence (Singing Daughters): first Florence, 158–59, 317n14; second Florence, 214, 218, 224–25
Frankel, Andrew, 241, 260, 326–27n18

Gallo Records, 68, 72, 303n43
GALZ (Gays and Lesbians of Zimbabwe), 222, 283
Garande, Tinaye, 186–89, 196, 198
Gelfand, Michael, 61–62, 305n18
Goddard, Keith, 135, 140–41, 179, 222; death of, 264, 329n1
Goldsmith, Chris (booking agent), 182, 195, 199, 320n4
gospel music, 77, 156, 193–94
Gramma Records, Gramma/ZMC, 78, 126, 128, 130, 139, 140, 144, 146, 152, 155, 213, 232, 259, 271, 323n8, 326n8; Julian Howard, 225–26, 325n2; licensing/sales, 315nn26–27, 316n1, 322n29, 325n2; Mapfumo confronts, 184–85, 225–26, 196, 209; merger with ZMC, 225, 234, 322n28. *See also* Teal Recording Co.
Great Sounds (band), 43–44, 68, 74
Great Zimbabwe, 16–17, 54, 73
Green, Al, 172, 236, 238, 241, 246, 249, 251, 259–60, 265, 279, 287, 296, 329n24, 330n5, 330n10; establishes aNOnym reCOrds, 231–34; plays drums with Blacks Unlimited, 330n9; rants/accusations against world music industry, 235, 241, 261, 270–

73, 276, 326–27n18, 328n3; saves Chaka Mhembere, 273; splits with Mapfumo, 278–79
Green Arrows (band), 68, 72, 99, 109, 111, 311n37. *See also* Manatsa, Zexie
Grier, Joseph (lawyer), 165, 167, 321nn23–24, 321–22n27
guitar, 1, 3, 26, 33, 36, 72, 79, 82, 166, 212, 285, 313n6; accompanying mbira, 157, 167, 180, 315n21; author plays, 9, 297–98n7, 317n13, 323n2, 327n19, 330n13; bass and mbira, 49, 69, 77, 96, 129–30, 200–201, 232, 322n29, 330n12; evoking mbira, 48–49, 53, 68–69, 74–76, 81, 94, 96, 114, 127, 154, 158; parts in Mapfumo songs, 105, 126–27, 131, 135, 138, 173, 185, 191–92, 205, 224–25, 237, 252, 275, 286, 292, 314n9; picking techniques, 127, 146, 302n28, 303n40, 303n43; players in Mapfumo bands, 6–7, 44, 73–74, 77, 88, 104, 128, 130, 136, 139, 141, 168–69, 192, 195–97, 207–8, 236, 242, 261–62, 273, 297n4, 316n6, 325n6, 330n12; players' styles described/compared, 129, 206, 253, 318n6. *See also names of individual guitarists*
Gukurahundi (slaughter of Ndebele), 132–33, 280
Gung-Ho Studio, 236, 242, 249, 325n6, 326n9
Guruve (Thomas's ancestral home), 13, 205, 234–35, 252, 287. *See also* Dande
Guveya, Zivai (guitarist), 242, 253, 255, 261, 273, 327n19

Hallelujah Chicken Run Band, 48–49, 54, 68–69, 71, 79, 96, 129, 277, 306n7, 313n8, 324n17
Harare (formerly Salisbury), 14, 22, 32, 73, 116, 120, 145, 172, 207, 211, 264, 266, 271, 274, 281–82, 327n22; descriptions of, in 1997, 2–3, 9, 59, 128–29, 213, 221–22, 226; Mapfumo in, 96–97, 104, 150, 159–60, 163, 181, 191–92, 195, 234, 237, 240, 247, 251, 258, 260, 261–63; mayors of, 73, 154, 269, 315n27; renamed from Salisbury in 1980, 114; song about, 106; unrest/violence in, 210, 215–17, 244, 268, 273, 275, 326n9, 330n8. *See also* Chitungwiza; Mabvuku; Mbare; Salisbury
Hayfron, Sally. *See* Mugabe, Sally Hayfron

Hendrix, Jimi, 31, 47, 72, 75, 159
"Hendrix, Jimi" (chimurenga fighter), 82
Herald (Zimbabwe newspaper), 212, 215; on Mapfumo and bands, 125–26, 130, 135, 140, 142, 235, 243, 251–52, 254, 258–59; support of Mugabe regime, 155, 216–17. *See also Rhodesia Herald; Sunday Mail*
homosexuality, 323n10; and Canaan Banana, 221; Cecil Rhodes suspected, 19; GALZ (Gays and Lesbians of Zimbabwe), 222, 283; Keith Goddard, activist, 264; Mandela and gay rights in South Africa, 222; Mapfumo views on, 222, 283; Mugabe homophobia, 221–22
hosho (gourd rattle), 45, 49, 55–58, 69, 167, 201, 304n6
Hove, Chenjerai, 21–22, 178, 244, 246, 320–21n14
Hunzvi, Chenjerai "Hitler," 210, 244; Liberation War Veterans Association, 209, 237; death of/song about, 249
Hwa Hwa (prison), Mugabe detention, 40, 91, 214

internal settlement, 93–94, 100, 102, 115, 309n13
Island Records, 137, 142, 156, 159–67, 174, 177, 317n15, 317–18n4, 319–20n2, 320n6, 327–28n3; end of contract with Mapfumo, 181–84, 188, 190–91, 232. *See also* Blackwell, Chris

Jackson, Michael, 212, 291, 316n1
Jamaica Inn, 72–73
jazz, 96, 107, 113, 118, 165, 172, 286, 300n7; African, 31–35, 41, 47, 138, 150, 300n7; in Mapfumo's music, 5, 68, 87, 196, 205, 259, 285, 292, 316n6; sidelined by rock in Rhodesia, 34; "Skokiaan," 320n6
Jera, Emmanuel (Manu), 129–30, 133, 146–47; death of, 264, 329n1; leaves band, 314n20
Jira, Sekuru. *See* Munhumumwe, John "Sekuru Jira"
jit/jiti (music genre), 30, 47, 65, 86, 193, 303n43, 319n20
Job's Nitespot (nightclub), 42, 117, 120, 215
Josam, Elisha, 48–49, 68

Kachingwe, Thompson (manager), 112, 120, 125–28, 136
Kaguvi, 22, 60. *See also* ancestors
Kanengoni, Alexander, 81–82, 155, 231, 245–46, 284
Karimaura, Ephraim (guitarist), 158, 167–71, 289, 317n13, 320n3, 322n29; death of, 195–97, 209; guitar style, 173, 192
Kaunda, Kenneth, 37, 91–92, 113, 309n7. *See also* Zambia
Kavhai, Washington (bassist), 135, 168–69, 176, 181, 198, 223, 315n23, 320n3; bass style, 130, 192; joins Blacks Unlimited, 130
keyboards, 194, 323n8; in Mapfumo band/music, 3, 96, 135, 138, 140–41, 146, 150, 186, 195, 200, 205, 235, 275, 286, 292, 325n4
Korekore (Shona subgroup), 13–14, 16, 63, 149, 224, 316n3
Kronos Quartet, 190, 192, 286, 321n22
Kuti, Fela, 74, 141, 143, 159, 160, 285–86
Kutsch, Ken, 165–70, 174, 181–83, 190–91, 317–18n4, 319–20n2, 321nn24–26, 322n27, 331n2
Kwanangoma College of Music, 46–47, 170, 318n11

Lancaster House talks, 107–8, 185, 321n15, 326n11
land, 118, 227, 249, 281, 300n6; cultural significance of, 18, 22, 59–60, 63–64, 90; debate/controversy over, 246, 249–50, 284, 293, 326n11; description of Zimbabwe's, 13–16, 63, 127; Land Tenure Act, 90; Mapfumo songs/comments about, 78–80, 175–76, 185, 249–51, 311–12n2; owned by Mapfumo, 288; reform/resettlement policy, 2, 108, 149, 221, 250, 254, 306n30, 326n11, 327–28n3; seizure of, 17, 19, 20–22, 79, 237–38, 246, 249–51, 265, 284, 293, 299n16, 327–28n3; and spirit mediums, 64; Tribal Trust (communal) Lands, 23, 80
liberation war/struggle, 4–6, 15, 23, 26, 34, 61, 107, 120, 133, 170, 207, 212–13, 220, 281–82, 288, 297n6, 300n4, 304n7; fought from Mozambique/Zambia, 34, 64–65, 68, 75–76, 81–82, 89, 92, 94, 101, 108, 148–49, 188, 311n41; internal settlement, 93–94, 100, 102, 115, 309n13; legacy/after-

math of, 61, 155, 221, 237–39, 255, 284, 293; Mapfumo songs/comments about, 70, 78–83, 89, 94–95, 97–98, 102–3, 111, 114–15, 120–21, 125–27, 130, 136–37, 141, 143, 149, 151, 155, 160, 176, 185, 209, 217–18, 226, 238–39, 268–69, 310n23, 313n2, 313n4, 315–16n20, 316n23; and Shona/Ndebele relations, 18, 40, 103, 131–32, 334n11; spiritual dimension, 60, 62–65, 82, 118–19, 268–69, 303n36, 305n26, 306n30; spreads throughout Southern Rhodesia, 41, 63, 76, 93. *See also* chimurenga; veterans
Liberation War Veterans Association, 209, 237
Lipopo Jazz Band, 43–44, 73, 303–4n43
Lobengula (Ndebele king), 18–21, 60, 108, 305n17
lobola (bride price), 14, 23, 300n32
Lonrho (mining company), acquires Teal Records, 69

Mabvuku (township), 95, 144; bulldozing of, 273; Mapfumo family home, 25–26, 28, 32–34, 281, 287
Machel, Samora, 76, 113; death of, 148. *See also* Mozambique
Macheso, Alick (sungura musician), 267, 313n7
Machipisa Nightclub, 77, 302n26. *See also* Mutanga Nightclub
Madzikatire, Safirio, 44, 69, 126, 267, 329n3
Mafundikwa, Saki, 196; album cover designs, 159–60, 166, 191, 195–96, 258, 318n9; U.S. unplugged tour management, 201–2, 205
Magwaza, Phillip, 209, 213, 234–36, 324n11
Makokowa, Charles (bassist), 95–96, 98, 101, 146, 181, 195, 198, 308n27, 308n32, 316n4; Acid Band, 77, 86, 88, 307n21; beaten by soldiers, 140, 316n29; death of, 200–204, 209, 215; friendship with Mapfumo, 130, 146, 169, 172, 174, 200–201, 215; jailing and release, 130, 134–35; as keyboardist, 138, 168; style on bass, 77, 96, 127, 129, 192, 200, 322n29
Makombe, Bezil (mbira player), 3, 5–6, 9, 190, 196, 201–2, 206, 225, 236, 275, 320n3, 321n21, 329n2, 331n5; childhood, 218–19; criticism of Mapfumo, 204, 271; criticized

by Mapfumo, 218, 223, 266–67; joins
Blacks Unlimited, 182; mbira prowess, 195,
218, 261, 298–99n7
Makombe, Ngoni (mbira player), 3, 5, 9, 196,
201–2, 204, 235, 250, 328n4; death of, 261
Makore, Jeremiah (paternal uncle), 71, 95,
234–35
Mambo, Hilton, 39, 85–86, 136, 144, 220
Manatsa, Zexie, 72, 99, 109, 113, 118, 126, 151,
307n12; and Webster Shamu/ZANU, 111,
311n37; wedding of, 106, 311n36. See also
Green Arrows
Mango Records, 156–57, 320n6. See also
Island Records
Mapfumo, Chiedza Chikawa (daughter), 25,
150, 189, 227, 255, 257, 266, 277, 290; on
move to America, 240–41
Mapfumo, Edith (sister), 29, 288
Mapfumo, John Kashesha (stepfather), 25–
29, 32, 34, 189, 281, 287; death of, 227
Mapfumo, Lancelot (brother), 29, 32, 43, 86,
100–101, 134–35, 157, 169, 195, 201, 253,
255, 266–67, 329n2; death of wife, 236;
in Eugene, Oregon, 272–77, 287–88; as
loveable uncle, 189–90; as percussionist,
140–41, 171
Mapfumo, Mati (daughter), 227, 255–57, 277
Mapfumo, Tabeth (sister), 26, 29, 288
Mapfumo, Tapfumaneyi (son), 129, 150, 227,
252–53, 255, 266, 277, 288–90
Mapfumo, Thomas: on African Americans, 175, 270, 293; and AIDS, 186, 206,
249, 322n38; and alcohol, 24, 47, 87, 271;
author's relationship with, 2, 297–98n7,
313n3; bandleader, 88, 136, 163, 169, 177,
182, 195, 197–98, 201, 214–15, 220, 223,
247, 315n22; birth and pastoral childhood,
13–16, 23–27, 151, 249–50, 281; BMWS
impounded, 240, 246, 250, 257–58, 288,
326n16, 328n17; businesses, 191, 198, 234,
236; at Carnegie Hall, 293; and cars, 33, 98,
152, 182, 191, 240, 255, 316n4; Chikawa, 4,
241; Chimurenga Guru, 4, 152, 234, 284; as
consumer/lover of pop culture, 31, 96, 150,
202–3, 283; criticized/accused/shunned,
5, 125, 144, 163, 178, 192–93, 198–99, 204,
213, 239, 243, 251–52, 254, 266, 278, 282,
322n33, 330n6; criticizes/embraces foreign

music influence, 31, 44, 68–69, 71, 75,
96, 128, 130, 142, 145, 158, 186, 245, 271;
defense of African culture, 80, 97, 103, 127,
158, 186–87, 282–83, 286, 290; detention
under Smith regime, 98–109, 113, 310n25;
divided parentage, 29, 36, 129, 204–5, 266,
282, 287; vs. DJs in Zimbabwe, 145, 158,
178, 184, 187, 226, 245, 254; early musical
career/influences, 26, 31–35, 38–44,
48–49, 307n20; education, 4, 25, 29–30,
32–34, 284; exile and its consequences,
241–43, 246, 269–70, 276, 283, 288; family
vs. career, 265–66; first recording with
mbira, 135, 315n21; first song/record,
29, 41; funny stories, 7–8, 134, 147–48,
189–90, 289; Gandanga, 4, 245; on God,
ancestors, and prayer, 10, 36, 142, 145, 186,
200, 204–5, 209, 222, 256–57, 268–69, 283,
287; and golf, 32–33, 48, 283; harassment
of, 240, 246, 252, 257–58, 262, 272; health
concerns, 232–34, 263, 266; as historical
figure, 1–3, 10, 126, 212–13, 221, 245, 285;
home/family life, 25, 29, 72, 91, 150, 189–
90, 227, 241, 248, 255–57, 265, 271–75, 277,
287–90; honored by universities/insti-
tutions, 220–21, 236–37, 239, 248, 324n4;
Hurricane Hugo, 4, 173; on Ian Smith, 216,
240, 274; at independence celebration in
1980, 118–21; on Jonah Sithole, 73–75, 88,
128, 208–9, 316n6; legal problems, 71, 85,
95–96, 134–36, 153, 194–95, 204, 207–8,
234–35; Lion of Zimbabwe, 6, 165, 199,
248, 289; managers, 7, 10, 86, 112, 125, 136,
140, 152, 162–63, 165–67, 170, 181, 191, 201,
205, 230–36, 241, 259–60, 265–66, 278,
286–88, 319–20n2, 321nn25–26, 326–
27n18, 329–30n5, 330–31n17; marijuana,
use of/views on, 7–10, 99, 117, 134, 139,
148, 152, 169, 203, 207–8, 216, 256, 267,
289; marriages and separation, 86–87,
104, 128–29, 265, 271; and mbira music, 15,
24, 29, 42, 49, 52, 69, 71, 76, 79, 150, 170,
173, 176, 179–80, 201, 204, 286, 329n20;
meets with guerrillas, 82–83, 200, 308n27;
on Morgan Tsvangirai and MDC, 223, 240,
259, 267, 273, 276, 279, 289; Mudhara, 4,
262; compared with Mugabe, 284; on Mugabe and ZANU, 107, 115, 121, 137, 149–50,

Mapfumo, Thomas (*continued*)
155, 178, 188, 206–7, 217, 233, 239, 240, 242, 250–51, 259, 267, 273–74, 284; Mukanya, 4, 9, 29, 118, 134, 141, 177, 195, 203, 213, 223, 224, 235, 239, 243, 251–52, 262; music, seductive power of, 3, 9–10, 164, 171, 253, 261; musical influences/adaptations, 86, 105, 135, 285; at Muzorewa rally, 102–4, 270, 310n28, 310n31; Muzorewa rally, damage to reputation, 101, 112, 125–28, 270; name variations, nicknames, 4, 9, 14, 83, 173, 188, 245, 262; on the Ndebele, 115, 131–32, 158, 192, 214, 267, 270–71, 313n4; and Oliver Mtukudzi, 77, 113, 224, 226, 239, 277; as a parent, 72, 153, 189, 241, 256–57, 290–91; personas, public/private, 47, 79–80, 86, 94–95, 127, 156, 171, 186, 236, 245, 281–82; physical descriptions, 5, 116, 167; plays guitar, 274; political conscious-ness, 18, 28, 38, 42, 70, 78, 81, 92, 97–98, 108–9, 154, 197, 238, 267–68, 270, 293, 306n5, 309–10n20; and politics in Rhode-sia, 45, 72, 76, 83, 97–98, 109; on politics/politicians in Zimbabwe, 137, 160, 177, 259, 292; on race relations, 21, 25, 44–45, 70, 95–96, 155, 175, 239, 249–50, 270, 293; on rap and hip-hop, 203, 270–71, 290–91; record deals/sales/royalties, 139, 156, 172, 183–85, 190–91, 195–96, 225–26, 230–32, 260, 271, 278, 292, 315nn26–27, 316nn1–2, 317–18n4, 318n6, 320n6, 321nn23–24, 321–22n27, 324–25nn1–2, 327–28n3, 330n10; recordings/recording studio, 85, 96, 141, 146, 157, 177, 182, 207, 225, 236–37, 249, 262, 275, 292, 307n19, 314–15n20, 322n29, 323n8, 325n4, 326n9, 327n19, 329–30n5, 331n18; on reggae, 118, 140, 142, 255; remixing old songs, 291; and Shona religion/Christianity, 60, 91, 142, 164, 200, 203–5, 208–9, 215, 234–35, 274, 283; as soccer (football) fan, 150, 188–89, 193, 203, 218, 257, 325n4; song composition/re-hearsal method, 130, 149, 151, 185, 195, 204, 218, 224–25, 275, 307n15; stage manner, 3, 138–39, 143, 167, 175, 182, 227, 253; Tafiren-yika, 4, 83; top four songs (in his view), 307n22; and traditional (non-mbira) music, 99, 104, 127, 141–42, 146, 193, 285, 303–4n43, 307n15; typical concert, 5–6, 8–9; urged to stop singing politics, 254, 267–68, 274; U.S. immigration status and political asylum, 263, 268, 277, 289; vocal style, 1, 8, 75, 80–81, 94, 115, 127, 133, 167, 178, 182, 286, 314n9; and Webster Shamu, 95, 105, 111, 155; women, views on, 10, 222, 256, 283; ZANU, criticism of, 139, 149, 155–56, 197, 217, 238, 249, 254–55, 259, 265, 284; and Zexie Manatsa, 99, 106, 109, 111–13, 118, 126, 151, 311nn36–37; on Zimbabwean police, 134, 216. *See also* Acid Band; Black Spirits; Blacks Unlimited; chimurenga: as popular music genre; Cosmic Four Dots; Hallelujah Chicken Run Band; Sporting Lions; Springfields; Zutu Brothers

Mapfumo, Vena Sibanda Dangarembwa (wife), 86–87, 134, 150, 173, 199, 207, 240–41, 246, 249, 255–57, 263, 268, 271, 275–79, 321n21, 326n16, 331n3; in business, 191, 234–36, 247; marriage to Mapfumo, 128–29, 159, 203, 227, 248, 265, 288–90; at Muzorewa rally, 104

Mapfumo, William (brother), 7, 29, 35, 39, 73, 76, 125, 198–99, 241, 250, 262, 268, 271–77, 321n21; as band manager, 136, 140, 162–63, 167, 183, 213–14; recruits guitar players, 157, 197, 242; relationship with Thomas, 32, 100, 169, 174, 190, 215, 266–67, 287–91

Maraire, Chiwoniso (singer): death of, 264, 329n1

Maraire, Dumisani, 170, 201, 264, 318nn11–12, 321n22; critique of Mapfumo, 221; death of, 324n5; feud with Ephat Mujuru, 319n14; teaching in Seattle, 302–3n34

Maridadi, James (DJ), 237, 244–45

marijuana (mbanje, fodya, ganja, daga, spliff), 7–10, 85, 117, 134, 138–39, 142, 162–65, 192, 207, 216, 271, 283, 289, 314n19, 324n1; issues with, during tours, 166–71, 173, 183, 194, 204; in Jamaica, 148; research on, 256

marimba, 46, 170, 321n22, 330n12

Marley, Bob, 5, 84, 94, 134, 137, 312n11, 312n14, 312–13nn16–17; at independence celebra-tion, 113, 116–20; Mapfumo's respect for/emulation of, 127, 158–59, 182, 212, 254, 285–87

Marondera (formerly Marandellas), 13–15, 25, 29, 277
Marudza, Kudzi, 178, 187, 226, 245
Mataure, Sam, 207, 328n14
Matema, Crispen (producer/manager), 69, 78, 85–86, 96, 308n27
Mattaka, Kenneth / Mattaka Family, 35. See also Cosmic Four Dots
mbaqanga, 76, 166, 326n9. See also South Africa
Mbare (township), 9, 28, 31–39, 48, 69, 130, 188–89, 216–17; culture/personality of, 281–82; mbira music in, 45, 47, 54, 63, 75, 302n32
Mbata, Sebastian (drummer), 129, 209, 215, 320n3; death of, 198
mbira, 62, 176, 194, 211, 283; amplification of, 3, 180; bands of the early '90s, 180–81, 193; in Blacks Unlimited repertoire, 176, 225, 257; buzzing of, 52, 180, 304n3; in ceremonies (mapira), 1–2, 15, 22, 24, 29, 45; ceremony (dandaro) described, 55–59; construction of, 24, 179–80, 304n3; definition/description of, 3, 297n1; dzavadzimu, 59, 318–19n13; early Mapfumo adaptations, 8, 48–49, 65, 68–70, 74–76, 80–82, 87, 127, 135–36; and guitar/bass, 6–7, 53, 69, 74–77, 79, 94–96, 127–30, 157, 192, 200–201, 303n40, 303n43; harmony and rhythm, 48–49, 55–56, 303n41; healing power of, 1, 171; Ian Smith's views on, 212; initiation into, 50–51; international profile/popularity of, 46, 137, 198, 204, 248, 286, 321n22, 329n20; and liberation struggle, 65–66, 82; music described, 8–9, 49–53, 167; mystification of, 52; notation for, 304n2; nyunga nyunga/ndima, 318n11; players/recordings with Blacks Unlimited, 5–7, 136, 145–46, 150, 157, 173, 182, 185–86, 196, 201, 206–7, 218–19, 225, 235–37, 252, 257, 261, 272, 285–86, 297–98n7, 314n20, 315n23, 315n25, 320n3, 322n29, 323n5, 325n4, 326n9, 330n13, 331n5; players' views of Mapfumo, 52–53, 79, 168, 180; in popular music generally, 42, 46, 76, 135, 147, 197, 302n32, 303n43, 315n21; on Rhodesian radio, 45–46; in the Salisbury townships, 45–46; singing with, 54, 56,

264; and spirits/ancestors, 59–60, 170, 206; stigmatized/banned by missionaries/educators, 53–54, 223, 303n4; tuning of, 150, 180, 236, 319n1. See also bira; Blacks Unlimited: mbira used in; guitar; Mapfumo, Thomas: and mbira music; and names of individual players and songs
Mbofana, Comfort (DJ), 244–45, 282
MDC (Movement for Democratic Change), 240, 244, 255, 259, 267, 269, 273, 275, 279, 289; formation of, 237–38. See also Tsvangirai, Morgan
Merz, Amy, 151–52, 159, 163–64, 317nn9–10; and Island Records contract, 156–57, 163
Mhangura (copper mine), 47–49, 68–69, 71–72, 277, 307n12, 313n8
Mhembere, Chaka (mbira player), 3, 207, 252, 255, 266, 271, 329n2; health issues, 273, 289, 311n5
Mhlanga, Chris, 53, 79, 179–80, 195, 198
Mhlanga, Louis, 154, 316n6
Miller, Benny, 162, 316n2, 323n8; death of, 264, 329n1. See also Shed Studio
Misty in Roots (band), 141, 147, 161–62
Moyo, Jonah, 250, 302n28, 313n7, 316n1. See also Devera Ngwena
Moyo, Jonathan, 153, 239; Mapfumo song about, 258; as minister of information, 250–54, 257–59; as musician, 250, 254
Mozambique, 13, 15, 20, 89, 110–11, 113, 127, 132, 152, 163, 181, 207, 267, 275; Mapfumo sings for, 148–50, 163; Radio Mozambique, 65, 89, 95, 111, 151; role in liberation war, 64, 68, 76, 81–82, 92, 101, 105, 108, 125, 137, 188, 311n41. See also Machel, Samora
Mtukudzi, Oliver, 73, 97, 105, 109, 118, 126, 137, 220, 224, 226, 234, 317n1, 322n36, 325n6, 328n14; AIDS song, 320n11; and Mapfumo, 77, 113, 239, 277–78, 289; and politics, 244–45; "Wasakara," 327n22
Muchabaiwa, Chris (bassist/drummer), 236, 253, 272, 278, 325n6, 330n13
Mude, Hakurotwi (mbira, spirit medium), 51, 54–58, 80–81, 105, 304n5; death of, 264, 329n1
Mudeka sisters (Anna, Mutsa, Patience), 197–98, 224–25; Anna, 225; Mutsa, 214, 218, 224–25; Patience, 198, 203, 225

Mudzuri, Elias, 67, 154, 269–70
Mugabe, Albert: death of, 206–7, 323n7, 323–34n10
Mugabe, Grace Marufu (Mugabe's second wife), 207, 217, 279, 324n3
Mugabe, Robert, 2, 4, 67, 99, 117, 125, 211, 213; actions after prison and before election, 91–92, 95, 108, 311n1, 321n15; childhood and youth, 37; conciliatory words/actions at independence, 119–20; corruption of family/regime, 92, 153–54, 192, 207, 217, 221, 233, 239, 270, 274–80, 288, 311n41; and cultural issues/policies, 111, 145, 243–44, 255, 257, 269, 303n36, 320–21n14, 327n22; death of brother Albert, 206, 323n7; and ESAP/economic reform, 187–88, 216; establishes one-party rule, 152–55, 178; imprisonment, 40, 91, 214; and Joshua Nkomo/ZAPU, 110, 113, 115, 131–32, 187, 312n6; and land policy, 108, 149, 238, 246, 265, 321n16, 326n11, 327–28n3; late career survival tactics, 274–76, 279, 289; Mapfumo praises/criticizes, 95, 178, 185, 188–89, 217, 223, 233, 240, 242, 251, 259, 267, 284, 289, 293; Mapfumo songs about/refer-encing, 115, 121, 126, 136–37, 145, 148–50, 249, 292, 306n5, 320–21n14; marriage to Grace Marufu, 207, 217, 279, 324n3; marriage to Sally Hayfron, 37, 111, 188, 207, 232n7; vs. MDC/Tsvangirai, 187–88, 237, 252, 273–75; meets/honors Mapfumo, 188, 221; political beginnings/philosophy, 37–38, 107; racism/homophobia of, 222, 269–70; responds to 1990s economic slump, 187–89; return to Zimbabwe after war and first election of, 110–13; and war veterans, 2, 132, 209–10, 216, 226, 237–38. *See also* elections; ZANU, ZANU-PF
Mugabe, Sally Hayfron (Mugabe's first wife), 37, 111, 207, 323n7; death of, 188
mujibas, 81, 102–3, 121
Mujuru, Ephat, 53–58, 61–63, 66, 80, 302n31, 304n8, 318–19n13; on AIDS, 196; as bandleader, 180, 197, 319n14; death of, 250; Dumisani Maraire, feud with, 319n14; and Mapfumo, 159, 172–73
Mujuru, Muchatera, 53, 61–63, 65, 173,

304n12, 305nn17–18, 308n27, 318n13; death of, 66
Mukanga, Samson (drummer), 3, 198, 220, 249, 252, 327n19; death of, 252–53
Mukanya, 29. *See also* Mapfumo, Thomas
Munhumumwe, John "Sekuru Jira" (uncle), 2, 6, 7, 15, 134, 150, 163, 190, 320n3; as band disciplinarian, 199, 213–14, 242; death of, 264, 329n1; during Mapfumo's detention, 98, 100
Munhumumwe, Kufera and Hamundidi (grandparents), 4, 14, 24
Munhumumwe, Marshall (uncle), 15, 74; death of, 250; Four Brothers band, 298n2, 307n13
Munhumumwe, Michael (Thomas's childhood name), 14–15, 23–25. *See also* Mapfumo, Thomas
Munhumutapas, 17
Munyama, Shepherd (bass player), 136, 194, 320n3, 322n30
Mupariwa, Tapfumaneyi (father), 13–14, 23, 26, 36, 129, 164; death of, 71
Mupawaenda, Lucky, 136, 138–39, 142, 307n21
Murambatsvina (Operation Drive Out Trash), 273–74
Mushandira Pamwe (nightclub), 73, 78, 87, 159, 178, 197, 224, 258, 307n19
Music Express, 184–85, 188, 320n7
Mutanga Nightclub, 42–44, 48, 77, 302n26
Mutare, 15, 216, 259, 275, 280; as Mapfumo proving ground, 72–79, 88–90, 136, 153
Muzorewa, Bishop Abel Tendekai, 255, 282–83; campaign and elections, 107–12, 309n11, 309nn16–17, 310n32, 312n6; death of, 264, 329n1; and Mapfumo in 1979 campaign, 100–106, 113, 115, 126, 252, 270, 310n29, 310n31, 312n7; rise and entry into politics and war, 89–94
Mwale, Allan (bassist), 3, 5, 40, 200–202, 205, 215–16, 220, 223, 232–33, 311n37; death of, 236, 311n37
Mzilikazi (Ndebele king), 17–18; Bulawayo neighborhood, 86–87

n'anga (traditional healer), 15, 51, 63, 94, 206, 282, 305n26; distinguished from spirit medium, 59, 64; Mapfumo's use of, 208–9, 234–35

Ndebele (people), 19–20, 30–31, 162, 302n28; arrival in Zimbabwe, 13, 17; customs, 23, 214; language (Sindebele), 66, 110, 214. *See also* Nkomo, Joshua; Shona (people); ZAPU

Ndlovu, Charles. *See* Shamu, Webster

Nehanda, 13, 22, 60–64, 238, 297n3, 299n29. *See also* ancestors

Nekati, Robert, 49, 69

ngoma. *See* drums/drumming: ngoma

Nkhata, Alick, 45–46, 49

Nkomo, Joshua, 37, 40; position post-independence, 110–15, 131–32, 152, 187, 237–38, 309n11, 312n6, 314n16; and Smith regime, 92, 105, 107, 110. *See also* Ndebele; ZAPU

Nkosi, West, 72

Nyarota, Geoffrey, 75–79, 83, 96–97, 120, 244, 282, 312n6, 326n14; breaks Willowgate scandal, 153–54, 269; founds *Daily News*, 238–39. See also *Daily News*

Osibisa, 68, 118

Parade (magazine). See *African Parade*

Pasipamire, 60, 62, 305n14, 305n17

Patriotic Front, 94–95, 107, 309n11. *See also* ZANU, ZANU-PF

Peel, John, 140

Pied Pipers, 78, 307nn19–20

Presley, Elvis, 5, 31–32, 34, 38, 41, 68, 107, 118, 138

press, 97, 135, 138, 146, 240, 251, 262, 310n29; independent in Zimbabwe (*Financial Gazette, Standard, Sunday Mirror, Zimbabwe Independent*), 153–54, 199, 217, 226, 239, 243–45, 254, 273, 324nn2–3; Mapfumo/music in foreign, 133, 140, 148, 183, 239, 268, 274. See also *African Parade*; *Daily News*; *Herald*; *Rhodesia Herald*; *Sunday Mail*; ZBC

pungwe (all-night gathering), 9, 58, 73, 77, 207, 223, 297n6, 304n7, 306n30

Queens Garden Hotel, 114, 117, 128, 135, 152, 163

radio: American, 148, 152, 165–66, 183; Capital Radio, 244–45, 327n23; Central African Broadcasting Service (CABS), 30; Federation Broadcasting Corp. (FBC), 30, 35; foreign music favored by, 44, 71, 145–46, 158, 184, 187, 226, 245, 258; LM Radio (Mozambique), 75; Mapfumo's music on, 41, 83, 95, 111, 185, 226, 274; mbira music on, 45–46, 49, 51, 302n31; propaganda jingles on, 254, 258; RBC (Rhodesia Broadcasting Corp.), 30, 41, 44–45, 51, 95, 97; in Rhodesia, 24, 31–32, 44–47, 54, 261; songs banned/restricted on, 31, 54, 70, 83, 97, 239, 243, 251–52, 259, 267; supporting liberation war from Zambia, 40, 89; as tool in liberation war, 65, 81, 89, 200; Voice of Zimbabwe (Mozambique), 65, 89, 95, 97, 106, 111, 151, 200. *See also* Afropop / Afropop Worldwide; ZBC

Rambanai (nightclub), 39, 42

Rappaport, Jerry, 163–67, 182–84, 317n8, 319–20n2, 321n26; Mango Records, 156

RAR (Rhodesian Army Rifles), 83

RBC (Rhodesia Broadcasting Corp.), 30, 41, 44–45, 51, 95, 97

Real World Records, 207, 323n9, 330n10. *See also* WOMAD

Redding, Otis, 31, 38, 172

reggae, 138, 156, 161, 165–66, 174, 194, 255; and Bob Marley, 113, 116–18, 137; Gregory Isaacs, 148; Reggae Sunsplash, 234; Zimbabwean, 187. *See also* Blacks Unlimited; Mapfumo, Thomas; Misty in Roots

Rettinger, Manny, 172, 205, 235, 323n2; and Al Green, 231

Rhodes, Cecil, 18–22, 30, 60, 67, 213, 280; "Confession of Faith," 299n16

Rhodesia, 4, 16–17, 28, 46, 63, 78, 91–97, 111, 216; becomes Zimbabwe, 107–8, 117–19; establishment of, 20, 23–24, 301–2n23; federation with Nyasaland, 29–30; legacy of, in Zimbabwe, 237–38, 255; life/art for black Africans in, 30–34, 41–45, 47, 53, 61, 69–71, 79–85, 95, 114, 127, 138, 300n6, 301n8, 303n36, 304n4, 311n1, 316n31. *See also* liberation war/struggle; radio; *Rhodesia Herald*; Smith, Ian

music, 3, 31–32, 46, 76, 86, 143–45, 147, 166, 257, 300n7, 326n9
spirit mediums, 2, 6, 57–62, 167, 170, 218, 301n9, 305n14; Mapfumo emulates/ turns to, 94, 159, 164, 209; persecution of, 305nn26–27; in war context, 22, 37, 51, 53, 63–66, 79–80, 82, 91, 98, 108, 173, 238, 299n3, 308n27
spirit possession, 1–2, 9, 57–60, 62, 305n26, 308n27; varieties of spirits, 59. *See also* bira
Sporting Lions (soccer club), 7, 198, 209, 215, 241–42, 251, 263; advancement/demotion of, 203, 256, 263; vs. Blacks Unlimited, 198, 220, 326n16; founding of, 188–89; sale of, 263, 267–68
Springfields (band), 38–44, 75, 159, 172, 200, 215, 236, 302n24, 307n19
Stein, Rikki, 141, 147–48
Stern's Music, 235, 260
Storm (band), 88, 308n32
Sunday Mail (newspaper), 126, 135, 137, 141–42, 144, 152, 158, 177, 186, 188, 199, 209, 234, 236, 237–39, 249–51, 258, 329n20; Mapfumo speaks to, 175, 213, 242, 268, 271–72, 315n27. See also *Herald*; press
sungura (music style), 127–28, 130, 137, 142, 148, 187, 193, 226, 244, 267, 313n7. *See also* Congolese music

Tawengwa, Solomon, 73, 307n19
Teal Recording Co., 68–71, 78, 83–85, 89, 96–98, 126, 306n8, 311–12n2. *See also* Gramma Records, Gramma/ZMC
Tekere, Edgar, 92, 117, 309n8, 321n15
television, 103, 126, 151–52, 157–58, 163, 212, 223, 258; Mapfumo a fan of, 33, 150, 227, 255, 257. *See also* press
Tembo, Biggie, 194, 209, 323n4; death of, 204–5. *See also* Bhundu Boys
Terrell, Tom, 161, 165, 168–74, 318n5, 329n1; death of, 264, 329n1
T'n'V Music Sales and Video Hire, 191, 198, 234
Toure, Sekou, 46–47
Tracey, Hugh and Andrew, 45–46, 49, 172–73, 302nn33–34, 302–3n34, 318–19n13
Tsvangirai, Morgan: attacked physically,

216–17, 275; leads MDC, 223, 237, 252, 259, 275–76, 279, 289; as trade union leader, 187–88, 209. *See also* MDC
Tuku. *See* Mtukudzi, Oliver
Turino, Thomas, 46, 49, 81, 155, 171, 286, 300n34, 302n24, 302nn31–32, 303n36, 303n40, 303n43, 306nn5–6, 309n17, 310n30, 315n21, 323n6, 329n20

UANC (United African National Council), 100–106, 111
UDI (Unilateral Declaration of Independence), 40, 90
U2 (band), proposed collaboration with, 156, 286, 331n2

Van Renen, Jumbo, 133, 137, 138–39, 141–42, 156, 163, 165, 183–84, 232, 314n17, 315n26, 327–28n3
veterans (of liberation war), 2, 8, 81, 132, 137, 185, 209–10, 262; demand/receive money, 2, 209, 213, 216, 226, 244, 249; land seizures and election violence, 210, 237–38. *See also* Hunzvi, Chenjerai "Hitler"; land: seizure of
villages, protected, 68, 93, 145, 309n16
Vori, Emmanuel, 69–71, 83, 85; on "Corruption," 155, 307n15; on Shona/Ndebele tension, 115–16
VOZ (Voice of Zimbabwe), 65, 89, 95, 97, 106, 111, 151, 200

Wagon Wheels, 77, 307n19
war veterans. *See* veterans
Wells, Mike. *See* Serengeti
Willowgate (scandal), 153–54, 160, 238, 269
WOMAD (World of Music and Dance): festival, 181–82, 233, 277; organization, 139, 207, 260; record label, 209, 323–24n10, 324–25n1. *See also* Real World Records

Zambia, 29, 34–35, 40–41, 48, 89–90, 110, 113, 127, 146, 181, 197, 316n29; death of Herbert Chitepo, 91–92. *See also* Kaunda, Kenneth; liberation war/struggle
ZANLA (Zimbabwe African National Liberation Army), 76–77, 81, 89, 92, 94, 108, 117, 132, 311n41

ZANU, ZANU-PF (Zimbabwe African National Union–Patriotic Front), 4, 280, 285, 289, 330n6; banning of, 94; first election, 108, 110, 117–19, 121; founding of, 38; governs Zimbabwe, 125, 149, 154–55, 221, 250, 258, 321n15; leaders of, 42, 95, 309n13, 310n32; in liberation war, 63–67, 76, 91–93, 101, 301n22, 309n7, 311n1; and Mapfumo, 111, 137, 177, 185, 217, 225, 238–40, 245–46, 250–55, 265–68, 317n12; and MDC, 237–38, 254–55, 269, 289; and violence/harassment, 188, 243–44, 246, 252, 269–70, 274; and war veterans, 208–9; youth members, 40, 252; and ZAPU, 104, 115, 131–32, 152–53, 158. *See also* Mugabe, Robert

ZAPU (Zimbabwe African People's Union), 37–38, 40–41, 66, 94, 110–11, 238, 309–10n20, 311n1; under ZANU rule, 104, 115, 131–32, 152–53, 158. *See also* Nkomo, Joshua

ZBC (Zimbabwe Broadcasting Corp.), 116, 155, 184, 212, 239, 251–52, 259. *See also* radio

ZCTU (Zimbabwe Congress of Trade Unions), 206, 223

Zexie Manatsa and the Green Arrows. *See* Manatsa, Zexie

Zig Zag Band, 262

Zimbabwe: devaluation of currency/inflation, 275–76, 279–80; independence ceremony, 113, 116–21; meaning of name, 16; the nation's birth, 119–21; plateau/geography, 13, 63. *See also* elections; liberation war/struggle; ZANU, ZANU-PF

Zimbabwe College of Music, 54–55, 135, 179, 222

Zimbob Records, 172, 191, 195, 205, 208, 231–32, 260, 322nn28–29. *See also* Diener, Bob

Zimunya, Musa, vii, 32, 43, 73, 125, 146, 184, 226, 240, 243, 280; Mapfumo, assessments of, 106, 108, 157, 220–21, 283, 303n39, 324n4; Mapfumo, early memories of, 26, 47, 70–71, 108–9, 281; on Mapfumo's music, 75, 82, 113, 137, 149, 177, 192, 307n15, 319n16; on mbira, 50, 211; return to Harare after independence, 113; on Rhodesian propaganda songs, 30, 300n6; on Robert Mugabe, 221, 257, 283–84

ZINATHA (Zimbabwe National Traditional Healers Association), 59

Zindi, Fred, 100, 104, 192, 259, 281, 300n35, 301n13, 302n25, 307n21

ZIPRA (Zimbabwe People's Revolutionary Army), 81, 94, 108, 131–32

ZMC (Zimbabwe Music Corporation). *See* Gramma Records, Gramma/ZMC

ZUPCO (Zimbabwe United Passenger Co.), 216

Zutu Brothers, 33–34, 301n11. *See also* Mapfumo, Thomas

Zvamaida, Gilbert (guitarist), 267, 272, 281, 289, 292, 329n2, 331n2; on guitar and music, 224, 307n15; joins Blacks Unlimited, 261–62; trapped in Zimbabwe in 2005, 274–75, 330n8, 331n2